GEOGRAPHY OF THE MUSLIM WORLD

For Senior/General Level
First Edition

Program of Islamic Social Studies

Mushtaqur Rahman & **Guljan Rahman**
Professor of Geography   Former Professor of Geography
Iowa State University   Sir Syed Girls College, Karachi
Ames, Iowa

Copyright: IQRA' International Education Foundation
Chicago, Illinois 60607

Part of a Comprehensive
and Systematic Program
of Islamic Studies

Program of
Islamic Social Studies

Geography of the Muslim World
Senior Level/General

Reviewers:

Dr. Akhtar H. Siddiqi
Bilal Ahmed
Dr. Ilyas Ba Yunus

Cover Art:

Aldin Hadzic

Language Editors:

Huseyin Abiva
Huda Quraishi-Ahmed
Heidi Liddle-Bhutt

Typesetting:

Uzma Rahman

Copyright © 1997

IQRA' International
Educational Foundation
All Rights Reserved

Note on Copyright
This book is part of IQRA's
comprehensive program of
Islamic Education.
No part of this book may be reproduced
by any means including photocopying,
electronic, mechanical, recording, or
otherwise without consent of the publisher.
In specific cases permission is granted
on written request to publish or
translate IQRA's work. For information
regarding permission, write to:
IQRA' International Education Foundation
7450 Skokie Boulevard
Skokie, Illinois 60077
Telephone: 847-673-4072
Fax: 847-673-4095

Printed by **Percetakan Zafar Sdn Bhd** (Co.No. 97878-H)
KUALA LUMPUR

To our loving grandchildren,
Yousef and Amal

PREFACE

Two major factors, Islamic faith and geographical environment, play an important role in shaping the development of the Muslim world. The religion of Islam provides the comprehensive guiding principles for Muslim life. The preservation and propagation of these principles have given impetus to the Islamic movement, and therein, led to the expansion of the Muslim world. With expansion to new and often unchartered territories, the Islamic movement faces new physical challenges set before them by formidable geographical environments. In establishing new communities, Muslims have had to learn to adapt to their geographical conditions for sustenance while upholding their social and religious obligations. Not only have they had to channel their natural resources, they have also had to invent ways to create new resources within the parameters their habitat would allow.

In light of these challenges, it is no wonder that the Muslim World is so richly diverse and exceptionally creative. During the lifetime of Prophet Muhammad, Islam was firmly established in Arabia. Within a decade, it spread rapidly to Africa at first, and from there, to Spain and Sicily. To the east, Islam spread along the trade routes to Central, South and Southeast Asia. With the growth of mercantile trade, the message of Islam readily gained prominence. Markets and mosques, serving as meeting places, became cultural centers, taking on a pivotal role in strengthening the local community. As one community led to another, mosques and minarets continued to be raised around the globe.

Markedly, there has been a surge in the Muslim population throughout the western hemisphere in recent decades. In the United States, the number of Muslims (estimated between 5 to 7 million) has shown a steady increase as immigration and conversion is on the rise. Hundreds of people, mostly African-Americans, are embracing Islam every year. As Islam places heavy emphasis on the sanctity of family values, we see more Muslim families staying together and giving rise to new generations of Muslims. These are just a few reasons why the Muslim population is growing more than any religious group. Currently, nearly one in every five people in the world is a Muslim, coming from any number of ethnic backgrounds and nations.

Geography of the Muslim World provides essential coverage of Muslim countries. It has been written for senior level school students or the interested reader seeking a well-balanced survey of the Muslim world. For easy reading, the text has been organized alphabetically by country. Efforts have been made to keep the reading meaningful and simple. For example, for one country, economics is emphasized, while for another, history takes focus. In certain cases, government and politics have been stressed, whereas in others, ethnicity is featured. A summary has been provided as an introduction at the beginning of each chapter. The information has been condensed to a length that may be more practical for school programs. The goal is to cover the essentials of basic geography in a concise manner.

Maps have been included to illustrate thematic subjects. Most of these maps are graphic representations of the most recent national boundaries and spatial information. Carefully selected colored photographs have been included as useful instructional aid, bringing geography to life by putting students right at the scene of their studies. Because of the limited space, many photographs depicting various physical landscapes and cultural sights could not be included.

The Muslim World is certainly not homogeneous. To the contrary, each region offers its own unique geographical environment, culture, linguistic variations, and racial diversity. Interestingly, this diversity does not just run across borders. In fact, within each country, there are often different terrain, subcultures, and dialects, adding to the heterogeneity of the Muslim population. In some regions, climates vary from snow-shrouded mountains to rain-soaked tropical forests and sun-scorched deserts. The land types differ from fertile plains to towering peaks, and highlands of gravel and sand. Some areas contain the largest known concentrations of human population, while others are empty quarters. In some areas, people have accepted Islam, yet maintained their own language. In others, pre-Islamic religions have survived, but the Arabic language has been accepted. In some areas, multiple languages and religions occur within the same country. To highlight these differences, a brief discussion of the history of the Muslim World follows the preface.

The specific content of this brief version owes a great deal to those reviewers who so kindly took the time, and expended the effort, made suggestions, offered criticism, and were helpful in improving the book. We have tried to incorporate most of their suggestions by rearranging and merging new chapters, adding photographs, eliminating superfluous text, adding tables and maps, among many other changes. We are extremely grateful to those who offered their help. We will remain appreciative of suggestions and constructive criticism.

Many officials of the embassies, consulates, universities, and other institutions made contributions of inestimable value. The authors gratefully acknowledge their help and wish to thank them for their cooperation.

We are especially grateful for the support of IQRA' International Educational Foundation in undertaking this effort. The pioneering efforts of IQRA' Foundation in the field of Islamic education needs no introduction. IQRA' is providing value-based Islamic education, combining the authenticity of information with modernity of methodology. Its efforts may go a long way to meet the goals of Islamic education in re-formulating an Islamic future. It is our good fortune to write this textbook as part of IQRA' Program of Islamic Studies. The textbook is written for both Muslim and non-Muslim readers.

Beyond our critics, reviewers and friends, we also received the strong backing of Association of Muslim Social Scientists. We have worked closely with Drs. Abidullah Ghazi and M. A. W. Fakhri. Our dear Dr. Ghazi spared no effort in supporting this venture and we thank him and IQRA' Foundation for the opportunities they created for us to complete this work.

Mushtaqur Rahman, Ames, Iowa
Guljan Rahman, Ames, Iowa

Jum`ah, 16 Sha`ban 1417
Friday 28 December 1996

IQRA'S NOTE
TO
PARENTS AND TEACHERS

Geography of the Muslim World, written by two prominent professors of geography, Dr. Mushtaqur-Rahman and Mrs. Guljan Rahman, is a unique textbook in a much needed yet very much neglected field of study. This textbook brings a wealth of basic information on the Muslim countries that are known for the unity of their faith and rich diversity of their cultures, environments, and languages. The textbook is written for senior level as well as for the general reader. It offers well-organized reading material for classroom for both public schools and Islamic schools.

The unity inspiring faith of Islam and its rich civilization gives Muslims a unique sense of unity and common destiny. Yet, the Muslim world is not a monolith; it is found in many continents, regions, colors, shades and cultural traits. Arabic, the basic language of the revelation and tradition, is spoken by only 20% of the Muslims, but it is studied by all Muslim communities across the world as the sacred language of their faith. Even those who cannot understand or speak know whole or part of the Qur'an, which they must recite each day as part of the daily prayer. Islamic faith, as opposed to most other faiths, has maintained amazing uniformity in its beliefs and practices, and the Qur'an, its Holy book, remains as it was originally revealed to Prophet Muhammad. The concept of one *Ummah* (Community) is still very strong, and pan-Islamic ideologies are found in all Islamic lands, both as political movements aspiring for Muslim unity or as spiritual yearnings of their faith.

Muslim people truly represent the humanity in all its forms and linguistic diversity. Muslims may be the only people in the world whose universal vision of One God, One Prophet, One Book, One Holy Sanctuary has given rise to spiritual solidarity that rises above cast, color, location, nation, and language.

Yet, Muslims are divided into almost 52 nation states. Muslim minorities, big and small, exist in almost all the countries in the world. We see the Muslim world in constant turmoil and political upheavals. Although Islamic solidarity does not recognize national boundaries, national sentiments many times have developed within national boundaries similar to the nationalism of the West. In the West, the national boundaries were largely drawn by national struggles based upon common language and race; in the Muslim world these are drawn primarily by colonial powers for their own political and economic considerations. We have regions where one culturally homogenous people (such as Kurds, Arabs, Malays, etc.) are divided into many independent nations or are parts of other nations. This has given birth to political instability, the arms race, and military conflicts. Muslim sentiment of political emancipation has led to several struggles of independence (such as in Palestine, Bosnia, Chechnia, Kashmir, Southern Philippines, etc.) at huge human and economic cost.

The Muslim world is one-fifth of humanity. It is enormously rich and has many strategic advantages. It is the staunchest ally and greatest adversary of the West. The West has exploited it, shunned it, rebuked it, and befriended it. The most educated and elitist part of the Muslim world now is found in the West. The misunderstanding of, as well as *not* understanding the Muslims is dangerous both for the West as well as for the Muslims. In this growing global village, a Muslim is literally a next-door neighbor whose existence the West has long ignored, but who can no longer can be ignored - much less denied.

Geography of the Muslim World fills a gap that has existed in the literature on this part of the globe, and we hope will generate a better understanding of a people in both their unity and diversity among those who strive for better understanding.

The Chief Editors
7450 Skokie Boulevard, Skokie, IL 60077
Tel: (847) 673-4072 Fax: (847) 673-4095

Jum`ah 17 Dhu al-Hijjah 1417
Friday, 25 April, 1997

CONTENTS

Preface	iii
List of Maps	xvi
List of Figures	xviii
List of Tables	xx
About the Authors	xxi

	INTRODUCTION	1-16
	Rise of Islamic Civilization	3
	The Basic Principles of the Islamic Faith	3
	Early Islamic Period	7
	Expansion in the Middle East and North Africa: 634-750 AD	8
	Expansion of Islam during the Middle Ages: 750-1400 AD	9
	Islam and the Ottomans: 1400-1900 AD	10
	Eastward Expansion of Islam: 750-1400 AD	11
Chapter 1	**AFGHANISTAN**	17-24
	Geography	17
	Evolution	19
	Population and Economy	22
	Industry	23
	Transport and Communication	24
Chapter 2	**ALBANIA**	25-30
	Geography	25
	Evolution	27
	Albanians outside of Albania	28
	Economy	29
	Agriculture	29
	Industry	29

Chapter 3	**ALGERIA**	31-36
	Geography	31
	Evolution	33
	Economy	33
	Agriculture	34
	Minerals	34
	Industry	35
Chapter 4	**AZERBAIJAN**	37-42
	Geography	37
	People and Population	39
	Evolution	39
	Economy	40
	Agriculture	40
	Minerals and Industry	41
Chapter 5	**BAHRAIN**	43-50
	Geography	43
	Evolution	45
	Population and Economy	46
Chapter 6	**BANGLADESH**	51-56
	Geography	51
	Evolution	53
	Economy	54
	Agriculture	55
	Industry	55
Chapter 7	**BOSNIA-HERZEGOVINA**	57-62
	Geography	57
	Religions and Population	59
	Evolution	59
	Economy	61
Chapter 8	**BRUNEI**	63-68
	Geography	63
	People and Population	65
	Economy	65
	Agriculture	67
	Evolution	67

Chapter 9	**BURKINA FASO**	69-72
	Geography	69
	People and Population	70
	Evolution	71
	Economy	71
Chapter 10	**CHAD**	73-78
	Geography	73
	People and Population	75
	Evolution	76
	Economy	77
	Minerals and Industry	77
Chapter 11	**COMOROS**	79-82
	Geography	79
	Population	80
	Evolution	80
	Economy	81
Chapter 12	**COTE D'IVOIRE**	83-88
	Geography	83
	People and Population	85
	Evolution	85
	Economy	86
	Agriculture	86
	Minerals and Industry	87
Chapter 13	**DJIBOUTI**	89-92
	Geography	89
	People and Population	91
	Evolution	91
	Economy	92
Chapter 14	**EGYPT**	93-100
	Geography	93
	People and Population	95
	Evolution	95
	Economy	98
	Agriculture	99
	Manufacturing Industry	100
	Transport and Communication	100

Chapter 15	**ERITREA**	101-106
	Geography	101
	People and Population	103
	Evolution	103
	Economy	104
	Agriculture and Industry	104

Chapter 16	**GAMBIA**	107-112
	Geography	107
	People and Population	109
	Evolution	109
	Economy	110

Chapter 17	**GUINEA**	113-118
	Geography	113
	Evolution	115
	Economy	116
	Agriculture	116
	Minerals	116

Chapter 18	**INDONESIA**	119-126
	Geography	119
	Evolution	120
	People and Population	122
	Economy, Agriculture	122
	Minerals, Oil, Trade, Industry	124

Chapter 19	**IRAN**	127-134
	Geography	127
	Climate	129
	People and Population	129
	Evolution	130
	Economy	132
	Agriculture	132
	Manufacturing	133

Chapter 20	**IRAQ**	135-140
	Geography	135
	People and Population	137
	Evolution	137
	Economy	138
	Agriculture	139
	Petroleum	140

Chapter 21	**JORDAN**	141-148
	Geography	141
	People and Population	143
	Evolution	144
	Economy	145
	Minerals and Industry	148
Chapter 22	**KAZAKHSTAN**	149-154
	Geography	149
	People and Population	151
	Evolution	152
	Economy	152
	Agriculture	152
	Minerals and Industry	153
Chapter 23	**KUWAIT**	155-162
	Geography	155
	People and Population	157
	Evolution of Kuwait	159
	Economy: Oil	161
	Industry and Development	162
Chapter 24	**KYRGYZSTAN**	163-166
	Geography	163
	People and Population	164
	Evolution	165
	Economy: Agriculture	165
	Minerals and Industry	166
Chapter 25	**LEBANON**	167-172
	Geography	167
	People and Population	167
	Evolution	169
	Economy	170
Chapter 26	**LIBYA**	173-180
	Geography	173
	People and Population	175
	Evolution	176
	Economy: Agriculture	177
	Oil and Development	179
	Manufacturing and Service Activities	179

Chapter 27	**MALAYSIA**	181-188
	Geography	181
	People and Population	183
	Evolution	185
	Economy: Agriculture	186
	Minerals and Manufacturing	187
Chapter 28	**MALDIVES**	189-194
	Geography	189
	People and Population	190
	Evolution	191
	Economy	192
Chapter 29	**MALI**	195-200
	Geography	195
	Evolution	197
	People and Population	197
	Economy: Agriculture	198
	Mineral and Industries	199
Chapter 30	**MAURITANIA**	201-206
	Geography	201
	People and Population	202
	Evolution	203
	Economy: Agriculture	204
	Minerals and Industry	204
Chapter 31	**MOROCCO**	207-212
	Geography	207
	People and Population	209
	Evolution	210
	Economy	210
	Agriculture	211
	Minerals and Industries	212
Chapter 32	**NIGER**	213-216
	Geography	213
	People and Population	215
	Evolution	215
	Economy	215
	Agriculture, Minerals, and Industries	216

Chapter 33	**NIGERIA**	217-222
	Geography	217
	People and Population	219
	Evolution	220
	Economy	221
	Agriculture	221
	Minerals and Industries	222
Chapter 34	**OMAN**	223-226
	Geography	223
	People and Population	225
	Evolution	225
	Economy	226
	Oil and Modern Development	226
Chapter 35	**PAKISTAN**	227-234
	Geography	227
	People and Population	229
	Evolution	230
	Economy: Agriculture	233
	Minerals and Industries	233
Chapter 36	**PALESTINE**	235-240
	Geography	236
	Population	237
	Evolution	237
	Economy	240
Chapter 37	**QATAR**	241-246
	Geography	241
	People and Population	242
	Evolution	243
	Economy: Agriculture	244
	Oil and Minerals	244
	Industries	245
Chapter 38	**SAUDI ARABIA**	247-252
	Geography	247
	People and Population	248
	Evolution	250
	Economy: Agriculture	250
	Oil and Industry	251

Chapter 39	**SENEGAL**	253-256
	Geography	253
	People and Population	254
	Evolution	255
	Economy: Agriculture	255
	Industries and Minerals	256
Chapter 40	**SOMALIA**	257-262
	Geography	257
	People and Population	259
	Evolution	259
	Economy	260
	Agriculture, Minerals, and Industry	261
Chapter 41	**SUDAN**	263-268
	Geography	263
	People and Population	265
	Evolution	266
	Economy: Agriculture	267
	Minerals and Industry	267
Chapter 42	**SYRIA**	269-274
	Geography	269
	People and Population	271
	Evolution	271
	Economy	272
	Agriculture: Minerals	273
	Industry	274
Chapter 43	**TAJIKISTAN**	275-278
	Geography	275
	People and Population	277
	Evolution	277
	Economy: Agriculture	278
	Minerals and Industry	278
Chapter 44	**TUNISIA**	279-284
	Geography	279
	People and Population	280
	Evolution	281
	Economy: Agriculture	282
	Minerals and Industry	282

Chapter 45	**TURKEY**	285-290
	Geography	285
	People and Population	287
	Evolution	288
	Economy: Agriculture	289
	Minerals and Industry	290
Chapter 46	**TURKMENISTAN**	291-296
	Geography	291
	People and Population	293
	Evolution	293
	Economy: Agriculture	294
	Minerals and Industry	295
Chapter 47	**UNITED ARAB EMIRATES**	297-302
	Geography	297
	People and Population	299
	Evolution	299
	Economy: Oil and Industry	301
Chapter 48	**UZBEKISTAN**	303-308
	Geography	303
	People and Population	305
	Evolution	305
	Economy: Agriculture	306
	Industries and Minerals	307
Chapter 49	**YEMEN**	309-316
	Geography	309
	People and Population	310
	Evolution	311
	Economy: Agriculture	313
	Minerals and Industry	314

Selected Bibliography　　317

LIST OF MAPS

1	Muslim World	2
2	Haram	6
3	Diffusion of Islam	14
4	Afghanistan	18
5	Albania	26
6	Algeria	32
7	Azerbaijan	38
8	Bahrain	44
9	Bangladesh	52
10	Bosnia - Herzegovina	58
11	Brunei	64
12	Burkina Faso	70
13	Chad	74
14	Comoros	80
15	Cote d'Ivoire	84
16	Djibouti	90
17	Egypt	94
18	Eritrea	102
19	Gambia	108
20	Guinea	114
21	Indonesia	120
22	Iran	128
23	Iraq	136
24	Jordan	142
25	Kazakhstan	150
26	Kuwait	156
27	Kyrgyzstan	164
28	Lebanon	168
29	Libya	174
30	Malaysia	182
31	Maldives	190
32	Mali	196
33	Mauritania	202
34	Morocco	208
35	Niger	214
36	Nigeria	218
37	Oman	224
38	Pakistan	228
39	Palestine	236
40	Qatar	242

LIST OF MAPS

(continued)

41	Saudi Arabia	248
42	Senegal	254
43	Somalia	258
44	Sudan	264
45	Syria	270
46	Tajikistan	276
47	Tunisia	280
48	Turkey	286
49	Turkmenistan	292
50	United Arab Emirates	298
51	Uzbekistan	304
52	Yemen	310

LIST OF FIGURES

#	Title	Page
1	The Ka'bah	5
2	A Haji wearing the Ihram	6
3	Istanbul Mosque, Turkey	11
4	Early Arab merchant, Malaysia	13
5	Afghan family migrating to Pakistan	20
6	A tent village near Peshawar, Pakistan	21
7	School for Afghan Refugees	21
8	Dilman Mounds, Isa Town, Bahrain	45
9	Bahrain airport, 1932	47
10	Trickle-Drip Irrigation, Bahrain	48
11	Government Avenue, Bahrain	50
12	Market in Bahrain	50
13	National Monument, Savar, Dhaka, Bangladesh	54
14	Tea plantation, Sylheth, Bangladesh	56
15	A camel nomad, Egypt	95
16	Port of Alexandria, Egypt	96
17	Al-Azhar University, Cairo, Egypt	97
18	Saqiyeh	98
19	Equatorial forest, Guinea	115
20	Coconut fiber, Guinea	117
21	Rice field, Indonesia	123
22	Coffee plantation in Indonesia	124
23	Cultural landscape, Java	125
24	Masjid-i-Shiraz, Iran	129
25	Shatt-el Arab, Iran	131
26	A modern farm, Iran	133
27	A Mosque in Baghdad, Iraq	138
28	A farm in Iraq	139
29	Dead Sea, Jordan	143
30	Amman, Jordan	145
31	Sheep Herding	146
32	Olive cultivation	147
33	Port of Aqaba, Jordan	148
34	A Mosque in China	151
35	Cultural landscape, Kuwait	157
36	Saudi Arabia-Kuwait Border	158
37	Kuwait City	159
38	Shuwaikh University, Kuwait	160
39	Libya's coastal settlements	175
40	A nomad, Libya	176

LIST OF FIGURES
(continued)

41	Central Mosque, Kuala Lumpur, Malaysia	183
42	Indian Mosque, Kuala Lumpur, Malaysia	184
43	A settlement in Maldives	191
44	Fishing activity, Maldives	192
45	Hotel Mamoura, Marrakesh, Morocco	209
46	Mausoleum of King Mohammed V, Rabat	211
47	Traditional dancing, Nigeria	219
48	General view of Lagos, Nigeria	221
49	City of Lahore	229
50	Minar-i-Pakistan, Lahore	230
51	Mausoleum of Quiad-i-Azam Jinnah, Karachi	231
52	Three Pillars (Symbols of Unity, Faith, and Discipline), Karach	232
53	Port city of Karachi, Pakistan	232
54	A Nomad, Qatar	243
55	Kabah, Mekkah, Saudi Arabia	249
56	Livestock in Somalia	261
57	Somalia: Fishing	262
58	Zikr Assembly, Sudan	265
59	A Maderssa (School), Sudan	268
60	Damascus	272
61	Aleppo	273
62	Tunis, Tunisia	281
63	Istanbul, Turkey	287
64	General view of Abu Dhabi, UAE	299
65	General view of Umm-al-Qaiwain	301
66	A clay Fort, Al-Mukalia, Yemen	311
67	A Mosque in Jibla, Yemen	312
68	Terraced farming, Yemen	314

LIST OF TABLES

#	Title	Page
1	Muslim nations, 1994	15
2	Countries with 25-49% Muslim population	16
3	Countries with 2 million Muslims	16
4	Major import/export of Afghanistan	23
5	Land use in Algeria	34
6	Azerbaijan's Agricultural Production	41
7	Azerbaijan's Output of Industrial Products	42
8	Tunisia's Mineral Production	283
9	Land use in Turkey	290
10	Population of Emirates	300

ABOUT THE AUTHORS

Mushtaqur Rahman is currently a Professor of Geography at Iowa State University at Ames, Iowa. He earned his Ph.D. at Louisiana State University and did his post-doctoral work at the University of Giessen, Germany and at South Asia Institute, University of Heidelberg, Germany. A specialist in the cultural geography of South Asia and the Muslim World, Dr. Rahman is interested in the contemporary Muslim World's problems and potentials. He served as President of the Association of Muslim Social Scientists in 1989-1991 and earlier as the Editor-in-Chief of the *American Journal of Islamic Social Sciences*. He has written on a wide variety of cultural topics of the Muslim World and South Asia, especially Pakistan. His scholarly books include *Land and Life in Sindh, Pakistan* (Ferozsons, 1993), *Agriculture in Pakistan* (Budapest, 1988), *Muslim World: Geography and Development* (Lanham, Maryland, 1987), *Rural Development in Pakistan: Its Policies and Problems* (Hong Kong, 1983), *Agrarian Egalitarianism: Land Tenures and Land Reforms in South Asia* (Iowa, 1981), and *Geography of Sind Province, Pakistan* (Karachi Geographers Association, 1975). He is also editing a special volume of the *GeoJournal (Germany)* on the Muslim World. John Wiley and Sons, New York has contracted him to edit a book on South Asia. For him, the most rewarding aspect of geography has been the field research in the Muslim World including Pakistan.

Guljan Rahman is a former Professor of Geography at Sir Syed Girls College, Karachi, Pakistan. She earned her Masters degree at the University of Karachi and another Masters degree at Iowa State University. She was associated with the *Iowa in Global Perspective* research project at Iowa State University and also taught courses in map making at the Department of Surveying at Iowa State University. She specializes in regional geography of Pakistan and non-computerized cartography. Her books for college include *Map Projections* (Oxford University Press, Pakistan) and Laboratory Exercises (Paracha Printers, Karachi).

INTRODUCTION

The Muslim World extends from Morocco to Indonesia and from the Horn of Africa to Central Asia. In addition, a sizable number of Muslim minorities can be found in India, China, Burma, Thailand, Philippines, the Balkans and many other countries. The total population of the Muslims around the world is estimated at a little over 1 billion. Islam is growing at a faster rate than any other religion. At the current rate of growth, the world's Muslim population could nearly double before the year 2020, accounting for 23 percent of the world's total population. As of now, Muslims constitute a majority in more than 52 countries (Table 1), (Map 1). In five countries, they represent between 25 to 49 percent of the population (Table 2), and in seven countries their population is less than 25 percent (Table 3).

In the United States, Muslims are increasing just as rapidly. By the end of this century, their number is likely to exceed eight million, giving them a larger total representation than the membership of Episcopal or the United Church of Christ.[1] According to the Islamic Research Institute, 85 percent of the Americans who convert to Islam are African-American, owing to Islam's strong emphasis on egalitarianism, equality, and brotherhood, and denouncement of racial and class discriminations.[2] Other Muslims in the United States have origins in the Middle East, South and Southeast Asia, Africa and Eastern Europe. Mosques and Islamic centers built in the United States, mostly during the last 15 years, number about 1,100, with heavy concentrations on the East and West coasts, the Midwest and the South.

Islam brought with it a new, advanced civilization to the world. During the reign of the Islamic empire, significant advances were made in agriculture, medicine, mathematics, science, and architecture. A vigorous intellectual life flourished in university cities of Cairo, Fez, Baghdad, Damascus, Istanbul, Cordoba, Toledo, Seville, and Granada.

Long confrontation with western colonialism and the struggle against it has left much of the Muslim world dilapidated, plagued by social fragmentation and internal unrest. Some may rightly contest that the West is too often used as a scapegoat for the existing problems; however, it cannot be denied that historically, there have been clear instances when an expression of popular will has been thwarted by blatant, external western interference. In fact, there are numerous examples of the imposition of an autocratic regime according to will of the Western powers that be in opposition to the will of the people. The continuation of injustices in Palestine, Bosnia, Chechnia, Lebanon, Kashmir and other parts of the Muslim world has left their people only with feelings of bitterness and disappointment. Anti-west feelings and polarization in Muslim society between the so-called camps of "modernism" and "fundamentalism" are a direct backlash of this state of affairs.

Despite the adversity, there has been a revival of the Muslim spirit throughout the world.

---

[1] Haddad, Yvonne, *The Muslim World Today*. Washington: D.C., Islamic Affairs Program. The Middle East Institute, 1993, p.1

[2] *USA Today*. January 27, 1994

There is a genuine yearning to return to traditional Islamic values and ethics in an effort to create a just and egalitarian political, social, and economic system. What is lacking is the development of a practical model for such values. Within the Muslim world, there is a wide range of opinions with respect to socio-political and economic issues and their solutions.

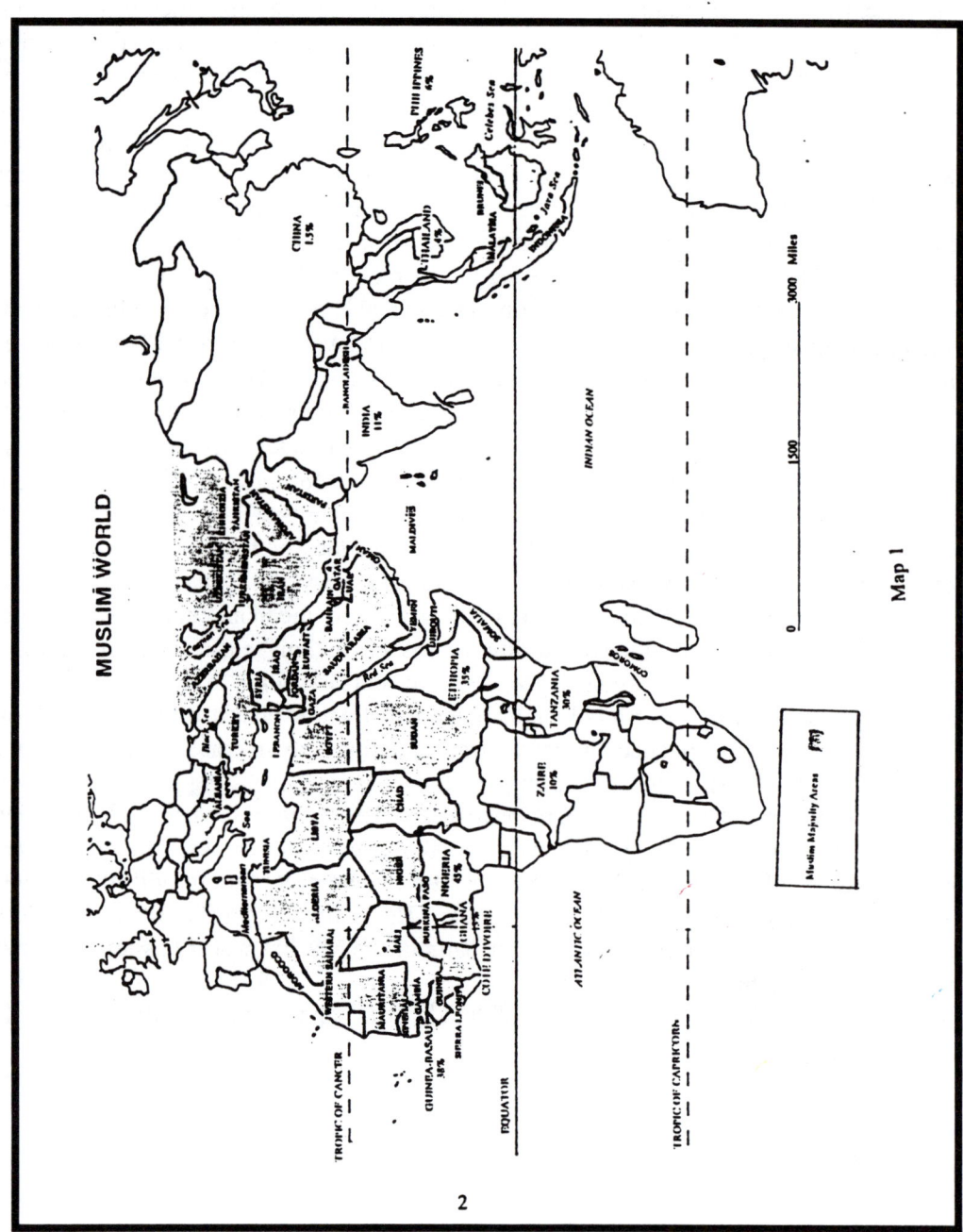

Map 1: Muslim World

However, the increased prominence of the Muslim community in the West has had a dichotomous effect: It has facilitated the understanding of Islam on a grassroots level, but it has also given rise to suspicion, prejudice, and suppressive attempts by many policy makers and much of the media. Unfortunately, from this suspicion and fear has come misinterpretation of Islam and distortion of its history. Rarely do we see a balanced coverage of events, accounting for the Muslim view as well as the opposing view.

While western media, information, books, and even church-related services continue to propagate anti-Muslim sentiment, at the same time, we are witnessing a slow change in attitude. The development of forums promoting better understanding; media reporting on Muslim festivals and social life; inter-faith dialogue groups; and growing Muslim participation in social, religious, and political life are all encouraging. In recent years, there has been a growing recognition of the Muslim existence in the West; Catholics, Lutherans, Unitarians and other mainstream Christians denominations and several Jewish groups, especially the American Jewish Committee, are working toward better understanding and communication. Prince Charles of Great Britain has become a great advocate of Islamic civilization and an eager champion of recognition of religious pluralism in the western world in recent years. All people of understanding must work to make our global community a place of harmony and peace. Muslims, especially, have a responsibility to contribute positively to this development.

We hope that the following brief review of the Islamic religion and tradition; its spread around the world; and its scientific, socio-cultural accomplishments will shed light on the dynamics of the Muslim World and give our younger generation a better understanding of a people who, in spite of large numbers and western roots, have often been misunderstood.

THE RISE OF ISLAMIC CIVILIZATION

The Basics Principles of the Islamic Faith

Islam is a complete way of life. This perhaps best sums up the faith better than any other statement. When one looks at the ideal of Muslim life, whether at the individual or community level, one soon finds that the guiding principles of the religion are present in everyday life. Even in situations where many aspects of Islam have been diminished by varying circumstances, ingrained religious attitudes are still apparent.

The paramount message of Islam is the belief in the Oneness of God and in the Messengership of Muhammad, who acted as the final vehicle of God's guidance. This twofold tenet of faith provides practical application in human life through the Qur'an and the *Sunnah*, the tradition of Prophet Muhammad (the role and nature of both will be discussed below). The very foundation of Islam requires humankind to acknowledge the absolute Oneness (*Tawhid*) and Omnipotence of God. There is no room in Islam for the acknowledgment of any other source other than one God. As a matter of fact the greatest sin in the eyes of God is *Shirk*, to associate partners with Him.

A Muslim must believe in the Angels (*Mala'ikah*), who are beings created by God to carry out certain duties. Of these countless numbers of creatures, four archangels have special distinction, Jibra'il (Gabriel), Israfil, Azra'il and Mika'il (Micheal). The angels, in Islamic tradition, are believed to have a pure and innocent nature, incapable of committing sins or acting at will against the Will of the Creator.

A Muslim is required to believe and accept all that God revealed throughout human history. The divinely revealed books were sent through chosen messengers to provide guidance to humanity. These divine books were sent by Allah to chosen prophets (*anbiya'*) and messengers (*Rusul*), the final of them being Muhammad. Islam enjoins its followers not only to accept Prophet Muhammad but all previous prophets and messengers of God. The Qur'an mentions by name twenty-five of these venerable figures, five of whom had divine books revealed to them. Many of these prophets and messengers mentioned by name in the Qur'an are encountered in the texts of the Old and New Testaments. These, however, have not been the only ones to have been ordained and Islam stresses that countless other guides and warners have come in the past to all people and nations. No people are left without guidance.

Islam also teaches that human existence continues beyond death. First, the soul continues to endure in the grave. This is followed by a period known as the *Qiyamah* or resurrection. At this point, everyone must stand to witness against himself on the Day of Judgment, a time when the good and bad actions and beliefs of this life are examined. This will decide whether the individual shall have eternal salvation and bliss or damnation in Hell.

The belief that God is the supreme cause of all actions and events, both good and bad, is one of the tenets of faith for the Muslim. Nothing can escape the decree of the Lord, who is All-Powerful in His Might. Therefore, a Muslim is one who can rest assured that even in bad times God is working His Divine Will. And if affliction can be borne out patiently, vast spiritual awards await the believer.

In Islam, these inner beliefs must be coupled with an outer display of good works. This, in its most basic form is what is commonly known as the Five Pillars. Every Muslim is to observe these practices, some which are daily occurrences, others yearly, and yet others, once in a lifetime. The Five Pillars are:

The Shahadah: This is to bear witness that that one believes in the Oneness of God, and that Muhammad is His servant and Messenger. The formal uttering of this phrase and believing it to be the ultimate of all truths brings one into the fold of Islam and makes him member of the *Ummah*, the community of Islam.

The Salah (Prayers): The five, daily, formal prayers. These are incumbent on all adult Muslims of sound mind and body. The prayers are to be performed punctually, facing the Ka'bah, the holiest Muslim shrine (Fig. 1).

The Siyam (Fasting): The yearly fast during the lunar month of *Ramadan*. Muslims are required to abstain from food, drink, and sexual activity from before dawn to sunset during the days of this month. Increased devotions are recommended, as the month of Ramadan is seen a time for renewing one's spiritual attainments and goals.

The Zakah: Another yearly duty is the payment of *Zakah*, the payment of a small portion of one's savings to the needy of the Muslim community.

Fig. 1: The Ka'bah

The Hajj (Pilgrimage): The *Hajj*, pilgrimage to Makkah, is required to be performed only once in a lifetime (if the means are available). It is truly a test of the individual's faith and endurance. In spite of the advent of modern travel amenities of life, the gathering of *Hajj* and the performance of its ritual over a period of five days requires great patience and perseverance. The Hajj represents the coming together of the human family in the worship of the One God. While performing the *Hajj*, one is required to wear the *Ihram,* a white seamless garment, as a symbol of equality and purity (Fig. 2). Nowhere on earth can one find the gathering of every conceivable race, color, language and nation dressed alike and performing the same ritual. Within the boundries of *Haram*, or sanctuary, all agression, even towards plants and animals is prohibited (Map2). Thus, *Hajj*, unlike any other event, signifies the unifying power of Islam.

The five pillars give Islamic life regularity, uniformity, unity and, social cohesion. Since there is no Church and priesthood in Islam, the Islamic ritual unites the worshiper directly with his Creator.

Fig. 2: A *Haji* wearing an *Ihram*

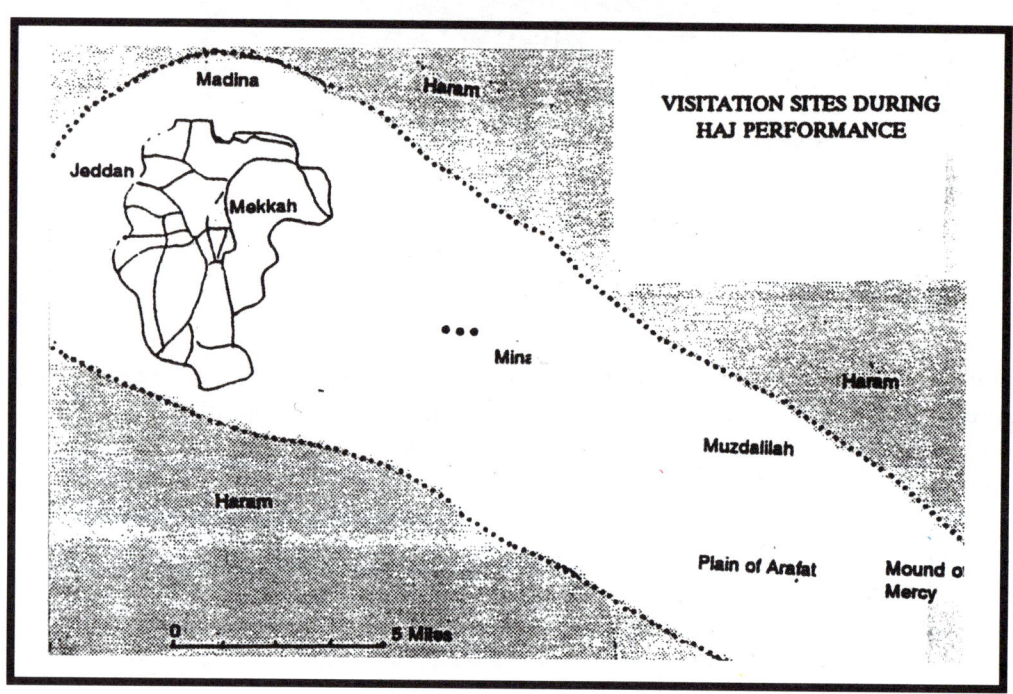

Map 2: Haram

Early Islamic Period

Prophet Muhammad was born in 570 AD in the Arabian town of Makkah, located some 45 miles (70 km) inland from the Red Sea. As a youth and young adult, he developed a reputation for humility, trustworthiness, and honesty to which even his later detractors had to admire. At the age of forty, after having engaged in a successful business career with his wife, he began receiving the Revelations of the Qur'an and the proclamation that he had been ordained to be the last Messenger of God.

At first, Islam was not accepted by most of the Arab tribes and clans that lived in and around Makkah. The Prophet and his followers encountered much opposition and persecution at the hands of these idol worshippers. A change in fortune came, however, in 622 AD, when he and his followers were invited by the people of the city of Yathrib (located some 200 mile north of Makkah) to come and settle there. These people embraced Islam and were known as the *Ansar* (the helpers). This migration of the Prophet from Makkah to Yathrib became known as the *Hijrah*, the event by which the Islamic calendar is reckoned. The city of Yathrib came to be known as *Madinat un-Nabi*, or simply, Madinah. Here, the Prophet was able to establish Islam as a complete code of life. Islam was now the ideology that not only managed the affairs of the new city-state but reflected itself in the individual's social and spiritual life.

This growth of Islam did not go unnoticed by the pagan tribes. They made several attempts to crush the nascent Muslim community which resulted in armed confrontation. However, after the battles of Badr, Uhud and Khandaq, they realized that the Muslim community of Madinah could no longer be overthrown by force of arms. They soon advocated a peace treaty, which they thought would buy time to their crumbling influence. During this short peace, more and more Arab tribes flocked to the banner of Islam and swore allegiance to the Prophet.

The pagans, however, breached the articles of the treaty, and as a result, a large Muslim army marched to the city of Makkah. The sacred home of the Ka`bah fell without bloodshed. The Prophet's conquest of the home which rejected him was truly magnanimous. Those who discarded his message soon embraced him as a result of his great mercy. With Makkah now in the hands of the Prophet, the influence of Islam began to make itself more and more apparent among the Arab peoples, and the majority of the tribes of the peninsula came into Islam during this period.

The Prophet passed away in 632 AD and was succeeded by one of his closest companion, Abu Bakr. This new position, *khalifah* (Caliph), encompassed the duties of leader of the *Ummah*, religious leader, supreme judge, and commander-in-chief of the army. Within a year, Islam reached Central Arabia, and by 634 AD, all of Arabia became Muslim. Not long after, the Islamic movement reached the borders of the Byzantine and Persian Empires to the North.

The advent of Abu Bakr as *khalifah* initiated a new age in the history of Islam known as the period of the *Khilafa'ar-Rashidah*, the "Rightly Guided Caliphates." During a span of some thirty years, the Islamic state was led by men of impeccable character who had been the closest of companions to the Prophet. These men, Abu Bakr, `Umar, `Uthman and `Ali, laid the foundation of what would become in decades following their deaths, the pre-eminent political institution on the face of the Earth.

Expansion in the Middle East and North Africa 634-750 AD

To the northwest of the nascent Islamic state lay the powerful Byzantine and Sasanid Persian empires. United under the banner of Islam, the Arabs began to push their way into these territories. Their first objective was to take Syria and Palestine and then provinces of the Byzantine Empire. In 635 AD, they succeeded in conquering Syria. A year later they smashed the Byzantine army at the Battle of Yarmuk, which effectively ended Byzantine resistance south of the Taurus Mountains. Thus, in just over two years, the Arabs succeeded in introducing Islam to the lands that now comprise Palestine, Syria, Lebanon and Jordan. By 650 AD, the Muslims even sent a naval expedition to the island of Cyprus, which they occupied for some time.

In 639 AD, Muslim soldiers advanced into Egypt. They conquered the great city of Alexandria and other towns and villages in the Nile Delta. After a siege of several months, Alexandria surrendered to the Muslims. From this base in Egypt, the towns and cities along the coast of North Africa as far as Tripoli soon came under the control of the Islamic state. The Islamic faith found a positive reception among the peoples of this area and within several centuries most of them had become Muslim.

Muslim advance westward gained new impetus in 667 AD. By the turn of the eighth century, all of North Africa up to the Atlantic ocean was under Muslim control. Here, despite initial resistance from the fierce Berber tribes, Islam also began to take root among the native people. In 711 AD, a small Muslim army led by the Berber general, Tariq ibn Ziyad, crossed over into Spain. He was able to crush the Visigoth King's attempt to repel him. This victory opened all of Spain for conquest. Within a decade, all of the Iberian peninsula, with the exception of the extreme northern provinces, was under Muslim control.

In Black Africa, Islam began to spread through trade along the east coast of Africa and through the caravan routes through the Sahara desert and down the Nile River. As would be the case in other lands, these Muslim traders and merchants demonstrated extreme honesty in their dealings, which made a good impression on the local people. Struck by such behavior, many of the African peoples began to enter into Islam. These new converts took up the task of preaching the faith to other African peoples who had yet to hear the Word. This is a process that is continuing even to this day.

Far to the East lay the Sasanid Persian Empire, which stretched all the way from Iraq to the Amu Darya River in Turkestan to the Indus valley. It was, however, nothing but a shadow of its former glory and after a few battles, the forces of Islam brought most of its provinces under its control. The Persian army collapsed after several disastrous engagements with the Muslim forces, namely, at Qadisiyyah in central Iraq.

The Arab victors were quite tolerant to their new Persian subjects, who had suffered for centuries under their oppressive royal dynasties that exploited them. The Muslims did not force people off their land, as many others had done. Very often the local administrators retained their jobs. The non-Muslims were allowed to administer justice to their own people. They could judge legal cases concerning members of their religion under their traditional codes of law. The non-Zoroastrian religious groups (mainly Christian), which had been persecuted under the rule of the Sasanid Shahs, were treated with much more tolerance by the Muslims. They were especially liberal with Jews and Christians, because both of these groups are considered *Ahl al-Kitab*, the People of the Book.

During this time period, Damascus became the administrative headquarters of the Muslim state. This was the era of expansion and consolidation. New internal ideological developments over the question of who should lead the new empire divided the community. This early ideological division evolved into three distinct religious sects, the *Ahl as-Sunnah* (*Sunni*), the *Shi'ah* (Shi'ites), and the *Khwarij* (Kharijites).

Ahl as-Sunnah, the majority sect, believes in the principle of the *Shūra* (consultation and consensus) in the election to the political office. The *Shi'ah* support the claim of Ali and his descendants to the spiritual and political office of the caliphate as the only legitimate successors. The *khawarij* was initially a political group that revolted against Ali, the fourth caliph. They believe in the *Shūra* of the community and right of the community to depose the leader. They are no longer a political or religious force in the community

Expansion of Islam during the Middle Ages: 750-1400 AD

By 750 AD, the armies of Islam had reached as far as Spain in the West, the borders of India in the East, and across Persian lands, all the way to Central Asia. During this era, the Turks, a nomadic people, roamed the vast lands north of the Islamic empire, from Mongolia to the Black Sea. Although initially shamanists, many Turkish tribes began to trickle into Islam, a trickle which, in time, would become a gushing flow. Around 970 AD, a Turkish clan under the leadership of a prince by the name of Seljuk led his people out of the Central Asian steppe and into the Middle East. They soon came to dominate the region, playing an important part in combating the Crusaders and weakening the remnants of the Byzantine Empire in Anatolia.

Also during this period, the Christian armies of Western Europe tried to make conquests into the Muslim lands in Palestine and Syria. Several Crusades were sponsored by the Church of Rome (beginning just before 1100 AD). The Christians wanted to recapture the lands they held to be holy to their faith, and at the same time, open trade routes between Europe and the East. They gained several footholds in Palestine, occupying Jerusalem, where they slaughtered every Muslim and Jew who did not escape. Using this holy city as a base, they established a Christian kingdom. In 1187 AD, the Christians lost control of their holdings (including Jerusalem) to the Muslim armies that were reorganized under the great Kurdish general Salahuddin al-Ayyubi (Saladin). During the sixth Crusade, which began in 1228 AD, the Christians were able to regain control of Jerusalem, which was again lost in 1244 to the Muslims. In 1291, the last Crusader stronghold in the Middle East was seized, ending almost two centuries of war.

The Crusades continued for another two hundred years to the far west in Spain. Beginning in the thirteenth century, the Christian kings of Spain attempted to regain the land that was conquered by the Muslims centuries before. This offensive is known as the *Reconquista*. It was a slow and brutal affair which did not end until 1492, when the last Muslim kingdom centered around the city of Granada fell to the armies of King Ferdinand and Queen Isabella. Most Muslims were forced by torture to convert to Christianity or flee to North Africa.

In the East, the lands of Islam were hit with a great disaster. In 1215 AD, with an army of

10,000, the Mongol warlord Genghis Khan invaded the Muslim lands of Central Asia and Persia. He sought revenge against the kings of the Khwarezm dynasty for their earlier treatment of some Mongol merchants. The invading Mongols looted, destroyed and massacred the population as they advanced. Tens of thousands of people were killed. Only craftsmen were spared, as they were useful as slaves. All of Persia was conquered in little more than seven years. Following these triumphs, Mongol armies turned their attention to the rich and fertile lands of the Middle East. The glorious city of Baghdad was captured and burned to the ground in 1258 AD. After pushing through Syria, the Mongols were stopped from further advance by the brilliant general of the Egyptian Mamluk army, Baybars at the Battle of `Ayn Jalut. Of the great Muslim centers of civilization that existed before the Mongol invasions, only Cairo escaped unscathed. By 1300 AD, after several decades of ruling Muslim lands, most of the conquering Mongols had embraced Islam, which was the religion of their subjects.

By the 14th century, the Mongol Empire began to deteriorate. The empire in Western Asia experienced a brief spurt of glory under the leadership of the Muslim king, Tamerlane. His armies swept out of their heartland in Transoxiana, conquering the Middle East as far as Palestine in the South and Anatolia in the West. By 1400 AD, his vassals had subdued parts of what is now Russia and briefly raided Indian lands as far as the Ganges River plain. Tamerlane's influence on the lands he conquered disappeared as quickly as it had come. All of these events gave rise to the next phase of Islamic expansion which came with the rise of the Ottoman Empire.

Islam and the Ottomans: 1400-1900 AD

After taking Adrianople (Edirne), the Ottoman Turks forced their way into the Balkans, skirting around what was left of the small Byzantine state in the shape of the city of Constantinople. They conquered Greece, Serbia, Bulgaria, and Albania, spreading Islam far up toward the Danube River. At the same time, they were conquering Southeastern Europe, the Ottomans were also strengthening their position in the Middle East by crushing the many petty kingdoms that dotted the land. This had the desirous effect of unifying the whole of the region. In 1453, Sultan Mehmet Fatih took the city of Constantinople in a great siege, after it had held off Muslim attacks for more than 700 years. Constantinople (later renamed Istanbul) became the proud capital of the Ottoman Empire (Fig. 3) and the seat of the *Khilafah*.

By the early sixteenth century, Ottoman rule extended throughout the lands bordering the eastern and southern shores of the Mediterranean. During the reign of Sultan Sulaiman al-Qanuni (1520-1566), the empire expanded all the way up to the gates of Vienna, where their armies were halted by the Hapsburg defenders. Following the death of Sulayman, the empire gradually slipped out of prominence, especially following the disastrous second attack on Vienna in 1683. As a result of this war, the Ottomans lost all of their Hungarian provinces. Eventually, the Christian armies pushed all the way to Skoplje in Macedonia, before the Muslims were able to regroup and push them back across the Danube.

Fig.3: Istanbul Mosque

During the 18th and 19th centuries, the European provinces were slowly detached. In 1910, Ottoman authority extended only in the Sanjak of Novi Pazar, Macedonia, Albania, the southern part of Bulgaria and Thrace. Asia Minor and the Arabic speaking regions of Southwest Asia were still under the banner of the Ottomans. The disastrous results of the First World War, in which the Ottomans allied with the Central Powers, resulted in the destruction of the Empire and the *Khilafah*. The collapse of the Ottoman Empire paved the way for the Europeans to take control of Muslims of North Africa and the Middle East. Syria and Lebanon came under French rule, as did Algeria, Tunisia and neighboring Morocco. The British took control of Egypt, Sudan, Iraq, Jordan and Palestine. To lay out their colonial holdings, the European created a framework of political boundaries which were not known in Muslims lands before. Those borders established the politico-geographical map of the region which have for the most part, remained in tact to this day. Such boundaries, often inadequately defined and delimited, were destined to produce conflict, and many did.

Eastward Expansion of Islam: 750-1400 AD

By 750 AD, the Muslim Empire had extended from Spain in the West across Northern Afric, and the lands east of the Mediterranean Sea as far into Central Asia. Muslim armies had also pushed eastward as far as Sindh and Punjab in the Indian subcontinent. While the Muslim Arab armies never invaded China (although they did fight the Chinese armies at the Battle of the Talas River in modern day Kazakhstan), Muslim merchants were active in the region. Sizable numbers settled in cities along the trade routes rimming the Taklamakan desert, which was the western gate into China. Arab and Persian tradesmen also sailed to the eastern coast of China, where they established Muslim neighborhoods in the coastal cities. Thus, they had influence beyond the political frontiers of the Muslim states. They maintained an enduring influence. In fact, these areas of modern China still have huge Muslim populations.

In India, the Muslims were very active in extending their influence by both land and sea. The main land route into India was through Afghanistan and from there into the Punjab region. In 712 AD, Arab Muslims gained control of the Sindh and Punjab provinces, which became, in time, Muslim dominated areas and a stage for further expansion of Islam. Later, Islam was carried deeper into India by the Turks, Persians, and Islamized Mongols.

The real breakthrough into India occurred after the year 1000 AD. Turkish Muslims pushed southeastward along the Ganges River plain as far as the junction of the Ganges and Jamuna Rivers. Near the end of the 1100s, a second wave of expansion began. This too, was led by a Turkish dynasty that rose to power in Western Persia. They won an important battle at Panipat near Delhi against the Hindu *rajas* (kings and princess), giving them control of the key routes to the East and South. Once again, the conquering Muslims remained as tolerant as ever and won over the hearts of the population. During their rule, forcible conversions were rare. The Sufi teachers and political environment brought many Hindus to the fold of Islam. Islam's vigorous presence in India brought far-reaching changes to Hindu society. The Muslim religion gained most of its converts in the cities and towns and, for the most part, did not reach out to the vast rural areas. Since the Muslims were not bound by the caste system, they freely associated with the lower levels of Hindu society and offered them employment (particularly in the army). When Hindu low-castes and outcasts accepted jobs with the Muslims, they achieved a degree of brotherhood that they could have never attained among their own people. Consequently, these urban Indians gradually began accepting Islam *en masse*.

Several strongholds of Islam were established by Arab traders in the coastal ports of India and along the Arabian Sea, such as in the Comoros, the Maldives, Sri Lanka, and along the east coast of Africa. Here again, the spread of Islam was by peaceful means rather than by conquest. Muslim retailers settled in these port cities, which were frequently visited by ships sailing along the trade routes to the Orient.

The same sea traffic that carried Islam to Indian and East African ports was responsible for spreading the religion by peaceful means to the islands of modern day Indonesia, Malaysia, and the Philippines. As a result of its trade with China, Muslim traders (some time before 1400 AD) had begun establishing themselves at the northern tip of the island of Sumatra, astride the sea route to China. From this base in northern Sumatra, Islam spread through the East Indies between 1400 AD and 1600 AD. An active trade was developed by the Arab, Persian, and Indian Muslims, particularly with ports on Java, Sumatra, and Ternate. Trade routes were eventually extended to other islands as well, including the island of Mindanao in the Philippines. At the same time, shortly after 1400 AD, a Muslim colony was established on Malacca on the Malay peninsula (Fig. 4). Often, the honesty and high moral character of the Muslim merchants in these ports swayed the local inhabitants to accept Islam. Sometimes, local princes converted to Islam, bringing all their people with them. The diffusion of Islam around the world is represented by Map 3, and the number of Muslim countries by Table 1. Tables 1 and 2 represent the number of Muslims and their percentages in the world.

Fig. 4: Early Muslim Traders in the Malay Islands

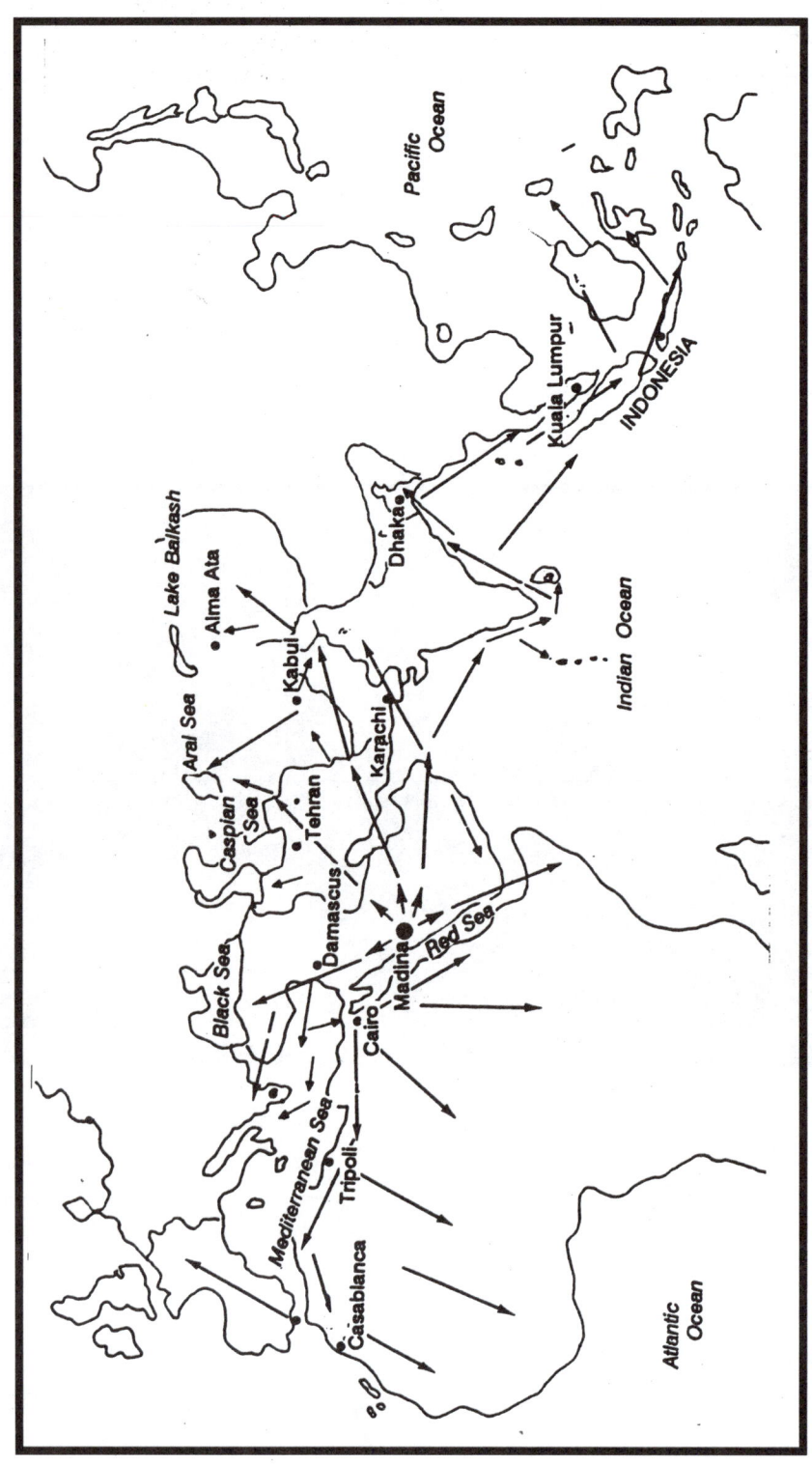

Map 3: Diffusion of Islam

Table 1 Muslims Nations, 1994			
Country	Percent Muslim Population	Muslim Population (Million)	Total (Millions)
Afghanistan	99	17.52	17.70
Albania	70	2.38	3.40
Algeria	99	27.23	27.50
Azerbaijan	83	5.81	7.00
Bahrain	99	0.59	0.60
Bangladesh	85	99.28	116.80
Bosnia-Herzogovina	40	1.75	4.50
Brunei	64	0.19	0.30
Chad	51	2.81	5.50
Comoros	100	0.50	0.45
Djibouti	90	0.45	0.50
Egypt	91	53.14	58.14
Eritrea	51	1.40	2.70
Gambia	87	0.87	1.00
Gaza	98	0.78	0.80
Guinea	69	5.68	8.20
Indonesia	88	169.99	190.90
Iran	98	62.43	63.70
Iraq	96	19.82	19.60
Jordan	95	3.67	3.80
Kazakhistan	60	10.42	17.40
Kyrgyzstan	74	3.18	4.30 (1988)
Kuwait	96	1.44	1.50
Lebanon	60	2.16	3.60
Libya	98	4.70	4.80
Malaysia	60	11.22	18.70
Maldives	100	0.20	0.20
Mali	80	5.60	7.00 (1988)
Mauritania	99	2.18	2.20
Morocco	99	27.42	27.70
Niger	87	7.70	8.90
Nigeria	51	48.76	95.60
Oman	99	0.50	0.50
Pakistan	97	125.32	129.20
Qatar	95	0.48	0.50
Saudi Arabia	99	17.00	17.20
Senegal	91	7.64	8.40
Sierra Leone	50	2.35	4.70
Somalia	99	8.71	8.80
Sudan	72	20.30	28.20
Syria	87	12.88	14.80
Tajikistan	60	3.42	5.70
Tunisia	99	6.73	6.80
Turkey	99	61.23	61.90
Turkemenistan	90	3.67	4.10
United Arab Emirate	90	2.43	2.70
Uzbekistan	69	25.43	22.20
Western Sahara	100	2.43	2.70
Yemen	99	10.99	11.10

Table 2
Countries in which 25-49 percent of the population in Muslim

	Percent	Muslim Population Million (1994)	Total Population
Burkina Faso	44	4.49	10.2
Cote d'Ivoire	25	4.87	13.9
Ethiopia	35	19.08	54.5
Guinea-Basau	38	0.38	1.0
Tanzania	30	8.82	29.4

Table 3
Countries in which a significant number of people (2 million or more) is Muslim, even though they represent less than 25 percent of the total population.

	Percent	Muslim Population (Million) (1994)	Total Population
Cameroon	22.0	2.97	13.5
Ghana	15.0	2.35	17.0
India	11.0	101.05	918.6
Zaire	10.0	4.03	40.3
Philippines	6.0	4.01	66.8
Thailand	4.0	2.32	58.0
China	1.5	17.94	1,196.2

Other Muslim population (country, percent Muslim, number Muslims in millions (1988); Belgium (0.9%) .069; Benin (16%) .720; Bhutan (5%) .075; Bulgaria (11%) .988; Burma (3.6%) 1.479; Burundi (1%) .052; Canada (0.6%) .157; Central African Republic (8%) .221; Cyprus (18.5%) .127; Equatorial Guinea (0.7%) .002; Fiji (8%) .059; France (1%) .559; Gabon (1%) .013; Greece (2.5%) .252; Guyana (9%) .069; Hong Kong (0.5%) .028; Israel (12.5%) 554; Kampuchea (2.4%) .160; Kenya (6%) 1.401; Liberia (21%) .517; Madagascar (2%) .218; Malawi (16%) 1.229; Mauritius (17%) .187; Mongolia (9.5%) .194; Mozambique (13%) 1.967; Nepal (5%) .913; Panama (4.5%) .104; Reunion (2.4%) .013; Romania (1.2%) .276; Rwanda (8.6%) .607; Singapore (18.3%) .483; South Africa (1.2%) .421; Sri Lanka (8%) 1.331; Suriname (14%) .055; Taiwan (0.5%) .099; Togo (16%) .554; Trinidad and Tobago (6.5%) .083; Uganda (6.6%) 1.086; United Kingdom (1.4) .799; United States (0.6%) 1.477; Vietnam 1%) .652; Zambia (1%) .075; Zimbabwe (0.9%) .068
Source: John R. Weeks, "The Demography of Islamic Nations." Population Bulletin, Vol. 14, No. 4 (December 1988). Population Reference Bureau, Washington, DC, 1988

CHAPTER 1
AFGHANISTAN

Afghanistan is a country where Islam pervades all aspects of life. The religious doctrines and codes provide the principal means of controlling conduct and settling legal disputes. Except for a rather small urban population in the principal cities, most of the people are divided into clan and tribal groups, and follow centuries old customs and religious practices in the conduct of affairs. Tragically, this nation has been involved in bitter violence over recent decades.

GEOGRAPHY

Afghanistan is a landlocked country, whose strategic location has had a major influence on its history. It borders Turkmenistan, Uzbekistan and Tajikistan in the north, Iran in the west, Pakistan in the south and southeast, and the Peoples Republic of China in the northeast. Its boundary with Pakistan is about 1,406 miles (2,250 km) long, drawn by Sir Mortimer Durrand in 1893 and accepted by the King (Amir) of Afghanistan in a treaty that same year. It is a topographically convenient boundary along the foothills of the Sulaiman mountains. The northern boundary with Turkmenistan, Uzbekistan, and Tajikistan (Former Soviet Union), which was confirmed in 1921 and revised in 1946, is 680-miles (1088 km) long. It runs east from Zulfikar on the Hari River to the Kushka River, then northeast to the Oxus River. Oxus is one of the great rivers of Central Asia, which rises in a lake in the Pamirs and runs for over 1230 miles (1,968 km). From the Pamirs to

Geographical Profile

Area: About 250,000 sq. miles (647,500 sq. km)
Population: 17.7 million (1994); 20.7 million (2000); 34.5 million (2010); (about 3.5 million live as refugees in Pakistan and 2 million in Iran)
Capital City: Kabul
Other Cities: Ghazni, Qandahar, Mazar-e-Sharif, Herat
Neighboring Countries: Pakistan (south and southeast), Iran (west), Turkmenistan, Uzbekistan, Tajikistan (north), and China (northeast)
Climate: Extremely hot, dry summers with cold nights, cold winters with moderate rain and snow in the mountains, scanty rain on the plain. Strong winds and dust storms are common.
Official Languages: Pushtu and Dari (a branch of Persian)
Other Principal Languages: Uzbek, Turkmen, Balochi, and Hazara
Ethnic Background: People identify mainly on the basis of languages, i.e., as Pashtuns (Afghans), Tajiks, Uzbeks and Turkmens. The Dari speaking Hazaras are distinguished from Tajiks by geographic location and traditions.
Principal Religions: Islam 99% (Sunnis 87%; Shi'ahs 12%)
Official Name: Islamic Republic of Afghanistan

Khamiab, it forms the northern boundary of Afghanistan. The Anglo-Russian Pamir Convention held in 1890 made the Wakhan panhandle a part of Afghanistan, to separate British and Russian forces.

Within these boundaries, Afghanistan lies wholly on the western portion of the Iranian plateau. The dominating feature is the great mountain range of the Hindukush and its continuations (Map 4). The Hindukush mountains fan out in a number of minor ranges with plateaus and valleys. The

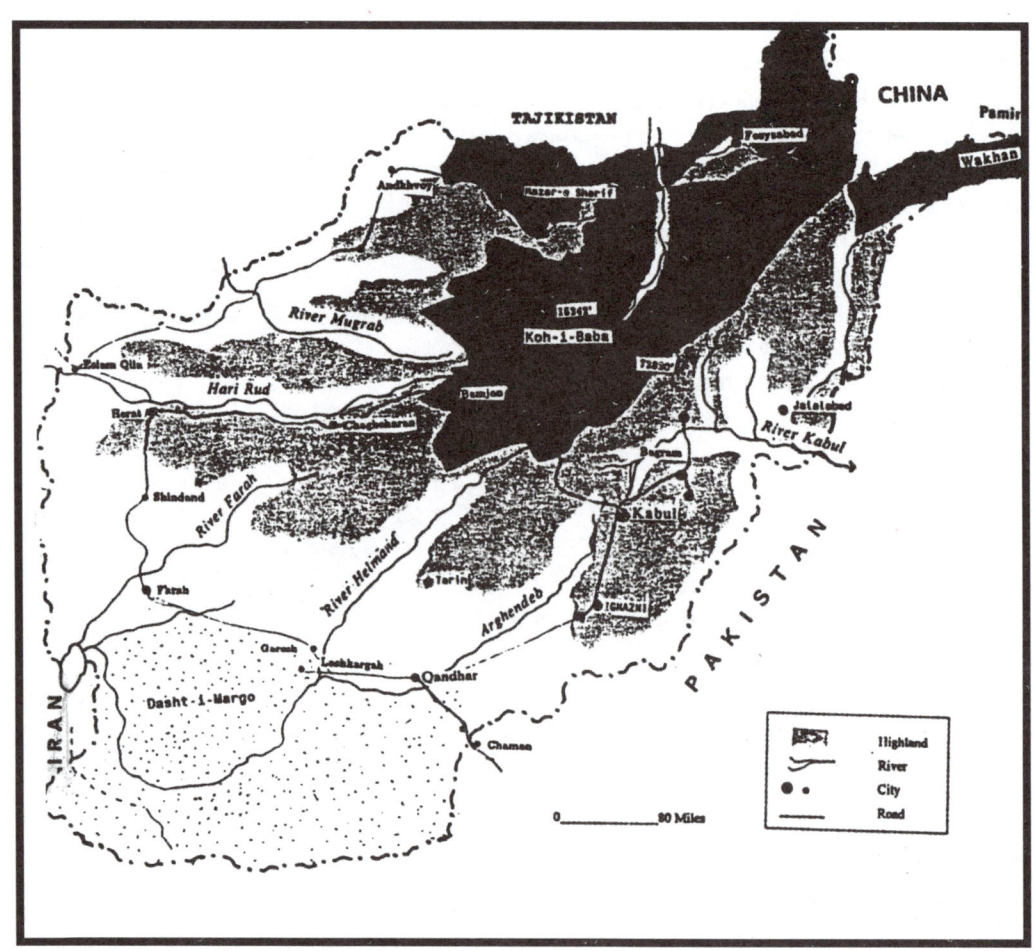

Map 4: Afghanistan

northern slopes of the Hindukush mountains form the region of Badakshan and Afghan Turkistan. This area is drained by a number of rivers running to the Oxus River (Amu Darya). In the Northwest, the Hari River is important. The Helmand River and its tributaries drain Southwestern Afghanistan. Kabul River drains about 35,000 sq. miles (90,650 sq. km) of Afghanistan. Kabul and its tributaries are all snow fed streams. Their valleys are the most fertile in the country, furnishing the chief routes of trade between Central and South Asia.

Afghanistan's climate is typical of the higher regions of central Asia: cold in the winter and hot and dry in the summer. Another characteristic of the climate is the range of temperature within short periods, from one season to another, and from place to place. For example, in the summer, the temperature is 16°C (60°F) at sunrise in Kabul (1829 m., 6000 ft.) and by noon it reaches 38°C (100°F). Kabul's mean temperature in January is 0°C (32°F). In the plains of Jalalabad (594 m., 1800 ft.), summer temperatures often reach 46°C (115°F). Precipitation is scanty, rarely exceeding 15 inches (38 cm.) annually, most of which comes from October to April. Rainfall varies greatly. The monsoon has little effect in Afghanistan, for hardly any rain crosses the barrier of the Sulaiman Mountains. No part of the country receives more than 10 inches of rainfall annually, coming mainly in the winter from westerly depressions which originate in the Mediterranean or the Caspian Sea.

EVOLUTION OF AFGHANISTAN

The land of Afghanistan has played an important role in history since the dawn of recorded history. This land was conquered by Alexander the Great during his campaigns of the fourth century BC. Most of the urban dwellers became Buddhist prior to the coming of Islam. The last great pre-Islamic Afghan kingdom, the Kushans Shahs, held considerable sway even up to the Indus valley.

Arabs conquered Afghanistan in 652 AD, and introduced Islam so effectively that it continues to be a supreme force there. Islam is invoked in almost everything done by the people. This faith dominates the land and society in Afghanistan, though the country came under different influences following the Arab rule.

The modern Kingdom of Afghanistan began in the 18th century. Through much of the 19th century its independence was jeopardized by the intrusion of British and Russian forces. But in 1907, because of resistance by the people of Afghanistan, the two powers agreed to maintain Afghanistan as an independent buffer state between their respective domains. British influence continued to be strong, however, until after World War I.

In 1973, a communist government, oriented towards the Soviet Union, overthrew the Afghan monarchy. People did not accept the un-Islamic communist rule and widespread rebellion ensued. In 1979, the armies of the Soviet Union were called on by the communist government for assistance against this armed resistance. The Soviets responded by sending in sizable military forces, and a long guerrilla war began. The Soviet invasion roused international outrage led by the United States. Widespread killing and maiming of civilians, destruction of villages, burning of crop fields, killing of livestock and pollution or destruction of irrigation systems by Soviet ground and air forces caused several million Afghani refugees to flee to Pakistan and Iran (Fig. 5). The Pakistani Government tried to accommodate the Afghani refugees, making temporary tent settlements along its border (Fig. 6) and establishing temporary schools for the children (Fig. 7). Meanwhile, arms from Pakistan, Saudi Arabia, Egypt and United States were provided to the Afghani *Mujahideen*, who kept up resistance in the face of heavy odds. Finally, in 1989, the Soviet government withdrew its forces, leaving the country dilapidated and in the hands of the Najibullah. The government of Najibullah tried to hold on to power, but was forced to resign on April 16, 1992. In wake of the anti-Communist victory, internal dissension led the country into a civil war. Despite the efforts of neighboring countries, the Organization of Islamic Conference, and the United Nations, Afghanistan's civil war is getting worse, even spreading to provinces previously spared from fighting. Kabul has been split into sectors controlled by half a dozen factions, resulting in house-to-house battle for control of the devastated capital.

Fig. 5: A family moving to Pakistan
as a result of Soviet Occupation of Afghanistan

Fig. 6: A Tent Settlement near Peshawar, Pakistan

Fig. 7: School for Afghan Refugees

POPULATION AND ECONOMY

Afghanistan's population before the Soviet invasion was estimated at 15 million. Except for a small population, the people live in the irrigated valleys around the fringes of high mountains occupying a large part of the country. The most heavily populated section of Afghanistan is the Southeast, particularly the fertile valley of the Kabul River, where the capital city of Kabul is located. Kabul is located at an elevation of 6200 ft. (2260 m) and has a population of 1.5 million people. Most of the inhabitants of the Southeast are Pushtuns, who are the largest and the most influential of the numerous ethnic groups that comprise the Afghan state. Their language, Pushtu, is related to Persian, which is widely used in Afghanistan, being the main language of administration and commerce.

Another populous area of Afghanistan occupies a belt of foothills and steppes on the northern side of the Hindukush Mountains. In this area, most of the inhabitants live in a series of oases forming an east-west belt along the base of the mountains. Southwestern Afghanistan comprises a large desert basin, part of which extends into Iran. An area of interior drainage, it receives the water of the Helmand and several other rivers originating in Afghanistan's central mountains. Extensive irrigation works supported a large population here in ancient times, but the water system was largely destroyed by Mongolian invaders in the 13th and 14th centuries, and the damage has never been fully repaired. The Afghan government, through its Helmand Valley Irrigation and Power project, has been reclaiming and resettling the land by providing irrigation water from storage and flood-control reservoirs on the Helmand and other rivers. *Karez* or *Qanat* is a traditional and important irrigation system. It is a subsurface irrigation system, which originated in nearby Iran about 3000 years ago.

Afghanistan is overwhelmingly a rural and agricultural or pastoral country. People gain their living from farming or livestock grazing. The country is so mountainous and arid that only an estimated 12 percent is cultivated. Enough rain falls in the major areas of population during the winter to permit nonirrigated growing of winter grains. Agriculture accounts for 44 percent of the Gross Domestic Product (GDP), employing more than 67 percent of the labor force. Yet, of the 160 million acres, only 35 million acres are considered suitable for agriculture. Of these 35 million, only 30 million acres were actually cultivated before the Soviets occupied the country. Wheat is the principal crop, covering a quarter of the cultivated area. Sugar cane, sugar beets, fruits, nuts, and cotton are also grown in the irrigated lands. In keeping with a long tradition, the skins and wool of *karakuli* sheep remain important exports. The United States has been one of the principal purchasers of Afghani goods, particularly of the skins of *karakuli* lambs.

In good crop years, the country is nearly self-sufficient in terms of cereal grains, but increasing population and frequent drought has required the import of other grains in most years. The high price of cotton in world markets has resulted in increased production of this crop. Overall, Afghanistan's agriculture bears many of the customary Middle Eastern earmarks: traditional methods, crude tools, inadequate fertilization, poor varieties of plants and animals, and low yields.

Fourteen years of war (1978-1992) devastated the economy of Afghanistan. Five million people, about one third of the population, were forced to flee to Pakistan or Iran, deserting their farms. Orchards were destroyed, and so were the industrial units. The government statistics published for the United Nations conference show the GNP prices as having declined by 1.3 percent per annum between 1978-79 and 1986-87.

The northern part of this country has large deposits of natural gas and some oil. Mineral resources, such as iron ore and coal in the Hindukush Mountains, have not yet been explored. Lead, copper, zinc and *lapis lazuli* (a blue semi-precious stone) have been located at several places. The best potential source of energy is hydroelectric power, the development of which requires a capital investment beyond the country's limited capacity.

Industry

Industry in Afghanistan, which is responsible for processing the raw material provided by agriculture, is rudimentary. The first cotton textile mills were established in the mid-1930s. Other plants manufacture rayon, woolen textiles, and refined sugar. Chemical fertilizer is produced from natural gas at Mazar-e-Sharif. In the Shibarghan gas field area, Nitrogenous Fertilizer Works and the Jangalak Engineering Factory were established by the Soviets. The volume of gas at Shiberghan is enormous. It is piped in two directions: one pipeline goes to the North, and the other towards Hajigak. Along its routes, factories, including a steel mill at Hajigak, are planned using the pipeline as a source of power. A few miles from Hajigak are substantial deposits of limestone. Extensive deposits of other minerals have been found throughout Afghanistan, but none of them is substantial enough to help industrialize the country.

Civil war and political instability has brought an end to tourist industry. Formerly, the main tourist attractions were Bamian, with its high statue of Buddha, the hundreds of painted caves in Bandi Amir, with its splendid lakes, the blue mosque of Mazar, Herat, with its grand mosque and minarets, the towns of Qandhar and Girishehk, Balkh (ancient Bactaria), "Mother of Cities" in the North, Bagram, and the high mountains of Hindukush.

The economy of Afghanistan is in shambles, because of continued internal warfare among various ethnic/tribal groups for political control of the country since Afghanistan's freedom from Soviet occupation. Table 4 gives the major imports and exports of Afghanistan. based on a 1993 publication of *Islamic Chambers*.

Table 4 Major imports/exports of Afghanistan			
Principal exports 1990	$ m	Principal imports 1988	$ m
Fruits & nuts	93	Capital goods	293
Carpets	44	Food	150
Wool	10	Textiles	117
Karakul skins	3	Petroleum products	99
Cotton	3	Sugar & vegetable oil	53
		Tyres	50
Total include others	253	Total include others	900

Transport and Communication

Afghanistan's progress has been much hampered by its poor transport and communications network. Even today, no rail line crosses Afghanistan to connect the Central Asian states or Pakistan. In fact, not a single mile of railway exists at all within Afghanistan, and surfaced highways are few. The foreign commerce is routed through the port of Karachi in Pakistan. Any major modernized road in Afghanistan date back to 1953. Both the United States and former Soviet Union contributed largely to these roads. A historic case of cooperation between the Americans and Soviets occurred in Afghanistan with the building of the bridge of Dilaram. The former Soviet Union built a road over a bridge built by Americans. The Americans also built a road from Kabul to Torkham at the Khyber Pass. The Americans additionally funded construction of the highway from Kabul to Kandhar and Spin Boldak, and from Herat to Tayibat on the Iranian border. The former Soviet Union constructed a road from Kabul to Qizil Qala through the Salang tunnel, which was inaugurated in August 1964. It took six years and a lot of money to construct this one and a half-mile tunnel. Previously, it used to take two days to drive from Kabul to Phul-i-Khumri, the first town on the other side of the mountains. Now, it takes hardly five hours. Another 465-mile road linking the Soviet frontier town Khushka with Kandhar via Herat was opened in August 1965.

———————————— **NOTES** ————————————

CHAPTER 2
ALBANIA

Most Albanians are followers of Islam, which was introduced by the Turks during their rule of over 500 years. A minority of Christian Orthodox and Roman Catholics had been in existence since the time of the apostles in the first century. In 1944, the Communists took over and abolished all religious institutions. Therein, Albania proclaimed itself as "the first atheist state in the world." However, many Albanians continued to practice their religions in the privacy of their homes. Since 1990, Albania began changing its policies to reorganize politically and economically. As a result, Islam and Christianity are slowly re-emerging in Albanian society.

GEOGRAPHY

Albania is one of the smallest and poorest nations in Europe. It stretches along the Adriatic shores, facing Italy across the narrow Strait of Otranto, leading into the Adriatic Sea. On the north and the east of Albania is Yugoslavia (Serbia and Montenegro) and Macedonia. On its southeastern borders lies Greece (Map 5).

The great Proklatije Range, sometimes called the North Albanian Alps, forms the frontier between former Yugoslavia and Albania. In this region, Albania is unique, having a triangular shaped lowland, seamed with lines of low hills. The bed of this lowland is the Adriatic coast between the Drin Gulf and Cape Glossa.

Geographical Profile

Area: 11,000 sq. mi. (26,249 sq. km.)
Population: 3.4 million (1994); 3.8 million (2000); 3.9 million (2010)
Annual Rate of Natural Increase: 3.5%
Capital City: Tirana
Other Cities: Durres, Vlora, Korce, Shkoder
Neighboring Countries: Greece, Yugoslavia, Macedonia. To the West is a 250-mile coastline along the Adriatic Sea
Official Language: Albanian
Ethnic Groups: Albanians (consist of two subgroups: Gegs and Tosks), small numbers of Greeks
Religion: 70% Muslims (80% Sunni, 20% Bektashi Shi'ah); 20% Orthodox and 10% Roman Catholics
Economy:
  GDP: $2.7 billion (1991)
  Per Capita Income: $820.00
  Agriculture: Labor Force: 50%
  Products: Wheat, corn, sugar beets, cotton, tobacco
  Industry: Textile, timber, construction material, semi-processed minerals
Official Name: Peoples Socialist Republic of Albania

The southern section of Albania consists of lofty mountain ranges, tending northwest to southeast, alternating with deep river valleys. The high mountain zone of interior Albania stretches south from the Drin River to the southern end of Lake Prespa. The western mountain zone consists of barren ranges through which rivers flow in difficult gorges to the lowlands, offering good facilities for hydroelectric power development.

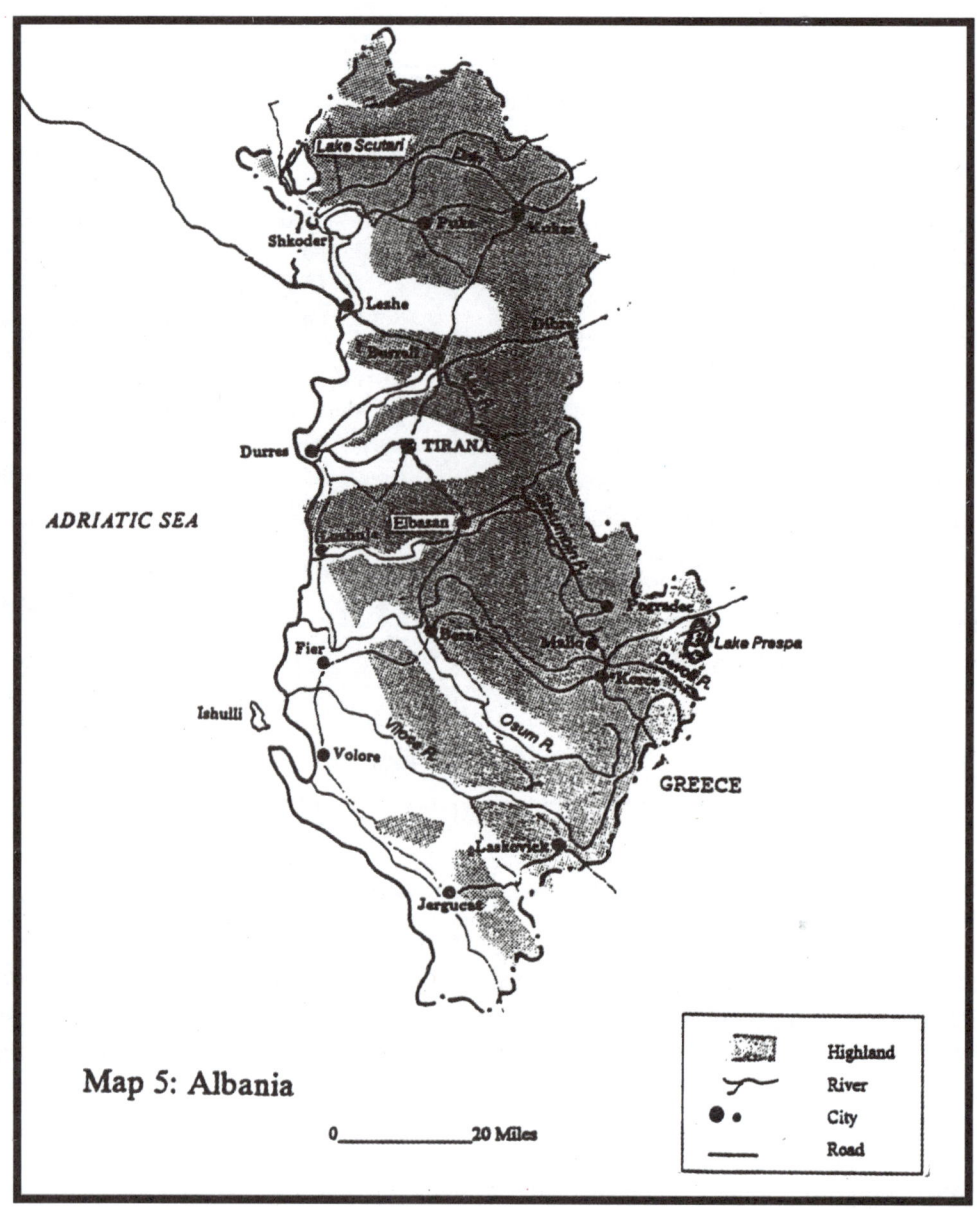

Map 5: Albania

The inner tectonic depression is occupied by the upper courses of various rivers and filled by young sediments. This discontinuous depression is succeeded eastward by the lofty central zone, where there are extensive forests which provide the raw materials for the timber industry.

About 20 percent of Albania consists of a flat to rolling coastal plain, poorly drained in some places. Most of the country consists of hills and mountains between the Dinaric highlands of former Yugoslavia and the ranges of northern Greece, often covered by scrub forests. Access to the hills above is difficult; yet the traffic and the native population refuse to desert them. Most of the population lives in the interior basins amid the hills.

Major cities are located on the coastal plain or in the larger upland valleys. Primary rivers, moderate in size, generally flow in an east-west direction. The Buna River, which forms the outlet for Lake Scutari along the Yugoslav border to the north, is the only navigable river. Along the coast, Albania has mild, wet winters with a January low of 5.5°C (42°F) and dry, hot summers with a July high of 28°C (83°F). The interior is cooler and with more rainfall.

EVOLUTION OF A NEW NATION

The Albanian nation represents one of the oldest human communities in Europe. They are the direct descendants of an ancient Indo-European people, the Illyrians. This race inhabited most of the western portions of the Balkan peninsula up to the Danube. During the days of the Roman Empire, the Illyrians proved difficult to conquer. During the massive Slav migrations of the seventh century AD, the Illyrian tribes were pushed back into the lands now occupied by the Albanians. Early on in the Middle Ages, Albanians embraced Christianity (both the Catholic and Orthodox brands).

In the early fourteenth century, the Ottomans began to make inroads into Albanian territory. At this point in history Albania could not be considered a unified state per se. The whole country was nothing more than a patchwork of tribes and feudal lords all in constant quarrel with each other.

The Ottomans were able to overtake the entire territory by exploiting the internal discord. It was during the nearly five centuries of Ottoman rule that the bulk of the Albanian people entered into Islam. This new faith offered the population a way out of the spiritual misery and exploitation that both of the Christian churches had for centuries afflicted Albanians with. Most Albanians belong to the Hanafi school of Sunni Islam. However, over centuries, Sufism has played a major role in shaping the religious traditions of the Albanians. Among the Albanians of Kosovo and Macedonia, the Sufi Orders were mainly Sunni (*Rifa'i, Qadiri, Mevlevi and Khalwati*) but in Albania proper, the Bektashi *Tariqat* brought the *Shi'ah* presence into this part of Europe.

During the era of the Ottomans, Albanians had shown exemplary service to the Sultans and the cause of Islam. In fact, it can almost be said that this Balkan people (along with the Bosnians) completely ran the affairs of state.

At the height of the Balkan War in November 1912, a provisional government was established in Albania. Seeing the inevitable collapse of the Ottoman Empire in the Balkans, Albanian nationalist leaders grudgingly declared independence from Turkey. Following the end of the First World War, some of the Allied Powers wanted to dismember Albania and divide it between the Serbs and Greeks. However, the Paris Peace Conference established Albania as an independent nation on the urging of President Woodrow Wilson. In 1920, Albania was admitted to the League of Nations and remained a member until Italy occupied it in 1939.

Germany occupied Albania in 1943. Many Albanians, seeing the success of the godless communist partisans on the battlefield, sided with the Germans. In 1944, Germans retreated from the Balkans, including Albania, and the Communist National Liberation Front took control of the country on November 29, 1944, initiating the blackest era in Albanian history. The new dictator of the country was the atheist Enver Hoxha (pronounced Hoja). As a Soviet stooge (from 1946 to 1962), Hoxha received much money and equipment for his country's economic development.

Extensive drainage and peat control made considerable areas suitable for agriculture, especially for grain. The region between the mouth of Drin River and Valona specialized in cotton, tobacco, and citrus fruits. The area north of Drin specialized in tobacco and dairy products.

Enver Hoxha's distate for the softer brand of communism introduced by Khrushchev in 1953 caused a rupture in Soviet-Albanian relations by 1960. The differences came to a head in 1961, when the Soviet Union openly denounced Albania, suspended diplomatic relations, and removed military bases from Albanian soil.

Enver Hoxha then turned to the People's Republic of China (PRC), and since 1962, the PRC has been a staunch ally of Albania, helping it in trade, industrialization and development programs. The PRC also provided military assistance and built a naval base at Valona as a showcase in Europe. However, political differences between the PRC and Albania soured following the Chinese decision to seek a relationship with the United States. After October 1976, Albania publicly denounced the PRC for its improved relations with the West.

Since the death of Enver Hoxha, in 1985, Albania has been trying to reorganize itself politically and economically, but the country has faced immense problems. The economy was completely depleted under communist rule. Today, Albania is not only the poorest state in Europe but in the entire Mediterranean region as well.

Religion was completely silenced during the decades of communist rule. Any open religious activity was punishable by imprisonment or execution. Many prominent members of the Sunni `ulama* and *babas* of the Bektashi *Shi'ah* order were murdered or made to suffer in prison camps. In 1990, a new Democratic government under the leadership of President Salih Berisha proclaimed an end to this barbaric repression. Since Albanians have been slowly rediscovering their Islamic roots. The vast majority of those born after the ban on religion in 1967 have virtually no awareness of Islam. This has proven to be a great challenge, as nearly two whole generations have grown up without religious knowledge.

ALBANIANS OUTSIDE OF ALBANIA

Nearly half of all ethnic Albanians live outside the borders of Albania. This is mainly the result of the desire of great powers of the West to prevent any powerful Muslim state in Europe. The worst repression of Albanians occurs in the Serbian province of Kosovo, where Albanian Muslims represent two million souls (95% of the province's population). Here, the dreams of "Greater Serbia" are being put into action in the face of through the worst forms of oppression. Nearly 700,000 Albanians, nearly all of them Muslim, live in the Republic of Macedonia. There used to be a large Albanian presence in Greece, but this was exterminated following the Second World War.

Historically, Albania has had the reputation of being the poorest country in Europe. At the outbreak of World War II, more than 80 percent of the Albanians were dependent on agriculture, which was the highest economic proportion of any European country. Even then, Albania was not self-sufficient in food. Relative neglect of agriculture in the post-war period has caused further damage.

Agriculture

Albania continues to be a net importer of foodstuffs and requires economic assistance from abroad to cover the deficit in its balance of payment. Even in 1993, an overwhelming majority of the people subsisted on livestock herding and farming. There is little chance that Albania will become self-sufficient in the near future. The break-up of cooperative farms in 1991, which were established during the communist regime resulted in severe dislocations.

Albania's agricultural resources are also not impressive. Arable land is estimated to cover 12 percent of the total area, which is the lowest of any agricultural country in Europe. This could be easily expanded with some reclamation and drainage of swamps, especially in the coastal plain. A variety of crops are raised, including tobacco around Shkoder on the lower Drin, cotton in the plain, and a great number of fruit trees, a specialty of the central part of the country around the capital.

Industry

Since 1994, the Communist government devoted its efforts to building an industrial infrastructure based on oil, tobacco, chromite, salt, asphalt resources and surplus labor. The economic model was that of the former Soviet Union under Stalin. Impressive gains in the industrial output were achieved, and goods were shipped through Albanian ports for ideological reasons, and not through former Yugoslavia or Greece, though it was more convenient. The construction of Albania's first railway after 1948 greatly assisted the development. Oil production and oil refining was greatly expanded along the Seman River, especially south of Elbasan. Durres was converted into a sizable, artificial port serving Northern and Central Albania. Tirana became the country's main industrial center with varied food, textile, timber, engineering and glass industries. There have been serious dislocations consequent to the break-up of Communist regimes in Eastern Europe, though the country still exports crude oil and natural gas to them. There are about 91 miles (145 km) of pipeline for petroleum, 37 miles (55 km) for petroleum products and 42 miles (64 km) for natural gas. Means of transportation have been improved as railroads and highways have extended their networks.

NOTES

CHAPTER 3
ALGERIA

Algeria fought seven long years for its independence from France and became an independent republic in 1962. Its successful revolution has assured the new state a place of prominence in the Muslim world as a fiercely independence loving country.

GEOGRAPHY

Situated in Northwest Africa, Algeria is the second largest country in Africa, after Sudan. Its area is 919,550 square miles (2.4 million sq. km) almost equal to one-third of the continental United States. In the south, Algeria's large Saharan desert is bordered by Libya, Niger, Mali, Mauritania, and Western Sahara. On its north is a 620 mile (900 km.) coastline along the Mediterranean Sea (Map 6).

Two Atlas Mountain ranges divide Algeria laterally into three zones. The first is a narrow fertile coastal plain - the Tell (Arabic for hill), between the northern Tellian Atlas and the Mediterranean. The Tell has a moderate year-round climate and rainfall adequate for agriculture. Stretching southward from the Tellian to the Saharan Atlas is the second zone of the High Plateau region. The Plateau region is 3,000 feet (914 meters) above sea level, with limited rainfall and great rocky plains and desert. It is generally devoid of vegetation except for a few oases of intermittent bush and plateau lands. The third and largest zone, south of the Saharan Atlas, is mostly desert. The mountains, desert, wasteland, and steppe are so large that they cover about 80 percent of the country.

Geographical Profile

Area: 918,497 sq. miles (92.4 million sq. km.)
Population: 27.5 million (1994); 32.5 million (2000); 37.0 million (2010)
Capital: Algiers (3 million)
Other Major Cities: Oran (59,818); Constantine (438,717); Annaba (310,106)
Neighboring Countries: Libya, Tunisia, Niger, Mali, Mauritania, Western Morocco, Morocco
Official Language: Arabic, Berber dialects, French widely spoken
Ethnic Groups: Arab and Berber
Religion: 99% Sunni Muslim
Economy:
  GDP: $59 billion
  Per Capita Income: $2,645.00
  Agriculture: 8% of GDP
  Products: wheat, barley, oats. olives, dates, citrus fruits, sheep, cattle
  Industry: 73% of GDP
  Types: crude oil, condensate and refined products, liquefied gas, mercury, phosphates
  Natural Resources: crude oil, natural gas, iron ore, phosphate, uranium, lead, zinc, mercury
Official Name: Democratic and Popular Republic of Algeria
Date of Independence: July 3, 1962

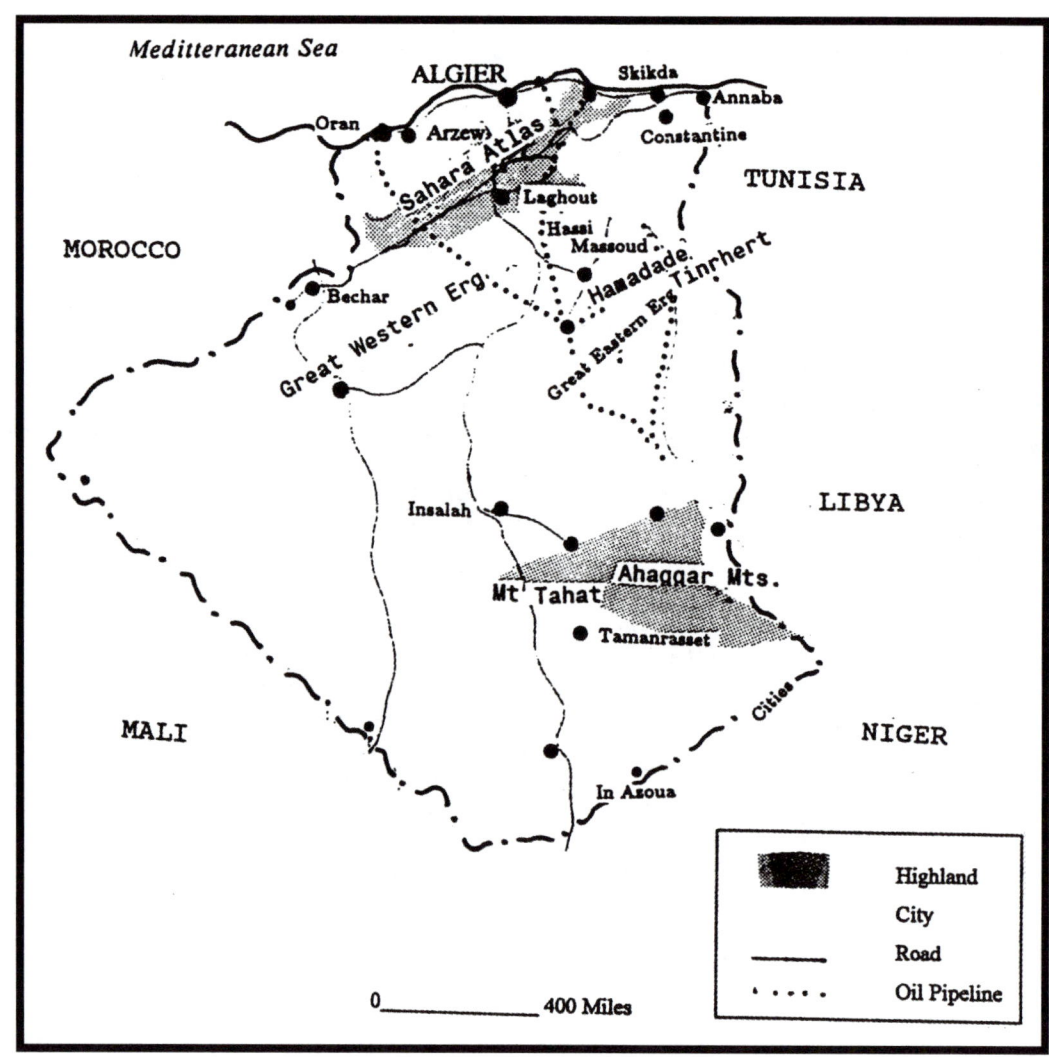

Map 6: Algeria

Algeria's weather is irregular from year to year. Generalizations about Algeria's climate apply without qualification. In the South, the summers are usually hot with little rainfall. In the North, the climate is of Mediterranean type, involving not only a modest annual precipitation but also a concentration of rainfall during the winter months. Winter brings rain to the North in October, but frost and snow are rare except in the Tellian Atlas. Dust and sandstorms occur most frequently between February and May.

EVOLUTION OF ALGERIA

Algeria's indigenous tribes, called "Berbers" by the Romans, were of Nilotic origin. They were successively invaded by the Phoenicians, Romans, Vandals, Byzantines, Arabs, Turkish, and finally the French in 1830. Of all these, the cultural impact of Islam has been the most significant. The Arabs introduced Islam and the Arabic language in Algeria between the 8th and 11th centuries. The French colonized the area in 1830 and with it began a major cultural conflict. The French tried to westernize Algeria, but the Muslims resisted to adopt it.

North African boundaries have frequently changed in history. The French created modern Algeria, whose colonization began in 1830. To benefit the French colonists, most of whom were farmers and businessmen, Northern Algeria was organized into overseas departments of France with representatives in the French National Assembly. France controlled the entire country, but Muslims in the rural areas remained outside the modernization orbit.

Muslims began their revolt against French rule on November 1, 1954. The revolution was launched by the National Liberation Front (FLN) which was a guerrilla war. The protracted war of seven years led to a cease-fire signed by France and the FLN on March 18, 1962, at Evian, France. The Evian Accord also provided for continuing economic, financial, technical, and cultural relations along with interim administrative arrangements until a referendum on self-determination could be held.

The referendum was held in Algiers on July 1, 1962. Favored by an overwhelming majority, France gave independence to Algeria on July 3. A constitution was adopted on September 8, 1963, which was abrogated two years later. Eleven years of rule by decree followed when a new constitution was approved by a popular referendum.

In recent years, Algeria has been the scene of much political turmoil. The national elections of 1992 were nullified when the Islamic Party (FIS) won landslide victories at all levels. The military (with the tacit support of the West) canceled the election and outlawed the FIS, arresting and killing its major proponents. Since then, FIS has launched an armed resistance campaign against the government.

ECONOMY

In the decade following independence, Algeria nationalized all major foreign business interests, as well as many private Algerian companies and about one-third of the arable farm land. Some land was redistributed to private owners in early 1985 and much larger redistribution occurred in 1987-88. Nationalization ranged from the assumption of a controlling interest to complete takeovers. The Algerian government has settled most of the claims for compensation of nationalized properties by foreign firms and in 1982 began settling individual claims.

Traditionally, the planning, development, and administration of the Algerian economy has been almost totally under state control. In recent years, the government has sought to reduce the level of its control. Government agencies and numerous state enterprises have controlled foreign trade and operated almost all major industries, much of the distribution and retail systems, all public utilities, and the entire banking and credit system. Recently, the government has launched an effort to foster greater autonomy in agricultural and other economic sectors as a means to improve production and economic performance.

Algeria has the most diverse and integrated economy of North African countries. It has a wealth of petrochemical resources and possesses rich agricultural resources in the northern and central sections of the country. The combination of minerals, such as iron ore, phosphates, lead, zinc, and mercury coupled with petroleum and farming, provides a breadth and richness to the Algerian resource base that is lacking elsewhere in North Africa.

Agriculture

Although 80 percent of the country is too dry or too steep to be productive for crops or pasture (Table 5), agricultural wealth of the country is derived from the limited area of fertile valleys and basins near the coast. Elsewhere, the mountains and steppes offer forests and grazing rather than agricultural opportunity. Of some importance are the high-quality dates produced in small desert oases for export. The northern region of Algeria is relatively fertile and well-watered. Once the granary of the Roman Empire, the area today grows wheat and other cereal crops, especially in the drier plateau country between the Saharan Atlas and the coastal mountain ranges. The coastal climate is ideal for cultivating grapes, olives, and other fruits and vegetables.

Outside the commercial agricultural zone, many peasants till poor soils for a low subsistence level of life. As a result, many people have left those areas and have moved to the coastal cities, where economic and social opportunities are greater. Also, many Algerians have migrated to France; their labor is important to the French economy.

Minerals

Algeria possesses valuable mineral resources, the most important being iron ore, phosphate, oil

Table 5
Land Use (in thousand hectares) in Algeria

Land Use	1981	1986	1991
Algeria			
Total land area	238,174	238,174	238,174
Arable land	6,885	6,967	7,085
Permanent cropland	625	566	568
Permanent pasture	31,661	31,155	31,000
Forest	4,384	4,252	4,050
Other	194,619	195,234	195,471

and natural gas. The iron ore is phosphorus free, with a high iron content and suitable for high grade steel-making. It is mined beside the Tebessa-Souk Ahras Railway near the Tunisian border and in the Cheliff valley of the Tell. Production is being increased, since it is being used in the Annaba iron and steel plant. Phosphates are mainly worked at Kouif, near Tebessa.

Algeria has a moderate position among oil producers. Oil production peaked in 1978, and has since declined. In 1980, reserves were down to 20 years' supply, and Western oil companies (most of whom had left when Algeria nationalized its oil industry in 1971) were persuaded to resume exploration. Oil was first discovered in Algeria in 1956 at Hassi Messaoud, 200 miles (350 km) south of Biskra. Other producing oil fields are at El Gessi and Edjele, and an enormous natural gas field is worked at Hassi R'Mel. Algeria is better supplied with natural gas than oil and is the world's largest gas exporter. Pipelines carrying oil and natural gas connect the main Saharan fields with Oran, Arzew, Algiers, and Sakida. Arzew and Sakida are major gas ports with plants to liquefy the gas (LNG) for export to industrialized nations in special tankers, with half of its LNG being shipped to the United States. To lessen that dependence on the United States, a pipeline to Italy was completed in 1981.

Industry

Until the Second World War, little industrial development was encouraged in Algeria, as France monopolized 90 percent of the trade in manufactured goods and regarded Algeria as a market and outlet for French products. In return, Algerian agricultural products and minerals were sent to France. This policy channeled most of the national capital and skill into agriculture and mining. During the war, the isolation of North Africa from France gave an impetus to the rise of varied industries, many of which have since continued. They are concerned with food processing, flour milling, fish canning, wine, oil, and olive oil manufacturing, and preserving fruit and vegetables, tobacco, and leather manufacturing. Other industries produce soaps, matches, glass and textiles. Not unexpectedly, most of these industries are located within the Tell and particularly in the three major port areas: Algiers, Oran, and Annaba.

In the years immediately following independence, both agriculture and industrial output declined drastically. Agriculture suffered because of the dislocation and resettlement during the war of independence, the hasty exodus of the French farmers (whose farms were the most productive), the reduced demand for Algerian wine by the French, and severe drought. Industrial production collapsed as French managers, teachers, clerks, and accountants left the country to be replaced by inexperienced workers' committees. Investment tailed off, and much French capital was withdrawn: unemployment soared. During this period, it was only the revenues from oil exports that kept Algeria from bankruptcy. These revenues increased. With aid from France and credit from the former Soviet Union, sales of natural gas became possible. Consequently, the earlier difficulties were overcome, and tentative economic planning on the socialist pattern began in the late 1960s. The early plans (1967-79) allotted 60 percent of investment to industrial and hydrocarbon development, notably into steel, mechanical and electrical engineering, oil refinery and petrochemicals, gas liquefaction and cement. Cheap power for industrial development was provided by establishing thermal electric plants using Saharan oil and gas.

The development plans throughout the 1970s paid little attention to agriculture (which at the time of independence employed 70 percent of the working population). Hence, food production declined by 25 percent since independence and with a heavy rate of population increased Algeria now produces barely one-third of her food needs. Agrarian reforms were introduced after 1972, but with the lack of resources for modernization, wider land ownership has had little effect upon productivity. It was not until the Third Plan (1980-84) that the proportion of investment in industry was decreased to 39 percent, and increased resources were given to agriculture, housing and education.

Algeria's external payments have been adversely affected by declining oil production and prices, as well as falling world prices of other hydro-carnon exports. In recent years Algeria has improved its relations with the World Bank and International Monetary Fund (IMF). It intends to overcome its debt problem by exporting and importing goods to and from Algeria.

CHAPTER 4
AZERBAIJAN

Azerbaijan is a Muslim stronghold in the corridor between the Black and the Caspian Seas. It has a beautiful, natural environment and offers a blend of traditional and modern development. Azerbaijan's political geography is complicated because of the existence of Nogoro-Karabakh (population 210,000), an enclave with sizable Armenian population, and Nakhichevan (population 325,000), an Azeri enclave landlocked by Armenian territory. Both Azeri enclaves were claimed by Armenia. Such action has led to continuing tensions and skirmishes. Because of its geographical location and its Islamic faith, its two Muslim neighbors, Iran and Turkey, and its powerful former colonial ruler Russia, have tried to pull Azerbaijan into their area of influence. Azerbaijan has both suffered and benefitted by these overtures.

Geographical Profile

Area: 41,000 sq. miles (106,000 sq. km)
Population: 7.4 million (1994); 8.3 million (2000); 9.5 million (2010)
Neighboring Countries: Iran, Armenia, Georgia, Daghestan (Russia)
Capital City: Baku
Other Cities: Gyanja or Gyandzha (formerly Kirovabad), Sumgait
Ethnic Groups: Azeris (78%), Russians (5.6%), Armenian (5.0%), Lezghi (2.4%), Others (3.7%)
Religion: 85% Muslims (75% Shi'ah, 25% Sunni), 15% Christians
Economy:
  GDP: $12,065 million (1991)
  Per Capita Income: $1,670
  Natural Resources: Oil, natural gas, iron ore, iron pyrites, cobalt, molybdenum
  Agriculture: Cotton, tobacco, grapes, tea
  Industry: Oil and oil refining, chemical, construction and machine building
Official Name: Republic of Azerbaijan
Date of Independence: October 18, 1991

GEOGRAPHY

The Republic of Azerbaijan (formerly the Azerbaijan Soviet Socialist Republic) occupies a corner of Transcaucasia that lies separated from Russia by mountains, from its western neighbors by religion and ethnicity, and from the Muslim republics to the east by waters of the Caspian Sea. It borders Iranian Azerbaijan in the south along the Aras River. To the west is Armenia, to the northwest is Georgia, and to the north is the Daghestan Autonomous Republic in the Russian Federation (Map 7). The Nakhichevan Autonomous Republic is a part of Azerbaijan, although it is separated from the rest of the country by Armenian territory. Azerbaijan also includes the Nagorno Karabakh Autonomous Region, which has a small Armenian presence. These three republics lie on the southern flanks of the Caucasian Mountains (Bolshoi Kavkaz) which is the traditional boundary between Europe and Asia. The country is characterized by a variety of landscapes. More than 40 percent of its territory is taken up by lowlands, about half lying at elevations from 1,300 to 4,900 feet (400 to 1,500 m) above sea level. Areas above 4,900 feet (1493 m) occupy a little more than 10 percent of the total area.

The highest peaks are Bazarduzi, Shakdagh, and Tufan, all parts of the Great Caucasus, which forms a natural northern boundary of the republic. The spurs of little Caucasus in southwest Azerbaijan form the second important mountain system which includes the Shakdag, Murovdag and Zangazur ranges and also the Karabakh uplands. The southern part of Azerbaijan is bordered by the Talish Mountain with Kumurk as the highest point. The Kara-Aras (Araks) lowland is named after the main river and its tributary. A well-developed network of canals between the Kara and Aras Rivers makes it possible to irrigate a major part of the lowland.

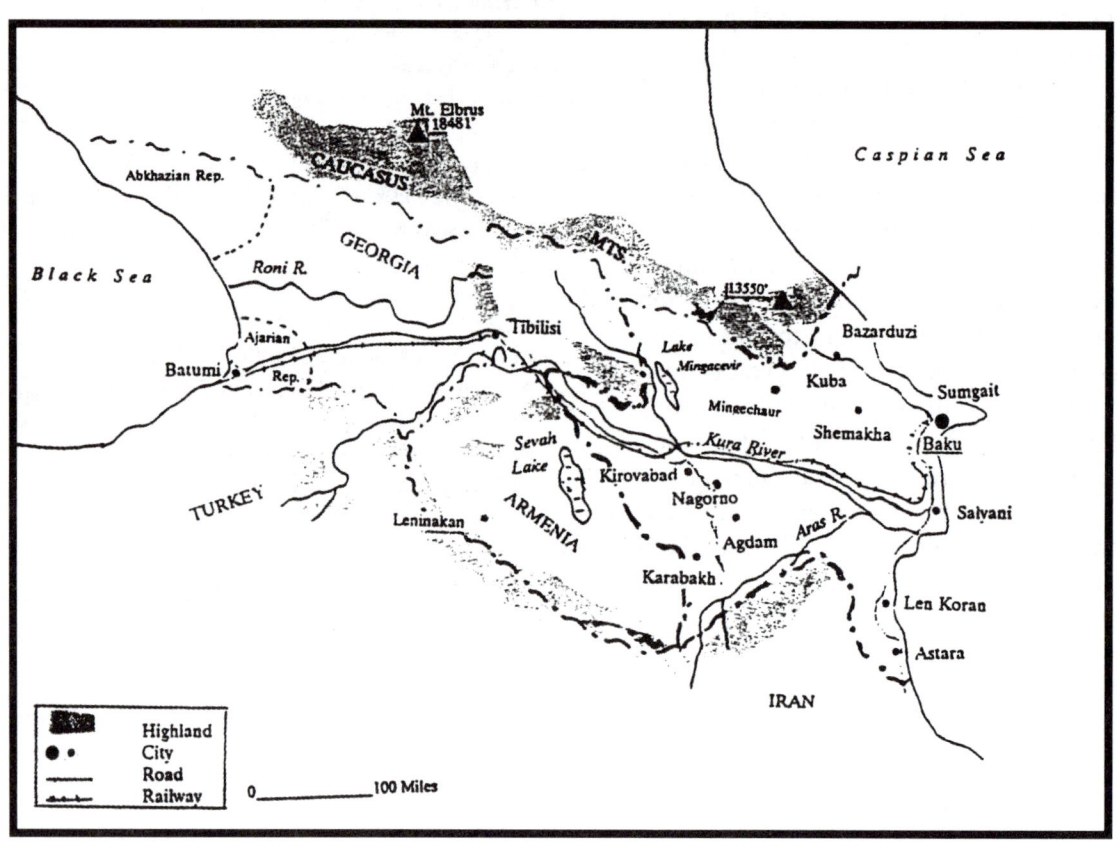

Map 7: Azerbaijan

The dry, subtropical climate prevailing in central and eastern Azerbaijan is characterized by a mild winter and a long (four to five months) hot summer, with an average temperature of 81°F

(27°C) and a maximum temperature of 109°F (27°C). Southeast Azerbaijan is characterized by a humid, subtropical climate and has the highest precipitation in the republic reaching 47-55 inches (1200-1400 mm) a year, most of which falls in the cold months. A dry continental climate, with a cold winter and a dry, hot summer prevails in the Nakhichevan Autonomous Republic at altitudes of 2,300 feet to 3,300 feet (700 to 1000 m). Moderately warm, dry, or humid types of climate are to be found in other parts of Azerbaijan.

PEOPLE AND POPULATION

The oldest inhabitants of Azerbaijan were of Persian stock. These people mingled with the Turkish tribes who migrated here in the 11th century. In the following centuries, the region came to adopt the Turkish language. Today, Azeris comprise about three-quarters of the republic's population. In the Nakhichavan region, almost all of the inhabitants are Azeris, whereas more than 40% of the population of Nogorno-Karabakh are Armenians.

The official language of the country is Azeri, one of the southwest Turkic group of languages. In 1992, the Turkish version of Latin script replaced the Cyrillic alphabet (which had been in use since 1939). Religious adherence corresponds largely to ethnic origins; almost all ethnic Azeris are Shi'ah Muslims, and the 25% Sunnis include some of the Daghestani groups within the country. There are also Christian communities, mainly representatives of the Russian Orthodox and Armenian Apostolic denominations. Shortly after the dissolution of the Soviet Union, fighting between Muslim Azeris and Christian Armenians broke out in the autonomous province of Nagorno-Karabakh. The Armenians in Nagorno-Karbakh hoped to cleanse the region of its Muslim element and join with the Armenian Republic. The initial conflict was very bloody, and the Armenians (with outside assisitance) were able to make gains against the Azeris. Iran and Turkey tried to broker a peace between the Azeris and Armenians, but this effort was rejected by radicals in the Armenian camp. More than twice as many Azeris live in the Iranian province called Azerbaijan (as in independent Azerbaijan). To stop any move by its Azeri population to unite with independent Azerbaijan, Iran very often supported the Armenian side. Turkey, however, backed the Azeris in their efforts to consolidate against Armenian nationalism and expansionism in the region.

In 1994, Azerbaijan's population stood at 7.4 million people with a 2.0 percent annual rate of natural increase. With this rate, the population of Azerbaijan would be 8.3 million people and 9.5 million in 2010. As a capital, Baku (1.8 million) has grown into Transcaucasia's largest city.

EVOLUTION OF AZERBAIJAN

Azerbaijan was a center of several ancient civilizations. It formed part of the Urartu and later of Median civilizations. In the 4th century BC, it was conquered by Alexander the Great and was named Atropatne after one of Alexander's generals, who established a small kingdom there. The area returned to Persian rule under the Sasanids in the 3rd century AD. Islam was introduced by the Arabs in Azerbaijan in the 7th century. In the 11th century, Turkish nomads overran the area. Thenceforth, the inhabitants of the region were Turkish speakers.

In the early 16th century, Azerbaijan was the cradle of the Safavid dynasty. It was the Safavid *Shahs* who introduced Shi'ism into Persian society. Subsequently, the area was fought over by the Ottoman Turks and the Safavids, until Nadir Shah expelled the Turks in the 1740s. During the 18th century, the Russians gradually encroached on the area, but the Persians managed to retain control of it. Under the Treaty of Turkmenchai of 1828, Azerbaijan was divided between Iran (which was granted southern Azerbaijan) and Russia (northern Azerbaijan). During the later half of the 19th century, oil was discovered in Azerbaijan and by 1900, the region had become one of the world's leading oil producers. In the early 20th century, Azerbaijan was the cradle of the revolutionary movements that gave Iran its constitution in 1906. The area was briefly occupied by the Ottomans in World War I. Azerbaijan was invaded by the Red Army in April 1920, and a Soviet Republic of Azerbaijan was established on April 28, 1920. In December 1922, the republic became a member of the Transcaucasian Soviet Federative Socialist Republic (TSFSR), which entered the USSR as a constituent republic on December 31, 1922. The TSFSR was disbanded in 1936, and Azerbaijan became a full Union Republic. In 1945, Soviets set up the short-lived Kurdish Republic in Western Azerbaijan, but Iranian forces regained control of the region in 1946-47 once the Soviet armed forces had withdrawn back across their border.

Independence was formally declared on October 18, 1991. However, the Supreme Soviet voted not to sign the treaty to establish an economic community, which was signed by leaders of eight other Soviet republics on the same day. In a further move towards full independence, the Supreme Soviet adopted legislation allowing the creation of national armed forces, and Azerbaijan units began to take control of the Soviet Army's military facilities in the republic. However, Azerbaijan did join the Commonwealth of Independent States on December 21, 1991.

ECONOMY

Azerbaijan is endowed with fertile land and ample mineral resources, including natural gas and iron ore. The country is also one of the leading manufacturers of oil drilling equipment, in addition to light industries. Traditionally, the industrial sector has accounted for 40 percent of the Net Material Product (NMP), with agriculture as a close second.

Agriculture

In 1992, agriculture contributed an estimated 33.5 percent of the Net Material Product (NMP). The arable land was 7 percent of the total country at that time. With fertile soil and a temperate climate, the country is a major producer of cotton, tobacco, tea, grain, vegetables and fruits. It is also a producer of livestock products like meat, milk and eggs. Silk is also an important product and one of Azerbaijan's oldest agricultural activities. In recent years agricultural production has suffered due to land reforms. Land reforms have called for land leases to farmers as opposed to outright sales. Agricultural production has also suffered from economic dislocation. At the beginning of 1980s, the country produced more than 20 percent of the former Soviet Union's wine grapes and was a major wine exporter. In 1984-86, vineyards under cultivation fell by 25 percent as a result of trouble in Nagorno-Karabach. Total agricultural exports plunged significantly. Table 6 gives the production of agricultural crops.

Table 6
Agricultural Production
('000 Tons)

	1992	1993	1994
Wheat	859	844	760
Barley	371	277	238
Cotton	111	95	90
Tobacco	63	70	68
Carrots	12	12	12
Other Vegetables	155	172	85
Grapes	1,126	900	860
Watermelon/melons	300	200	300
Citrus Fruits	10	8	6
Tea	7	4	4

Minerals and Industry

Azerbaijan is richly endowed with mineral resources. The most important resource is oil, extracted mainly from the Apsheron Peninsula, where Baku is situated. At the turn of the 20th century, Azerbaijan produced more oil than the United States. However, as the 20th century progressed, Azerbaijan's role in oil production decreased, as the industry was developed in other parts of the world. A considerable amount of oil is also extracted from the offshore fields in the Caspian Sea. Oil is refined at Baku. Other minerals include natural gas (mainly offshore), iron ore, alumite (alum-stone), iron pyrites, copper, cobalt, and molybdenum.

Azerbaijan has a diversified industrial base, with heavy industry and its leading branches: power, manufacturing, and chemicals predominate. Industry contributed an estimated 48.3 percent of the Net Material Product in 1992. The principal sector is oil extraction (with important associated industries of refining and petroleum equipment). Other heavy industries include chemical processing, petrochemicals, construction, and machine-building. Sumgail, Baku, Kirovabad and Mungechaur have emerged as the major industrial centers.

Light industrial manufacturing includes cotton and woolen textiles, knit wear, traditional household items, footwear, and other consumer goods. The cities of Shaki, Stepanakart, Kirovabat, Mingechaur, and Baku are the main centers of the industry. Food processing plants are distributed fairly evenly throughout the republic. Azerbaijan fisheries are of particular importance because of the Sturgen of Caspian Sea, which is made into caviar.

In recent years, there has been a shift from oil-based industries to sectors like finished metal goods, including pipes, machine tools, and computers. The centralized planning of the former Soviet Union made Azerbaijan the center of regions air-conditioning assembly plants. Other important manufacturing sectors include textiles, food, and beverages (Table 7).

Table 7
Output of Industrial Products

	1986	1987	1988	1989	1990	1991
Metal industry						
Steel ('000 tons)	739.0	772.0	726.0	696.0	501.0	462.0
Steel pipes ('000 tons)	541.0	566.0	604.0	584.0	493.0	411.0
Machinery & Equipment						
Oil extraction equipment ('000 tons)	6.2	6.4	6.2	5.4	5.2	4.1
Drilling equipment ('000 tons)	95.3	92.1	87.3	79.3	73.0	73.0
Pumping equipment ('000 tons)	420.0	323.0	465.0	494.0	527.0	462.0
Electric motors ('000 tons)	6,985.0	7,223.0	7,105.0	6,496.0	4,860.0	3,761.0
Transformers ('000 tons k/Va)	2,587.0	2,502.0	2,082.0	2,410.0	1,996.0	1,883.0
Constructional material						
Reinforced concrete (m.cu. meters)	2,074.0	2,105.0	1,912.0	1,688.0	1,295.0	1,089.0
Bricks (m.)	1,436.0	1,523.0	1,465.0	1,454.0	1,317.0	1,172.0
Roof tiles (m.)	100.0	116.0	92.0	85.0	66.0	78.0

CHAPTER 5
BAHRAIN

Bahrain is a small welfare island state in the Arabian Gulf. Its history goes back 5,000 years when it was an important link on a trade route between the Indus Valley and Sumerian civilizations. It became independent in 1971 and has since been actively trying to serve its people and the region.

GEOGRAPHY

Bahrain consists of a group of thirty-three islands in the Gulf, midway between the mainland of Saudi Arabia and Qatar peninsula. It is 22 km off the eastern coast of Saudi Arabia and slightly further from the western coast of the Qatar peninsula. In addition to the main island of Bahrain, the most important islands in the archipelago are Al-Muharraq, Umm Na'san, Sitrah, An-Nabi Salih, and the Hawar group. The other islands in the archipelago are not inhabited. The total area of all inhabited and uninhabited islands is 268 sq. miles (693 sq. km), about four times the size of Washington, D.C. (Map 8). The area is steadily increasing due to enormous land reclamation activity taking place in Bahrain. The island of Bahrain, 30 miles long (north to south) and 10 miles wide, is largely a desert, but it has some gardens and groves near the northern coast watered by springs fed by underground sources originating on the mainland. It has 190 to 200 ft. (30-60 m) high

Geographical Profile

Area: 231 sq. miles (598 sq. km.)
Population: 600,000 (1994);600,000 (2000); 800,000 (2010)
Neighboring Countries: Saudi Arabia (west), Qatar (southeast)
Capital: Manama (pop. 122,000 (1985 est.)
Other City: Al-Muharraq
Terrain: Low interior plateau and hill on main island
Climate: Hot and humid from April-October, temperate from November-March
Official Language: Arabic
Other Principal Languages: English and Persian
Ethnic Background: Arab (90%) with Iranian, Pakistani, Indian and other minorities
Principal Religions: Shi'ah and Sunni Muslims
Economy:
  GDP: (1998) $3.4 billion
  Per Capita Income: (1989) $7,300
  Natural Resources: Oil, natural gas, fish
  Agriculture: 1% GDP
  Types: Eggs, vegetables, dates, fish
  Industry: (36% GDP) Manufacturing, oil, aluminum, ship repair, natural gas, fishing
  Services: (62% GDP) Banking, real estate, insurance
Former Colonial Status: British Protectorate, 1861-1971
Independence Date: August 15, 1971

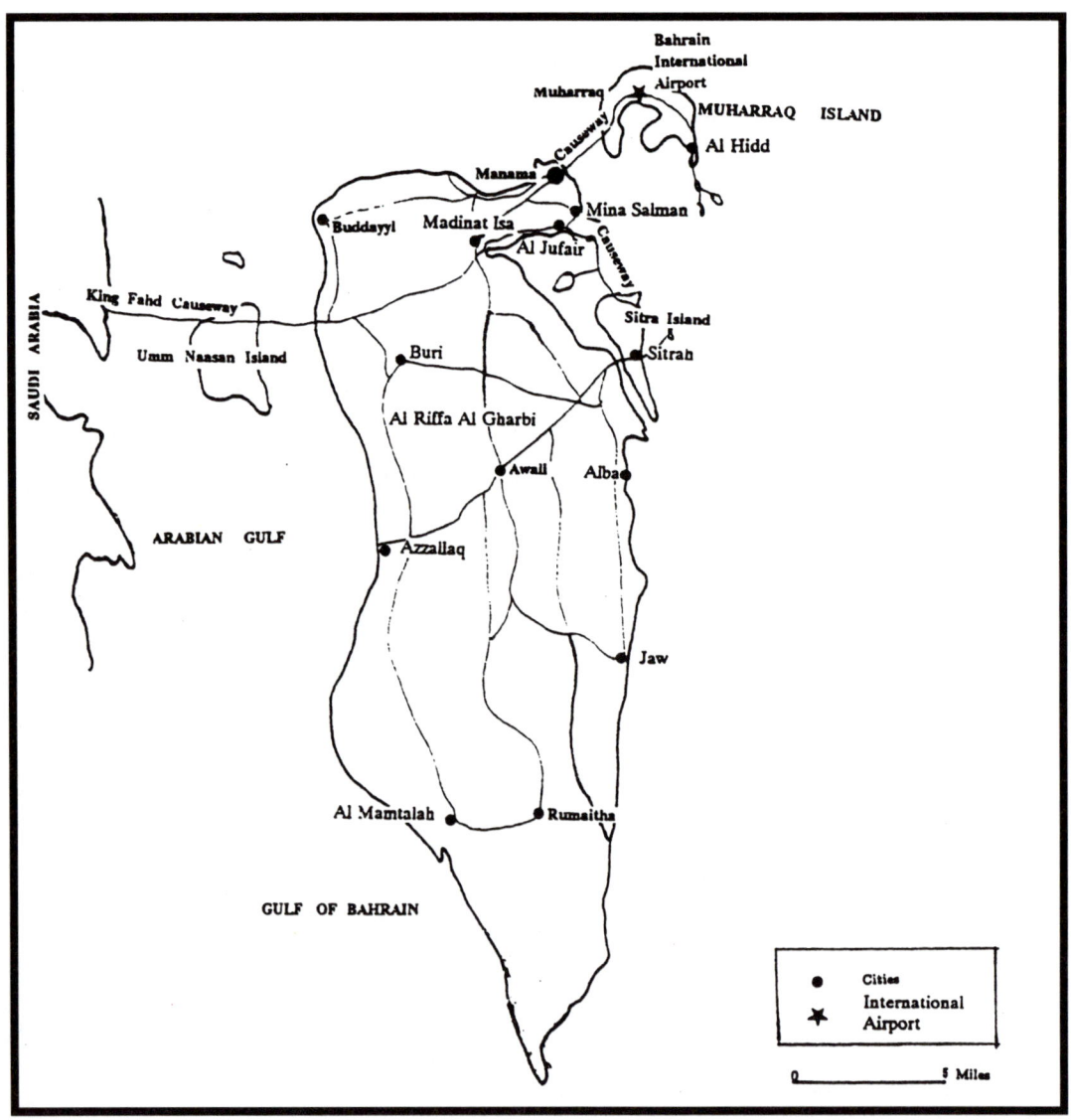

Map 8: Bahrain

interior plateau with a hill (*Jabal* Dukhan) which rises to 445 ft. (135 m), the highest point on any of the islands.

Bahrain is connected to Al-Muharraq by a causeway 1-3/4 miles (2.8 km) long, to Sitrah by another causeway, and to Saudi Arabia by another 25 km long King Fahd causeway. There is also an active program to reclaim low-lying coastal areas. Bahrain also claims title to the island of Hawar, near the Qatar Coast, and jurisdiction over a tribe around the village of Zubara on the shore of Qatar (Map 8).

The climate is hot and humid most of the year. Daytime temperatures regularly reach 106°F (41°C) and the relative humidity is 70 to 80 percent. In the summer, the highest temperature usually climbs to 45°C. The winter temperatures range between 14°C to 20°C with less than 4 inches of rainfall annually. Between the years 1931 and 1990, the highest monthly rainfall was 135.9 mm, which was recorded in January 1959. However, as a result of industrialization, Bahrain is experiencing rising temperatures at a rate of 0.014°C per year, and a declining rainfall at a rate of 0.16 mm per year.

Date palms, vegetables, and forage crops are grown in Bahrain and on some of the smaller islands, although Al-Muharraq is barren of vegetation. Efforts are being made in Bahrain to grow trees and create green areas through trickle-drip irrigation. Bahrain also has some gardens and groves near the northern coast watered by Alat and Khobar springs fed by underground sources originating on the mainland. However, piezometric head of Khobar aquifer is falling at a rate of more than 100 mm per year. As a result, the sea water is intruding, causing anxiety in the island country.

EVOLUTION OF BAHRAIN

Bahrain was a part of the ancient civilization of Dilmun and served as an important link in trade routes between the Indus Valley Civilization and Sumeria about 5000 years ago (Fig. 8). Mounds and other archaeological remains of such trade connections have been discovered at a number of

Fig. 8: Dilmun Mounds, Isa Town, Bahrain

places in and near Isa town in Bahrain. Islam was introduced in Bahrain during the lifetime of Prophet Muhammad. It is said that the Prophet came to know twenty Bahrainis who were studying Islam in Madinah. He instructed them to go back home after their studies and establish study centers (*hauzas*) in Bahrain, like those in Madinah. These Bahraini *ulemas* were Al-Muntahir ibn Aith, Al-Jarood al-Abdi, Al-Hakim Ibn Jiba, Al-Abdi, Rashid ibn-al-Hujri, Sa'sa'ah ibn Sawhan, Al-Abdi, Shaikh Naseer al-Bahraini, Shaikh Mohammad ibn Sahl al-Bahraini, Shaikh Allam al-Bahraini and Mas'ood al-Abdi. Since the late 18th century, Bahrain has been governed by the Al-Khalifa family, originally of the Utbah clan of the large Anaiza tribal confederation of the Arabian Peninsula. The Khalifa family also claimed Qatar as a part of their kingdom.

The political relations persisted until 1868, when at the request of Qatari nobles, the British negotiated the termination of Bahraini claim, requiring payment of a tribute. The treaties ended with the occupation of Qatar by the Ottoman Turks in 1872. The rulers of Bahrain entered into relations with the United Kingdom in 1805, and the first treaty between the two parties was signed in 1820. A binding treaty of protection, known as the Perpetual Treaty of Peace and Friendship, was concluded in 1861 and further revised in 1892 and 1951. This treaty was similar to those entered into by the British government with the other Arabian (Persian) Gulf principalities. It specified that the ruler could not dispose of any of his territory except to the United Kingdom and could not enter into relationships with any foreign government without British consent. The British promised to protect Bahrain from all aggressions by sea and to lend support in case of land attack.

During and after World War II, Bahrain supplied Britain's main naval and military needs in the Gulf and became the center for British administration. The British Political Resident in the Persian (Arabian) Gulf moved his headquarters there in 1946. In the following years, Britain directed the modernization of the state's administration and economy, but the inability of the citizens to participate in government created unrest. The most serious demonstrations occurred in 1956 and were suppressed with the aid of British troops. In 1968, when the British government announced its decision (reaffirmed in March 1971) to end the treaty relationships with the Gulf sheikhdoms, Bahrain joined the other eight states (Qatar and the other seven Trucial Sheikhdoms, which are now called the United Arab Emirates) under British protection in an effort to form a union of Arab emirates. By mid-1971, however, the nine sheikhdoms still had not agreed on terms of union. Accordingly, Bahrain sought independence as a separate entity and became fully independent on August 15, 1971, as the State of Bahrain.

POPULATION AND ECONOMY

Most of the people in Bahrain are Arabs, belonging to three main tribes: Tameem Banu Madar, Abdoul Qays Banu Rabia, and Bakr ibn Wail of Banu Rabia. All these tribes have been in Bahrain since the first Islamic century.

Bahrain is an active center of oil refining, seaborne trade, ship repairs, air transportation, business administration, international banking, aluminum manufacturing (based on imported alumina), and local natural gas. Even before oil and natural gas, Bahrain was one of the richest areas in the northern Gulf. Its pearls were the best in the region, and pearling employed nearly half of the male working population, which totaled 162,500 people according to 1985 estimates. Fifty five percent of the working population was composed of expatriates. Of the total number employed in 1985, women accounted for about 12%. Unemployment among Bahrainis was estimated at 15%.

Most of the population of Bahrain is concentrated in the two principal cities of Manama and Al-Muharraq. The indigenous people (80 percent of the population) are from Arabian Peninsula and Iran. The minorities are composed of South and East Asians as well as Europeans. Islam is the major religion, with the Sunni sect predominating in the urban areas, and the Shi'ah sect in the rural areas. There are both Roman Catholic and Protestant churches in Bahrain as well as a small indigenous Jewish community.

Bahrain was one of the first Arabian countries where oil was discovered in 1932. Because of the oil, the first airplane landed there in 1932 (Fig. 9). Now the airport located at Muharraq can handle the largest aircraft in the world and is considered one of the most modern and efficient airports in the Middle East. The airport is the Gulf's main air communication center. An expansion program was initiated in 1990, in which a new passenger terminal with a capacity of 10 million passengers a year was opened in 1991.

Fig. 9: Bahrain Airport, 1932

Bahrain was also the first to have a refinery in 1935. Since then, petroleum and natural gas dominate the economy and provide about 60 percent of budget revenues. From the region's economic boom in the late 1970s and 1980s, Bahrain benefited greatly and emphasized infrastructural development and other projects to improve the standard of living; health, education, housing, electricity, water, and roads all received specific attention. Prior to oil, the profession of

Bahraini people was pearl diving, fishing, and weaving. The natural pearl industry declined due both to a depression and to competition from the cultured pearl industry. Agriculture is of little significance in the economy, and only 10% of the land is arable.

During the last ten years, efforts have also been made to irrigate frontyards and agricultural places through trickle-drip irrigation (Fig. 10). Bahrain has stabilized its oil production at 40,000 barrels per day and has also worked to diversify its economy by actively pursuing a policy of encouraging foreign investment. A notable development was the international consortium formed in 1968 to construct a $72 million aluminum smelter at Sitrah. The plant operates at full capacity,

Fig. 10: Trickle-Drip Irrigation, Bahrain

though facing marketing problems. To continue diversification of the economy, the state has also purchased 60 percent of the refinery from Caltex, a US company, which now owns only 40 percent of the refinery. Saudi Arabia provides most of the crude oil through an undersea oil pipeline for refinery operations via pipeline. In addition, Bahrain receives one-half of the net output and revenues from Saudi Arabia's Abu Saafa offshore oil field. The Bahrain National Gas Company operates a gas liquefaction plant that utilizes gas piped directly from Bahrain's oil fields. Gas reserves should last about 50 years at the present rate of consumption and oil may last for another 10-15 years.

Bahrain's role as an entry port, transportation, and service center in the Arabian Gulf supplements the petroleum industry's contribution to the economy. Figure 11 represents the view of a section of Bahrain. An important development in 1977 was the passage of legislation which encouraged the establishment of Offshore Banking Units in the Gulf aimed at channeling Arab capital through Bahrain. The aggregate assets/liabilities of the Offshore Banking Units of Bahrain were 60.2 billion at the end of December 1993. Customer analysis at the end of December 1993 indicates that loans to non-Bank clients stood at 20% of total liabilities. Deposits from Arab countries were $30.2 billion (52% of the total assets), while claims on them were $21.6 billion (35.9% of total assets), Western European countries deposits were $12.2 billion (20.2% of the total liabilities), while claims on them amounted to $13.7 billion (22.8% of the total assets). Other offshore countries' deposits amounted to $5.2 billion (8.6% of the total liabilities), while claims on them were $4.6 billion (7.6% of the total assets). The US Dollar accounts comprised 71.1% of total assets and 69.7% of total liabilities, while other currencies comprised 16.9% of total assets and 19.6% of total liabilities. Thirty-eight international banks, including several American ones, have begun operations under this legislation. To provide its increasing links within the Middle East and foreign areas, Bahrain's international airport handles over 300 flights per week to over fifty destinations. The decision of the Arab Petroleum Exporting Countries to build a dry dock for supertanker at Sitrah provided another economic asset. Since 1958, there has been no custom duty on goods in transit, and warehouses have been reserved for merchandise intended for re-export. Harbor facilities are well-developed and have helped to make Bahrain a leading transit center in the Gulf. The deep water harbor at Mina Sulman has fourteen berths and two container terminals, as well as one roll-on/ roll-off berth. Plans for further development in a new port, industrial area and a free trade zone at Hidd have been revised following the Gulf war in 1991.

Like many other countries in the Middle East, there is no exchange control legislation in Bahrain. No import or export licenses are required (except for arms and ammunition, gambling machines, and alcohol). However, the importers and exporters are required to register with the state, and must be members of the Bahrain Chamber of Commerce and Industry. Major imports of Bahrain are manufacture goods, food stuff, and live animals. In addition, machines, transport equipment, chemicals, beverages, and tobacco products are imported. In addition to modern outlets for imported goods, traditional markets (Suqs) are also common in Bahrain (Fig. 12).

Fig. 11: Government Avenue, Bahrain

Fig. 12: Market in Bahrain

CHAPTER 6
BANGLADESH

Bangladesh or "Bengali Country" was a part of Pakistan until 1971. In 1971, Mujibur Rahman came to office with immense personal popularity, espousing autonomy, and with India's help, amputated Pakistan to establish an independent nation of Bangladesh. Since independence, Bangladesh went through a number of political changes and severe economic strains, being the most densely populated agricultural nations in Asia, yet remaining one of the poorest in the world.

GEOGRAPHY

Bangladesh is a low-lying, flood plain country of South Asia located on the northern edge of the Bay of Bengal. It is surrounded on three sides by India. On the fourth side is a 120-mile frontier with Mynamar (Burma) in the southeast. The irregular border, some 1500 miles long, is not based on any natural feature of landscape but was determined according to religious and political considerations in 1947. Its marshy coastline is about 370 miles long.

The geography of Bangladesh is largely a function of its rivers. The land is chiefly deltaic, an alluvial plain formed by the confluence of the great Ganges, Brahmaputra, and Meghna Rivers, and their tributaries. These rivers lose their identities as their waters mingle into a waterway maze which flows on an alluvial ridge of its own making, the higher parts of which are the levees immediately adjacent to the river's channel. From the levee crest, the land slopes away gently into the back swamp depressions. Much

---

Geographical Profile

Area: 55,813 sq. mile (148,998 sq km) (about the size of Wisconsin)
Population: 116.8 million (1994), 134.3 million (2000), 165.1 million (2010)
Capital City: Dhaka (pop,. 7 million)
Other Cities: Chittagong (2.8 million), Khulna (2.8 million), Rajshahi (1 million)
Neighboring Countries: Surrounded by India on three sides; a short border with Myanmar on the southeast.
Official Language: Bangla (also known as Bengali)
Other Principal Languages: Urdu and English (in schools and commerce)
Ethnic Background: 98% Bengalis; small minority, Biharis and tribal groups
Principal Religions: Sunni Islam 83%, Hindus 16%, Christians, Buddhist, others (1%)
Economy:
  GDP: (1991) $23 billion
  Per Capita Income: $198
  Agriculture: 37% of GDP
  Products: Rice, jute, tea, sugar, wheat
  Industry: 17% of GDP
  Types: Jute goods, garments, frozen shrimp, tea, leather, metal, reprocessing, pharmaceutical, newsprint
Official Name: Peoples Republic of Bangladesh
Date of Independence: December 17, 1971

of the country is less than 30 feet above sea level. Hills rise above the plain only on the Chittagong Hill tracts in the southeast and in Sylhet in the northeast (Map 9).

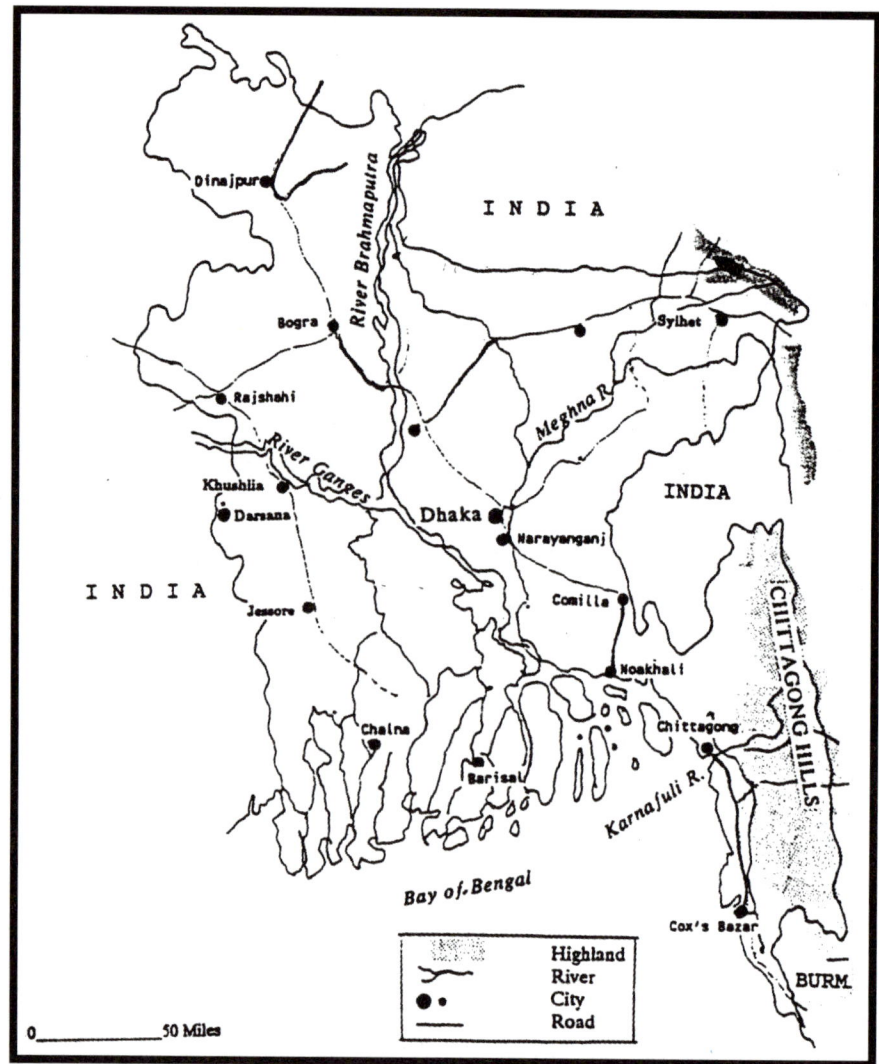

Map 9: Bangladesh

Located at about the same latitude as the Bahamas, Bangladesh has a tropical, monsoon climate. The average temperature is 84°F, with some seasonal variation. It has one of the highest annual rainfalls in the world, averaging 85 inches in the Northeast. Since much of the country is partially submerged or subject to flooding during the rainy season, land travel can be difficult. Thus, it is no surprise that boating is the lifeblood of its transportation system.

Until the middle of the century, the area of Bangladesh produced an agricultural surplus, and the fertile soils earned it the nickname of *Shonar Bangla*, or Golden Bengal. In recent years, however, agricultural productivity has not kept pace with the steady population growth. Its population growth rate is currently estimated at 2.4 percent per year; a conservative estimate projects a population of 140 million by the year 2000. Every year, the population is jeopardized by four scourges: (i) river flooding, (ii) cyclonic storms (hurricanes), (iii) disease, and (iv) famine. The climate and lack of adequate sanitation gives rise to disease, especially after floods or storms. Overpopulation leads to periodic starvation. The pressure of increasing numbers has forced people into southern deltaic areas, formerly considered uninhabitable, and made them vulnerable to the devastating cyclones which sometimes strike the country.

EVOLUTION OF BANGLADESH

Bangladesh has a rich historical and cultural past, the product of the repeated influx of varied peoples: Dravidians, Aryans, Mongol-Moghul, Arab, Persian, Turks, and European cultures. About 1200 AD Islam, through the Sufi teachings, supplanted the Hindu and Buddhist religions, and converted most of the population of eastern Bengal to Islam. Since then, Islam has played an important role in the region's history and politics. In the 16th century, Bengal was absorbed into the Moghul Empire.

During the 18th and 19th centuries, the British East India Company gradually extended their commercial contacts and administrative control beyond Calcutta into the remainder of Bengal and in the Northwest up the Ganges River Valley. In 1889, the East India Company, was replaced by the British Crown, which extended British dominion from Bengal in the east to the Indus River in the west.

In the 19th and 20th centuries, Muslim and Hindu leaders began to press for a greater degree of independence. At the movement's forefront was largely the Indian National Congress dominated by the Hindu majority. Growing concern about Hindu domination of the movement led Muslim leaders to form the All India Muslim League in 1906. In 1913, the League formally adopted the same goal as the Indian National Congress, self-government for India within the British Empire. The Congress and the League were unable, however, to agree on a formula to ensure the protection of Muslim religious, economic, and political rights. Over the next two decades, mounting tension between Hindus and Muslims led to a series of bitter inter-communal conflicts.

The idea of a separate Muslim state emerged in the 1930s. It gained popularity among Indian Muslims after 1936, when the Muslim League suffered a decisive electoral defeat in the first elections under the 1935 constitution. On March 23, 1940, *Quaid-i-Azam*, Muhammad Ali Jinnah, publicly endorsed the "Pakistan Resolution" that called for the creation of an independent state in regions where Muslims were a majority. The resolution was proposed by A. K. Fazlul Haq, a Bengali leader, and seconded by Chaudhry Khaliquzzaman, a leader from the United Province.

As a result of mounting disaffection against the British rule, and considerable international pressure to reduce the size of its Empire, in June 1947 the British government announced that it would grant full dominion status to two successor states - India and Pakistan. Pakistan would consist of the contiguous Muslim majority districts of Western British India, including parts of Bengal. The various princely states could freely join either India or Pakistan. These arrangements resulted in a bifurcated Pakistan separated by more than 1,000 miles (1,600 km) of Indian territory.

Pakistan's history for the next 26 years was marked by political instability and economic difficulties. The growing demands for a greater autonomy in the eastern province of Pakistan led Sheikh Mujibur Rahman's Awami League to win 167 out of 313 seats in the National Assembly. However, the political leaders of East and West Pakistan were unable to reconcile their differences over fundamental constitutional questions relating to the sharing of power between the central government and the provinces. When no agreement was reached among the leaders, and the situation was deteriorating, the army sought to repress Bengali dissidence. Sheikh Mujibur was arrested, his party banned, and most of his aides fled to India, where they established a provisional government. India and Pakistan went to war in late November 1971. On December 16, 1971, Pakistan forces surrendered in Dhaka, and the new but heavily war-damaged nation of Bangladesh emerged. Bangladesh has constructed a monument in Savar, a suburb of Dhaka, to commemorate its separation and independence (Fig. 13).

Fig. 13: National Monument, Savar, Dhaka

ECONOMY

Bangladesh's predominantly agricultural economy depends heavily on an erratic monsoon cycle, which leads to periodic flood and drought. It struggles constantly to produce or import enough food for its rapidly increasing population. As one of the world's poorest and most densely populated countries, an estimated 10 to 15 percent of its population is at serious nutritional risk, and the majority faces food insecurity.

Economic reform efforts began in 1975, when the government gradually increased private sector participation in the economy, including privatization of more than 30 state enterprises. In the mid-1980s, encouraging signs of progress appeared. In the following years, economic policies to denationalize public industries including jute, textiles, and banking were accelerated. In 1985, the government also began an economic structural adjustment program with the International Monetary Fund.

Agriculture

Most Bangladeshis earn their living directly or indirectly from agriculture. Rice and jute are the primary crops, while wheat is assuming greater importance. Tea is grown in the hilly regions of the Northeast (Fig. 14). Bangladesh's fertile soil and normally ample water supply yield three rice crops in many areas. Through better flood control and irrigation measures, more intensive use of fertilizers and high-yielding seed varieties, increased price incentives, and improved distribution and rural credit networks, Bangladesh's labor-intensive sector has achieved steady increases in food grain production. Food grain production in 1992 was about 20 million metric tons, a 5 percent increase over the previous year. Rice is Bangladesh's principal crop, although yields per hectare are among the lowest in Asia. Rice output rose 3.2 percent in 1992, much of which can be attributed to the irrigated spring crop, which has increased steadily due to the greater availability of fertilizer and irrigation equipment. Wheat production is expected to rise. Jute, which historically has accounted for the bulk of Bangladesh's export receipts, faces an uncertain future due to competition from synthetic fiber substitutes. Fishing, especially for shrimp, has become an increasingly important source of export earnings.

Industry

Bangladesh has virtually no mineral resources except for an estimated 17 trillion cubic feet of proven natural gas reserves (which meets two-thirds of Bangladesh's commercial energy needs), coal reserves, estimated at 250 million metric tons in the Northwest, and estimated oil reserves of 7.5 million barrels. It has a weak industrial base and a largely unskilled labor force.

Although small, the industrial sector contributes significantly to export income; it also provides employment and a market for cash crops. Jute products (mainly burlap-sacking and carpet-backing for export) and cotton textiles for domestic consumption are predominant.

Since the early 1980s, production of ready-made garments for the United States market has grown rapidly. Bangladesh is the fifth largest supplier of cotton apparel to the United States, and it has begun exporting such products to European markets. Breaking up ships for scrap through methods that are highly labor intensive, now meets most of Bangladesh's domestic steel needs. Other industries include sugar, tea, leather goods, newsprint, pharmaceutical, and fertilizer production.

The government continues to court foreign investment. To this end, the United States and Bangladesh signed a bilateral investment treaty which took effect in 1989. Bangladesh has also established an export processing zone (EPZ) in Chittagong and plans to create additional zones. The government has offered special incentives and simplified procedures for potential investors.

Fig. 14: Tea Plantation, Sylhet, Bangladesh

CHAPTER 7
BOSNIA-HERCEGOVINA

Yugoslavia (a land of the south Slavs) was a region of seven major and seventeen smaller ethnic and cultural groups that was unified into a country after World War I. By late 1993, this multinational and multicultural state split into five new republics, one of which is Bosnia-Hercegovina. Muslim dominated Bosnia-Hercegovina is wedged between the twin prongs of Croatia and Serbia. Serbian minority in Bosnia dominates the eastern region, and in its effort to secede from Bosnia and become a part of "Greater Serbia," it has been waging war against Muslims and Croats.

GEOGRAPHY

Any discussion of Bosnia-Herzegovina is necessarily linked with Yugoslavia. Yugoslavia was formed in 1918 as a union of the Kingdom of Serbs, Croats, and Slovenes. After World War II, it became a Communist-ruled federation under the iron fist of Marshal Tito. When the Communists ruled the country, they divided it up into six internal "republics" on the Soviet model, one of which was Bosnia-Herzogovina.

The name Bosnia (Serbo-Croatian: Bosna) has been derived from the Bosna River and is probably of Illyrian origin. Herzegovina, the southern part of the republic, takes its name from the title *herzog* (German: *herzog*, "duke."). The capital of the republic is Sarajevo.

Geographical Profile

Area: 19,781 sq. mi. (1,369 km.)
Population: 3.3 million (1994); 3.5 million (2000), 4 million (2010)
Population Growth: 0.77%
Population Doubling Time: 80.02 years
Neighboring Countries: Croatia (northwest and west), Serbia and Montenegro (east)
Capital: Sarajevo
Terrain: Mountains and valleys
Climate: Hot summers, cold winters
Languages: Bosnian, Croatian and Serbian
Ethnic Divisions: Bosnjaks 44%, Serb 30%, Croats 17%
Religions: Sunni Islam 52%, Orthodox Christians 31%, Catholic 15%, Protestant 4%
Economy:
  GDP: (1991) $14 billion
  Natural resources: Coal, iron, bauxite, manganese, timber, wood products, copper, chromium, lead, zinc
  Agriculture: 8.6% GDP
  Types: Wheat, corn, orchards, vineyards
  Industry: steel production, mining, manufacturing, oil refining
Former Status: A part of Yugoslavia
Independence Date: April 12, 1992

The republic is roughly triangular, located in the west central part of former Yugoslavia. It is located south of the Sava River, and for the most part, it lies between the Una River in the north and west, and the Drina River in the east. Its western boundary runs southward from the town of Bihac in the north, across the Dinaric Mountains to a point near the mouth of the Neretva (Narenta) River, and then for a short distance upon the Adriatic it turns inland again. The coastline stretches for 13 miles (20 km) on the Adriatic Sea, but there are no harbors. The Republic of Montenegro is Bosnia-Herzogevina's neighbor to the south. On the east, it is bordered by Serbia, and on the north and on the west, by Croatia (Map 10).

Map 10: Bosnia-Herzegovina

In climate, Bosnia differs considerably from Herzegovina. In both regions, the sirocco winds bring rain from the southwest. In the north, the fearful *bora* winds sweep down the Dinaric Alps, overwhelming everything in their path. The snowfall is slight. In the summer, the weather is generally mild, although it can be bitterly cold in the winter. The weather in Herzegovina, by contrast, is characterized by excessively hot summers, with the heaviest precipitation between

October and January. Much of the country is covered with deciduous forests. At higher elevations, evergreen trees like pine, fir, and juniper are common.

RELIGIONS AND POPULATION

The Christianization of most of Bosnia was not affected until the tenth century, although Herzegovina was one of the Mediterranean areas where conversion to Christianity of the pre-Slavic populations occurred very early. Bosnia (like Albania) was a crossroad of religious ideas. At least four religious groups were represented in the Medieval state: Roman Catholicism, Bogomilism, the Bosnian Church, and Greek Orthodoxy, which had the weakest representation.

The Ottoman conquests were followed by massive acceptance of Islam. The Muslim element began to decline in importance after the 1690s, mainly because of the immigration of Orthodox Serbs from the south and the constant drain on the Muslims populations to fight in the wars of the empire. In 1800, Muslims constituted only 45 percent of the total population; their numerical strength fell to 39 percent in 1879 and to 31 percent in 1921. The Orthodox element has remained more or less stable since 1879: 43-49 percent of the population. The Roman Catholic element increased from 18 percent in 1879 to 23.5 percent in 1921.

For the most part, the Muslim population is concentrated between the Vrbas and Drina and north to Neretva. In 1994, the Muslim population in Bosnia-Herzegovina stood at 52 percent. In 1994, the total population of the republic was 3.3 million. With less than one percent annual rate of natural increase, the population was expected to rise to 3.5 million in 2000.

EVOLUTION OF BOSNIA-HERZEGOVINA

Until the settlement of a people called Dalmats and Illyrians (second and first millennia BC), very little is known of Bosnia's past. The Dalmats and Illyrians were the chief settlers of the province until the fourth century BC, when groups of Celts moved in from the north. The Romans occupied the present territory of Bosnia-Herzegovina in the first century BC and made it part of the larger province of Illyrium.

In the sixth and seventh centuries, a wave of Slavic tribes overran the Balkan Peninsula. The Slavs destroyed the colonies of the Eastern Roman (Byzantine) Empire but inter-married with the partly Romanized Celto-Illyrians, to whom they gave their language. The language of Bosnia-Herzegovina thus became Slavic.

During the Middle Ages, Bosnia was the last of the South Slavic provinces to develop a separate state organization and the last to be Christianized. Geography isolated the central area from the southern cultural influences of Byzantium, from the northern cultural influences of Germany and the Holy Roman Empire, and from the western, or maritime, cultural influences of Italy and Byzantium. The northern periphery, however, came under the political and cultural influence of Croatia and the southern periphery (Herzegovina) under that of Zeta (Montenegro) and Rascia (Serbia).

At the beginning of the twelfth century, Hungary occupied part of Bosnia, including the valley of the Rama River, flowing 20 miles (32 km.) southeast near Prozor. The Hungarian king assumed the title of "Lord of Bosna" and appointed *bans*, or viceroys, to administer the new province. Emperor Manuel Comnenus of Byzantium then removed Bosnia from Hungarian control and made it into a Byzantine vassal state.

For a century, the *bans* were tied to the politics of Hungary and the religion of Rome. The Bosnian nobility, on the other hand, allied themselves with the Bosnian Church and sought to throw off the authority of the *bans*. The alliance of nobles and heretics aided the spread of feudalism, thus depriving the Bosnian Church of the socially revolutionary doctrines espoused by their possible Bogomil ancestors and predecessors in Bulgaria and Macedonia.

Most of Bosnia fell to the Turks in 1463. Herzegovina resisted somewhat longer, but in 1482, the two provinces were joined by the Turks under a single administration. The last of the Bosnian territories (the district of Jajce) fell to the Turks in 1528. All of Bosnia-Herzegovina remained under Ottoman rule until 1878, when some territory was transferred for three decades to the Austro-Hungarian Empire.

During Turkish rule, Bosnians accepted Islam on a massive scale. The Muslims of Bosnia today are mainly the descendants of the followers of the Bosnian Church. There has been recent contoversy as to the actual influence Bogomilism played in Bosnian history. Many Croats and Serbs who were Roman Catholic and Orthodox Christians also accepted Islam. During the four hundred years of Turkish rule, these people were integrated in a single polity, as there was more religious tolerance during the Turkish rule than anytime before. During the days of the Ottomans, the capital cities of Bosnia were both Sarajevo and Travnik. From 1580, Bosnia was raised to the status of an *eyalet* (province) of the Ottoman Empire, and its area was bigger than the present Bosnia-Herzegovina.

At the congress of Berlin, following the disasterous Russo-Turkish War of 1877-88, Bosnia-Herzegovina was assigned to be administered by Austro-Hungary, although it was still officially an Ottoman province. The land, however, was openly annexed to Austria-Hungary on October 7, 1908, when a new constitution divided the territory into three electoral colleges. The electoral colleges, Orthodox, Roman Catholics, and Muslims were assigned a fixed proportion of seats. This antagonized the Serbian nationalists and culminated in the assassination of the Austrian archduke Franz Ferdinand and his wife on June 28, 1914, by a Bosnian-Serb student, which led to the beginning of World War I.

When the war ended in 1918, the Austro-Hungarian Empire had disappeared. It was divided into the four republics of Austria, Hungary, Czechoslovakia and Poland. Serbia-Montenegro were combined with Slovenia and Croatia to form a new kingdom of Serbs, Croats and Slovenes. The name was changed to Yugoslavia in 1929. It became a communist-ruled federation after World War II, more precisely in 1945.

The eight-member Presidency was collective, with one member from each of the six republics and two from the Serbian provinces. The two Serbian provinces were Kosovo and Vojvodina. The chairman's job rotated annually. The presidency commanded the armed forces, but day-to-day control was in the hands of the defense minister and senior officers. This arrangement collapsed in 1992, when Yugoslavia split into five new countries, including Bosnia-Herzegovina. Bosnia's population of 4.3 million has three components: Muslims, the largest group (about 52 percent of the total), Serbs, and Croatians. Here, the Serbs saw an opportunity to expand their domain. They laid siege to the capital, Sarajevo, and drove the Muslims into ever-smaller pockets of territory. There was also a systematic attempt to destroy the entire Muslim presence in Bosnia, resulting in the mass extermination of tens of thousands at the hands of the Christian forces. The Croats also pushed the Muslims back as well, to the extent that by the autumn of 1993, the Muslims, while still 52 percent of the population, held a mere (estimated) 15 percent of their country's land.

The carnage in Bosnia went on despite attempted United Nations intervention, and in early 1994, it appeared doubtful that a Bosnian state could emerge from the war. Islamic countries in Asia and Africa called for armed support of the beleaguered Bosnian Muslims, but the Western countries and United Nations did not allow it. Western countries, unwilling to stop the flow of arms and fuel to Serbs, argued that arming the Muslims would "raise the death toll."

ECONOMY

Northern, Central, Eastern, and Southeastern Bosnia is heavily forested, while Herzegovina and the western areas neighboring Dalmatia are mostly karst (limestone plateau). The forest or timber resources of the republic are supplemented by abundant supplies of lignite, brown coal, iron, siderite and limonite iron ores, copper, manganese, lead, zinc, chromite, mercury, silver, bauxite, salt, and petroleum. The ample hydroelectric resources began to be extensively developed only during the 1950's, when the republic underwent spectacular economic development, transforming it from an economically backward to a relatively industrialized area able to sustain further economic growth largely from its own resources.

There are some light industries, and during the 1970s and 1980s, the Sava Valley (along the northern border of the republic) became the favored development area for heavy industries. There are iron and steel plants in Zenica. The armaments manufacturing industry is also important. Service industries, notably, tourism, are not well developed, compared to Croatia and Slovenia. Prior to independence, the republic was dependent on transfer of resources from the central government.

Bosnia-Herzegovina is mainly an agricultural country. Corn, wheat, sugar beets, and tobacco are grown in the fertile valley of the Sava. The livestock sector is also of economic importance. Hogs, cattle, and horses are raised in many parts of the country. Sheep are grazed in the mountainous terrain, where timber reserves are also exploited.

The sharecropping system of land tenure was abolished in Bosnia-Herzegovina in 1919, after the province became part of the united Yugoslavia state. A portion of the land was thereupon transferred to the peasantry, the old landlords being indemnified by the state. After World War II, new land reforms were adopted.

Bosnia-Herzegovina's economy has been severely affected by the civil war, which began in June 1991. The naval blockade of the Croatian ports, through which Bosnia and Herzegovina's petroleum supplies are delivered, added to the republic's economic difficulties. By late May 1992, Bosnia and Herzegovina had suffered extensive material damage, and it was estimated that about four-fifths of the republic's industrial plants had fallen to 17% of the normal production capacity.

There are extensive mineral resources, the republic being a major source of copper, lead, zinc and gold. Iron ore is mined, and there are resources of lignite (a poor quality brown coal). Federal government policy favored the development of Bosnia-Herzegovina and the other poorer regions of the former Yugoslavia, but industrialization has not become a significant feature of the local economy.

NOTES

CHAPTER 8
BRUNEI

Brunei is a Muslim welfare state in Southeast Asia, located south of Catholic Philippines. The people of Brunei and their government eagerly follow Islam, build mosques, and establish Qur'anic schools. Education is free to all, and so is medical care. Food, housing, and fuel is subsidized, and everybody receives a generous pension. For a small service charge, the national bank offers easy loans with no interest to build homes or buy consumer goods. People go to perform *Hajj*, often financed by the Sultan of Brunei.

GEOGRAPHY

Brunei is a small enclave on the north coast of Borneo island. Actually, it is a two-part enclave, surrounded by Sabah and Sarawak, both parts of Malaysia. Between the two enclaves is Sarawak's Limpung valley. The total area of the country is 2,227 sq. miles (5,769 sq. km), which is twice as big as Luxembourg, and nine times the size of Singapore. In 1994, its population was estimated at 3 million and its per capita income at $13,300 (1989) which has made it one of the richest countries in the world (Map 11).

> **Geographical Profile**
>
> **Area:** 2,227 sq. miles (5,769 sq. km)
> **Population:** 3,000,000 (1994)
> **Capital:** Bandar Seri Begawan
> **Terrain:** East: flat coastal plain with Beaches, West: hilly with a few mountain ridges
> **Climate:** Equatorial; high temperatures, humidity, and rainfall
> **Ethnic Groups:** Malay (40%); Chinese (30%); Indigenous tribal groups (29%)
> **Nationality:** Brunians
> **Religion:** Sunni Islam, Chinese religions, Christianity
> **Languages:** Malay (Official); English, Chinese, Iban and others
> **Economy:**
>   **GDP:** $3.3 billion (1989)
>   **Per Capita GDP:** $13,300
>   **Natural Resources:** Oil and Natural Gas - 47% of GDP
> **Work Force:** (1989) 86,400: Government-50%; petroleum sector-5%; foreign workers-33%
> **Official Name:** Brunei Darussalam
> **Independence Date:** January 1, 1984

The eastern enclave, or eastern wing of the country, is the district of Tembrong. From east to west, the Tembrong district is 7 to 15 miles (11 to 24 km) wide and 45 miles (72 km) long from north to south. Tembrong is sparsely populated and hilly. In this area, Buket Pagan Peak has an elevation of 6,070 ft. (2,023 meters), which is the highest in Brunei. Much of its interior is covered with thick forests, and on the coast are mangroves. The forests are the source of lumber, and the rocks in the northeast have stone quarries.

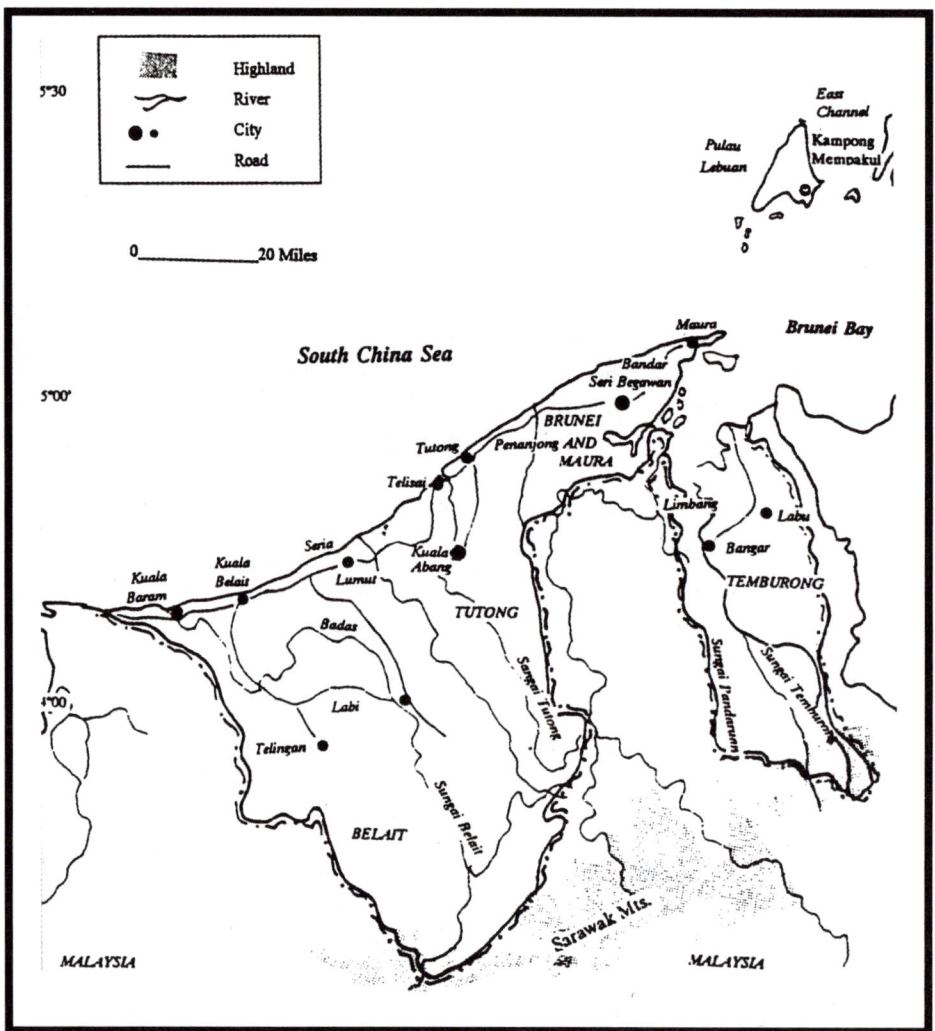

Map 11: Brunei

The western enclave, or western wing of Brunei, has a long coastline and lovely beaches. Most of the towns are located along the coast, including Kuala Belait, capital of the western wing. Seria, the oil capital of Brunei, and Lamut, the world's biggest natural liquefication center are also located along the coast. Other coastal towns are S. Liang, Banau, Sinau, Kilanas, Tungku Gadong, Muara, and Bandar Seri Begawan, the capital of Brunei. Until 1970, Bandar Seri Begawan was called Brunei Town, but the present ruler, Sultan Hassan Ali Bolkiah changed the name when he succeeded his father, which means the "town of the former ruler."

The climate of Brunei is equatorial, with high temperatures, humidity, and about 100 inches of rainfall. Consequently, there are too many rivers in the hilly region of the western wing. Belait is the biggest river, which flows from the southern border to Kuala Belait. In the central region are the Labi Falls, and nearby are the hot springs. In the east center is Tasek Merimbum, the biggest freshwater lake in Brunei.

PEOPLE AND POPULATION

In 1981, the population of Brunei was less than 260,000, which reached to 300,000 in 1994. It is estimated that the population will jump to 400,000 by 2010. About 40 percent of the people of Brunei are Malays, about 30 percent Chinese, and about 29 percent belong to indigenous tribal groups (described as Malays for census purposes and considered as *bhumiputras*, or sons of the soil). The Chinese dominate the private sector of the economy and engage in oil and gas business, construction, and retail trade.

The Department of Religious Affairs is heavily funded by the Government of Brunei to build mosques, establish Qur'anic schools and undertake missionary activities. It is reported that every year, two to three hundred persons embrace Islam, the majority of whom belong to Iban and other tribal groups.

ECONOMY

Brunei's economy changed after oil was discovered in 1929, and its production began in the early 1950s. When the petroleum prices increased in the 1970s, the gross domestic product soared to a peak of $5.7 billion in 1980. It declined slightly for the next 5 years, then fell by almost 30 percent in 1986. This drop was caused by sharply lower petroleum prices in the world market and voluntary cuts in Brunei. The GDP has recovered somewhat since 1986; it grew by 12 percent in 1987 and 1 percent in 1989. However, in 1989, the GDP was $3 billion, far below the 1980 peak.

Brunei Shell Petroleum (BSP), a joint venture, owned in equal shares by the Brunei Government and the Royal Dutch Shell group of companies, is currently the only oil and gas production company in Brunei. It also operates the country's only refinery, BSP, and four sister companies. A second joint venture between the locally owned company Jsra International Petroleum and the French Oil company ELF Aquitaine recently became active in petroleum exploration in Brunei. This company has discovered commercially exploitable quantities of oil and gas in three of the four wells drilled since 1987, including a particularly promising discovery announced in early 1990.

Japan has traditionally been the main customer for Brunei's oil exports, but its share dropped from 45 percent of the total in 1982 to 25 percent in 1989. In contrast, oil exports to South Korea increased from only 8 percent of the total in 1982 to 25 percent. Other major customers include Thailand, Singapore, and Taiwan. Brunei's oil exports to the United States amounted to 23 percent of the total in 1987 and 1988. Exports resumed again in 1989 but accounted for only a 5 percent share.

Almost all of Brunei's natural gas is liquefied at Brunei's Shell Liquefied Nitrogen Gas (LNG) plant and exported to Japan under a long agreement, which will expire in 1998. The Japanese company, Mitsubishi, is a joint venture partner with Shell and the Brunei Government in Brunei LNG, Brunei Coldgas, Brunei Shell Tankers, which together produce the LNG and supply it to Japan. Brunei's LNG plant opened in 1972, and is the largest in the world. Brunei is the fourth largest exporter of LNG after Indonesia, Algeria, and Malaysia.

Regular shipping service operates from Singapore, Hong Kong, and from ports in Sarawak and Sabah to Bandar Seri Bagawan. Private companies operate a passenger ferry service every day between Bandar Seri Bagawan and Labuan. The main port in the state is Muara, eighteen miles from the capital, Bandar Seri Bagawan. There is another port at Kuala Belait, at the other end of the state. Brunei Shell maintains a single buoy at Seria mooring and a special jetty at Lumut for the export of crude oil and liquid natural gas. The port of Kuala Belait on the Belait river serves the oil fields and Seria. There is also a jetty at Bandar Seri Bagawan, which is now used only by vessels less than 100-feet long and drawing less than 15 feet carrying general cargo for direct deliveries. The Mauara port is a deep one which was opened in 1973, and since then, extensive improvements in accommodation and other facilities have been made to it.

Other port facilities include 175,000 square feet of warehouses for long-term rental, 135,000 square feet of transit godown, 15,000 cubic feet cold store room, container freight station and various general cargo and container handling equipment. Regular freight services operate to Singapore, Malaysia, Hong Kong, Thailand, Japan, and Taiwan.

Over the years, the government has undertaken a succession of 5-year national development plans. The stated aims under the 1986-90 plans were to strengthen, improve, and further develop the economic, social, and cultural life of its people, with priority on employment and accelerating development of agriculture and industry. The need for economic diversification was given renewed emphasis in January 1989, with the formation of the new Ministry of Industry and Primary Resources, tasked with developing a strong, export-led private sector.

Labor shortages in almost all job categories constrain Brunei's industrial development. The government is unwilling to allow much foreign labor, for fear it might disrupt Brunei's society. As a result, labor sneaks in illegally, especially from Indonesia and Sarawak, and an underground network operates to facilitate their entry. It is also difficult for the resident Chinese to obtain Brunei citizenship. Of the 66,000 Chinese in Brunei, only 6,000 have citizenship. Others are the "British-Protected Persons" with British passports, which do not allow them to live in the United Kingdom. Citizenship for the Chinese in Brunei has become even more difficult after 1984, when it was decided that the Chinese could qualify for citizenship if they have resided continuously for 25 years in 30 years prior to their application.

One of the government's most important priorities is to encourage the development of Brunei Malays as leaders in industry and commerce. There are no specific restrictions for foreign equity ownership, but local participation, both shared capital and management, is encouraged.

The government owns a cattle farm in Australia which supplies much of the country's beef. At 2,262 square miles, this ranch is larger than Brunei itself. Eggs and chicken are mostly produced locally, but most of Brunei's other food needs must be imported. Agriculture and fisheries are among the sectors which the government has selected for highest priority in its efforts to diversify the economy.

Agriculture

Agriculture, including forestry and fishing, provided only 2.2 percent of the Gross Domestic Product in 1984. About 15 percent of the total land area was cultivated. Rice, cassava, banana, and pineapple were the main crops. In addition to agriculture, fishing provided more than one-half of the domestic consumption. Livestock consisted of 1,600 buffaloes, 5,200 pigs, 32,599 goats, and 1.42 million chickens.

EVOLUTION OF BRUNEI

Historians believe there was a forerunner to the present Brunei Sultanate, which the Chinese called Po-ni. Chinese and Arabic records indicate that this ancient trading kingdom existed at the mouth of the Brunei River as early as the seventh or eighth century AD. This early kingdom was conquered by the Sumatran Empire of Srivijaya in the early ninth century, which later controlled northern Borneo and the Philippines. It was subjugated briefly by the Java-based Majapahit Empire, but soon regained its independence and rose to prominence once again.

The founder of the current Sultanate was a pagan ruler who married a princess from Malaysia. He embraced Islam and took the name Muhammad, and with him, Brunei became a Muslim state. According to official records, Sultan Muhammad's reign began in 1405. He was succeeded by his brother Ahmad, who later died without a male heir. Ahmad was succeeded by his daughter's husband Sharif Ali, an Islamic leader from the Middle East.

The Brunei Empire had its golden age from the 15th to the 17th centuries, when its control extended over the entire island of Borneo and north into the Philippines. Brunei was particularly powerful under the fifth Sultan, Bolkiah (1473-1521), who was famed for his sea exploits and even briefly captured Manila.

After Sultan Hasan, Brunei entered a period of decline due to internal battles over royal succession. The rising influences of European colonial powers in the region added to the decline by disrupting traditional trading patterns and destroying the economic base of Brunei and many other Southeast Asian Sultanates. In 1889, the English adventurer James Brooke arrived in Borneo and helped the Sultan crush a rebellion. As a reward, he became governor and later "*Rajah*" of Sarawak in northwest Borneo and gradually expanded the territory under his control.

Meanwhile, the British North Borneo Company was expanding its control over the territory in northeast Borneo. In 1888, Borneo became a protectorate of the British government, retaining internal independence but with British control over external affairs. In 1906, Brunei accepted a further measure of British control when executive power was transferred to a British resident, who advised the ruler on all matters except those concerning local custom and religion.

In 1959, a new constitution was written declaring Brunei a self-governing state, while its external affairs, security, and defense remained the responsibility of the United Kingdom. An attempt in 1962 to introduce a partially elected legislative body with limited powers was abandoned after the opposition party launched an armed uprising, which the government put down with the help of British forces. In the late 1950s and early 1960s, the government also resisted pressures to join neighboring Sabah and Sarawak in the newly formed Malaysia. The Sultan eventually decided that Brunei would remain an independent state.

In 1967, Sultan Omar abdicated in favor of his son, Hassanal Bolkiah, who became the 29th ruler. The former Sultan remained as the Defense Minister and assumed the royal title of Seri Begawan. In 1970, the national capital was renamed Bandar Seri Begawan in his honor, which means the "town of the former ruler." The Seri Begawan later died in 1986. On January 4, 1979, Brunei and the United Kingdom signed a new treaty of friendship and cooperation. On January 1, 1984, Brunei Darussalam became a fully independent state.

CHAPTER 9
BURKINA FASO

Burkina Faso is one of the poorest countries in Africa. The poverty is reflected by its low life expectancy (39 years) and a low per capita income ($190). The literacy level is only 5 percent and only 10 percent of the population has access to reasonable water supply. There is only one doctor available for every 55,000 people.

GEOGRAPHY

Burkina Faso is a landlocked Sahel country that shares borders with six nations (Map 12). It lies between the Sahara Desert and the Gulf of Guinea, south of the loop of the Niger River. The land is green in the south with forests and fruit trees. In the north, the country is semi-arid. Most of central Burkina Faso lies on a savanna plateau 650-1,000 ft. (198-305 m) above sea level, with scattered fields and brush. Burkina Faso's game preserves contain lions, elephants, hippopotamuses, monkeys, warthogs, and antelopes.

Annual rainfall varies from about 40 inches (100 centimeters) in the south to less than 10 inches (25 centimeters) in the extreme north and northeast, where hot desert winds accentuate the dryness of the region. Burkina Faso has three distinct seasons: warm and dry (November-March); hot and dry (March-May); and hot and wet (June-October). Rivers are not navigable.

Geographical Profile

Area: 106,000 sq. miles (274,200 sq. km); about the size of Colorado
Population: 10.2 million (1004); 12.4 million (2000); 17.0 million (2010)
Capital City: Ouagadougou (pop. 500,000)
Other Cities: Bobo-Dioulasso (250,000), Koudougou (70,000)
Neighboring Countries: Cote D'Ivoire, Ghana, Togo, Benin, Niger, and Mali
Climate: Sahelian; pronounced wet and dry seasons
Terrain: Savanna; brushy plains and scattered hills
Official Language: French
Other Language: Moré
Ethnic Groups: Mossi, Bobo, Mande, Fulani, others
Religions: Sunni Islam about 50%; Christians 15%; traditional African 35%
Work Force: Agriculture 92%; industry 2.1%; commerce, services and government 5.5%
Economy:
    GDP: (1987 est) $1.6 billion
    Annual Growth Rate: (1982-87) 4.3%
    Per Capita Income: $174
Official Name: Burkina Faso
Date of Independence: August 5, 1960

PEOPLE AND POPULATION

Burkina Faso's 8.7 million people belong to West African tribal cultural groups. The Voltaic are in the majority which include the Mossi, who are about one-half of the population. The Mossi claim descent from warriors who migrated to present day Burkina Faso and established an empire that lasted more than 800 years. Predominantly farmers, the Mossi are still bound by the traditions of the emperor, the Mogho Naba, who holds court in Ouagadougou.

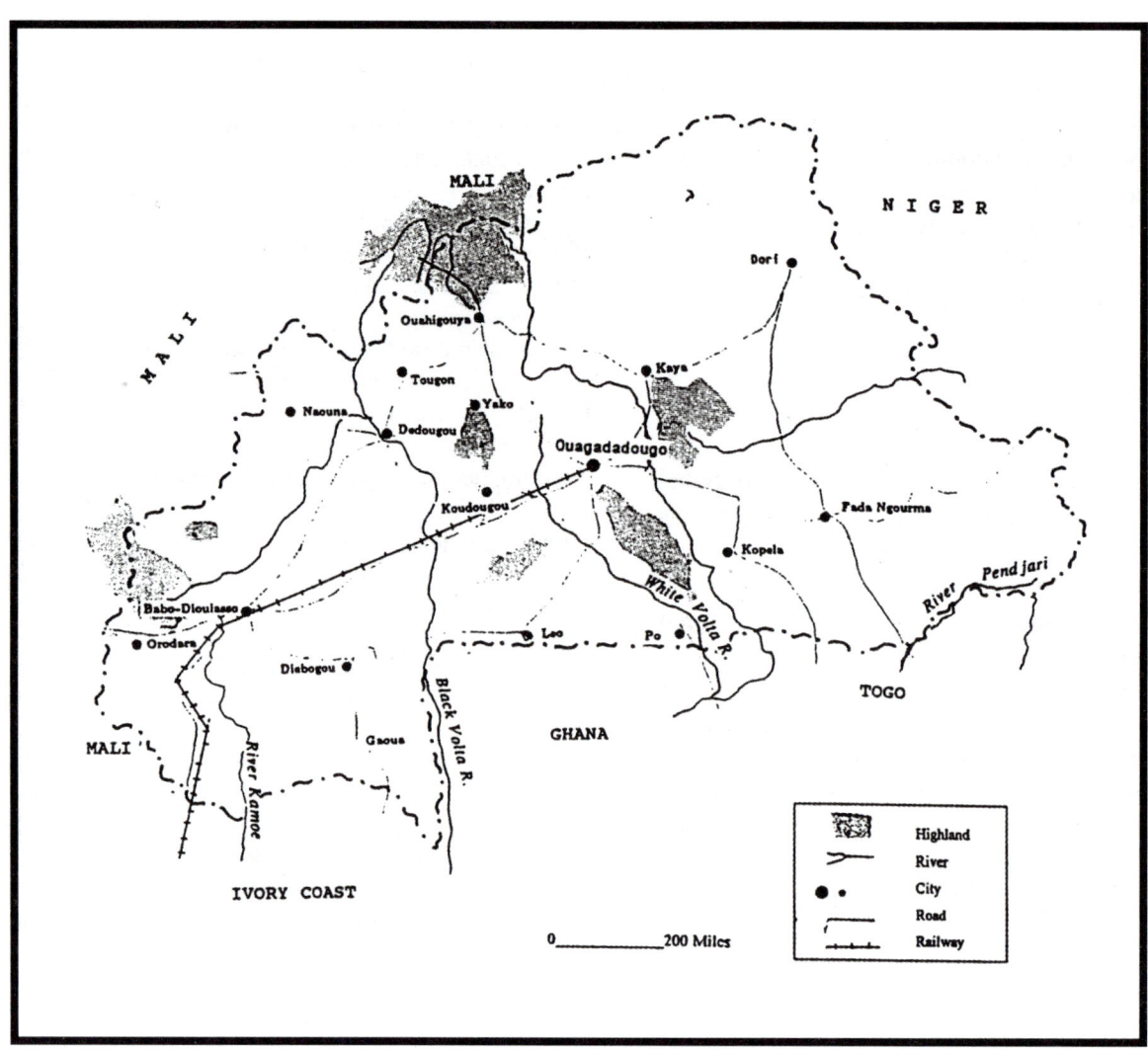

Map 12: Burkina Faso

Most of Burkina Faso's people are concentrated in the southern and central regions of the country, sometimes exceeding 125 persons per sq. mile (48 per square km). This population density (high for Africa) causes annual migrations of hundreds of thousands of Burkinables to Cote d'Ivoire and Ghana for seasonal agricultural work.

A plurality of Burkinabe adhere to traditional African religions. Although the introduction of Islam was initially resisted by the Mossi rulers, Muslims now constitute more than 50 percent of the population. Christians, predominantly Catholics, are largely concentrated in the urban areas.

EVOLUTION OF BURKINA FASO

Until the end of the 19th century, the history of Burkina Faso was dominated by the empire-building Mossai, who were believed to have come from Central or Eastern Africa some time in the eleventh century. For centuries, the Mossai peasants were both farmers and soldiers, who were able to defend their religious beliefs and social structure against the introduction of Islam by the Muslims from the northwest.

When the French arrived and claimed the area in 1896, Mossai resistance ended with the capture of their capital at Ougadougou. In 1919, certain provinces from the Ivory Coast were united into a separate colony, called the Upper Volta, in the French West African Federation. In 1932, the new colony was dismembered as an economic measure. It was reconstituted in 1937 as an administrative division, called the Upper Coast. After World War II, the Mossai renewed their pressure for a separate territorial state, and on September 4, 1947, the Upper Volta became a French West African territory in its own right.

A revision in the organization of French Overseas Territories began with the passage of Basic Law (*Loi Codre*) of July 23, 1956, followed by reorganizational measures approved by the French parliament early in 1956. These reforms ensured a large degree of self-government for individual territories. Upper Volta became an autonomous republic in the French Community on December 11, 1958 and achieved independence on August 5, 1960. The 1960 constitution required the election of a president and a national assembly for a 5-year term. Soon after coming to power, President Yaméogo banned all political parties other than his own party. His government lasted until 1966, when after much unrest, mass demonstrations and strikes by the students, labor unions and civil servants, the military stepped in.

The Army remained in power for 4 years, and on June 14, 1970, the Voltans ratified a new constitution that established a 4-year transition period toward complete civilian rule. Since then, factional internal unrest developed, resulting in yet another military *coup d'etat* on August 4, 1983. The country changed its name to Burkina Faso, meaning the "country of upright people."

ECONOMY

Burkina Faso is one of the poorest countries in Africa. Approximately 88 percent of the population relies on subsistence agriculture, with only a small fraction directly involved in industry and services. The agricultural economy remains highly vulnerable to fluctuations in rainfall.

Drought, poor soil, lack of adequate communications and other infrastructure facilities, a low literacy rate, and a stagnant economy are all long-standing problems. The export economy also remains subject to fluctuations in world prices. About 87 percent of the labor force works in the agricultural sector. These subsistence farmers eke out a living amidst problems of climate, soil composition, soil erosion, and rudimentary technology. The staple crops are millet, sorghum, maize (corn), and rice, and the cash crops are cotton, peanuts (groundnuts), karite (shea nut) and sesame. Livestock, once a major export, has declined.

Although still in its infancy, industry is located primarily in Bobo-Diolasso, Ouagadougou, Banfora, and Koudougou. Manufacturing is limited to food processing and textiles. Some factories are privately owned, and government policy shows increasing support for expansion of the private sector. Burkina Faso's exploitable natural resources are limited, although a manganese ore deposit is located in the remote northeast. Gold mining has increased greatly since the mid-1980s. In 1988, gold replaced cotton for the first time as the country's leading export money-earner.

Many Burkinabes migrate to neighboring countries for work, and their remittances provide a substantial contribution to the balance of payments. Burkina Faso is suffering from a chronic budget, balance of payments deficits, and an increasing debt. It is attempting to improve the economy by developing its mineral resources, improving its infrastructure, making its agriculture and livestock sectors more productive and competitive, and by stabilizing the supplies and prices of food grains.

CHAPTER 10
CHAD

In area and population, Chad is the largest country of former French Equatorial Africa. Contrary to its present-day dry conditions, ancient Arab manuscripts and modern archaeological investigations reveal that well-developed societies flourished more than 1000 years ago around Lake Chad. From that time to the present, Chad has served as a crossroads for the Muslim people of the desert and savanna regions as well as animistic Negroid tribes of the tropical forests.

GEOGRAPHY

Landlocked in the heart of Africa, Chad is surrounded by Libya to the north, Sudan to the west, Central African Republic to the south, and Cameroon, Nigeria and Niger to the southwest and west (Map 13). It is the largest and least accessible of the West African Sahelian states. In the middle of the western border is Lake Chad, the seventh biggest lake in the world. Eastern shores of the lake are in Chad, and the western shores in Niger and Cameroon. The country is shaped like a shallow basin which rises gradually from 750 feet (228 m) above sea level at Lake Chad in the west to more than 12,000 feet (3,638 m) in the Tibesti mountains in the north. Rivers of the southern watershed flow into Lake Chad, while the north is desert. Chari (Shari) and

---

Geographic Profile

Area: 496,000 sq. miles (1,284,634 sq. km)
Population: 5.5 million (1004); 6.4 million (2000); 7.7 million (2010)
Annual Rate of Natural Increase: 2.5 percent
Capital City: N'Djamena (600,000)
Other Cities: Sarh (100,000), Moundou (90,000), Abeche (70,000), and Bourgou (50,000)
Neighboring Countries: Libya, Central African Republic, Sudan, Niger, Nigeria, and Cameroon
Climate: Savannah, Sahelian, and Saharan
Ethnic Groups: More than 100 ethnic and linguistic groups
Principal Religion: Sunni Islam, Christians, Animists
Economy:
  GDP: (est.) 1 billion
  Per Capita Income: (est.) $200
  Natural Resources: Petroleum (unexploited), natron (sodium and carbonate), kaolin
  Agriculture: Products: Cotton, gum arabic, livestock, fish, peanuts, millet, sorghum, rice, sweet potatoes, cassava, dates
  Types: Agriculture and livestock processing plants, natron mining
Official Name: Republic of Chad
Independence Date: August 11, 1960

Logone are the important rivers which join at N'Djamena before draining into Lake Chad. Chari (Shari) is 746 miles (1,200 km) long and Logone, 603 miles (970 km) long.

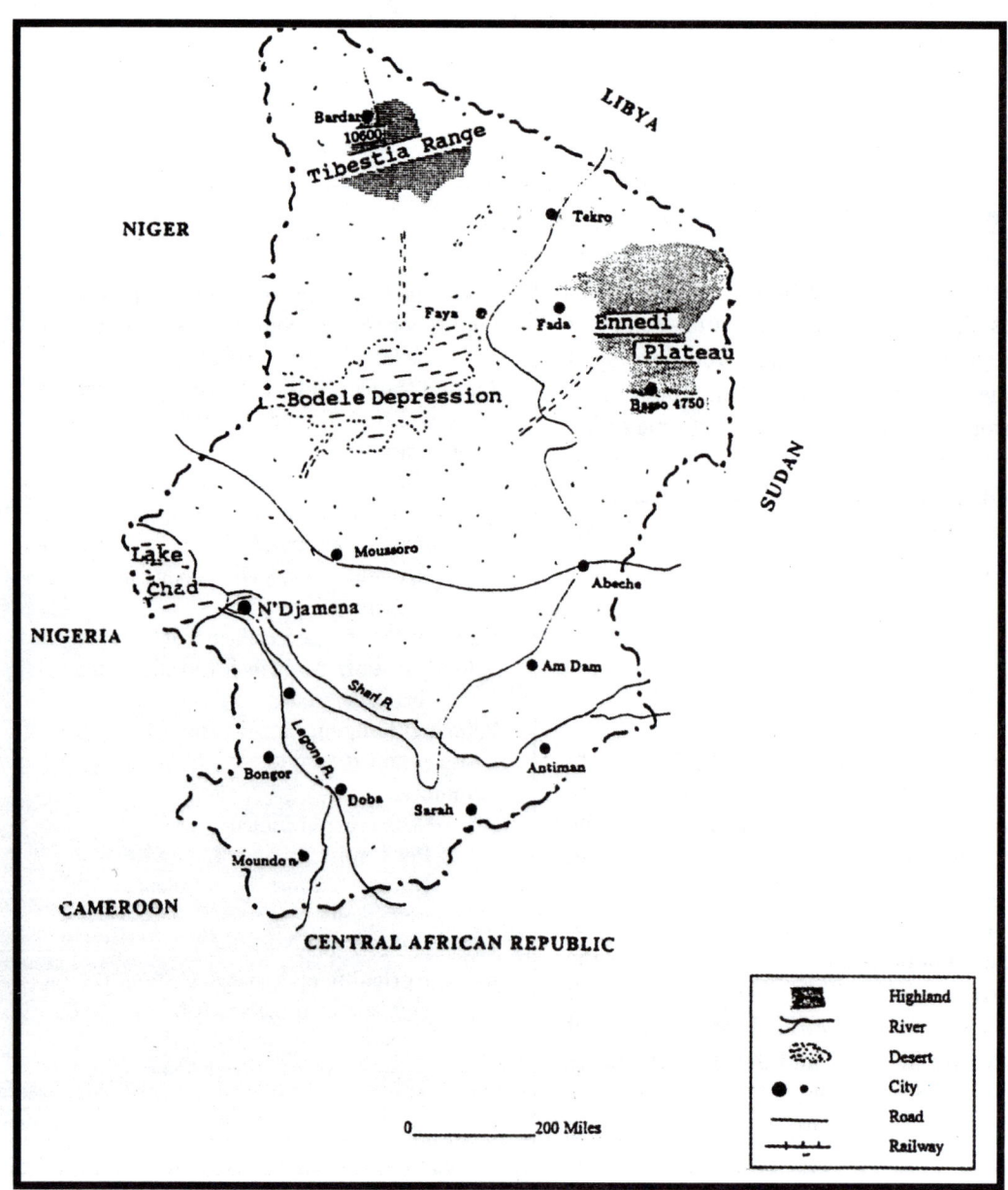

Map 13: Chad

Extending over 1000 miles (1,600 km) from 8º N to 23º N, Chad has four principal climatic zones. The northern third of the country is pure desert with negligible rainfall, except in the Tibesti mountains where some orographic precipitation supports sedentary population in small basins flanking the mountains. There is a narrow zone of sub-desert with rainfall from 4 to 12 inches (100 to 300 mm). Southward is a zone of Sahel type climate with totals of 12 to 31 inches (300-800 mm), with 2-4 months in excess of 4 inches (100 mm). In the extreme south, rainfall increases over 45 inches (1200 mm.) and the mean season extends to some 5-7 months. Except in the southern zone, the season and variability of the rainfall creates serious problems of water availability for much of the year. A reflection of this rainfall variability is Lake Chad itself, which varies from 932 miles to 2361 miles (1500 to 3800 km). Only at the margins of some of the higher ground in the north and in depressions where springs provide water are pastures, but in the better-watered south, the numerous permanent water-courses often flood large areas during the rains.

PEOPLE AND POPULATION

In 1994, the population of Chad was estimated at 5.5 million with an extremely diversified distribution. In the north, the density is extremely low. The northern province with half of Chad's land surface contains less than 100,000 people, while the five provinces lying in the south of Chari (Shari) River, namely Mayo-Kebbi, Moyen Chari (Shari), Tandjile, Logone Oriental, and Logone Occidental, contains more than 2.5 million people. The World Bank figures indicated that in 1989, 29 percent of Chadians lived in towns in the southern part of the country. The capital N'Djamena has a population of 600,000 people.

Chadians are divided into hundreds of ethnic groups and speak more than 100 different languages. The people of Chad can be divided into the Arab and Arabized north and the pagans or Kirdi of the south. Because of Islam, the north is relatively homogenous in culture, religion, languages and geographic unity. The ethnic groups and subgroups in the pagan south are close to 375 groups. No single group dominates any region in the south. Only Saras, which form 24 percent of the country's population, live in the south of the Chari (Shari) River. They were a favored group of the French, and as a result, quickly adopted Christianity and western education.

Arabs form 14 percent of the population. They mostly live in the northern half of Chad, not including the Tibesti and Ouaddai Mountains. They are largely nomadic or semi-nomadic, and wander with their livestock in search of pastures after the rainy season. The Arabs resisted French intrusion and hence were left out of French colonial developments in Chad. After independence, the Arab traders and merchants were established in the towns. As a result, Chadian Arabic (or Turku) has become a language of trade. Conventional Arabic also continues as an important language.

The next largest group are the *Mabas* who form five percent of the population. They created Wadai Sultanate (Ouaddai in French) in the early 17th century and are concentrated in the Ouaddai Mountains. They are semi-nomadic people and grow millet during the rainy season. The *Toubous* live in the Tibesti Mountains and are 3.9 percent of the population. Some of the *Tadas* are nomads and some are semi-nomads. Closely related to *Toubous* are *Dazas*, who speak a language of the same name. *Dazas* live between the Tibesti Mountains and Lake Chad and are semi-nomads. Ethnic divisions prompt rivalry and inhibit economic development. The per capita income is $110, which makes Chad the third poorest nation in the world. The life expectancy is 43 years and infant mortality only 20 percent in the first few years. There are four hospitals in the country and one doctor per 42,000 of the population.

EVOLUTION OF CHAD

Perhaps as early as the 8th century, some Arabs entered Chad across the Libyan desert, bringing Islam with them. Islam is the strongest religion in the country. Then, after the fall of Christian Nubia in the 14th century, an Arab and Islamic influx began from the east. The population of Chad is divided between Saharan Muslims and indigenous animist Negroid people in the south. The latter group has retained their traditional animist practices, with the exception of a small minority, who became Christian.

In 1194, the pagan dynasty of Ume was replaced by a Muslim Sultanate, which shifted its capital to Bornu. Another Sultanate was established at Banguirmi towards the end of the 15th century. In the 17th century, Islam was introduced by Sufi Salih to the Ouaddai Mountains (or Wadai) in the east-central part of Chad. Towards the close of the nineteenth century, the French penetrated and established their authority through military expeditions, primarily against Muslim kingdoms. Chad was finally conquered by capturing the capital city of Dik on April 22, 1900.

In March 1894, the French, British, and Germans signed an agreement under which they divided the territory around Lake Chad among themselves. Chad fell to the share of French. By 1913, France annexed the entire country, establishing an administration by 1920. During World War II, Chad served as a base for the Allied forces to launch their campaign in Libya, Algeria, and Tunisia. As they loudly proclaimed, the aim of the war was to champion democracy so the French felt obliged to give some internal autonomy to Chad in 1944. In 1947, elections were held and a legislative assembly was set up. In 1957, the first government was formed by the Chadians in which a West Indian, who had settled in Chad, was elected as the president of the country.

In 1958, General deGaulle placed his constitution to a referendum and offered the West African French colonies the choice of staying within the "French Community" as self-governing member states or becoming independent. In 1959, the territory of French Equatorial Africa was dissolved, and the four states, now Gabon, Central African Empire, Congo (Brazzaville), and Chad became autonomous members of the French Community. In 1960, Chad became an independent nation.

The ethnic religious groups fueled dissension which ensued in a civil war. Resistance against the south and their control on bureaucracy began in 1965-66 in the Muslim Tibesti and Ouaddai Mountains of the north, led by Toubou tribe. This resistance later took the form of an ideological movement when some Chadian expatriates in Sudan formed the Front de Liberation National du Tchad (FROLINAT) in 1966. Later FROLINAT moved its headquarters to Tripoli.

The French intervened and sent assistance to the government led by President Tombalbaye and the southerners. In April 1975, Tombalbaye was killed in a military coup. The struggle continued with Libyan and French help. In March 1979, a conference of the representatives of the countries neighboring Chad and all Chadian factions met at Kano and decided on a compromise government called GUNT (Government d'union National de Transition). This also could not resolve the ethnic rivalry and internal fighting. Libya now controls a part of the north.

ECONOMY

About 46 percent of Chadians are engaged in subsistence agriculture, fishing and stock raising, with extremely low productivity. Only one-third of the country south of the 10° latitude is *le Chad utile* (useful Chad). This region is well-watered by rainfall and rivers, hence, it is ideal for agriculture. Subsistence production, which never entered the market economy, accounted for more than half of the GDP. Among the obstacles to economic development are three factors: (i) a desert area as large as Texas, (ii) scarcity of known minerals, and (iii) an isolation caused by size of the country, landlocked position, soil, and climate.

Livestock is the largest source of income, representing half of the cash earnings. Chad has one of the largest livestock populations. Livestock products contribute about 18 percent of the GDP and are the second largest export earner, after cotton. Cattle wealth is considered a status symbol, and livestock breeding is invariably combined with agriculture. More than half of the country's livestock is owned by the nomads.

Food crops, produced mainly for local consumption, include millet, sorghum, rice, sweet potatoes, yams, and cassava. Peanuts are grown in rotation with cotton. Cotton cultivation was imposed on Chad by the French to make their occupation profitable. About 400,000 farmers raise cotton on 434,303 acres (175762 ha.) south of the Chari (Shari) River. The purchase, ginning, and marketing of cotton is a state monopoly exercised by a company known as Cottonchad. Seventy-five percent of the Cottonchad is owned by the government and 19 percent by France. Cotton is the backbone of Chad's economy and a substantial source of income to the government. Date production is also becoming important. Fishing in rivers and Lake Chad is an important economic activity. Most of the fish caught is consumed locally, but an appreciable quantity of dried or smoked fish is exported, mainly to Nigeria.

Chad's main export is raw cotton, accounting for 75% of the total value in 1991. Other exports are meat and live animals, hides and skins, netron, gums, and resins. Main destinations of these exports are Portugal, Germany, China, Japan, Cameroon, Nigeria, and Congo. The imports are machinery, transport equipment, and petroleum from France, United States, Cameroon, and Belgium - Luxembourg. Chad is heavily dependent on imports of mineral fuel for generation of electricity. Until recently, imports from South Africa were not permitted.

Minerals and Industry

The only mineral now being exported is natron (native sodium carbonate), in spite of the fact that production is low. A substantial deposit of kaolin (a clay used in ceramics and brick) has been located. A US company has been exploring for oil in three areas of the country and has found petroleum deposits in the Lake Chad region. But drilling was suspended in 1986 when oil prices fell. There appears to be enough petroleum to meet Chad's internal requirements and greatly improve its economic situation.

Cotton processing, centered in Moundon and N'Djamena, is the main industry in Chad. In the early 1980s, there were 26 cotton gins with a capacity of 184,000 tons, although half of these have been closed. In 1986, the ginning capacity of Chad was estimated 120,000 tons. Cotton seed is the source of the country's self-sufficiency in edible oil and soap. There is a cotton textile mill at Sarh, but its working has been hampered by the civil war and by smuggling from Nigeria. It had to close down for some time in 1990. Sugar refining is the monopoly of the of Sonasut, partly owned by the state. Beer and cigarettes are other manufactured products produced in Chad.

CHAPTER 11
COMOROS

Islam was introduced in the Republic of Comoros around 1500 AD by the "Shirazi" Muslims. Since then, Islamic culture dominates the islands, in spite of the fact that the French tried to uproot it during their occupation. The establishment of Qur'anic schools all over the islands has reinforced the religion.

GEOGRAPHY

North of Madagascar and 312 miles (500 km) off the coast of Mozambique lies a group of four volcanic islands: Grande Comoros, Anjouan, Mayotte, and Moheli. Grade Comore is the largest of the four islands (Map 14). In area and rock structure these islands compare with islands southwest of the Cameroon mountains. They lie from 11º to 13º south of the equator within the southeasterly wind belt, which loses much of its moisture in Madagascar. As such, Comoros has a marked dry season. The climate is tropical, affected by Indian Ocean Monsoon winds from the north, which give the country a wet season from November to April. The temperatures differ from island to island.

Formerly, the islands were governed by France. Since 1975, they have been independent with the exception of Mayotte island, which continues to remain under French administration.

Geographical Profile

Area: 838 sq. miles (2,171 sq. km)
Major Islands: Grande Comore (1,025 sq. km), Anjonan (424 sq. km), Mayotte (374 sq. km), and Moheli (211 sq. km)
Capital: Moroni (pop. 30,000)
Other City: Mutsamudu (20,000)
Population: 500,000 (1004), 700,000 (2000), 900,000 (2010)
Annual Growth Rate: 3.1 percent
Ethnic Groups: Antalote, Cafre, Makoa, Oimatsaha, Sakalava
Religion: Sunni Islam 98%, Roman Catholic 2%
Languages: Shikomoro (a Swahili dialect), Malagasy, French
Economy:
    GDP: (1990 est.) $240 million
    Per Capita Income: $448
    Agriculture: 37% of GDP
    Services: 25% of GDP
    Industry: 4% of GDP mainly perfume distillation
    Trade: Exports- $22 million: vanilla, cloves, perfume essences, copra
    Major markets: France, United States, Germany
    Major imports: Rice, petroleum, meat, wheat flour, cotton textiles, cement
    Major suppliers: France, Madagascar, Pakistan, South Africa
Official Name: Federal Islamic Republic of Comoros
Date of Independence: July 6, 1975

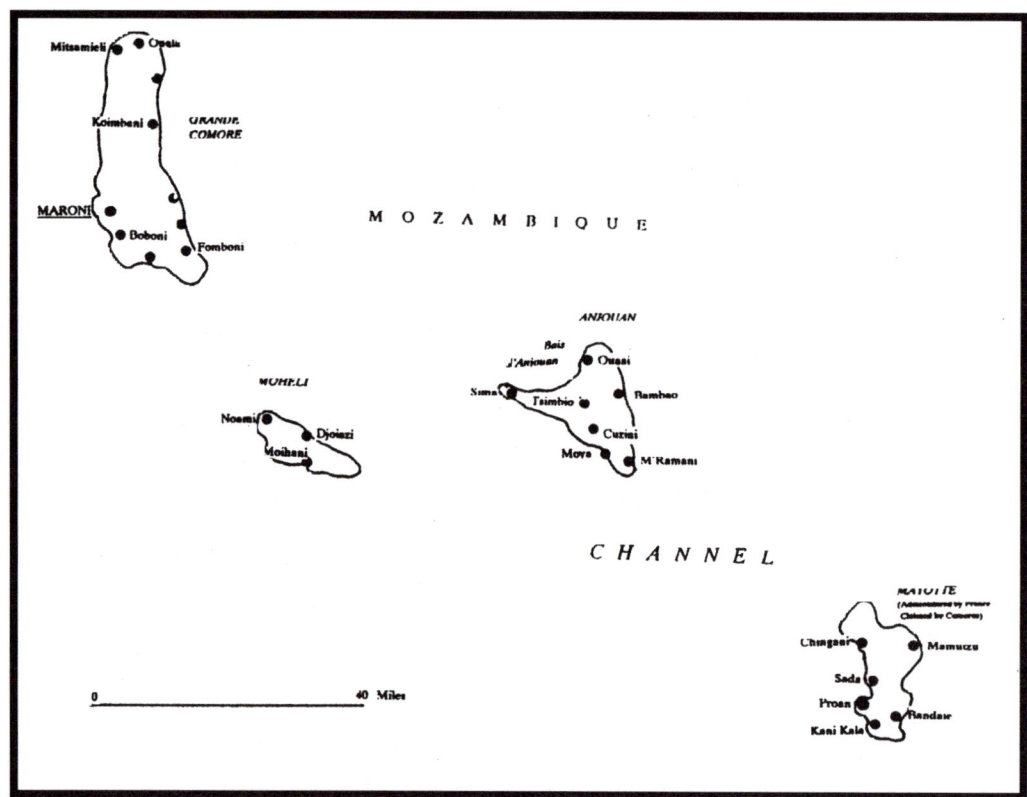

Map 14: Comoros

POPULATION

The population of Comoros was 503,000 according to 1990 estimates. The annual average growth rate was reported as 3.7 percent. The indigenous population is a mixture of Malagasy, African, Malay, and Arabs. The vast majority speak Comoran and about 27 percent of the population live in the urban areas.

EVOLUTION OF COMOROS

Over centuries, the Comoros Islands were invaded by a succession of diverse groups from the coast of Africa, the Persian (Arabian) Gulf, Indonesia, and Madagascar. Portuguese explorers visited the islands in 1505. At about the same time, "Shirazi" Arab migrants introduced Islam in the islands. Between 1841 and 1912, France established its colonial rule over the islands and placed them under the administration of the French Governor of Madagascar. Later, the French settlers and the French-owned companies and wealthy Arab merchants established a plantation-based economy that now uses about one-third of the land for export crops. After World War II, the islands became a French overseas territory with representation in the French National Assembly. Internal political autonomy was granted in 1961 under the terms of De Gaulle's Fifth Republic.

A political crisis arose in 1975, when the voters of Mayotte islands decided to stay with France, a position that clashed with independence-minded peoples of Grande Comore (largest and most populous island), Moheli (the smallest), and Anjouan. Mayotte's population is mainly Christian, but Islam prevails elsewhere.

On July 6, 1975, the Comorian parliament passed a resolution declaring unilateral independence. The deputies of Mayotte abstained, and as such, the Comorian Government took effective control over the three islands (Grande Comore, Anjouan, and Moheli). Mayotte continues to remain under French administration. After independence in 1975, Ahmad Abdallah was designated President of Comoros. After barely a month in office, he was overthrown by foreign mercenaries who installed Ali Soilih. Soilih embarked on the "socialist" revolution, relying on undisciplined youth committees that often terrorized the public. They burned government archives and fired civil servants. Soilih openly challenged the dominance of Islam, alienating much of the devout Muslim population. As a result, a revolution took place in 1978, which restored the former President Abdallah to power. Soilih was killed by the revolutionaries. A constitution was adopted by popular referendum on October 1, 1978, and Abdallah was elected President in the same year. In early 1990, Said Mohammed Djohar won the presidential elections. Since then, the country has been engaged in rewriting its constitution and is on the path of economic progress.

ECONOMY

Comoros, with an estimated gross domestic product (GDP) of $240 million and per capita income of $450, is among the world's poorest and least developed nations. Agriculture, involving more than 87% of the population and 37% of the gross domestic product, provides virtually all foreign exchange earnings. Much of the quality land is either owned by the French settlers or wealthy Comorians. Large plantations occupy about one-third of the total area. Major crops include sugar cane, bananas, cassava, sisal, and copra. Extracts from plants such as lemon grass, citronella, and patchouli are exported to France as a basis for perfumes. Comoros is also the world's second largest producer of vanilla. Corn and rice are staple foods, and there is heavy dependence on the coco palm. Pressure on farming land is very heavy, and many people emigrate to Madagascar. Services including tourism, construction, and commercial activities constitute the remainder of the GDP.

The country lacks the infrastructure necessary for development. Some villages are not linked to the main road system, or at best, are connected by tracks usable only by four-wheel drive vehicles. The islands' ports are rudimentary, although a deep-water facility was recently completed in Anjouan. Only small vessels can approach the existing quays in Maroni and Grande Comoro, despite recent improvements. Long-distance ocean-going ships must lie offshore and be unloaded by smaller boats. During the cyclones, this procedure is dangerous and ships are reluctant to call the island. As a result, most freight is first sent to Mombasa or Reunion and transshipped from there.

There is no manufacturing to speak of, not even in the capital of Maroni, except for the distillation of essences, vanilla-processing, soft drinks, and wood works. In 1989, industries including manufacturing, construction, and electricity contributed about 10% of the Gross Domestic Product. The labor force employed in the industries was only 10% in 1980.

In April 1994, the International Monetary Fund (IMF) approved a credit for $1.9 million to support the government's economic policies over the years ahead. The background to the Comoros need for an IMF loan lies in economic deterioration since the mid-1980s, marked by a worsening trade and external current account deficits.

CHAPTER 12
COTE D'IVOIRE (IVORY COAST)

Cote d'Ivoire is the richest and, economically, the most diversified country in former French West Africa. It produces a wide range of crops and forestry products, the most important being coffee, cocoa, palm oil, and lumber. Besides other things, it benefits from its coastal location and relative political stability since its independence in 1968.

GEOGRAPHY

Cote d'Ivoire is located on the south side of the West African bulge. Its 340 mile (550 km) coastline on the Gulf of Guinea has heavy surf and no natural harbors. The coastal zone displays a contrast between stretches of low rocky cliffs and headlands with small, sandy embayments and smooth unindented sections with sand bars and backing lagoons. Economic development came after the deep water lagoon of Abidjan, which was opened in 1950 by linking the sea through the Virdi Canal. The generally narrow coastal plain gives way to a low interior plain. Much of the northern part of the country is described as a plateau (Map 15).

> **Geographical Profile**
>
> **Area:** 124,500 sq. mi. (322,500 sq. km)
> **Population:** 13.9 million (1994); 17.2 million (2000); 25.5 million (2010)
> **Annual Growth Rate:** 3.6% (1988)
> **Terrain:** Mostly flat
> **Climate:** Tropical
> **Capital:** Yamoussoukro
> **Other Cities:** Abidjan (2.7 million pop.), Bouake, Daloua, Gagnoa, Korhogo, Man
> **Ethnic Groups:** More than 60
> **Religions:** Sunni Islam 55%, Indigenous Pagan 25%, Christianity 20%
> **Languages:** French (official), tribal languages
> **Economy:**
>   **GDP:** $10 billion (1988)
>   **Per Capita Income:** $680
>   **Natural Resources:** Oil
>   **Agriculture:** 29% of GDP; Products: Coffee, cocoa, timber, rubber, corn, rice, tropical foods
>   **Industry:** 19% of GDP; Types: Food processing, textiles
> **Official Name:** Republic of Cote d'Ivoire
> **Date of Independence:** December 1968

Where the coastal alignment crosses the path of the moist, south westerly winds in the southeast and southwest, the rainfall is between 60 to 80 inches (1,500 and 2,000 mm). The central coast lands have less than 60 inches (1500 mm) of rainfall. In consequence of this rainfall pattern, dense forest extends to the sea in the western half of the country; scrub savanna covers a narrow strip, stretching from Fresco to the Ghana frontier. A lush tropical forest extends inland to a line about halfway between Dimbokro and Bouake. North of the forest lies an inland savanna zone of sandy soils, where vegetation is sparse and the landscape is unbroken. Only the Guinea Highlands in the northwest break the monotony of the inland plain, which rises 4,800 ft. (1,460 m) above sea level.

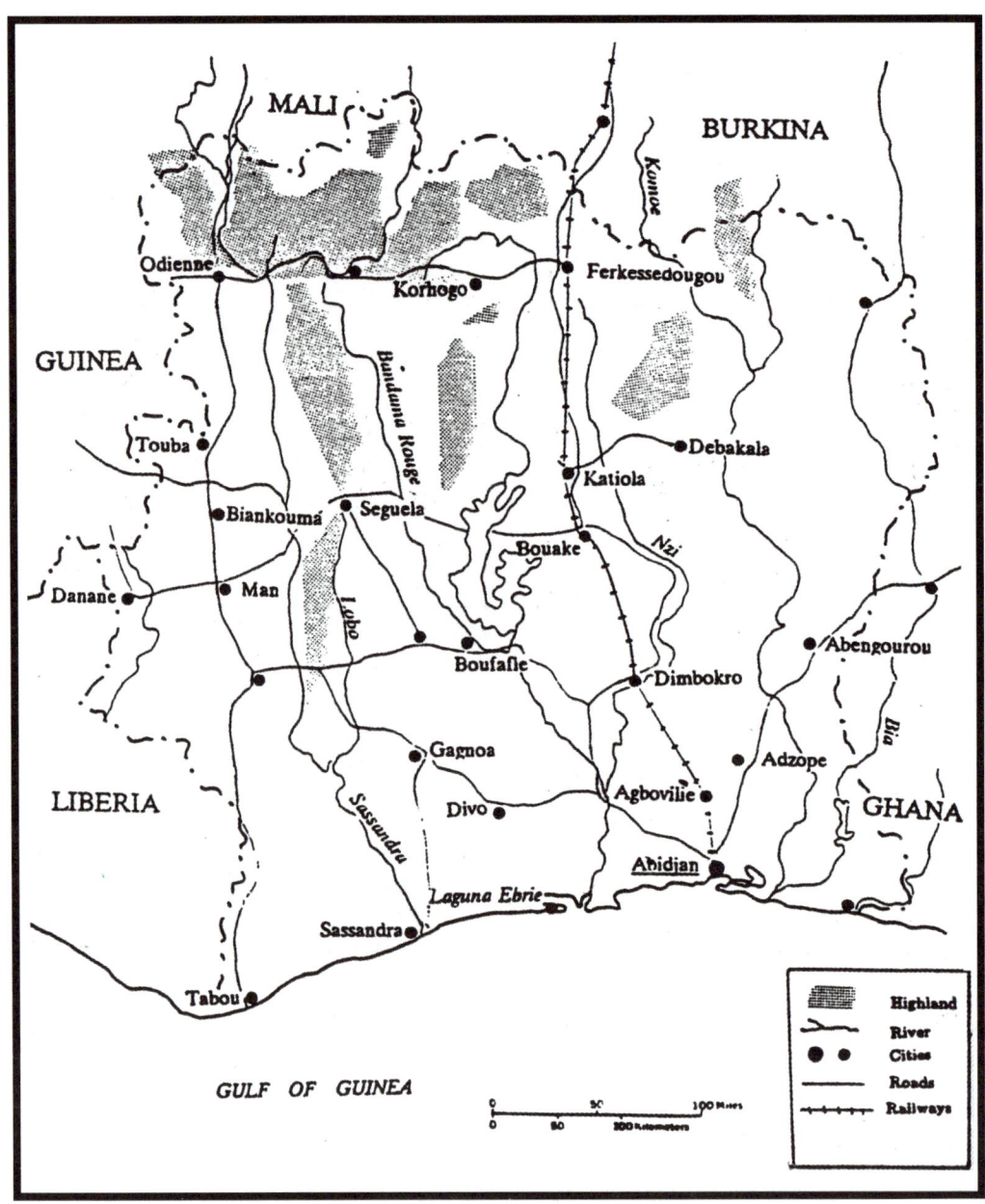

Map 15: Cote D'Ivoire (Ivory Coast)

The southern part of Cote d'Ivoire falls into the tropical zone, with hot, humid weather and heavy rainfall. Daily temperatures vary from a minimum of 22°C (72°F) to a maximum of 32°C (91°F), and the heaviest rainfall is generally between mid-April and mid-July, with a shorter rainy season in October and November. As one moves from the coast, the weather gets drier and the climate grows more savanna-like. Temperature differences become more extreme, with nighttime temperatures in January dipping as low as 12°C (54°F) and daytime temperatures in the summer rising to above 46°C (well into the hundreds).

PEOPLE AND POPULATION

More than 60 ethnic groups of Cote d'Ivoire are classified into seven principal divisions: Akan, Krou, Lagoon, Nuclear Mande, Peripheral Mande, Senoufo, and Lobi. Baoule is probably the largest single ethnic subgroup in the Akan division, with about 20 percent of the overall population. They live in the central region around Bouake. The Bete, in the Krou division, and the Senoufo in the north are the second and third largest groups, within roughly 18 and 15 percent of the population, respectively. Most of the principal divisions have centers in one of the neighboring countries.

Of the 5 million non-Ivorian Africans living in Cote d'Ivoire, one-third to one-half belong to Burkina Faso; the rest are from Ghana, Guinea, Mali, Nigeria, Benin, Senegal, Liberia, and Mauritania. A non-African expatriate community includes roughly 20,000 French and at least 100,000 Lebanese.

The total population of Cote d'Ivoire was estimated at 13.9 million (1944) with an annual increase of 3.6 percent. It is estimated that the population would increase to 17.2 million in the year 2000 and 25.5 million in the year 2010.

EVOLUTION OF COTE D'IVOIRE

The early history of Cote d'Ivoire is virtually unknown, although it is thought that a notable, neolithic culture existed there. In the medieval times, the camel caravans linked western regions of Cote d'Ivoire with the Mediterranean and brought Islam across the Sahara. In the fifteenth century, the Songhai people extended their influence to the west. Under Mohammad Askia, their empire became the most powerful state in the Western Sudan Zone. Later, it came to include the Hausa states on the Niger-Chad watershed and adjoining areas, which had been established in the eleventh century.

The French made their initial contact with Cote d'Ivoire in 1617, when missionaries landed at Assinie near the Gold Coast (now Ghana) border. Early contacts were limited to a few missionaries because of the inhospitable coastline and settlers' fear of the inhabitants. In 1843-44, the French signed treaties with local kings taking their territories under the French control.

Cote d'Ivoire officially became a French colony in 1893. Soon after, the colonial administration negotiated boundary treaties with Liberia and Ghana (then Gold Coast). From 1904 to 1958, Cote d'Ivoire was a constitutional unit of the Federation of French West Africa (now Mauritania,

Senegal, Guinea, Mali, Niger, Benin, Burkina, and Cote d'Ivoire). Until the period following World War II, governmental affairs in French West Africa were administered from Paris through governor generals and territorial governors.

In December 1958, Cote d'Ivoire became an autonomous republic within the French community as a result of a referendum that brought community status to all members of the old Federation of French West Africa except Guinea, which had voted against the association. Cote d'Ivoire became independent on August 7, 1960 and permitted its community membership to lapse.

ECONOMY

Rapid economic development since 1950 was assisted by the opening of the Vridi Canal, which made Abidjan a deep water port, and the Abidjan-Ouagadougou Railroad, which traverses the whole country. In recent years, railroad operations have not been as successful as in March 1987, because Cote d'Ivoire and Burkina Faso decided to form two different companies. A system of highways, most of which are paved, now connect the major urban centers. Many of these urban centers are also served by the national airline, *Air Ivoire*. *Air Afrique* and other African carriers provide regular international services.

Agriculture

Agriculture has been the keystone of Cote d'Ivoire's development into one of Africa's most prosperous economies, with an annual growth rate of nearly 7% from 1960 to 1980. Coffee, cocoa, and tropical woods were the key products. In recent years, Coffee has lost to cocoa, but is still the second most important export crop. Originally introduced in the lagoon area of the southeast, cultivation spread westward, and now there are important concentrations of production around Abidjan, Agboville, Daboa, Dimbokro, Gangoa, and Man. The general policy for coffee is to improve its quality rather than expand the quantity. Efforts are also being made to improve the flavor of the *robusta* by crossing it with higher quality *arabica* variety.

Cocoa was introduced from Ghana in the late nineteenth century, and its main producing area still is an extension of that in Ghana. In recent years, Cote d'Ivoire has surpassed Ghana to become a leading cocoa producer. Farmers receive guaranteed cash payments from the government, despite the fluctuations in world prices. Cocoa and its ancillary services now benefit about 650,000 people.

The banana was first introduced in the early 1930s. Production expanded rapidly, once suitable export facilities became available at Abidjan in the 1950s and as the road network improved. Production is now mainly from the area around Abidjan. The area around Sarsandra is the secondary area of banana export.

Pineapple is mainly grown on company plantations around Abidjan. It provides income for about 15,000 farmers. In the last 15 years, the pineapple production has increased twelve times. Much of this crop is now conserved as fruit or juice in local canneries.

Oil palm is a natural tree of the West African forest. Its cultivation has greatly increased by the development of village and large scale plantations, especially after the creation of the *Societe pour le Developpement Palmiste* (SODEPALM). Cultivation mostly occurs in the coastal regions, and a good part of the vegetable oil produced is marketed locally.

Cote d'Ivoire is trying to diversify its cropping pattern, which includes rubber, cotton, sugar, citrus, and rice. The bulk of the production is now from two large industrial producers (*Societie Africaine de Plantations d'Heveas* and *Societe des Caoutchoues de Grand Bereby*).

A temporary world shortage of sugar in the early 1970s prompted an Ivoirian surge in sugar cultivation, but far more successful has been the cotton cultivation. Main areas of cultivation are around Bouake and Korhogo. After 1961, the Mono variety was gradually replaced by the higher-yielding Allan variety.

Industry and Minerals

Since independence, rapid development of the industrial sector has been oriented toward import substitution, agriculture processing, energy, and construction. Half of manufacturing employment is in agricultural processing. The next largest category, employing about 17%, is textile and apparel industry, largely utilizing domestically grown cotton.

Cote d'Ivoire joined the ranks of petroleum producers when in 1980, an ESSO-led consortium brought the offshore Belier field into production. In 1982, a Phillips-led consortium brought the larger Espoir field into production. However, in recent years, oil production, which at one time met most of the country's needs, fell sharply, and Phillips wells had to be capped. However, ESSO is now undertaking additional exploration of its existing field, and the government intends to solicit bids both for the development of a known natural gas field and for the exploration of new offshore fields.

Cote d'Ivoire also has constructed a regional oil refinery, SIR, which moved in 1986 from being a loss center to generating some profits. Non-oil mineral production is negligible. Limited amounts of diamonds and gold are produced irregularly. A large deposit of low-grade iron ore has been found near Man, and a nationwide geological survey turned up deposits of nickel and manganese.

From 1981 through 1984, the economy slowed down. Over-ambitious state investment in the late 1970s, at a time of high coffee and cocoa prices, was financed largely by external borrowing. A subsequent sharp decline in commodity prices, high rates of interest, and a drought in 1982-83, brought the country to a real financial crisis at the end of 1983.

NOTES

CHAPTER 13
DJIBOUTI

The importance of Djibouti (formerly the French Territory of Afars and Issas) is based on the port of Djibouti, which was created in 1888. Djibouti is also the terminus of the only railway to the central highland in Ethiopia. More than 90 percent of the people are Muslims of Issa and Afar tribes. Based on the importance of two tribes, the name of the country was changed in 1967 from the French Somali Coast to the French Territory of Afars and Issas in July 1967. In 1977, when the country became independent, its name was changed to the Republic of Djibouti.

GEOGRAPHY

The Republic of Djibouti is located in Northeast Africa, near the southern entrance to the Red Sea. It is bordered on the north, the south and the west by Ethiopia, and on the southeast by Somalia (Map 16). The Republic has three regions: (i) a rocky coastal plain, (ii) foot hills of Ethiopia, and (iii) the interior plateau in the north and west. The coastal plain is narrow, parched, hot and treeless, with an elevation of about 650 ft. (200 meters) above sea level. The mountain area is about 3,000 ft. (1,000 meters) above sea level. Along the northern coast of the Gulf of Tadjouri are the Mabla and Gouda mountains, where elevations exceed 6,000

Geographical Profile

Area: 9,000 sq. mile (23,310 sq. km)
Population: 500,000 (1994); 700,000 (2010)
Annual Rate of Natural Increase: 2.9%
Doubling Time of Population: 24 years
Life Expectancy: 48 years
Capital City: Djibouti
Other Cities: Dikhil, Ali Sabieh, Obock, Tadjourah
Ethnic Groups: Somalis (Issas), Afars, French, Arabs, Ethiopians, Italians
Religion: Sunni Islam 94%, Christianity 6%
Languages: Arabic, French (Official), Somali, Afar
Economy:
  GDP: (1985): $339 million
  Per Capita Income: $450
  Natural Resources: Salt, limestone, gypsum, partite, diatoms, geothermal energy
  Agriculture: (10% of GDP): Products: livestock, limited fruits, and vegetables
  Agriculture Land: 2%
  Industry: (49% of GDP) banking (49% of GDP), public administration, construction, manufacturing
Official Name: Republic of Djibouti
Independence Date: June 27, 1977

feet (1,828 m). The plateau is behind the mountains, which rises from 1,000 to 5,000 ft. (300 to 1,500 meters) above the sea level. The land is bare, dry and desolate, marked by sharp cliffs, deep ravines, burning sands and thorny shrubs. Some depressions are below sea level, including Lake Assal.

The two transitional months of May and September are periods of high humidity. Winds generally blow from the east during the cool season, and from the west during the hot season, with occasional strong gusts. The climate is hot from May to September, and somewhat cooler from October to April. When the monsoon blows from the northeast from May to October, temperatures average 33°C (92°F), although they have been recorded as high as 45°C (113°F). The rainfall is sparse and erratic. Humidity is high all year.

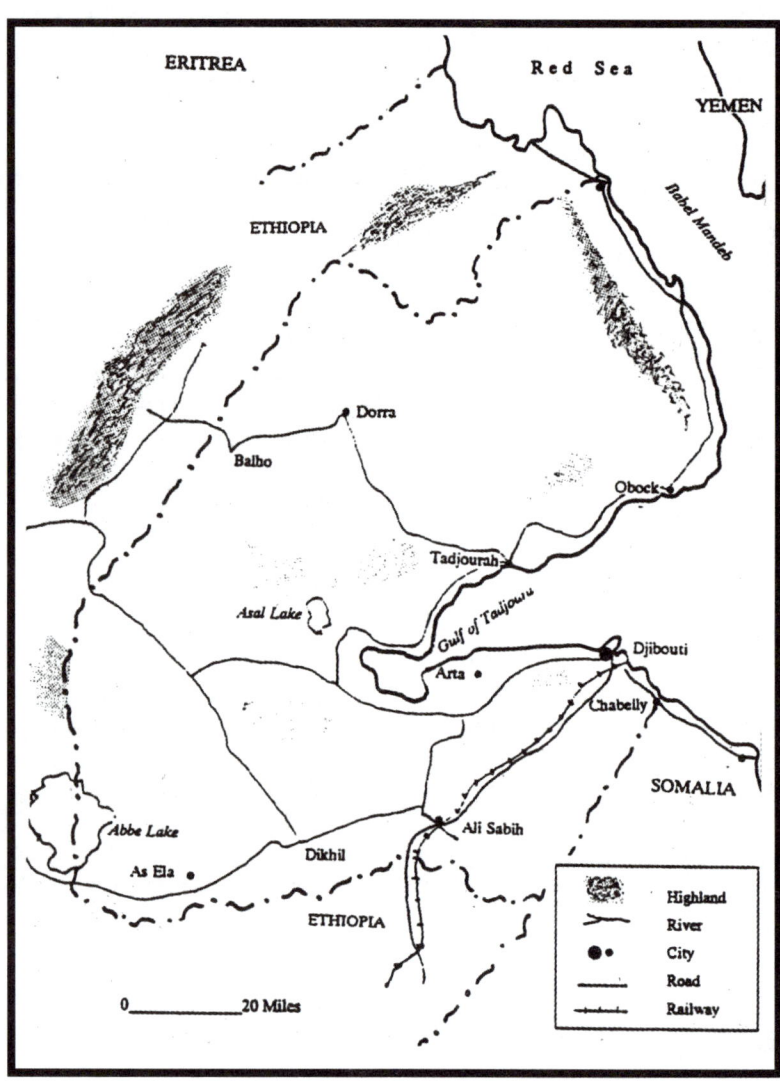

Map 16: Djibouti

PEOPLE AND POPULATION

The population of Djibouti is divided between the Somali and Gadabouur tribes. Somalis include Issas, Afars, Danakil, and Ishaak tribes. The Afars have ties with Ethiopia, and the Issa have ties with Somalia. Both groups are Muslims, both speak Cushitic languages, and both are nomadic beyond the towns. Among the 15,000 foreigners residing in Djibouti, French and Arabs are the most numerous by far. However, the small foreign community also includes Greeks, Indians, and Italians. Somali, Afar, and Arabic are all widely used languages, but French is the official language.

In 1994, the population of the Republic of Djibouti was estimated to have 500,000 people with an annual natural increase of 2.9%. With such an increase, the population of the Republic is likely to increase to 700,000 people in 2010.

EVOLUTION OF THE REPUBLIC OF DJIBOUTI

Thousands of years ago, Djibouti traded in spices, perfumes, hides, and skins with the Egyptians and Chinese. Before the beginning of Islam, contacts were also developed with the Arabian Peninsula. As a result, the Somali and Afar tribes were the first on the African continent to adopt Islam. Ever since, Islam has remained their religion, permeating every aspect of Djibouti's life and influencing their relationship with nature and their neighbors.

The modern history of Djibouti began in 1862 when Afar (Danakil) chiefs sold the anchorage of Obock and its environs to France (Map 16). French interest in Obock had much to do with the fact that it was a good natural harbor at the southern end of the Red Sea. As Italian and British interests in the Horn of Africa and Red Sea expanded, France signed a treaty of friendship and assistance with the *Sultans* of Raheita, Tadjourah, and Gobaad. Later, they acquired additional land to the south from the Issa Somali. They subsequently built a coaling station and naval base at Djibouti.

Growing French interest in the area took hold against the backdrop of British activity in Egypt and the opening of the Suez Canal in 1869. In 1884-85, France expanded its protectorate to include the shores of the Gulf of Tadjourah and the hinterland, designating the area as the French Somaliland. In 1896, Ethiopia, formally recognized French Somaliland, signed agreements with the French initiating the construction of the railroad from Djibouti to Addis Ababa. Boundaries of the protectorate, marked out in 1897 by France and Emperor Menelik of Ethiopia, were affirmed by agreements with Emperor Haile Selassie in 1945 and 1954.

The administrative capital was moved from Obock to Djibouti in 1892. Djibouti, which has a good natural harbor and an easy access to the Ethiopian highlands, attracted trade caravans crossing East Africa. By 1895, it grew from almost nothing to a small, but booming town, with more than 5,000 inhabitants. Two years later, a railway line linking Djibouti to the heart of Ethiopia was begun, which reached Addis Ababa in June 1917, further facilitating the increase of trade. By that time, Djibouti was firmly established as an entreport for the Red Sea trade and as an important bunkering port on the busy sea lane connecting Europe and the Far East through the Suez canal.

By the mid-1960s, more than 3,000 ships were calling at the port, and Djibouti was handling roughly two-thirds of all Ethiopia's trade. In 1967, the Suez Canal was closed as a result of Arab-

Israeli war leading to the abrupt decline in the Red Sea traffic. Although the Suez was reopened, Djibouti still has not regained the level of trade it had before 1967. Another setback was the war between Somalia and Ethiopia in 1977-78, during which sections of Djibouti-Addis Ababa railway were blown up by the guerrillas. The railway line remained closed for more than a year, and during this time, Ethiopia invested heavily in opening another overland trade route through the port of Assab.

On July 22, 1957, the colony was reorganized to give the people a considerable degree of self-government and the right to elect their own government. In August 1966, French President Charles de Gaulle's visit was marked by public demonstration by Somalis demanding independence. A month later, the French Government decided to hold a referendum to determine whether the people wanted to remain within the French Republic or become independent. In a March 1967 referendum, 60% chose to continue the territory's association with France.

A July 1967 directive from France changed the name of the territory from French Somaliland to the French Territory of Afars and Issas. The directive also reorganized the governmental structure of the territory, making the former governor general a high commissioner. The Executive Council also was redesignated as the Council of Government, with nine members.

In 1975, the French Government began to accommodate increasingly insistent demands for independence. In June 1976, the territory's citizenship law, which had favored the Afar minority, was revised to reflect more closely the weight of the Issa Somali. In a May 1977 referendum, the electorate voted for independence, and the Republic of Djibouti was inaugurated on June 27, 1977, after 114 years of colonial rule.

ECONOMY

Djibouti's economy rests jointly on four factors: (i) the maritime and commercial activities of the port of Djibouti, (ii) the airport, (iii) the operation of the Addis Ababa-Djibouti Railroad, and (iv) a large foreign expatriate community. Mineral resources include small quantities of salt from Lake Assab, limestone, gypsum, perlite and geothermal energy. Agriculture comprises about 10 percent of the GNP. Main agricultural products include livestock, fruits, and vegetables. About 89% of the country is desert wasteland, 10% is pasture, and 1% is forested. Djibouti has no industry; services and commerce provide most of the gross domestic product.

The port of Djibouti is the major resource, which has seven deep water berths, four fueling stations, quay space for coastal shipping, large storage areas and a modern container terminal. It has become a main Red Sea center for transshipment of fruits, vegetables, and coffee from landlocked countries in the region. High value cargo is flown to Djibouti and shipped from there by sea.

Most imports are consumed in Djibouti, while the remainder goes to Ethiopia and Northern Somalia. Principal exports from the region transiting Djibouti are coffee, salt, hides, dried beans, cereals, and wax. Djibouti has few exports, most of which come from France. The country's unfavorable balance of trade is offset partially by invisible earnings such as transit taxes, harbor dues and, railway profits. In recent years, Saudi Arabia's improvement of port facilities at Jeddah, and Ethiopia's development of its port at Assab have decreased the volume at Djibouti's port.

CHAPTER 14
EGYPT

Egypt is the most populous country in the Arab world and the second most populous nation on the African continent. The country became Muslim in 641 AD when the Muslim Arab army defeated Byzantine forces. A mosque was built where a solitary dove descended on the camp of the Muslim General, where the capital city of Cairo now stands. Later, the process of Islamization and Arabization began from Cairo, which influenced many areas in Africa. The Arabic language replaced the indigenous Coptic language; however, this tongue still exists among the Coptic Christians which are 10% of the Egyptian population. Since 641 AD, Egypt has been one of the major cultural and intellectual centers of the Muslim World.

GEOGRAPHY

Egypt lies astride the land bridge between Africa and Southwest Asia and between the Mediterranean and Red Sea. It is linked to Asia and Europe through the Sinai peninsula. Geometric boundaries separate it from Libya to the west, and Sudan to the south. The Mediterranean Sea is on its north, and the Red Sea on its south (Map 17).

In simplest terms, the physical geography of Egypt consists of the Nile valley, flanking deserts, and the barren highlands. In upper and middle Egypt, the

---

Geographical Profile

Area: 386,650 sq. miles (1,001,450 sq. km)
Population: 58.4 million (1994); 67.3 million (2000); 81.3 million (2010)
Annual Rate of Natural Growth: 2.4%
Capital: Cairo (pop. 12 million)
Other Cities: Alexandria (4 million), Aswan, Asyut, Port Said, Suez, Ismailia
Terrain: Desert except Nile Valley and Delta
Climate: Dry, hot summer, moderate winters
Ethnic Groups: Arab, Nubian, Copt
Religions: Sunni Islam 90%; Coptic Christian 10%
Languages: Arabic (official), English widespread
Economy:
    GDP: $34.5 billion (1987-88)
    Per Capita GNP: $680 (1987)
    Natural Resources: Petroleum and natural gas, iron ore, phosphate, manganese, limestone, gypsum, talc, asbestos, lead, zinc
    Agriculture: Products: Cotton, rice, onions, beans, citrus fruits, wheat, corn, barley, sugar
    Industry Types: Food processing, textiles, chemicals, petrochemicals, construction, light manufacturing, iron and steel products, cement, military equipment
Official Name: Arab Republic of Egypt

Nile valley varies from 3 to 15 miles (5 to 24 km) in width. East of the Nile valley, the Arabian desert slopes upward to a string of highlands along the Red Sea. Separated by the Gulf of Suez, the lower end of these highlands is the rugged desert territory of the Sinai Peninsula, bordered on the east by the Gulf of Aqaba. The Red Sea has mile-deep basins that contain exceptionally hot and salty water, the bottom sediments being rich in a variety of minerals. West of the Nile is the Libyan Desert, sloping northward to the Qattara Depression where there are several small oases. Southward is a string of depressions and in the desert are isolated groups of oases, such as Kharga and Dakhla.

The Nile is the aggregate of two branches upstream: the White Nile and the Blue Nile. The White Nile originates in the streams that fill Lake Victoria in East Africa. The source of the Blue Nile is Lake Tana in Ethiopia. The two branches of the Nile converge at Khartoum, in Sudan, from where it flows towards Egypt like a narrow ribbon. The dual origin of the Nile assures a fairly regular natural flow of water, making the annual floods predictable both in terms of timing and intensity. The Nile rises during July, August, and September to its flood stage in October, when it may be more than 20 ft. (7 m) above its low stage.

After a rapid fall during November and December, the river declines gradually until its minimum in the month of May. The Nile dwindles in volume, as it crosses Egypt where an annual inch of rain cannot make

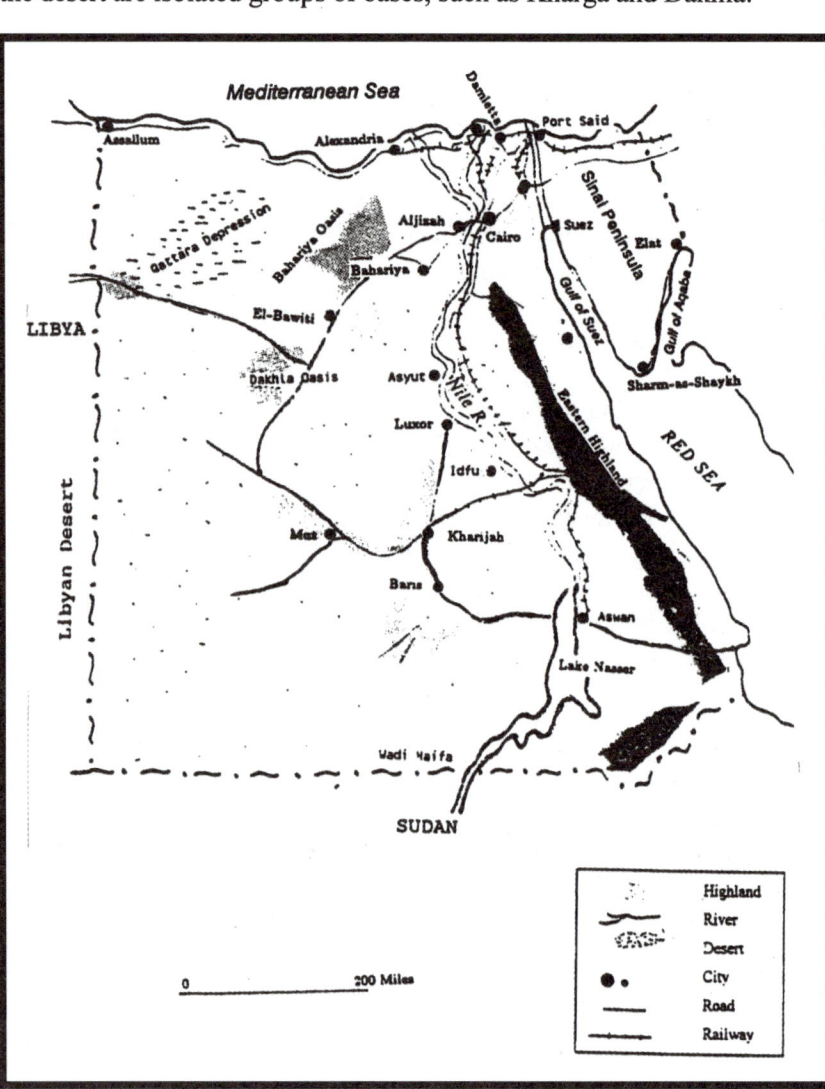

Map 17: Egypt

up for evaporation and irrigation losses. Today, the Nile is a highly artificial river, and very little water reaches the Mediterranean through its delta channels.

Climatically, the Egyptian year falls into two parts - a mild winter from November to April, and a hot summer from May to October, which is often ushered in by the scorching wind from the south known as *khamsin*. There are no spring or fall seasons in Egypt. The virtual absence of the cyclonic disturbances result in a monotony of climatic conditions. During most of the year, sudden variations of temperatures are rare, except occasionally in the winter.

PEOPLE AND POPULATION

The Egyptians are fairly homogenous: Mediterranean and Arab influences appear in the north, as well as some mixing in the south with the Nubians of northern Sudan. Ethnic minorities include a small number of Bedouin Arab nomads dispersed in the eastern and western deserts and in the Sinai, as well as 50,000-100,000 Nubians clustered along the Nile in upper Egypt (fig. 15). Before construction of the Aswan High Dam, Nubian villages stretched irregularly along the Nile. They have since been relocated along the banks of Lake Nasser.

Of the country's 58.4 million people, 99% live in the Nile valley and the Nile Delta. The Delta is 150 miles (250 km) wide at the seaward base and about 96 miles (160 km) from south to north. These regions are among the world's most densely populated areas, containing an average of over 3,600 persons per square mile (1,450 per sq. km). Small communities covering the desert regions of Egypt are clustered around oases, and historic trade and transportation routes. The government has tried to encourage migration to the newly irrigated land reclaimed from the desert. However, the proportion of the population living in rural areas has continued to decrease as people move to the cities in search of employment and a higher standard of living.

Fig 15: An Egyptian Bedouin

EVOLUTION OF EGYPT

Second only to Mesopotamia in ancient times, Egypt is an isolated land that has been spared conquest, invasion, and unsettling contacts to a remarkable degree. To the east and west are deserts. To the north is a desolate and harborless coast and the inhospitable, marshy delta. Above Aswan the Nile is studded with a series of rapids, or cataracts, and further south are the broad savanna marshes. Thus enclosed, Egyptians remained aloof for much of their history.

Largely because of its isolation, Egypt continued as one state for more than 5,000 years under different rules. The pyramids at Giza (near Cairo), which were built in the 4th dynasty of Egyptian rule, show the power of the pharaonic religion and state. Ancient Egypt reached the peak of its power, wealth, and territorial extent in the period called the New Empire (1567-1085 BC). In 525 BC, Persians dethroned the last pharaoh of the 26th dynasty. The country remained a Persian province until it was conquered by Alexander in BC 332. He founded the port city of Alexandria, which became one of the great centers of the Mediterranean world (Fig. 16), the location of the light house of Pharaohs, and the largest libraries of the ancient world. After Alexander's death in 323 BC, the Macedonians took control of Egypt, which ended in 30 BC with the suicide of Queen Cleopatra.

Fig. 16: The port city of Alexandria

For six centuries after 30 BC, Egypt was a Roman province. Christianity was brought to Egypt by St. Mark in 37 AD, and the church in Alexandria was founded about 40 AD. The new religion spread quickly, reaching upper Egypt by the second century, though many adhered to the eastern form after the country came under Byzantine control.

Arabs conquered Egypt in 642 AD, after which a process of Islamization and Arabization began. Cairo was founded in 969 AD, just 14 miles north of Memphis, a city which was founded in 3000 BC. The Arabs modernized the settlement and made it their metropolis, calling it *Al-Qahirah*, "victorious." Al-Qahirah was made the capital of Egypt. It soon became a university town (Al-Azhar University was established there in 1000 AD), a major center in the spice trade, an area of unmatched power and the focus of Islamic learning (Fig. 17). There was no greater city in Africa or Europe at that time. Although a Coptic minority remained and still remains, the Arabic language replaced the indigenous Coptic tongue. For the next 1,300 years, a succession of Turkish, Arabic, Mameluke and Ottoman *caliphs*, *beys*, and *sultans* ruled Egypt.

Fig. 17: Al-Azhar University
Cairo, Egypt

The conquest of Egypt by Napoleon Bonaparte in 1798 AD brought it again into the sphere of European commerce, and laid the foundation for the future role of Egypt in the life around the Mediterranean Sea. Napoleon developed Egypt in the colonial mold, to supply cotton and sugar cane to France. The framework was in place until a few years later when an Albanian potentate, Mohammad Ali Pasha, became the ruler of Egypt.

Napoleon was the first to contemplate a canal through the isthmus of Suez, linking the Mediterranean and the Red Seas to provide a seaway from Europe to South Asia and the Far East. As British interests in South Asia expanded, they became more interested in the project. Actually, British personnel and goods of the East India Company passing to and from Britain to India were taken by ship to the old port of Alexandria (Egypt). They traveled by river boats up the Nile to a point above Cairo, where they were transferred to desert caravans for land passage to the shores of the Red Sea, their point of re-embarkation on the journey to South Asia.

Later developments and a revolt by the Egyptian army in 1882 led the British to occupy Egypt, which ended in 1936, when a monarchy was established. The King of Egypt was overthrown and a republic established in 1953, which soon became a military-dominated dictatorship.

Fig. 18: An ancient irrigation method

ECONOMY

Egypt is still essentially an agricultural country with nearly one-third of its labor force engaged in farming. Although women form a sizable chunk of the labor force, they still have a fairly low standard of living. Egypt moved to improve the conditions of its farmers (*Fellahin*) with land reforms in 1952, which were revised in 1961 and 1969. The unequal distribution of land ownership had created social unrest. Until 1952, two-thirds of the farmland was owned by 6 percent of land owners, whereas 2 million peasants owned only 13 percent of plots of less than a *feddan* (about one acre or 0.4 ha) each, and another 2 million were landless. In 1952, family holdings were limited to 300 *feddans*. The surplus was expropriated and allotted in small plots to landless farmers. Then in 1961 and 1969, the land holdings were further slashed to 100 and 50 *feddans*.

Agriculture

The Egyptian economy is largely agricultural, based essentially on irrigation and the Nile River. In its 690 mile-long course through Egypt, the Nile usually flows near the eastern side of its valley. To irrigate higher fields, water is lifted by *shadufs*, which consists of a bucket made from a bag of skin. It is suspended from the end of a long pole and balanced by a counterweight. Another method of lifting the water a short distance is the Archimedes Screw. A more elaborate type of water lifting device, *saqiyeh*, is operated by the cattle or donkeys (Fig. 18).

The traditional form of irrigation in Egypt is basin irrigation. At the time of a flood, the waters of the river are let off into carefully constructed inundation or flood canals. From there, it passes into a basin where the flat field or fields are enclosed by low earth banks.

The modern system of canal irrigation may be regarded as having begun in 1861, with the construction of the delta barrage below Cairo. The barrage of Zifta was added to this system in 1901, and the year 1902 marked the completion in Upper Egypt of the great Asyut Dam, followed by the barrage at Esna (Isna), and still later, by the dam at Nag Hammadi in 1930, about 150 miles above Asyut.

Although these dams increased the area of cultivable land during the flood water, a reservoir was needed along the southern border of Egypt to provide water during the dry season when the level was low. It was for this purpose that the great dam at Aswan was constructed. First constructed in 1903, it was enlarged in 1907, 1912, and 1933.

The ever-growing population, however, outgrew these improvements. To meet the increasing needs and to provide power for industrialization, the "High Dam" was constructed a short way upstream. This dam has created a massive reservoir extending 310 miles (500 km) to the south and averaging 14 miles (22 km) in width. In so doing, 70,000 people both in Egypt and the Sudan, and the Sudanese town of Wadi Haifa were shifted. Many ancient monuments of the Nile Valley have been totally submerged, although the most famous of all, the giant statues of the rock temple of Abu Simbel, have been raised above the waters.

In 1990, more than one-third of the Egyptian labor force was engaged in farming, and many others worked in the processing or trading of agricultural products. Practically all Egyptian agriculture takes place in some 6 million acres (2.5 million hectares) of fertile soil in the valley of the Nile and the delta regions. Although some desert lands are being developed for agriculture, fertile lands along the river are being lost to urbanization and erosion.

The climate and availability of water, especially since the building of the Aswan Dam, permit several crops a year on the same piece of land. Although improvement is possible, agricultural productivity is high. Egypt has little subsistence farming. Cotton, rice, onions, and beans are the principal crops. Cotton is the largest agricultural export earner.

Egypt has few natural resources other than the agricultural capacity of the Nile Valley. The major minerals are petroleum, phosphate, and iron ore. The fall in the world oil prices during the mid-1980s had a severe impact on Egypt. However, petroleum exploration continues, particularly in the Western Desert.

Manufacturing Industry

Egypt is the most industrialized country of Muslim Africa. Most industrial development has occurred within the last 35 years, although its beginning goes back to 1930, when tariffs were first imposed on manufactured imports. The population pressure, the need to diversify the economy, and a desire to satisfy the aspirations of nationalism have contributed to these developments.

In 1952, when the revolution took place, the manufacturing industry contributed no more than 10 percent of the national income. The revolutionary government invested public money in services like roads, railways, and power supplies. After nationalization of the Suez Canal (1956), the government gradually nationalized industry, banks, and insurance companies.

Textile is the largest industry in Egypt, which includes spinning, weaving, dying, and printing of cotton, wool, silk and rayon. In addition to meeting the domestic demand, textiles are exported to Sudan and other Arab states. Most of the output comes from large modern factories located at Mehalla el Kubra and Kafr el Diawal. Other industries include sugar refining, oil-seed crushing, vegetable preserving and the manufacture of shoes, leather goods, alcohol, soaps, paints, varnishes, razor blades, and cars. The chemical industry has expanded with the growth of oil refining and petrochemicals - pharmaceutical, cosmetics, medical supplies, and fertilizers. The Helwan iron and steel plant, just south of Cairo, leads the metallurgical industry. Another mill has been constructed at Al Dikheik, near Alexandria. Aluminum (from imported bauxite) is produced at Nag Hammadi in Upper Egypt. There are oil refineries at Suez and Alexandria.

Transportation

Transportation facilities in Egypt follow the pattern of settlement along the Nile. The major rail line runs from Alexandria to Aswan. Other important lines lie along the north coast to the Libyan border and eastward to the Suez Canal. Most paved and improved roads are found in the Nile Valley and Delta, near the Suez Canal, and along the Red Sea and Sinai coasts. The Nile River system (about 1,000 miles or 1,600 km) plus another 1,500 km of navigable canals are important for inland transport. Major ports are Alexandria, Port Said, and Port Suez.

CHAPTER 15
ERITREA

Around 700 BC, a wave of advanced agriculturists crossed the Red Sea from Yemen to settle in Eritrea. They were Semitic-speaking people who accepted Christianity in 330 AD. Later in the twelfth century they accepted Islam. Now Islam and Christianity coexist in Eritrea.

GEOGRAPHY

Eritrea is bordered on the north and northwest by Sudan, on the south by Ethiopia, and on the southeast by the Republic of Djibouti. It stretches along the Red Sea from Cape Kasar to the Strait of Bab el Mandeb, a distance of about 620 miles (1,000 km). Eritrea also includes the Dahlak islands, a low-lying coral archipelago off shore from Massawa. The plain rises to the highlands in the central part (Map 18).

Eritrea's nearly 50,000 square mile (125,500 sq. km) area is either highland or desert, bush country or volcanic wilderness. The surface features can be divided into four types: (i) highland plateau, (ii) Red Sea coastal plain, (iii) hill country in the north and northwest, and (iv) the broad western plains. The Highlands range between 6,000 and 8,000 feet (1825 m to 2430 m) above sea level. The plateau sharply descends into the Red Sea coastal plain, which runs from 10 to 40 miles (16 to 64 km) in width, for the entire length of the Eritrean barren and treeless sea coast. The country's main rivers flow westward, cutting valleys through the central highlands and western low lands. The main rivers include the Baraka and the Garh. The Garh is called the Marab for a part of its length.

Geographical Profile

Area: 36,170 sq. mi. (121,144 sq. km)
Population: 2.7 million (1984);
3.3 million (1994); 4.2 million (2000)
Capital: Asmara; Other cities: Massawa, Assab
Ethnic Groups: Afar, Bilen, Hedareb, Kunama, Nara, Rashaida, Saho, Tigre
Religions: Sunni Islam 51%, Christianity 48% Animists and others 1%
Terrain: Includes many islands of the Dahlak archipelago, low coastal plains in the south, mountain ranges in the north
Climate: Hot, dry, rainfall between 500 mm to 1000 mm
Economy:
  GDP: not known
  Per Capita Income: not known
  Natural Resources: Petroleum deposits
  Agriculture Products:- Barley, dairy products, lentils, millet, sorghum, wheat, and teif
  Industry: Construction materials, leather goods, processed foods, and salt
Official Name: Republic of Eritrea
Date of Independence: May 28, 1993

With minor exceptions, the plateau has very sparse vegetation. The hill country to the north and west of the Eritrean plateau lacks both exact definition and internal uniformity. It is between 2,500 and 4,000 feet (760 and 1220 m) above sea level and is higher in the south around Karen. The broad western plains lie west and southwest of the River Baraka and north of the river Setit (or Takazzo, as it is known in Ethiopia). Here, between the rivers Garh and Setit, the soils are rich and dark, vegetation is thick, and during the rainy season the grass is plentiful.

Along the coast, rainfall ranges between 6 to 10 inches (15 to 25 cm) a year in the lowland areas, increasing up to 24 inches (61 centimeters) in most parts of the country. The heaviest rains occur in June and July. The temperatures average 80°F (27°C) along the coast and 60°F (16°C) in the highlands. In the southeast, the Danakil depression, which is more than 500 ft. (130 meters) below sea level, experiences some of the highest temperatures recorded on earth, frequently exceeding 122°F (50°C).

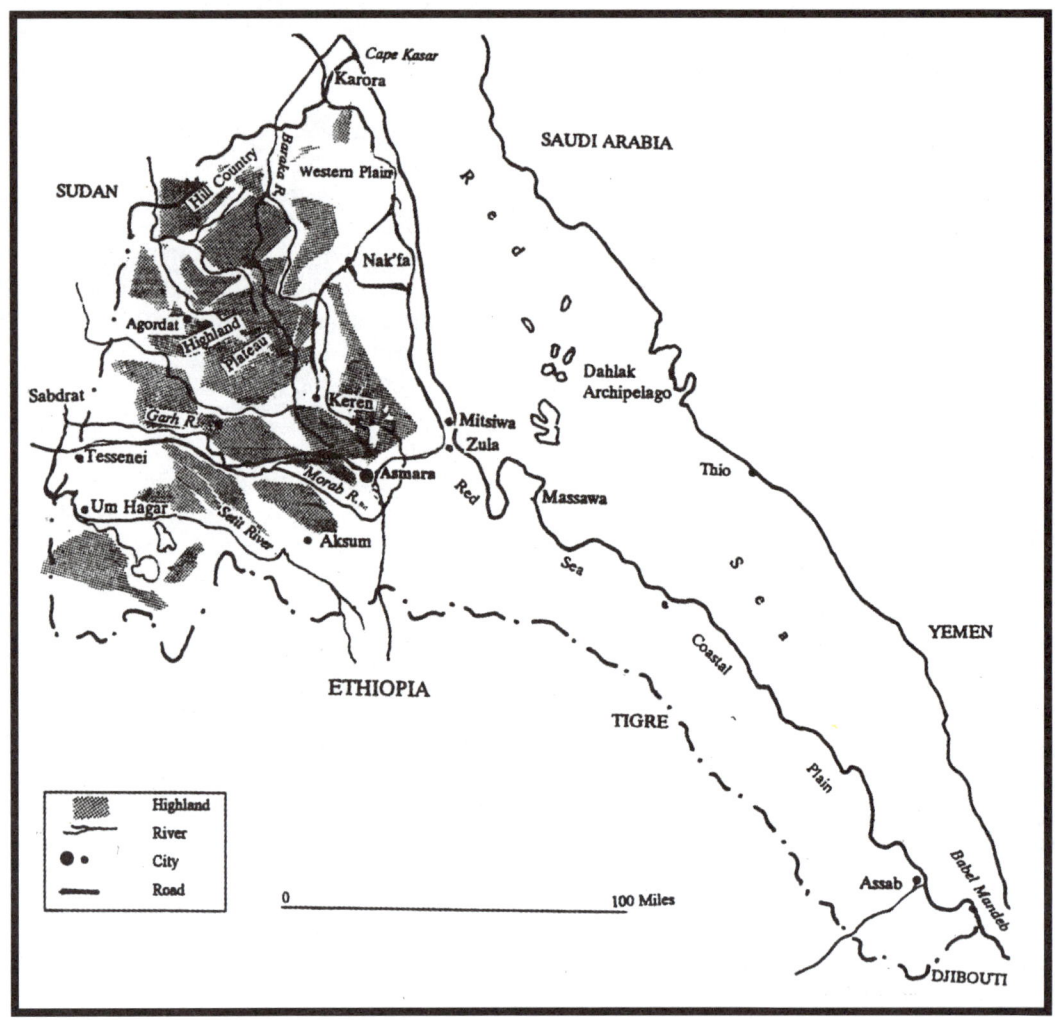

Map 18: Eritrea

PEOPLE AND POPULATION

An accurate census was conducted by the British in the early 1950s. Since then, there has been no census in Eritrea. The present population is estimated between 2 million and 3.5 million by various sources. According to some experts, the present population (1994) of 3.5 million will reach 4.15 million by the year 2000.

Eritrea is inhabited by a mosaic of diverse people. These people have varied origins, and all have links outside Eritrea proper. The Eritrean highland area from Asmara to the south is dominated by the people who were similar to their Tigrinya-speaking Ethiopian kinsmen. A great majority of the highlanders are Coptic Christians. For the most part, these people are settled agriculturists and are organized in village communities of extended families.

In the north and west of the central highlands, along much of the coastal plain, northern highlands and Naraka lowlands are Tigre speaking people, the oldest spoken derivative of the classical Ethiopian language. Most of these people are Muslim nomads or semi-nomads. The most notable exception is the Karen area, where agriculture is practiced. The southern portion of the coastal plain is sparsely inhabited by the Danakil Muslims, who speak a Hamitic dialect called Afar. The Danakils are organized in small clans and are highly mobile. One of the few permanent settlements in this part of Eritrea is the Red Sea port of Assab.

The other group is Saho, who live between the Danakil and the highland plateau. These people are Muslims, and the majority of them are either pastoral nomads or semi-nomads. In the Karen region live a small number of families known as Belain. Some Belain families also live in the Gash-Setit lowlands.

EVOLUTION OF ERITREA

Around 2,000 BC, people from the interior of Africa settled in what is now Eritrea. More people began arriving from the Arabian Peninsula. The Aksum Kingdom became the first important state in the area around 1,000 BC. The kingdom reached its height as a trading and cultural center between 300 AD and 600 AD. During the 600s, Muslims gained control of the area.

In modern times, Eritrea first emerged as an entity in the 1880s following Italy's occupation of the Red Sea port of Massawa and other coastal enclaves. In 1889, Italy signed a Treaty with the Ethiopian Emperor, and in 1890, named its new possession "Eritrea." This treaty gave control of the colony to the Italian Government. The borders agreed upon therein are now the borders of modern-day Eritrea. Italian farmers were then encouraged to settle on the fertile highland area. Italian exploitation continued until the Second World War. After the Second World War, Italy renounced its rights to Eritrea, leaving the United Nations to decide upon the territory's future. Several commissions were given the task of determining the most acceptable course of action, but none managed to provide a suitable recommendation. Eventually, the General Assembly itself recommended a federation of Eritrea with Ethiopia. The decision took effect in 1952, but a decade later, Eritrea was unilaterally absorbed into Ethiopia as a province.

Soon after, a war of secession erupted, led by the Eritrean Liberation Front (ELF) and the Marxist Eritrean Popular Front (PLF). Both were supported by Libya, Somalia, Iraq, and other Arab states. Following the 1974 revolution in Ethiopia, thousands of new recruits joined the EPLF. Even greater numbers joined after the regime launched its 'red terror' campaign in Asmara. The arms struggle intensified and was eventually transformed into full-scale conventional warfare. In 1989, the EPLF captured the port of Massawa, and succeeded in severing a major supply route to the Ethiopian forces. In May 1991, EPLF established an interim administration in Asmara.

In 1991, a conference of representatives of the EPLF and Ethiopian Government was convened in London under the chairmanship of the United States Assistant Secretary of State for Africa. All parties agreed that the EPLF hold a referendum on independence in 1993. The referendum was held in which 99.8% people voted for independence. As a result of this referendum, May 24, 1993 was proclaimed as independence day, and on May 28,1993, Eritrea became the 182nd member of the United Nations.

ECONOMY

Little statistical information is available on the Eritrean economy. It is estimated that Eritrea is one of the poorest countries in Africa with an annual income ranging between $75 and $150 per person. Although Eritrea has the distinction of being one of the few non-debtor nations in Africa, many of its people are without a basic subsistence income.

Agriculture

By far, the most important sector of the economy is agriculture, which sustains 90% of the population, despite a reduction in food production between 1980 and 1990. Most sedentary agriculture is practiced in the highlands, where rainfall is sufficient to cultivate the main crops. Teff (an indigenous grain), corn, wheat, sorghum, and millet are the main subsistence crops. Other major crops are cotton, coffee, and tobacco. In 1992, which was described as a satisfactory year in agricultural terms, some 778,050 acres (315,000 ha) of land was cultivated, and the harvest was good enough to satisfy an estimated 54% of the food requirement. But, 1993 was a disastrous year, following the almost complete failure of the rains and the problems caused by crop pests. As a result, 80% of the crop was lost.

In an effort to stimulate production, the Eritrean authorities have exempted agricultural (and industrial) exports from sales tax. However, lack of animal power, seed grains and capital equipment will hamper the long-term development of the agricultural sector. In 1993, Eritrea had only 47 tractors. Owing to the problem of water scarcity and unreliable rainfall, careful management and conservation are essential.

Industry

Eritrea has no industry. Its shattered industrial base was traditionally centered on the production of glass, cement, footwear and canned goods. Although some of the 40 public-sector factories -

producing textiles, footwear, beverages and other light industrial goods - were operating in 1991, they were doing so at only one-third capacity. A new investment code has been issued, which prescribes tax allowances on income, low import and export duties for up to five years, and duty free imports of materials required to establish industrial enterprises.

NOTES

CHAPTER 16
GAMBIA

Both in area and population, the Republic of Gambia is the smallest country on mainland Africa. Islam was introduced here by the Arab traders in the 12th century, and it spread widely in the middle of the 19th century. Now, 90% of the people of Gambia are Muslims.

GEOGRAPHY

Gambia is located on the bulge of West Africa and comprises a narrow strip of land 7 to 20 miles (11-32 km) wide along the lower reaches of the Gambia River (Map 19). Except for the sea coast, Gambia is completely surrounded by the Republic of Senegal. The maximum east-west distance of Gambia is 292 miles (470 km), and the north-south distance is 29 miles (47 km.), with only one or two villages on either side of the Gambia River.

Its form represents a bizarre politico-geographical legacy of the colonial period. It is enclosed by geometric boundaries which are the most artificial of all African states. A series of arcs were drawn with the compass placed at regular intervals along the Gambia River, and two parallel lines were extended from near the mouth of the river to connect with these arcs which formed the boundaries.

Geographical Profile

Area: 4,361 sq. mi. (11,300 sq. km)
Population: 1.0 million (1994); 1.1 million (2000); 1.6 million (2010)
Annual Rate of Natural Increase: 2.6%
Doubling Time of Population: 27 years
Capital City: Banjul (pop. 44,000)
Ethnic Groups: Mandinko 42%, Fula 18%, Wolof 16%, Jola 10%, Serkuli 9%, others 4%; non-Gambian 15%
Religions: Sunni Islam 90%, Christianity 9%, Paganism 1%
Languages: English (official), Mandinka, Wolof, Fula, other indigenous languages
Economy:
  GDP: (1991) $331 million
  Per Capita Income: $373
  Natural Resources: Possibility of Oil
  Agriculture: (20% of GDP)
  Products: Peanuts, rice, millet, sorghum, fish, palm kernel, vegetables, livestock, forestry
  Industry: (12% of GDP). Types: Peanut products, construction, brewing soft drinks, agricultural machinery assembly, small wood working and metal working, clothing
Official Name: Republic of Guinea
Independence Date: February 18, 1965

The Gambia River rises in the Fouta Djallon plateau of Guinea. It enters Senegal in the southeast, flowing through it for about 200 miles (320 km) before entering Gambia. The Gambia

River is deep and navigable from the Fatoto River wharf to Banjul seaport at the mouth of the estuary. The indented coastline strongly suggests that the land has sunk relative to the sea and that the Gambia River Valley has drowned to give it the great depth. The depth of the Gambia River has made it an important waterway. Even in the dry season, the river remains tidal and navigable for about 300 miles (500 km) inland. Kuntaur can always be reached by ships drawing 17 ft. (3 m) of water. Smaller crafts can go as far as Georgetown, 180 miles (283 km) upstream.

Gambia is a low-lying country with a maximum altitude of 120 feet (73 m) above sea level. Thick mangrove swamps border the lower half of the Gambia River, where vegetation often rises to 100 feet (30 m). Behind the mangroves are river "flats", which are completely submerged during the wet season, in some cases with salt water. Sand hills and rolling plateaus lie farther back from the river.

The climate of Gambia is subtropical, with a marked hot and wet season from June to October, and a cooler dry season from November until April. Annual rainfall varies from 30 to 55 inches (76-140 cm), and it comes only during the summer season. Temperatures range from 16º to 43ºC (60º to 110ºF) with daily temperatures exceeding 32ºC (90ºF) from April to June.

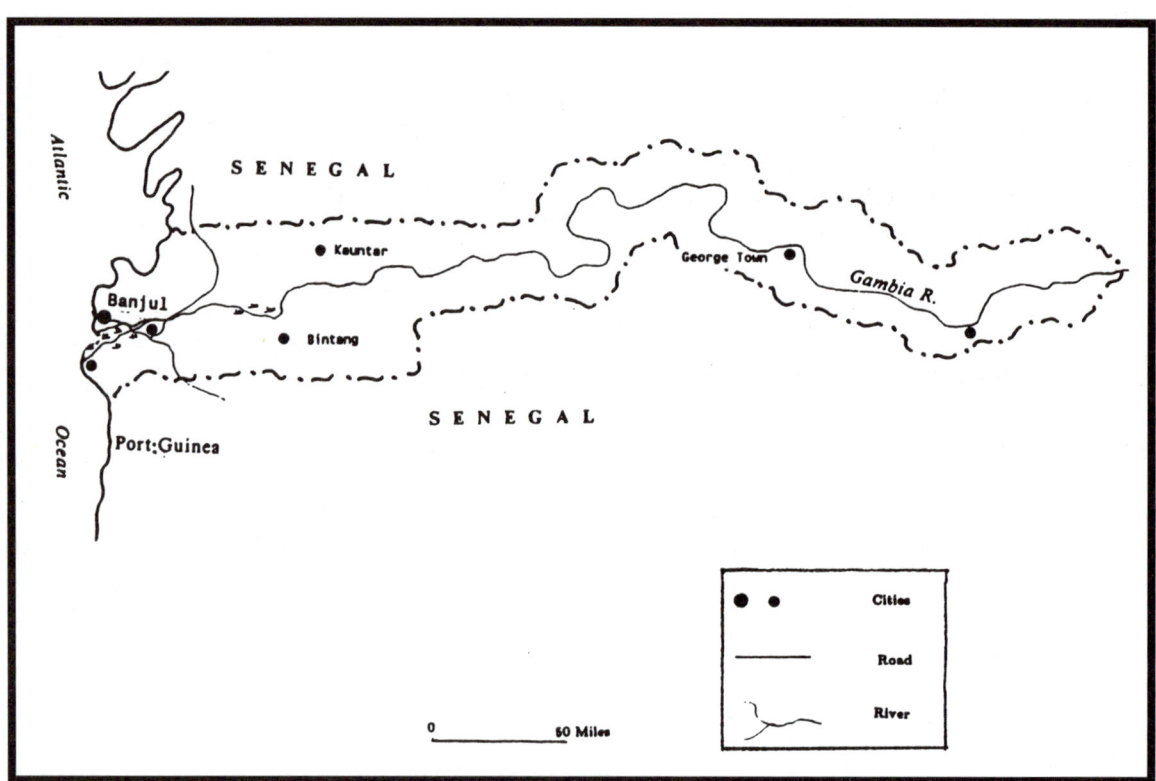

Map 19: Republic of Gambia

PEOPLE AND POPULATION

A wide variety of ethnic groups live side-by-side in Gambia with a minimum of inter-tribal friction, each preserving its own language and traditions. The Mandinka is the largest tribal group, followed by the Fula (or Peul), Wolof, Jola, and Serahuli groups. The Mandinka constitute about 42% of the population, and they are mainly peanut farmers. In Nigeria, they are known as Fulanis. Fulanis are mainly pastoralist and wander with their cattle in search of pastures. Wolofs are the third largest group. They are concentrated in the western part of the country and are the most educated group in Gambia. The Serahulis live in the extreme eastern part of the country and are a mixture of Mandingo, Berber and Fula. Jolas live along the river. In addition, approximately 2,500 non-Africans live in Gambia, including Europeans and many families of Lebanese origin.

In 1994, the population of Gambia was estimated at 1 million people, with a density of 217 persons per square mile. The annual rate of natural increase was 2.6 percent. With such an increase, the population is expected to rise to 1.1 million in the year 2000 and 1.6 million in 2010. The life expectancy is 44 years.

Muslims constitute over 90% of the population. Christians of different denominations account for most of the remainder. Gambians officially observe the holidays of both religions and practice religious tolerance. Gambians are liberal, but the traditional emphasis on the extended family, as well as indigenous forms of dress and celebrations, remain integral parts of everyday life.

EVOLUTION OF GAMBIA

Gambia was once part of the Ghana Empire and the Kingdom of the Songhais. In the 15th century, it became a part of the Kingdom of Mali. By the 16th century, Portuguese slave traders and gold seekers had settled in the lower river area. In 1588, the Portuguese sold exclusive trade rights on the Gambian River to the British merchants. In 1618, Britain granted a charter to one of its companies to trade with Gambia and the Gold Coast (now Ghana).

During the late 17th and throughout the 18th centuries, Britain and France struggled continuously for political and commercial supremacy in the regions of the Senegal and Gambia Rivers. The 1783 Treaty of Versailles gave possession of Gambia to Great Britain, but the French retained an enclave at Albreda on the north bank of the river. Albreda was later ceded to Britain in 1857.

As many as 3 million slaves may have been taken from the region during the three centuries that the trade operated. Most of those taken were sold to Europeans by other Africans, some were prisoners of inter-tribal wars, some were sold because of unpaid debts, while others were kidnapped. Slaves were initially sent to Europe to work as servants until the market for labor expanded in the West Indies and North America in the 18th century. Kunta Kinte, hero of Alex Haley's novel, *Roots,* was also from Gambia. Kunta Kinte's village, Juffurh, has now been declared as a national monument by the Gambian Government.

In 1807, slave trade was abolished throughout the British Empire, when the British also tried unsuccessfully to end the slave traffic in Gambia. They established the military post at Bathurst (now Banjul) in 1816. In the following years, Banjul came under the jurisdiction of the governor general in Sierra Leone. In 1843, it was made a separate British colony but in 1866, Gambia and Sierra Leone were reunited under a single administration. However, in 1888, Gambia became a separate entity once again.

In 1889, an agreement with France established the present boundaries, and Gambia became a British Crown Colony, divided for administrative purposes into the colony (the city of Banjul and the surrounding area) and the protectorate (the remainder of the territory).

During World War II, Gambian troops fought with the Allies in Burma (now Myanamar), and Banjul served as an air stop for the US Army Air Corps and a port-of-call for allied naval convoys. US President Franklin D. Roosevelt stopped overnight in Banjul en route to and from the Casablanca Conference in 1943, marking it the first visit to the African continent by an American president in office.

After World War II, the pace of constitutional advance quickened, and following general elections in 1962, full internal self-government was granted to Gambia in 1963. Gambia achieved full independence on February 18, 1965, as a constitutional monarchy within the British Commonwealth. Shortly afterwards, the government proposed its conversion to a republic, with an elected president.

In 1982, Senegal and Gambia signed the Treaty of Confederation. As a result, Senegal and Gambia united and renamed itself as Senegambia. The confederation claimed eventually to combine the armed forces and unify economies and currencies of the two nations. However, fundamental differences of attitude, approach, and mutual suspicions continued because of their different colonial pasts. Gambia ultimately withdrew from the confederation in 1989.

ECONOMY

The Gambian economy is characterized by traditional subsistence agriculture, historic reliance on peanuts or groundnuts, re-export trade around its ocean port, low import duties, minimal administrative procedures, and a fluctuating exchange rate with no exchange controls. Over 80% of its people depend on agriculture for their livelihood, but even in the best years, food production satisfies only 70% of the requirements. In 1979, production fell because of widespread pest infestation and in 1983-84, food production fell by 50% as a result of low rainfall. The basic traditional food crops are millet, guinea corn, cassava, and dry rice, although swamp rice has been increasing in importance. Animal husbandry is important in the drier areas, and Gambia has begun exporting Ndama breeding cattle to Gabon and Nigeria.

During the recent years, three sectors of the economy - agriculture, fisheries, and tourism have experienced significant growth in Gambia, which are expected to be the focus of export-oriented investment in the 1990s. Agriculture accounts for 20% of the gross domestic product (GDP) and employs 75% of the labor force. Within agriculture, peanut production accounts for 5%, other crops 8.3%, livestock 4.4%, fishing 1.8% and forestry 0.5% of the GDP. Industry accounts for 12% of GDP, of which manufacturing, primarily located in Banjul, contributes 6%. The limited amount of manufacturing is primarily agriculturally-based (e.g., peanut processing, bakeries, a brewery, and a tannery). Other manufacturing activities include soap, soft drinks, and clothing. Services account for the remaining 46% of GDP.

Gambia is also a smuggling base for manufactured imports into Senegal and an illegal recipient of Senegalese cattle and peanuts (groundnuts).

In 1991, nearly all domestically produced exports were agricultural products, amounting to about 17% of the GDP. Of that percentage, peanuts, the major commodity, accounted for half, making Gambia a prime example of monocrop dependence. The other 50% included fish, lobster, and shrimp (24%); horticultural commodities (9%); and other products such as cotton, hides, and live cattle (17%). By far, the most important export is peanuts (groundnuts), which is a cash crop for many farmers, especially in the sand hill terrain.

NOTES

CHAPTER 17
GUINEA

Guinea has considerable resources. It possesses an estimated one-third of the world's proven bauxite, high grade iron ore, significant quantity of diamonds, gold, and uranium deposits. In addition, it has considerable potential for growth in the agricultural and fishing sectors.

GEOGRAPHY

Surrounded by Guinea-Bissau, Senegal, Mali, Cote d'Ivoire, Liberia, and Sierra Leone, Guinea is located on the "bulge" of West Africa (Map 20). It is a land of considerable variety, physiographically, ethnically, and economically. Its physiography is dominated by the highland mass of the Fouta Jallon, rising several thousand feet and consisting of a dissected plateau with prominent peaks and deep valleys. The ancient Fouta Jallon (Fouta Djallon) is one of West Africa's main mountain and river source regions, with extensive areas of over 2700 ft (9000 m) near the Senegal border. The Fouta Jallon dips toward the Atlantic Ocean and gives rise to the Senegal River. In the north, elevations of over 5000 ft (1525 m) are sustained, and in the south, crystalline Guinea Highlands are shared by Liberia and Sierra Leone. The highlands support cattle rearing and plantation agriculture of coffee and bananas.

Geographical Profile

Area: 95,000 sq. mi. (246,048 sq. km.)
Population: 8.2 million (1994); 9.5 million (2000); 11.6 million (2010)
Annual Rate of Natural Increase: 2,5%
Doubling Time of Population: 28 years
Life Expectancy: 42 years
Capital City: Conakry
Other Cities: Kankan, Kindia, Labe, N'Zerekore, Siguri
Ethnic Groups: Foulali, Malinke, Soussaou, 15 smaller tribes
Religions: Sunni Islam 85%, Christianity 10%, Paganism 5%
Languages: French (official), national languages
Economy:
  GDP: (1988) $2.48 billion
  Per capita Income (1989) $400
  Natural Resources: Bauxite, iron ore, diamonds, gold, water power, uranium, fisheries
  Agriculture: (44% of GNP);
  Products: Rice, cassava, palm products, pineapples, livestock, forestry
  Industry: (28% of GNP)
  Types: Mining, small manufacturing, construction
Official Name: Republique de Guinee
Date of Independence: October 2, 1958

By virtue of its coastal location and areas of higher relief, Guinea generally has high rainfall, especially during the months of July and August, but lasting from March to December. Conakry, on the western flank of Fouta Jallon and Guinea Highlands, receives about 70 in. (1778 mm) of rainfall annually which results in luxuriant growth of forests. Okume tree is the national symbol of Guinea (Fig. 19). In the lee of the mountains it rains rapidly and savanna conditions prevail.

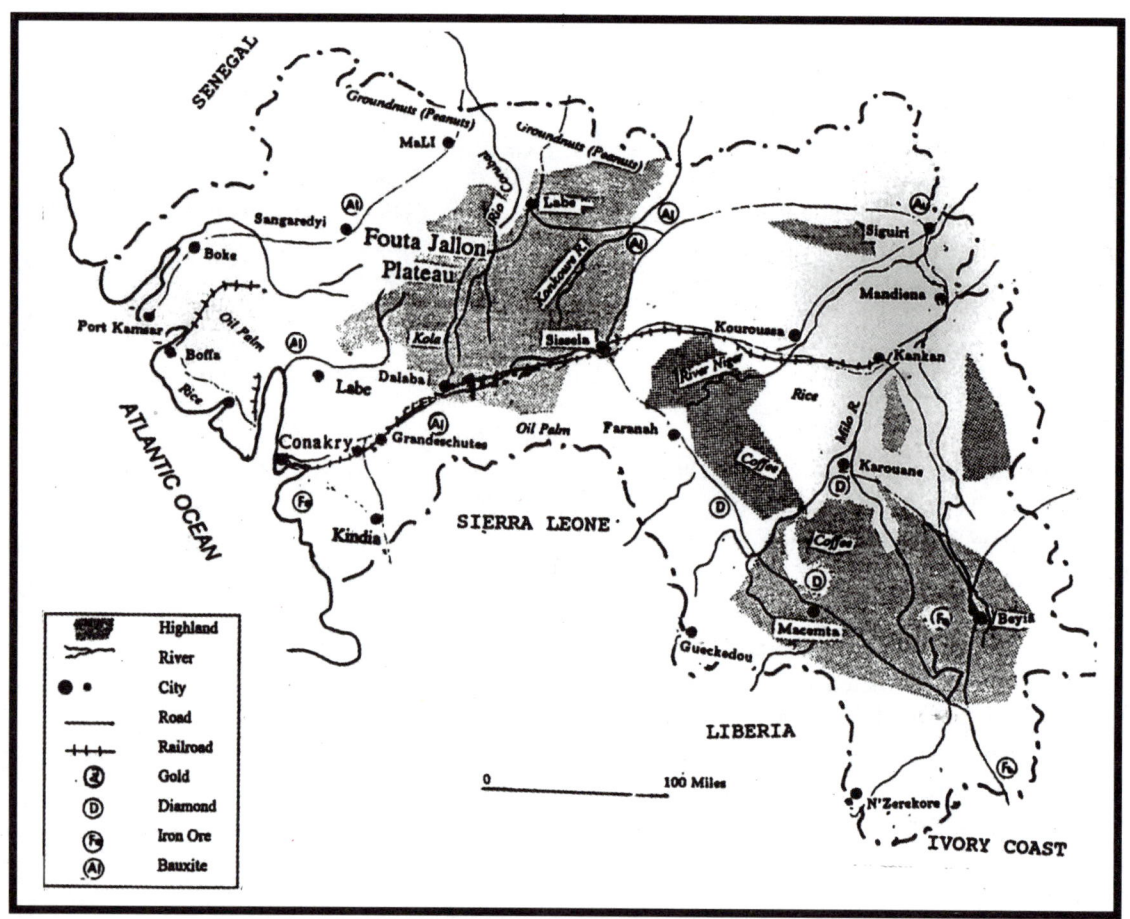

Map 20: Republic of Guinea

The coastal plain is less than 50 mi (80 km) in width. It is hot and humid, and is wedged between the swampy coast and slopes of the Fouta Jallon.

Fig: 19: The Equatorial Forest

EVOLUTION OF GUINEA

Guinea is partial heir to the series of West African empires. At its height, it cast a degree of political and commercial influence over many ethnic groups from Guinea's Atlantic coast to the southern edge of the Sahara before the arrival of Europeans. The empires of Ghana, Mali, and Songhai spanned the period from about the tenth to the fifteenth centuries. French military penetration into the area began in the mid nineteenth century. By signing treaties with the French in the 1880s, Guineas's Malinke leader, Samory Toure, secured a free hand to expand eastward. In 1890, he allied himself with the Toucouleur Empire and Kingdom of Sikasso and tried to expel the French from the area. He was defeated in 1898 when France gained control of Guinea and Cote d'Ivoire.

France negotiated Guinea's present boundaries in the late 19th and early 20th centuries with the British for Sierra Leone, the Portuguese for their Guinea colony (now Guinea-Bissau), and the Liberians. After 1984, Guinea was governed by the French Ministry of Colonies.

Following World War II, the French labor confederation and political parties became active in Guinea. The labor unions were modeled on French unions and usually became affiliated with them. Ahmed Sekou Toure, Guineas's former President, first gained a mass following as a leader of the colonial section of the French union, *Confederation General du Travail* (CGT). In 1956, Toure withdrew from the CGT to organize a separate African confederation.

In 1947, the Democratic Party of Guinea (DPG) was founded as a section of the new International African Democratic Rally (ADR), giving Toure and his associates a political membership in the general population. The ADR broke with the communists in 1950. Toure, as head of the DPG, asserted that the Marxist doctrine of class struggle was inapplicable to Africa, and the movement must be freed of any vestige of European control. In the 1957 elections, the DPG won 56 of 60 seats in the Territorial Assembly. It played the leading role in Guinea's decision in 1958 to reject membership in the proposed French Community. Guinea became an independent republic in 1958, the only French colony to vote against entering the community. Guinea's decision of not joining the French community brought reprisals. To help tide over the French's hostile attitude and the cut in aid, initial support came from the former Soviet Union. Guinea adopted a "socialist" approach, with state control of commercial activities - banking, imports, industry, farmers' collectives, and even a state tax-in-kind on farmers. The agricultural sector supporting the bulk of the population declined, import substitution industries stagnated, and the economy was further distorted by an emphasis on mineral exploitation and the servicing of heavy foreign debts.

ECONOMY

Guinea has considerable potential for growth in the agricultural and fishing sectors. Soil, water, and climatic conditions provide opportunities for large-scale irrigated farming and development of agro-industry. Possibilities for investment and commercial activities exist in all these areas, but Guinea's poorly developed infrastructure continues to present obstacles to investment projects.

Agriculture

Cassava is widely grown, and swamp rice is important in the coastal areas and on river flood plains in the Fouta Jallon, Niger Plains and Guinea Highlands. Upland rice, and corn (maize) are also grown widely. Livestock husbandry, mainly by Fulani people, is especially important in the Labe area of Fouta Jallon and traditionally provided some export to Sierra Leone and Liberia. The main cash crops are bananas, largely from the coastal zone just north of Conakry to the Sierra Leone border; pineapples are from the same area and from around Kindia and Mamou in the Fouta Jallon, kola and oil palm from the coastal zone, and coffee from the Guinea Highlands. Coconut is also grown, and its fibers are made into ropes and reeds for domestic use (Fig. 20). But Guinea has experienced difficulty finding markets and controlling distribution. Some Guinean farmers find it more profitable to smuggle their produce over the borders into Sierra Leone and Liberia than to market through state channels. It is for this reason that one-third of the coffee crop is smuggled out of the country.

Minerals

Guinea is richly endowed with minerals. It possesses one-third of the world's proven reserves of bauxite, more than 1.8 billion metric tons (MT) of high grade iron ore, significant diamond and gold deposits, and undetermined quantities of uranium. In the early 1960s, minerals made up 70% of the exports, although now that has increased to around 95%.

Joint venture bauxite and alumina operations in northwest Guinea provide about 90% of Guinea's foreign exchange. Important bauxite areas are Kassa Island near Conakry and Tamara Island, the town of Fria located 144 miles (230 km) from Conakry and Sangaredi. The *Companie des Bauxites de Guinea*, a joint venture in which 49% of the shares are owned by Guinea and 51% by an international consortium, produces about 10 million MT annually. The Office *des Bauxites de Kindia* produces some 3 million MT, nearly all of which was exported to the former Soviet Union and Eastern Europe. The Friguia Consortium produces about 500,000 MT of alumina annually.

Fig. 20: Using coconut fiber

Diamonds are the only other mineral being mined in the Guinea Highland and exported on a large scale. The potential of diamond mining was, however, diminished by poor management, illicit mining, and smuggling. To improve diamond mining, a new concession for alluvial mining was granted in 1984 to Aredor. Aredor is a joint diamond-mining venture between the Government of Guinea (50%) and an Australian, British, and Swiss consortium, which mines diamonds that are 90% of gem quality. Union Miniere (Belgium) is developing a joint-venture gold mine with the government in the Koron-Dial region near Kouroussa. Other concession agreements have been signed for diamonds and gold but most of these projects are in the exploratory stages.

Oil exploration is being held up by a dispute over the offshore boundary with Guinea-Bissau. When the dispute is resolved, oil may be a possibility. Guinea also has considerable hydroelectric potential.

Guinea did not have any economic or ideological support from its neighbors. Following the break with France and the Francophone group, Guinea followed an almost isolationist course. In 1970, a force of Guinean dissidents and Portuguese troops led a commando raid from Guinea-Bissau. Most neighboring states were accused by the Government of Guinea of aiding and abetting anti-Guinean sentiment, which resulted in Guinea's withdrawal from the Organization of Senegal River States - an organization composed of Senegal, Mali, Mauritania, and Guinea for development.

In 1975, Guinea re-established its relations with France and the Republic of Germany. Relations with neighboring Cote d'Ivoire and Senegal which had broken in early 1970s were also resumed in 1978. Increasing efforts to seek aid from Western and nonaligned countries and to accelerate economic development marked Guinean policy since late 1970s.

CHAPTER 18
INDONESIA

Indonesia is, by far, the largest Muslim state, and the fifth most populous country in the world. Islam was introduced in this country by the Indian and Arab traders in the 1440s. The fragmented morphology of the country and its central location in the Southeast Asian realm has made Indonesia the crossroad of international trade in today's world.

GEOGRAPHY

The Republic of Indonesia consists of more than 13,500 islands. It extends for 3,000 miles (4,800 km) along the Equator, from the mainland Southeast Asia to Australia. With so many islands stretching over such a wide area, Indonesia is the world's most expansive archipelagic state. With so many islands, the Indonesian archipelago encircles a number of important commercial and strategic waterways. These waterways include the Sunda straits, between Sumatra and Java; the Makasser straits, between Kalimantan and Swalesi; and Lambok, between Sumatra and peninsula Malaysia. More than half of Indonesia's land is forested, and a significant portion is mountainous and volcanic. Of its five largest islands, New Guinea is shared with independent state of Papua New Guinea. The other four large islands include Java, Sumatra, Kalimantan

---

Geographical Profile

Area: 736,000 sq. mi. (2.0 million sq. km)
Population: 190.9 million (1994), 211.6 million (2000), 238.8 million (2010)
Annual Rate of Natural Increase: 1.7%
Capital: Jakarta (1988 est. pop. 8.8 million)
Other Cities: (1987 est.) - Surabaya 3.5 million, Medan 1.7 million, Bandung 1.4 million, Semarang 1.1 million
Terrain: More than 13,500 islands, the larger ones consisting of coastal plains with mountainous interiors
Climate: Equatorial but cooler in highlands
Ethnic Groups: Javanese, Sundanese, Madurese, coastal Malays, many others
Religions: Sunni Islam 88%, Protestantism 6%, Catholicism 3%, Hinduism 2%, Buddhism and paganism 1%
Languages: Indonesian (official), local languages largest of which is Javanese
Economy:
 GDP: (1988 est.) $75.4 billion
 Per Capita Income: $435
 Natural Resources: Oil, tin, natural gas, nickel, timber, bauxite, copper
 Agriculture: (24% of GDP): Products: Rubber, rice, palm oil, coffee, sugar, Land 8.6% cultivated
 Industry: (37% of GDP) Types: Food and beverages, textiles, cement, fertilizer, light manufacturing, wood processing, minerals, and petroleum (18% of GNP)
Official Name: Republic Indonesia
Year of Independence: 1945

(Indonesian portion of Borneo), and Swalesi (Celebes). Collectively, these four islands are known as the Greater Sunda Islands. East of Java are the Lesser Sunda Islands, which include Bali and Timor. Another important island chain within Indonesia is constituted by the Moluccan Islands which lie between Sulawesi and New Guinea. The central water body of Indonesia is the Java Sea (Map 21).

The Indonesian islands form a natural barrier between the islands of the Indian and Pacific Oceans, making them strategically and politically important. Indonesia shares land borders with Malaysia and Papua New Guinea and sea borders with Australia, India, Singapore, Vietnam, Philippines, and the United States administered Trust Territory of the Pacific Islands.

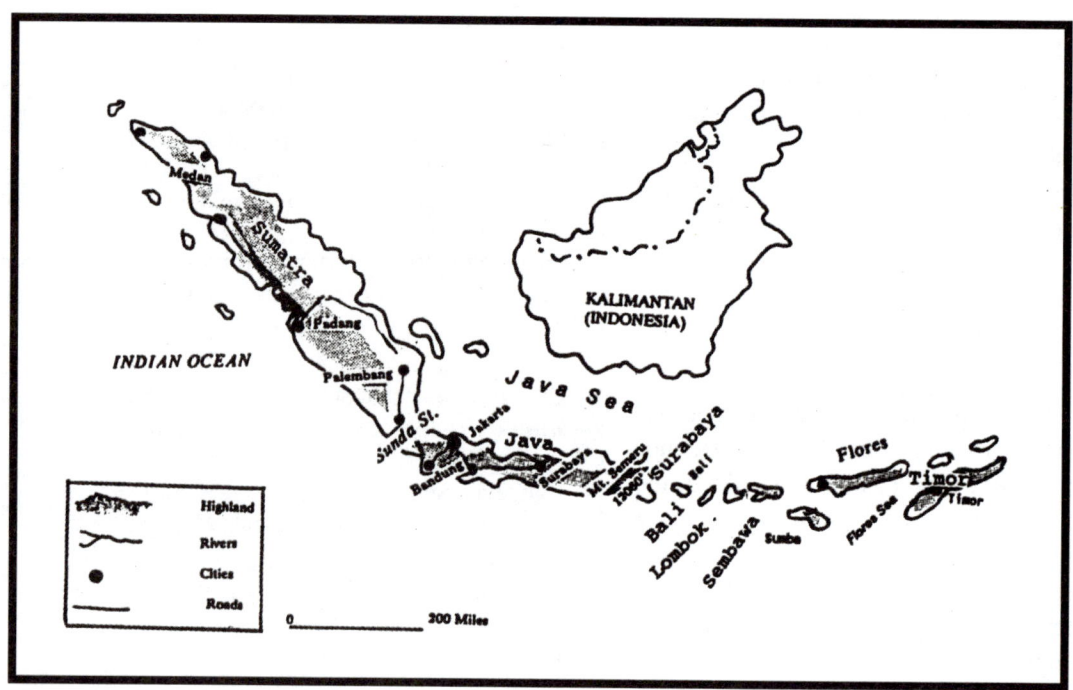

Map 21: Indonesia

Although Indonesia has an equatorial climate, it is mountainous and volcanic, and the upland areas on the principal islands provide a temperate contrast to the constant heat of the lowlands.

EVOLUTION OF INDONESIA

Historically, Indonesia has never functioned as a single political state. The constraints of distance, numbers of islands, varieties of ecological environments, ethnic subdivisions, and cultural separatism has constrained easy integration of these islands into a cohesive political entity. In addition are the diverse, deeply rooted feelings of regionalism and sectionalism that are inhibitory to the emergence of strong politico-cultural nationalism. In some cases, ethnic distinctiveness, common history, a rebellious tendency, and a strong ethnic communalism do not yield easily to a sense of Indonesian identity like in Atieh in Northwest Sumatera. The same may be said of South Suwalesi, and also of the Ambon island cluster in the eastern zone. A modernized and romanized form of the "Market Malay" is becoming popular as *Bahasa Indonesia*. English is widely spoken by the educated persons in Indonesia. There is no *lingua franca* for the whole political territory. Islam is the only force which binds the people together as a nation.

Islamic missionaries came from India and the Hadramaut coast of Arabia with the Arab traders in the thirteenth century to introduce their religion. These men (most of them Sufi masters) had a strong impact on the island of Java, where they are known as the *Wali Sanga* (the Nine Saints). Until the 1440s, their contacts were limited to some of the spice islands in the Halmahera group. By 1480, these contacts were extended to the southern Philippines. Honest dealings with the local people and Muslim tolerance of local traditions were the important factors to invite people to Islam. After local *rajahs* became Muslim, they were called *sultans* and organized small regional principalities and states. The Islamic faith spread so rapidly and effectively in Indonesia that it effectively altered the Indianized Malay culture, except in the interior and Bali island. The architecturally simple mosques replaced the ornate and costly Indian temples, social customs changed, the principalities replaced the extensive political state, and economic decentralization followed political decentralization.

In the beginning of 1602, the Dutch established themselves as rulers of all the islands of Indonesia except the eastern half of the island of Timor, which was occupied by the Portuguese until 1975. During their rule (interrupted only by a brief British interregnum during the Napoleonic period), the Dutch developed the Netherlands East Indies into one of their richest colonial possessions.

The Indonesian independence movement began during the first decade of the 20th century and expanded rapidly between the two World Wars. Its leaders came from a small group of young professional men and students, some of whom had been educated in the Netherlands. Many were imprisoned for their political activities, including Indonesia's first President Seokarno.

The Japanese occupied Indonesia for three years during World War II and for their own purposes encouraged a nationalist movement. On August 17, 1945, three days after the Japanese surrendered, a small group of Indonesians led by Sukarno proclaimed independence and established the Republic of Indonesia. Dutch efforts to reestablish complete control met strong resistance from the new republic. After 4 years of warfare and negotiations, the Dutch transferred sovereignty in 1949 to a federal Indonesian entity.

At the time of independence, the Dutch retained control over the western half of New Guinea, known as West Irian. Negotiations with the Dutch on the incorporation of West Irian into Indonesia failed, and armed clashes broke out between the Indonesian and Dutch troops in 1961. In August 1962, the two sides reached an agreement, and Indonesia assumed administrative responsibility for West Irian on May 1, 1963. East Timor was also recovered from the Portuguese in 1975.

PEOPLE AND POPULATION

Indonesia's 190.9 million (1994) people make it the world's fifth most populous nation. This also makes it the most populous Muslim nation. The island of Java is the most densely populated area in the world, with more than 105 million people living in an area the size of New York State. The population of the state of New York is 18.18 million (1992 est.). Since about 1800, Java has grown rapidly and has regularly been the most heavily populated region. Efforts to shift population from Java to outer islands have been made since 1920, but they have not been successful. Much of the population has been migrating in recent years from the Outer Islands to Java.

Indonesia includes numerous related but distinct cultural and linguistic groups; many of them are ethnically Malays. Since independence, Indonesian (the national language, a form of Malay) has spread throughout the archipelago and has become the language of all written communication, education, government, and business. However, local languages are still important in many areas.

Constitutional guarantee of religious freedom applies equally to all the five religions recognized by the state: Islam, Catholicism, Protestantism, Buddhism, and Hinduism. More than 88% of Indonesians are Muslim and 9% are Christians. The island of Bali retains its Hindu heritage, and in some remote areas, animism is still practiced in some of the outer islands.

ECONOMY

The Dutch introduced a system of government-controlled agriculture in Indonesia, conveniently termed the "culture system." Coffee, sugar, and indigo were the chief exports of the East Indies during this period. The Dutch government introduced new crops to the islands. Tea, tobacco, manioc, and oil palm were the most important of the new plants. Late in the century, cinchona came into production. Interest in minerals led to the exploration of tin, coal, and a few other minerals.

Since 1986, Indonesia has embarked upon an ambitious program of eliminating regulatory obstacles to economic activity as a member of the Association of Southeast Asian Nations (ASEAN). Its plans since joining the ASEAN are helping Indonesia make progress in agriculture, oil, and mineral sectors.

Agriculture

Indonesia's agriculture can be divided into three types: shifting cultivation, sedentary field and dooryard gardening, and plantation agriculture, a pattern that has significance for the Indonesian socioeconomic society. Shifting cultivation or *ladang* is the most widespread activity in the Outer Islands. In the western half of Indonesia, upland rice is the basic crop of shifting cultivator, and the taros, yams, sweet potatoes, manioc bananas, sago, and a few minor items are produced for local consumption.

The sedentary field and dooryard gardening system in its modern pattern is the basic system of cropping in Java, Madura, portions of Sumatra and some of the Eastern Sunda Islands. This system involves the traditional wet-field rice cropping *(sawah)* and the dooryard garden (*pekarangan*). Rice is the basic crop (Fig.21). The entry of new crops into the traditional cropping systems such as peanuts, maize, manioc, soybeans, and others did not alter the basic aspects except coffee, which did is flourishing well and is one of Indonesia's main export commodities (Fig. 22). On the contrary, they gave elasticity to the cropping combinations, permitted a closer ecological fit to local soil and climatic regimes, and further intensified the basic elements of local systems.

Fig. 21: Harvesting rice

Estate, or plantation agriculture, no longer holds the importance it once did in Indonesia, following the expropriation of Dutch-owned estates and gradual reduction of leases formerly given to Europeans. In the earlier periods, sugar plantations had been most productive, but rubber plantations increased in acreage and in importance. By 1937, rubber became the chief plantation product. Spices (clover, nutmeg, ginger, pepper, and other spices), for which Indonesia was once famous, are no longer important. The agricultural economy of Indonesia in a way is in a dangerous condition. The production of food is insufficient and the pressures on the land of Java, Madura, the Lesser Sundas, Sulawesi, and portions of Sumatra are extremely heavy. As of now, Indonesia presents a picture of happy, satisfied and developing landscape (Fig. 23) with an uncertain future.

One of Indonesia's greatest natural resources is its fishing grounds, concentrated primarily on the straits of Malacca and around the coast of Kalimantan. These productive fishing areas yield a significant harvest of fresh and salt water fish, in terms of a share of the Gross Domestic Product.

Minerals, Oil, Trade and Industry

It is notable that the commodities in trade for which the East Indies became most famous are no longer very important, in production or in international trade. The Moluccas, once the most important Spice Island, no longer holds monopolies over cloves, nutmeg, and mace. Small volumes of each still move into the export trade, but the products are minor trade items now. The export products that leave Indonesia today are the commodities of the modern industrial world; among these rubber, petroleum, and tin are the leaders, followed by coconut products, tea, tobacco, palm

Fig. 22: Coffee Plantation on the isle of Sumatra

kernels, coffee and sugar. The mineral and oil sectors have been critical to Indonesia's modern economic development. Although comprising only 21% of the country's gross national product, these sectors contribute about half the foreign exchange earnings and half the government tax revenues.

These sectors have been the focal point of foreign participation in the Indonesian economy. Indonesia's constitution decrees total sovereignty to the state over mineral resources. Therefore, foreign companies must operate as contractors to the government or one of the state enterprises. Since 1967, 144 contracts have been signed between Pertamina, the state oil company, and foreign contractors. Seventy-eight of these contracts are currently in effect with 46 foreign operators and even more foreign partners. In1988, twenty contract areas produced more than 1.3 million barrels of oil per day and a total of 869 trillion BTUs (British Thermal Unit) of liquefied natural gas (LNG). About 755,000 barrels of oil were exported per day as well as all of the LNG. American oil companies have developed 80% of Indonesia's oil and gas resources.

Fig. 23: The lush Javanese landscape

The country's major oil fields are maturing. With domestic demand for petroleum fuels expanding, Indonesia faces becoming a net importer of oil by the early 21st century, unless new reserves are found. Proven oil reserves are reported at 8.25 billion barrels of oil and 84 trillion cubic feet of gas. Development of additional refinery capacity for product export, expansion of LNG facilities and increased domestic gas utilization are expected.

Non-oil minerals have had a resurgence associated with an improving market for traditional exports during 1987-88 tin, copper, nickel, and a mini-gold rush attracting 103 new contracts for precious metal exploration. Over the next five years, the strongest mineral growth will be in coal, with production expected to expand five-fold to more than 15 million tons per year, including nearly half for export. U. S. companies involved in minerals include Freeport Minerals in copper, Pennzoil in gold, and Mobil in coal.

──────────────── **NOTES** ────────────────

CHAPTER 19
IRAN

Iran has a very old, rich, and sophisticated culture, with Islam as its official state religion. Nearly a quarter of its people live in 25 large cities and towns. The remaining three-quarters of the people live in small rural villages.

GEOGRAPHY

Iran controls the entire corridor between the Caspian Sea and Arabian (Persian) Gulf. To the west are Iraq and Turkey. To the north (west of the Caspian Sea), it borders Azerbaijan, Armenia, and Turkmenistan. To the east, Iran meets Pakistan and Afghanistan. At many places Iran seems to spill over its neighbors; the Kurdish domain connects it to Iraq and Turkey, and Azerbaijan is both an Iranian province and an adjacent independent state. Balochistan is divided between Iran and Pakistan. In the Persian (Arabian) Gulf, Iran reaches outward. In 1993, Iran asserted sovereignty over several small islands located in the Gulf of Hormuz (Map 22).

Within such borders, Iran consists mainly of mountains and interior desert plains. The heart of the country is a plateau, which is dissected by deep valleys and gorges and a few plains. The plateau is surrounded by even higher mountains including the Zagros in the west, the Elburz Mountains along the southern shores of the Caspian Sea, and the

---

Geographical Profile

Area: 636,294 sq. mi. (1,648,000 sq. km), slightly larger than Alaska
Population: 63.7 million (1994), 77.0 million (2000), 105.0 million (2010)
Annual Rate of Natural Increase: 3.3%
Capital: Tehran (6.2 million (1986);
Other Cities: Isfahan (1 million), Tabriz (1.5 million), Mashed, Shiraz
Ethnic Groups: Persian, Azeri Turks, Kurds, Armenians, Arabs, Turkmans, Balochis, Lur, Bakhtiari and Qashqai tribes
Religion: Shi'ah Muslims 93%, Sunni Muslims 5%, small minorities of Christians, Zoroastrians, Yezidis, Ali-Ilahis and Baha'is
Language: Persian, Azeri, Kurdish, Arabic
Economy:
  GNP: (1986) $75 billion
  Per Capita Income: (1986) $1,664
  Natural Resources: Petroleum, natural gas, and some mineral deposits
  Agriculture Products: Wheat, barley, rice, sugar beets, cotton, dates, raisins, tea, and tobacco
  Arable Land: 30%, Cultivated land: 11.5%
  Industry: Petroleum production, oil refining, textiles, cement and other building materials, food processing, metal fabricating
Official Name: Jumhorieh-i Islam'e-i Iran

mountains of the Kurdistan region to the northwest. The southern coast of the Caspian Sea is below sea level, and is called the garden of Iran created by abundant rainfall and warm waters. The Iranian Plateau is therefore actually a high land basin marked by salt flats and wide expanses of stone and

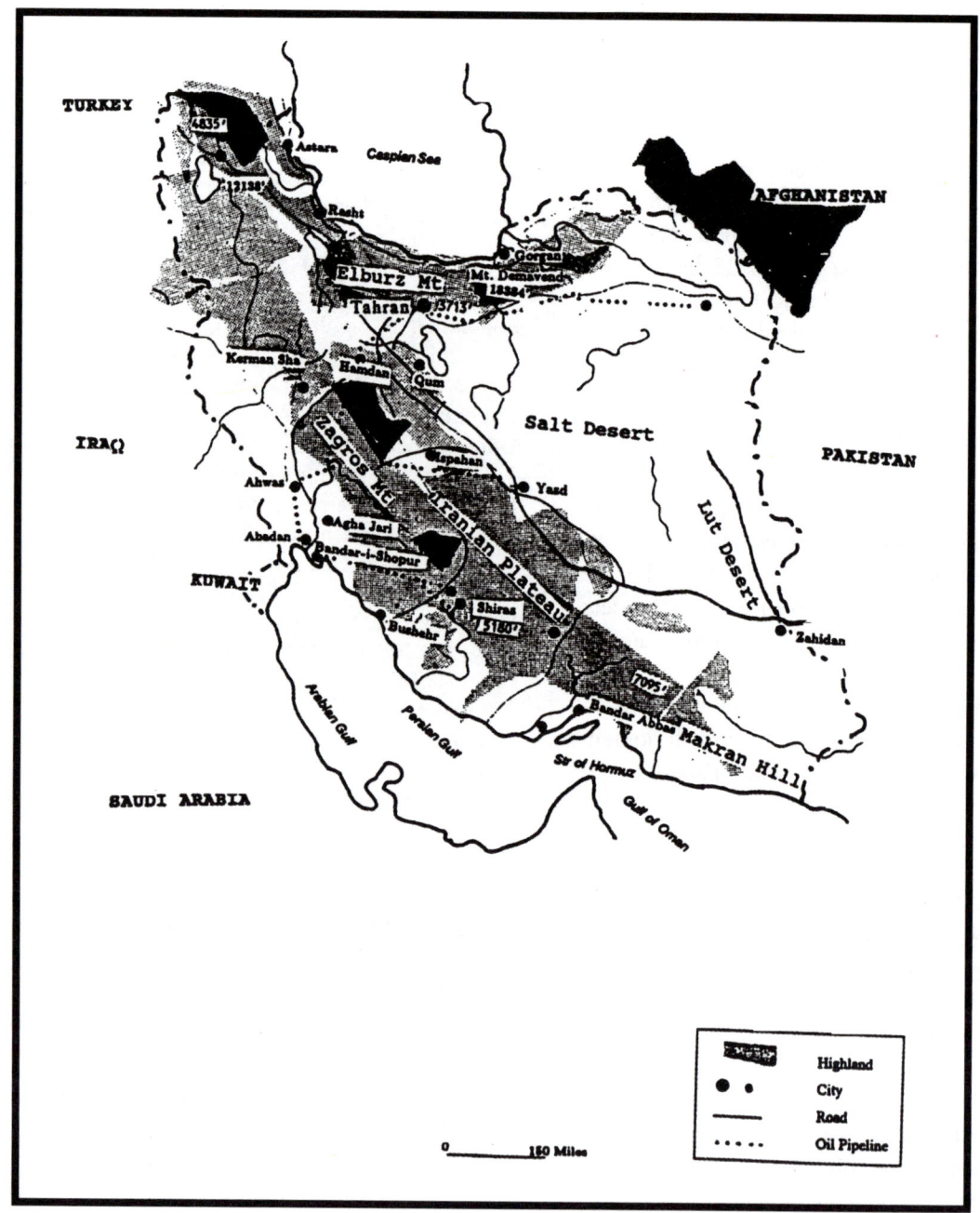

Map 22: Iran

sand. This area is largely uninhabited except for nomads who make great seasonal wanderings from north to south. The soil of the hillsides is fertile where some moisture becomes available; elsewhere, the arid monopoly is broken down by some oases.

Climate

Iran's climate is diversified, primarily because of its topography. Annual precipitation ranges from 40 inches (86 cm) along the Caspian Sea coast to less than 8 inches (17 cm). Winter and early spring comprise the rainy season. Practically all the winter rainfall is the result of Mediterranean depressions which govern the weather patterns of the country. These depressions cause rain at low altitude and snow at high elevations. The elevation of the central plateau (3,000 to 6,000 feet) produces great extremes of temperature: 110 °F or 115°F during the day in the summer. During the winter, nighttime temperatures drop below freezing. Summers are hot in all parts of Iran except at the highest elevations. The moist zone along the Caspian Sea coast supports a ribbon of settlement, and the area north of the head of the Persian Gulf, centered on Abadan, also contains fertile soil.

PEOPLE AND POPULATION

About two-thirds of Iran's people are Aryans, who speak related Indo-European languages such as Persian, Kurdish, Gilani, Mazandharani, Baloch, Lur, and Bakhtiari. About one-fourth of the people are Turkic speaking, including Azerbaijanis, Turkmens, and Qashqais. Semitic Arabs, Armenians, and Assyrians constitute smaller ethnic groups.

The distribution of Iran's population is strongly influenced by its climate and geography. Most Iranians live in the north and northwest, with the heaviest concentrations along the Caspian Sea coast, in and around Tehran, and in the provinces of East and West Azerbaijan. Tehran has grown in the last two centuries from a village to a huge city and has become the center of trade, roads, and railroads. Industry is also concentrated here. The other major cities are Tabriz and Isfahan, all of which are commercial and old handicraft centers. The city of Shiraz has several beautiful mosques and holy places (Fig. 24).

Fig 24: The Mosque of Shiraz

About 70 percent of the country is either mountainous or desert area and is virtually uninhabited. A large scale migration of Iranians from rural to urban areas has occurred on account of Iran's rapid industrialization. Now, almost half the population lives in urban areas.

EVOLUTION OF IRAN

Although Iran (formerly Persia) has been overrun many times and has had its territorial composition altered throughout the centuries, it is counted among the world's most ancient nations. It was invaded by the Arabs in 637 AD to introduce Islam. Iranian culture was so old and advanced that Iran accepted the religion but maintained its own Persian language. Later, Iran was invaded by the Seljuk Turks, the Mongols, and others. Though often caught up in the affairs of larger powers, Iran always reasserted itself and reemerged as a political and cultural entity. In recent years, it has faced three traumatic events: the Islamic revolution of 1979, the Iran-Iraq war (1980-87), and the Gulf War in 1991 (operation Desert Storm). The first led to a large scale exodus of government personnel, rich landlords, and anti-revolutionaries from Iran. The second brought the economy to shambles and led to the destruction of oil installations. The Desert Storm invasion resulted in an influx of thousands of Shi`ite refugees to Iran from Iraq. But again, Iran overcame these problems and reemerged as a regional power.

Numerous dynasties have ruled Iran during its lengthy history. Its first period of greatness was under the Achaemenians (550-330 BC), a dynasty founded by Cyrus. After the Hellenistic period (330-250 BC) came the Parthian (260 BC to 226 AD) and the Sasanid (226-651 AD) periods. The Arab conquest of Iran in 637 AD was followed by conquests of the Seljuk Turks, Mongols, and the great king, Tamerlane. Iran underwent a revival under the Turkic Safavid Dynasty (1501-1736). It was during this era that Iran became a predominantly Shi'ah nation. In the early eighteenth century, Persia was threatened by Turkey on the west, Russia on the north, and Afghans on the east. After Nadir Shah (1736-1747), the Qajar Dynasty came to power and maintained power until 1925. It was the early Qajar named Agha Mohammad Khan who made Tehran his capital in 1788. The Qajar Dynasty was succeeded by the Pehalvi Dynasty (1925-1979). The Pehalvi Dynasty was succeeded by the revolution which established the Islamic Republic of Iran.

Iran's modern history began in 1906 with the convening of Iran's first *Majlis* (Parliament) and the signing of Iran's constitution. At that time, rivalry between the Russian and British Empires tended to concentrate on Persia (Iran). Russia was looking for expansion to the warm water ports of the Persian Gulf, while Britain was concerned primarily for the security of India. Russia enjoyed more influence in Persia. Finally in 1907, Britain and Russia agreed to divide Iran into zones, without any consideration of Persian desires in the matter. Russia would have influence in the northern part of the country and Britain in the southern part, while a strip of less important territory in the middle was left as a neutral zone.

Dissatisfaction against the monarch and the *Majlis* increased substantially since the Anglo-Russian Agreement, because both these agencies were ineffective. In 1821, Reza Khan, an Iranian officer of the Persian Cossack Brigade, seized control of the government. In 1925, he became Shah and ruled Iran as Reza Shah Pahalvi for almost 16 years. During his reign, Iran began to westernize, and the central government reasserted its authority over the tribes and the provinces. In September 1941, Reza Shah was forced to abdicate in favor of his son, Mohammad Reza Pahlavi.

During the Second World War, Iran was a vital link in the allied supply line to the former Soviet Union. After the war, the troops of the former Soviet Union stationed in northwestern Iran not only refused to withdraw but backed Communist revolts, which established pro-Soviet regimes in the northern regions of Azerbaijan and Kurdistan. Iranian actions, supported by the United Nations and United States, resulted in Soviet withdrawal in 1946.

The ensuing period was characterized by a growth of Iranian nationalism that culminated in the nationalization of the British-owned oil industry in March 1951. After a political crisis in 1953, and a subsequent period of political uncertainty, Iran initiated a series of economic, social, and administrative reforms in 1961. These reforms were formalized at a national referendum in January 1963 and became known as Iran's White Revolution. The core of this program was land reform, widely considered to be one of the more successful land reform projects in the world. To further prevent opposition in the *Majlis*, the Shah sponsored his own party. This was formed in 1963 as the *Iran Novin* (New Iran) Party and then in 1973 enlarged and renamed to *Rastakhiz* (Resurgence) Party, while other parties were banned.

Fig. 25: Shatt-al Arab Waterway

While failing to meet the needs and desires of the majority of the citizens, the Shah attempted to assert himself as a responsible regional power with large and well-equipped military forces. For instance, in March 1975, an agreement was reached with Iraq after decades of border tensions. Iran obtained half of the Shatt al-Arab, the river connecting Abadan with the Gulf (Fig. 25), in return for a promise to Iraq to stop sending supplies to Kurdish rebels in the northern part of the country. Two months earlier, a much acclaimed visit to Egypt by the Shah ended years of rivalry. In early 1978, a visit to India showed Iran's interest in participating in the economic development in the Indian Ocean region.

A riot at Qum in late 1977, and another in Tabriz in early 1978 revealed serious dissatisfaction with conditions. Also in early 1978, there were mass demonstrations in Tehran and elsewhere despite of official bans. An Ayatollah or religious leader named Ruhullah Khomeini, who lived in exile in France for the last fifteen years, made himself the nominal leader of the movement against the Shah. He spread the idea of the "Islamic Revolution" for Iran. After months of confusion and strikes, oil production and exports halted, and the economy was in chaos. The Shah left the country on January 16, 1979, for a vacation. Khomeini returned to a triumphant welcome on February 1, and ten days later, his armed followers overthrew the government left by the Shah. The Islamic Republic of Iran was established on April 1, 1979.

ECONOMY

During 1990-91, the oil and gas industry contributed 19.4% to the Gross Domestic Product which was more than any other sector. Agriculture's contribution was 17.8% followed by industry and mining at 15.8%. The remaining 47% was provided by services.

Agriculture

Agriculture is of paramount importance to Iran's economy. Since the rise of Reza Shah to power, there have been some changes, such as the gradual introduction of cash crops in the system of subsistence farming. Iran has a total area of 407 million acres (165 m. ha) of which 19 million acres (8 m. ha) (11.5%) are cultivated, including seasonally fallow land. In addition, 76 million acres (31 m. ha) (18.9%) are potentially cultivable. Pastures and meadows cover 24.7 million (9.9 m. ha.) (6.1%) acres, forests cover 46.9 million acres (19 m. ha) (11.5%), and unused land cover 212, million acres (86 m ha) (52.1%).

The most productive area is the northwest (Azerbaijan province), the northeast (Khorasan province), and the southern shores of the Caspian Sea (Mazandran province) (Fig. 26). Together, these areas produce 60% of the wheat, 70% of the cotton, 75% of the tobacco, 80% of the rice and fruit, and 100% of the tea, jute, and silk. Until 1959, the country was self-sufficient in food. Currently, however, agriculture suffers problems with transportation, organization, poor methods, inferior seeds, lack of water, lack of capital for improvement, and the oppressive system of land ownership.

In spite of opposition of powerful landholders, the Shah began a program of redistributing farm land in 1963. In the first phase, the holdings of one person were reduced to no more than one village; previously, some 10,000 of the country's 50,000 villages had belonged to landlords owning five or more villages. Later phases concentrated on further reducing the amount of land controlled by individuals, but the program did not achieve real economic advantages.

Iran has 50 million acres of forests. They were all taken over by the government in 1963 and are now cared for as a national resource by the forestry service. Fishing is a large industry - the largest volume of fish is taken from the Persian Gulf, but the best known is from the Caspian Sea. Fishing in the Caspian Sea is becoming less profitable as pollution increases.

Fig 26: A Modern Farm in Iran

Manufacturing

Oil production is easily the most important single industry in Iran, not only because of its size, but because it supplies large amounts of foreign exchange. With the nationalization in 1951, these revenues were almost entirely lost. They were not restored until a settlement was concluded in 1954 with a consortium of international companies: the U. S. (40%), British (40%), Dutch (14%), and French (6%). In 1957, the Iranian government and the Italian state-owned oil company signed the first joint venture oil agreement. In 1969, the National Iranian Oil Company pressed for higher royalties from the group of foreign companies operating the major oil fields. Finally, in March 1973, the government took control of all oil production in the country, while promising to sell to the same group for marketing.

Textile is the second largest industry in order of importance, although a distant second to oil in cash returns. Cotton is grown in several parts of the country, especially in the vicinity of Isfahan.

Competition with the imported cloth is proving to be a big difficulty. The coast of the Caspian Sea has long been famous for its production of Persian silk.

The mineral resources of Iran other than oil have not yet been surveyed thoroughly. At present, lead, chromite and turquoise are exported, while coal and iron ore are mined for domestic use, along with some sulfur and salt. The steel mill at Isfahan is a source of pride for Iran.

Although handicrafts are losing importance, Isfahan, Tabriz, and other cities remain famous for their metal-work, carpets, ceramics, and textiles. Carpets are next to oil in export. Using its oil revenues on a massive scale, Iran has contracted entire factories to be built and put in operation by industrialized nations. A number of different cars and trucks are assembled in the country, while dozens of other industries are being aided. The post-revolutionary regime continues to give high priority to industrial development.

───────────────── **NOTES** ─────────────────

CHAPTER 20
IRAQ

Iraq, which is the size of California, has the greatest agricultural potential in the Middle East. With large areas of irrigated farmland and oil reserves, Iraq is best endowed with natural resources. It is here that the early Mesopotamian states and empires emerged.

GEOGRAPHY

Iraq is bordered by six countries. To the north is Turkey, the source of both of its vital rivers. To the east is Iran, and at the head of the Persian (Arabian) Gulf is Kuwait. Saudi Arabia lies vastly to the south. To the west, Iraq is adjoined by Jordan and Syria (Map 23). The country slopes from 10,000 feet (3,000 meters) high mountains along the borders of Iran and Turkey to reedy marshes in the southeast. Much of Iraq's land is desert or wasteland. Four major geographic regions can be identified in Iraq. The high Zagros Mountains are in the northeast. These mountains are an extension of the Alpine system that runs eastward from the Balkans into southern Turkey, northern Iraq, Iran, and Afghanistan, terminating in the Himalayas. At lower altitudes, Zagros provide a hospitable landscape. This area is a part of the "Fertile Crescent", where most wheat and barley is grown. Between the Tigris and Euphrates Rivers is the *Jazira*, a barren land frequented by nomads.

Central and southern Iraq is an alluvial plain formed by the deposition of sediments of the Tigris and Euphrates Rivers. Both these rivers rise in the mountains of southern Turkey and flow southeastward into Iraq. The Euphrates has only one large tributary, the Khabur, which joins the

---

Geographical Profile

Area: 167,924 sq. mi. (434,934 sq. km)
Terrain: Alluvial plains, mountains, and deserts
Climate: Mostly hot and dry
Population: 19.6 million (1994), 24.3 million (2000), 34.1 million (2010)
Annual Rate of Natural Increase: 3.7%
Capital: Baghdad (pop. 3.8 million)
Other Cities: Basra, Mosul, Kirkuk
Ethnic Groups: Arab 75%, Kurd 15-20%, Turkman and others 5%
Religion: Islam 90% (Shi'ah 70%, Sunni 30%), Christians 5%, Yezidis and Ahli Haqq 5%
Languages: Arabic, Kurdish, Turkish, Chaldean
Economy:
  GDP: (1984) $27 billion
  Per Capita Income: $1,740
  Natural Resource: Oil, Natural Gas, Phosphate, Sulfur
  Agriculture: (less than 10% of GNP)
  Products: Wheat, barley, rice, cotton, dates, poultry
Official Name: Al-Jumhuriyah al-Iraq
Date of Independence: 1932

mainstream in Syria. The Tigris has four tributaries, all of which join with the mainstream in Iraq. The largest of these, the Greater Zab, has its source in Turkey, while the Lesser Zab and the Diyala rise in Iran. All of the catchment zone of Adhaim, the smallest stream, is situated in Iraq.

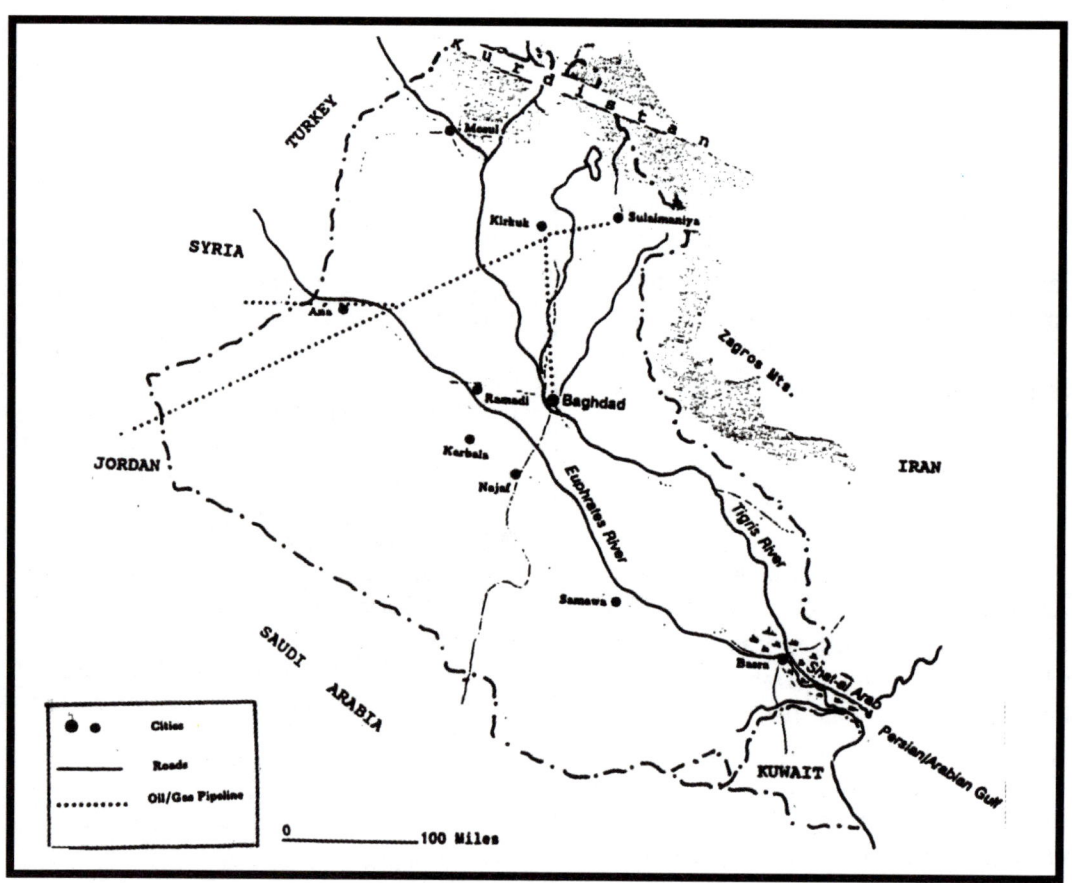

Map 23: Iraq

In southern Iraq, the Tigris and Euphrates unite to form the Shatt-al Arab waterway, which in turn flows into the Gulf. Both the Tigris and Euphrates carry about 70 million cubic meters of silt annually to the delta. Known in ancient times as Mesopotamia, the region is the legendary locale of the Garden of Eden. The ruins of Ur, Babylon, and other ancient cities are here as well. This is also the main agricultural region of the country, and the site of some of the earliest civilizations in the world. To the west of the alluvial plain, covering more than half the total area of the country, is the desert extending into Syria, Jordan, and Saudi Arabia.

Average temperatures range from more than 120ºF (48ºC) in July and August to below freezing in January. Most of the rainfall occurs between December and April and averages between 4-7 inches (10-18 cm) annually. Most of the precipitation falls in the belts of rugged mountains. In these mountainous regions, annual rainfall of more than 39 inches (1,000 mm) is often recorded.

Very little of this precipitation occurs during the summer months, and much of it comes as snow. Lowland Iraq is dry and provides one of the harshest environments for man in the Middle East.

PEOPLE AND POPULATION

Iraq's two largest ethnic groups are Arabs and Kurds. Other distinct groups are Assyrians, Turkmans, and Persians. Arabic is the most commonly spoken language. Kurdish is spoken in the north along with Turkish, and English is the most commonly spoken western language.

As many as 9 million Iraqis are Shi'ites, most of whom are concentrated in the south. The Sunni population is made up of both Arabs and Kurds. Small communities of Christians exist. Several anomalous groups, such as the Yazidis and Ahli Haqq, exist among the Kurds and Turkoman populations. The Yazidis are known for their veneration of Shaitan, and the Ahli Haqq (also known as the Ali Ilahis, Shabak etc.) worship Imam `Ali as the incarnation of God. Most Kurds, however, are Sunni Muslim but differ from their Arab neighbors in language, dress, and customs.

An estimated 68 percent of the people are urban dwellers - a proportion considerably higher than in most Middle Eastern countries. The rest of the population consists largely of villages which depend on agriculture for a living. Much of the agriculture is carried on by Egyptians who have immigrated from the overcrowded, irrigated land along the Nile. Such immigrants can become Iraqi citizens with relative ease after a certain period of residence. Iraq prides itself on adherence to the concept of a greater Arab nation, transcending present political boundaries. Small bands of nomadic Bedouins still raise camels, sheep, and goats in Iraq's western deserts. Some of the Kurdish tribesmen in the north are semi-nomadic graziers.

In 1994, Iraq's population stood at 19.6 million, with 3.7% as an annual rate of natural increase. With such an alarming rate of yearly growth, the population of Iraq is expected to reach 24.3 million in 2000 and 34.1 million in 2010.

EVOLUTION OF IRAQ

Once known as Mesopotamia, Iraq was the site of flourishing ancient civilizations, including the Sumerians, Babylonian, and Parthian cultures. Muslims conquered Iraq in the seventh century AD. In the eighth century, the Abbasid caliphate established its capital in Baghdad, which became a famous center of Islamic learning and the arts (Fig. 27). By 1638, Baghdad had become a frontier outpost of the Ottoman Empire.

At the end of World War I, Iraq became a British-mandated territory. When it was declared independent in 1932, the Hashemite family ruled it as a constitutional monarchy. In 1956, the Baghdad Pact allied Iraq, Turkey, Iran, Pakistan, and the United Kingdom into a defense pact, which established its headquarters in Baghdad.

Gen. Abdul Karim Qasim took power in a July 1958 *coup d'etat*, during which the Hashemite King Faysal II and his Prime Minister Nuri as-Said were killed. Qasim withdrew Iraq's membership in the Baghdad Pact in 1959, which was later reconstituted as the Central Treaty Organization (CENTO). Qasim was assassinated in 1963, when the Ba'ath Party (Arab Socialist Renaissance

Party) took power under the leadership of Gen. Ahmad Hasan al-Bakr as prime minister and Col. Abdul Salam Arif as president.

Fig. 27: A Mosque in Baghdad

Nine months later, Arif led a coup ousting the Ba'ath government. In April 1966, Arif was killed in a plane crash and was succeeded by his brother, Gen. Abdul Rahman Mohammad Arif. On July 17, 1968, a group of Ba'athists and military elements overthrew the Arif regime. Ahmad Hasan al-Bakr re-emerged as President of Iraq and the Chairman of the Revolutionary Command Council (RCC). In July 1979, Bakr resigned and his chosen successor, Saddam Hussein, assumed both offices.

ECONOMY

Iraq's economy is characterized by a heavy dependence on oil exports and an emphasis on development through central planning. Prior to the outbreak of war with Iran in September 1980, Iraq's economic prospects brightened. Oil production had reached a level of 3.5 million barrels per day, and oil revenues were $21 billion in 1979 and $27 billion in 1980. By 1983, however, reduced export earnings and the unexpectedly high cost of the Iran-Iraq war depleted Iraq's foreign exchange reserves, despite massive infusion of aid from the Arab Gulf states.

Iraq has four existing oil export pipelines: (i) north via Turkey; (ii) south via offshore terminals in the Gulf, (iii) south via Saudi Arabia, and (iv) west via Syria. The Iran-Iraq war and Syria's alignment with Iran have prevented the use of the pipeline via Syria and via offshore Gulf terminals. Desert Storm and United Nations restrictions on oil exports from Iraq have created critical conditions for the country. The country's economy was shattered. There were no medicines or hospitals, little food, and wide-spread unemployment.

Agriculture

The total area of cultivated land in Iraq is 13.5 million acres (5.45 m. ha). An unknown area remains fallow each year. Wheat and barley are by far the most important crops and make up well over half of the cropped area in a year. Production of cereals is concentrated in the northern, wetter parts of the country and in the Tigris-Euphrates lowlands (Fig. 28). In the uplands, wheat and barley are grown by dry farming methods, while on the lowlands irrigation has to be employed. Actual production totals of wheat and barley are highly susceptible to changes in precipitation. Rice is the only other crop of major significance. The other major crops are vegetables, fruits, and dates. The agriculture in Iraq is still non-mechanized. Much of the field work is done by men, but sometimes women work in the fields and orchards as well.

Fig. 28: A Farm in Iraq

An important change in the agricultural structure of the country took place with the passing of the Land Reform Law in 1959. The law limited the size of private holdings to 1,000 *donums* (250 ha) of irrigated land and 2,000 *donums* (500 ha) of rain fed land. As a result, large areas were redistributed among landless farmers. In 1970, another land reform program was introduced, which further reduced the maximum size of the individual holdings. The agricultural system of Iraq was dominated by state farms and cooperative villages until 1980. The government abandoned its farm collectivization program in 1981, allowing a greater role for private enterprise in agriculture.

Despite its abundant land, water resources, and agriculture, Iraq is a net importer of food. It exports limited quantities of fruits, such as dates, meat, poultry, and dairy products. The Agricultural Cooperative Bank targets its low-interest, low collateral loans to private farmers for mechanization, poultry projects, and orchard development. Modern large-scale cattle, dairy, and poultry farms are under construction. Obstacles to agricultural development include labor shortages, inadequate management and maintenance, salinization, urban migration, and dislocations resulting from previous land reform programs and the collectivization program.

Petroleum

The petroleum sector dominates the Iraqi economy. Iraq claimed proven oil reserves of 79.5 billion barrels at the end of 1986 and estimated natural gas reserves of 28.8 trillion cubic feet. Petroleum accounts for 99% of Iraq's merchandise export. Petroleum capacity has remained virtually intact despite the Iran-Iraq war, but actual export capacity has been reduced by almost 3 million barrels per day. Syria closed another Iraqi export pipeline, and the restrictions imposed by the United Nations on oil exports consequent to Iraq's occupation of Kuwait in 1991 further reduced the exports from Iraq.

In 1990, Iraq invaded and occupied Kuwait claiming it historically as a part of Iraq before the British demarcated its boundary in 1961. An outraged United Nations, coalition led by the United States, began a major military build up that resulted in the attack (known as Desert Storm), on January 16, 1991. After 45 days of one-sided air war that culminated in a brief but decisive ground invasion, Iraq was overwhelmingly defeated on the battlefield and ousted from Kuwait. Most of the after-effects of the Gulf War are felt within Iraq itself, being hard hit by bomb damage and UN trade embargo.

———————————— **NOTES** ————————————

CHAPTER 21
JORDAN

Jordan is a country without oil, without much farmland, without military strength, and overwhelmed with refugees. Originally created as a British mandated territory, Jordan suffered heavily when Israel came into existence in 1948. Jordan lost the West Bank including Jerusalem to Israel in 1967. In 1988, it formally renounced its claim on the West Bank and Jerusalem to the Palestine Liberation Organization (PLO).

GEOGRAPHY

Jordan takes its name from the Jordan River, which is the only real river in the area. The principal tributary of the Jordan River is the Yarmuk River, which forms the boundary between Syria, Jordan and Israel. The second main tributary is the Az-Zarqa River which flows within the territory of the East Bank (Map 24).

Except for the river valleys, Jordan is a country of rocky deserts, mountains, and rolling plains. About 88% of the country is desert or wasteland, 11% is agricultural, and only 1% is forested. Prior to the war with Israel in 1967, Jordan included two upland areas, the Palestinian Hills on the west and the Transjordan Plateau on the east, separated by a deep rift valley. This is a branch of the African Rift Valley system. The Rift Valley is the deepest depression on the earth's land surface, being about 600 feet (183 m) below sea level at Lake Kinneret and nearly 1300 feet (400 m) below

---

Geographical Profile

Area: 35,000 sq. mi. (91,000 sq. km)
Population: 3.6 million (1994), 4.1 million (2000), 4.9 million (2010)
Annual Growth Rate: 3.65%
Capital: Amman
Other Cities: Irbid, Az-Zarqa
Neighboring Countries: Israel, Saudi Arabia, Iraq, Syria
Religions: Sunni Islam 95%, Christians 5%
Languages: Arabic (official), English
Ethnic Groups: Mostly Arab, small communities of Circassians, Armenians, and Kurds
Economy:
　GDP (1986) $4.3 billion
　Per Capita Income: $1,530
　Natural Resources: Phosphate, potash
　Agriculture: 11% land arable. Products: Fruits, vegetables, wheat, olive oil
　Industry: (20% GDP): Types: Phosphate, mining, manufacturing, cement, and petroleum production
Official Name: Hashemite Kingdom of Jordan
Date of Independence: May 25, 1946

sea level at the Dead Sea. The Dead Sea bottom reaches 2600 feet and is 10 times more salty than ordinary water (Fig. 29).

The Jordan River divides the flood plain in half, with Jordan on the east and Israel and the Israeli-occupied West Bank on the west. Immediately to the east of the river and the Dead Sea is the edge of a high plateau, which receives moderate rainfall. Although the annual precipitation increases northward to an average of more than 12 inches (30 cm) in the vicinity of Lake Kinneret, most of the valley bottom lies in deep rain shadow and receives less than 4 inches (10 cm) a year. However, the bordering uplands, rising to 2,000 feet (610 m) or more and lying in the path of moisture bearing winds from the Mediterranean, receive precipitation during the cool season that

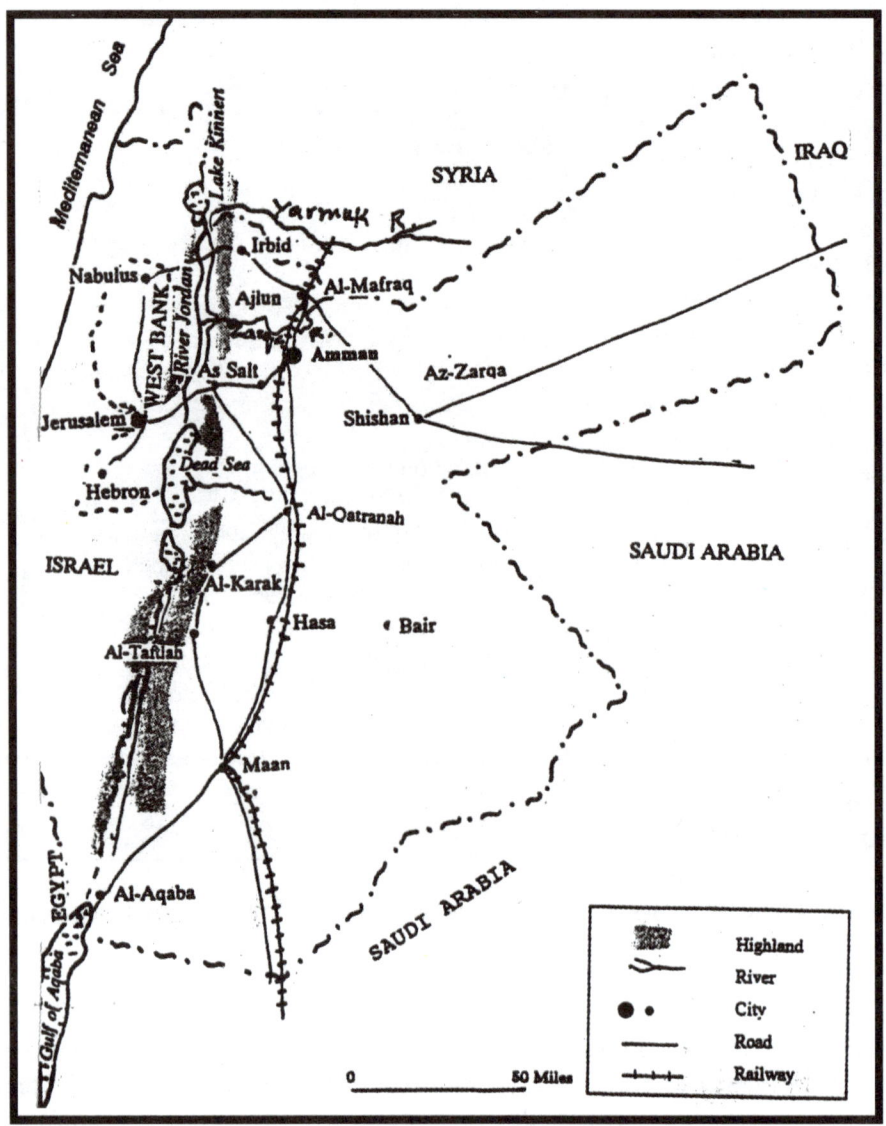

Map 24: Jordan

averages 20 inches (50 cm) annually within two north-south strips. Overall, the climate is Mediterranean with a rainy season from November to March and dry season for the rest of the year. Amman's temperature ranges from an average of 50°F (10°C) in January to an average of 90°F (32°C) in August. The East Bank, which is an extension of the Syrian and North Arabian dessert, has a semi-arid type of climate.

Fig. 29: A view of the Dead Sea

PEOPLE AND POPULATION

Jordanians are of Arab stock except for a few small communities of Circassians, Armenians, and Kurds that have long since adopted the Arab culture. The official language of Jordan is Arabic, but English is used widely in commerce and government.

Jordan's population comprises three elements: (i) the pre-1948 settled Arab population of Transjordan (the area east of the Jordan River), (ii) Palestinians, and (iii) nomads. In 1946, when the British mandate ended and Transjordan became independent, its total population was only about 400,000, which included nomads, peasants, villagers, and a few urban dwellers. Then, with the partition of Palestine and the creation of Israel, Jordan received more than half a million Arab refugees who were pushed out of their homes by the Jews. Soon after, they received another half a million Palestinians who were incorporated into the state. Thus, refugees outnumbered residents by more than two to one. About 55% of Jordan's population is urban, slightly more than 40% is rural, and less than 6% is nomadic or semi-nomadic. Most people live where the rainfall is sufficient to support normal cultivation.

About 1.5 million Palestinian Arabs, including more than 850,000 registered refugees and displaced persons, reside in Jordan. Unlike many Arab countries, virtually all Palestinians living in Jordan are its citizens.

EVOLUTION OF JORDAN

Jordanian history began around 2,000 BC when Semitic Amorites settled around the Jordan River in the area called Canaan. As a part of the Fertile Crescent, Canaan was a strategic location along a perennial river, which faced a number of invasions and conquests. Invasions and conquests included those by the Hittites, Egyptians, Israelites, Assyrians, Babylonians, Persians, Greeks, Romans, Arab , Christian Crusaders, Mameluks, Ottoman Turks, and finally the British. At the end of World War l, the territory now comprising Israel, Jordan, West Bank, Gaza and Jerusalem was awarded to the United Kingdom as the mandate called Palestine and the Transjordan. In 1922, the British divided the mandate and installed Amir (Prince) Abdullah as ruler of Transjordan in a special treaty arrangement, continuing the administration of Palestine under a British High Commissioner. Amir Abdullah was one of the sons of Sharif Hussain of Makkah (Mecca), who had fought with the British against the Ottoman *khalifah* during the First World War.

The Arab legion, composed of Arab soldiers with British officers, was the instrument which brought order to Transjordan. As the government of Amir Abdullah showed more competence, the treaty with British was revised in several stages. Finally, on May 22, 1946, a treaty was signed which recognized the independence of Transjordan. Three days later, Prince Abdullah proclaimed himself as the King of Transjordan. When the British mandate over Palestine ended, the Jews living in Palestine proclaimed the State of Israel on May 14, 1948 under the leadership of Ben Gurion. Transjordan suffered more than any other Arab state with the creation of Israel.

Transjordan moved with the neighboring Arab states to assist the Palestinian people who were opposed to the creation of Israel. This resulted in open warfare between the Arab states and Israel. The Armistice Agreement of April 3, 1949, established armistice demarcation lines between Transjordan and Israel, leaving Transjordan in control of the West Bank. In December 1948, King Abdullah convened a congress of Palestinian notables and had them proclaim him as the King of Palestine. He then formally annexed those parts of Central Palestine which his troops controlled. He also became ruler of holy places in Jerusalem, Bethelem, and Khalil (Hebron).

In 1950, the country was renamed the Hashemite Kingdom of Jordan to include those portions of Palestine which were annexed by King Abdullah. In 1951, King Abdullah was assassinated. His popular son, Talal, succeeded him, but after a short time, he was declared mentally ill. Talal's son, Hussain, then 16 years old, was installed as the King in 1952. Jordan established three governates on the West Bank: Nablus, al-Kuds, and al-Khalil, with Amman as the capital of the country (Fig. 30).

Jordan signed a mutual defense pact in May 1967 with Egypt. It participated in the June 1967 hostilities between Israel and the Arab states of Syria, Egypt, and Iraq. The six-day war resulted in the extension of Israeli control to the Jordan River, including the Jordanian controlled sector of Jerusalem. The 1967 war brought a large increase in the number of Palestinians living in Jordan. Its Palestinian refugee population (700,000 in 1966) swelled by another 300,000 refugees and displaced persons from the West Bank. The period following the 1967 war saw an upsurge in the power and importance of Palestinian resistance elements in Jordan.

Fig. 30: Amman, Jordan

ECONOMY

Jordan is a small country with limited natural resources. Of a total land area of nearly 24 million acres (9.7 million ha), about 11% is arable, and the effective use this land is reduced to 4% by the shortage of water. Other parts of the arable land are used to graze sheep and goats (Fig. 31). Rainfall is low and highly variable, and much of Jordan's available ground water is expensive to use. Even with such a low and variable rainfall, agriculture was a major source of income. However, agriculture is no longer the main stay of Jordan's economy. This shift came mainly as a result of growing urbanization and loss of the West Bank to Israel. After it lost the West Bank, Jordan became a net importer of food goods. Even in a good year, wheat production meets only

25% of food requirements. About 92% of the cultivable land is dependent on rainfall. Water resources are becoming increasingly strained by the demand of irrigated water for mechanized agriculture. Main crops are wheat and barley (cultivated mainly in the north and east around Irbid), while fruits, vegetables, olives, lentils, and tobacco are grown in the Jordan Valley (Fig. 32). Private irrigation projects are becoming common with government support in the southern and eastern desert.

Jordan's most important natural resources are phosphates, potash, and limestone. It has virtually no forests or known coal deposits, and with few water resources, its hydroelectric potential is extremely limited. Unlike many of its oil-rich Arab neighbors, Jordan is dependent on imported crude fuel oil. In addition, Jordan's distance from other markets makes it difficult for the country's exports to compete in the international market. The political disputes among its natural trading partners in the region also restrict regional trade and development.

Fig. 31: Sheep Herding

Before 1967, Jordan's trade used to flow through Haifa, which Jordan lost to Israel in the 1967 war. After 1967, Jordan had to depend on Lebanon's harbors or the tedious route via Aqaba in the far south, which further burdened Jordan's economy (Fig. 33). Despite the handicaps, Jordan's economy grew rapidly in the 1960s and 1970s. Through effective use of foreign assistance, the gross domestic product (GDP) rose from about $140 million in 1954 to more than $4 billion in 1967.

All major sectors of the economy expanded. Jordan established a number of light industries, brought thousands of acres under cultivation, developed its phosphate deposits, and began to exploit its tourism potential. Jordan was also able to take advantage of its location east of the Suez canal to dominate South and East Asian markets for phosphates, phosphate fertilizers, and potash. Although the 1967 war was a setback - Jordan lost the income producing West Bank and was burdened with thousands of refugees - the Jordanian economy recovered quickly following the war. Jordan also succeeded in meeting most of the targets of its ambitious first 5-year plan (1976-80), which called for $2.3 billion in investment and growth of 10% a year.

During the next few years, Jordan will have to continue to adjust to lower sources of external income. Whether or not oil prices increase, the country will be affected by the delayed, albeit indirect, effect of lower oil revenues in the gulf. Of the most serious difficulties it will face is the decline in foreign exchange reserves, which plummeted from more than $1 billion in 1980 to $212 million in 1987. A second major problem is unemployment. The growth of the labor force, estimated at 6% per year, far exceeds the growth of the domestic economy. With the shortage of new employment opportunities in the gulf, some Jordanians expect unemployment to reach as high as 20% by the end of this decade. Although Jordan will have to tap the international loan market to finance its current account deficit, its debt should not be a major problem given the limited scale of past borrowing.

Fig. 32: Olive Cultivation

Jordan will continue to depend on foreign grants and concessional loans to further its development efforts. Formerly, the main source of aid was Great Britain; more recently, large financial support has come from the Arab states and the United States as Jordan is a front-line state in the Muslim world's conflict with Israel. Jordan's central position vis-à-vis Syria, Iraq, Saudi Arabia, Egypt, and Israel also gives it a strategic significance for western nations interested in spreading their influence in the Middle East.

Minerals and Industry

The mineral wealth of Jordan includes phosphate, potash, oil, and gas. These minerals constitute a major source of its gross output manufacturing. The industrial sector of Jordan has two tiers. On the one level are the large-scale wholly or partially state-owned industrial establishments that produce chemicals, petrochemicals, fertilizers, and mineral products. On the other level are privately owned enterprises which produce a wide array of consumer products. Many of them are included in cottage or *bazaar* industries.

Fig. 33: Port of Aqaba, Jordan

CHAPTER 22
KAZAKHSTAN

Culturally, Kazakhstan is a part of the same Muslim core of Central Asia as Iran and Afghanistan. Only northern and northeastern sections of the country have been partly "Russified." The national boundaries were artificially imposed by the former Soviet Union to divide the Muslims. With independence, Islam is reviving, and the feelings for Muslim solidarity are strengthening.

GEOGRAPHY

Kazakhstan is one of the largest countries in the world, with Almaty (also written as Alma Ata) as its capital. It borders Siberia in the north, China in the east, Kyrgyzstan, Uzbekistan, and Turkmenistan Republics in the south, and the Caspian Sea on the west (Map 25). From the Caspian Sea in the west to the Chinese border in the east, Kazakhstan is a land of vast desert and steppe with scattered population clusters, few surface communications, and nomadic herding. The capital city of Almaty is separated by a vast desert from the populous north. Geographically, the country can be divided into three regions: (i) lowlands in the north and west, (ii) hills in the center, and (iii) mountains in the southeast.

Kazakh uplands in the northeast act as a water divide. They separate streams into those that flow into the Arctic Ocean and those that remain in the desert basin. Besides the Caspian Sea, Kazakhstan incorporates about half the Aral Sea and all of Lake Balkash, a large lake in the east. Its rivers include the Ural, flowing from the Ural Mountains into the Caspian, the Syr *Darya*, flowing from the high Pamirs and emptying into the Aral Sea, the Illi, flowing into Lake Balkash, and the

---

Geographical Profile

Area: 1,094,200 sq. mi. (1,750,720 sq. km)
Population: 17.4 million (1994); 18.9 million (2000); 21.9 million (2010)
Capital: Almaty or Alma Ata
Other Cities: Karaganda, Chimkent, Semipalatinsk, Artyubinsk, Kustany, Kzylodra
Neighboring Countries: Russia, China, Kyrgyzstan, Uzbekistan, Turkmenistan
Ethnic Groups: Kazaks (40%), Russians (37%), Germans (6%), Ukrainians (5%); Minor Groups: Uzbecks Belorussians
Official Language: Kazakh, Russian
Economy:
   GDP: $41.6 billion
   Per Capita Income: $2,470
   Minerals: Copper, coal, tungsten, iron ore, zinc, chromium, silver, lead, nickel, oil, bauxite
   Agriculture: Crops- Wheat, flax, hemp, millet, sunflower, rice, potatoes, cotton
   Industry: Steel, cement, shoes, textile
Official Name: Kazakhstan Republic
Year of Independence: 1991

Irtysh, flowing down from China to join the Ob River in Siberia. From 1961 to 1983, the Aral's water level has dropped by 40 feet (13 m), its area shrunk by 30 percent, and its volume decreased by 50 percent. The water coming to the Aral Sea has been channeled into a series of irrigation canals. As a result, Aral Sea has decreased in area and depth.

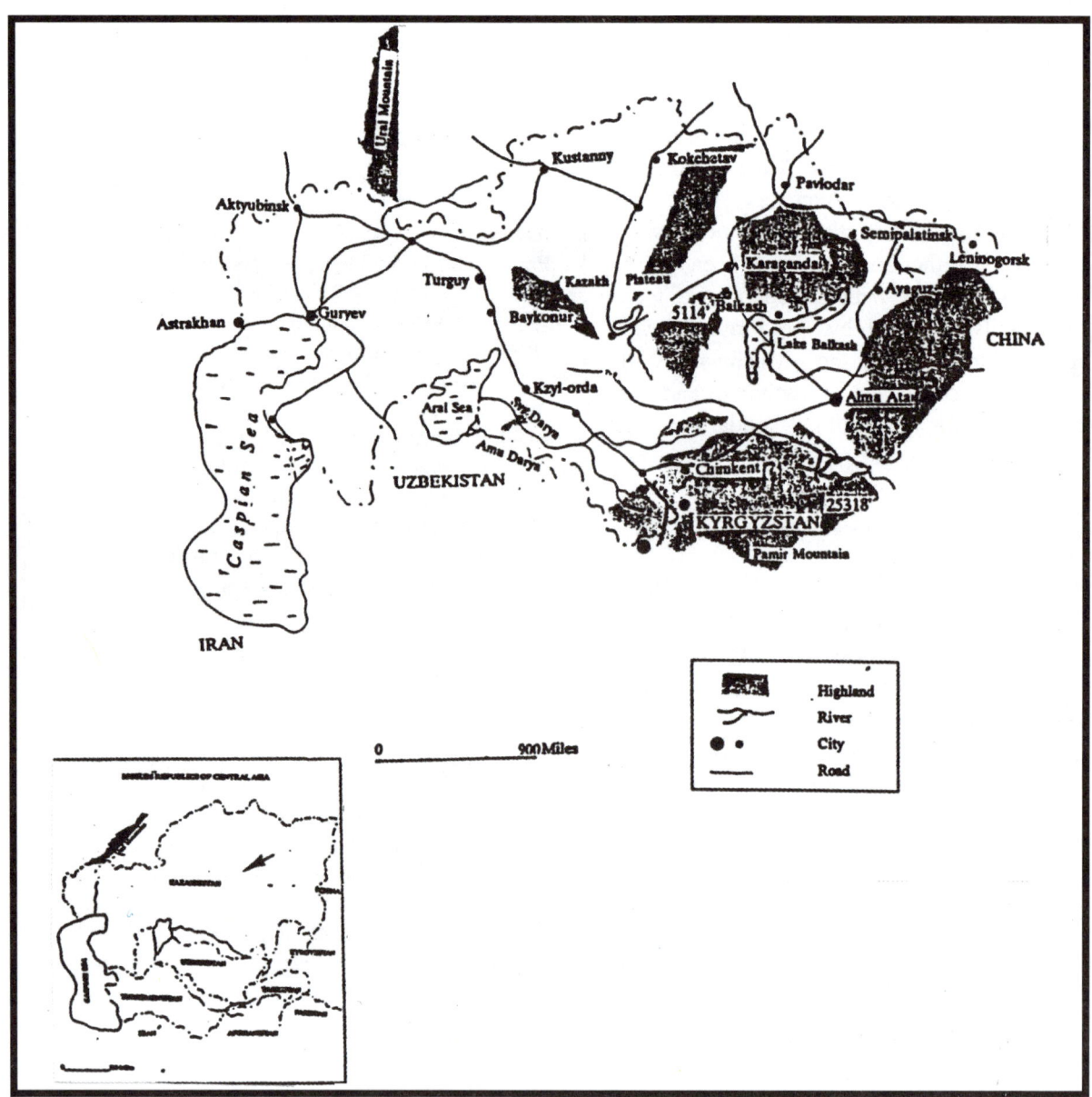

Map 25: Kazakhstan

Most of Kazakhstan is desert, and precipitation is low in most of the area. Some precipitation occurs in the high eastern mountains which is less than 12 inches (30 cm) a year. Where the Illi River flows into Lake Balkash, the lake is fresh; however, on the other end where evaporation is high, the lake is salty.

In northern Kazakhstan, winter snowfall is equal to approximately four inches of rain. In the north, the January average temperature is 4°F, while the July average is 68°F (20°C). In the south, the January average is 18°F, and the July average is 85°F (29°C).

PEOPLE AND POPULATION

The Kazakhs are united by their common descent, language, and religion. However, most of the people in Kazakhstan were not allowed to follow the main precepts of Islam by the communist regime. Many people can neither read the Qur'an nor do they have much religious knowledge. When the Soviets came to power there were mosques in every town, now only three hundred mosques are left in Kazakhstan (Fig. 34). Since independence, there is an awakening of new national and religious consciousness.

Fig. 34: A Mosque in Xinjiang Province, China

Kazakhstan's population in 1994 stood at 17.2 million people, with an average annual increase of 1.9 percent. Of these people, Kazakhs make up 40 percent, and Russians 37 percent of the population. Prior to the dissolution of the Soviet Union, these numbers were reversed. There are also many Germans (6%) and Ukrainians (5%) among the population. Minority groups are the Uzbeks and Belorussians. The transplanted Europeans are mostly Eastern Orthodox. Several groups were exiled to the region during the great purges of Josef Stalin. During World War II, Crimean Tartars and Lower Volga Germans were moved here. Koreans were also sent to the area. Most of these people have remained, but the Muslim Tartars want to return to Crimea and reclaim their ancestral homes and lands. About 100,000 have already left for Crimea.

EVOLUTION OF KAZAKHSTAN

Kazakhstan's pastoral economy based on grazing and herding has existed for centuries. The nomads have worked out a pattern of migration based on the availability of grass during different seasons. This way of life came into conflict with the Communists, who insisted upon settled farming and irrigation. The Kazakhs resisted collectivization by slaughtering their livestock and hiding their grain. The Soviets sent the Red Army to enforce the new decree, and in the process, millions of Kazakhs perished. Since independence, there has been a return of pastoralism. In 1994, there were about ten million cattle, 37 million sheep, and about four million pigs. Pigs are the result of Russian influence, as Muslims neither eat nor raise pigs.

ECONOMY

Between 1949, and 1989, Northeastern Kazakhstan became the Soviet Union's main testing ground for nuclear weapons. Over 500 atomic bombs were detonated south of the city of Semipalatinsk. Missiles with nuclear warheads remain and are presumably aimed at China. Spacecraft and satellites were launched from Baykonur, a desert area located between Karaganda and the Aral Sea. This was an important facility to the Soviet Union, and Russia still contracts to use it today.

Agriculture

Kazakhstan was one of the countries affected by the Soviet Virgin Lands Campaign or the idle Lands Scheme. Agriculture was redistributed and intense irrigation projects constructed. The Virgin Lands Campaign reclaimed marginal lands, which equaled more than all the arable land of Canada. A small Kazakh village became the central city of the Idle Lands Campaign. Today, about one half of the Virgin Lands remain under cultivation.

In the north, main crops are wheat, flax, hemp, millet and sunflowers. In the irrigated south, wheat, barley, rice, potatoes, cotton, and vegetables are grown. On the dry steppe, farmers watch for the *sukhovey*, a dry wind which blows north through Turkmenistan. It speeds up evaporation and transpiration, causing crops to wilt. Grain harvests are severely affected by the *sukhovey*.

Minerals and Industry

The central Kazakh Plateau produces copper, coal, and tungsten. Iron is produced in the northeast and zinc is mined east of Lake Balkash. Chromium, silver, lead and nickel are also mined. Oil lies just north of Caspian Sea which is being developed by major American Oil companies. Phosphate rock and tungsten are on the Caspian Sea eastern shore. Bauxite is produced at Arkalyk in the northern steppe. A major source of power is the hydroelectric station at Zaysan on the Irtysh River. Natural gas is also produced on the northeast Caspian lowland. Recently, two uranium deposits have been discovered west and south of Lake Balkash. Large deposits of bituminous coal are found at Karaganda in Southern Kazakhstan.

Kazakhstan's major industries produce steel, cement, shoes, and textiles. Its chemical industries produce fertilizers, acids, artificial fibers, synthetic rubber, and medicines. The wool industry is famous for producing *karakul* wool, a very fine wool sheared from newly born baby lambs. Most of the industries are located in large settlements. Alma-Ata (apple place) holds meat-packing, leather tanning, fruits and tobacco processing industries.

The city of Karaganda lies in a coal mining region. It produces iron and steel. Chimkent is the center of zinc and lead industry that produces small machinery.

_____ **NOTES** _____

NOTES

CHAPTER 23
KUWAIT

The degree of modernization Kuwait has experienced in a single generation is greater than what other countries experience in a century. In spite of such a rapid modernization, Kuwait still maintains its Islamic-Arab character. Islamic antecedents of Kuwait are visible in art, architecture, landscape, culture, and ethos (Fig. 35).

GEOGRAPHY

Located in the northeastern corner of the Arabian Peninsula, Kuwait is a small country of flat desert. It is bordered by Iraq on the north and west, Saudi Arabia on the south, and the Arabian (Persian) Gulf on the east (Map 26). Kuwait's northern border with Iraq dates back to 1932. Kuwait's boundary with Saudi Arabia (Fig. 36) was set by the Treaty of Uqair in 1922. The Treaty of Uqair also established the Kuwait-Saudi Neutral Zone. The Neutral Zone adjoins Kuwait's southern border and has an area of about 2000 square miles (5,180 sq. km.). In December 1969, Kuwait and Saudi Arabia signed an agreement dividing the Neutral Zone (now known as the Dividing Zone) and demarcated a new international boundary. However, efforts to reach agreement on the northern boundary of the Divided Zone territorial waters have been unsuccessful. Both countries equally share onshore and offshore oil of the Divided Zone. In Kuwait, there are only a few natural oases and no supply of fresh water for the city of Kuwait, which gives its name to the state.

> **Geographical Profile**
>
> **Area:** 6,880 sq. mi. (17,818 sq. km)
> **Population:** 1.5 million (1994); 1.7 million (2000); 3.2 million (2010)
> **Capital:** Kuwait
> **Other Towns:** Ahmadi, Jahra, Fahaheel
> **Neighboring Countries:** Iraq, Saudi Arabia
> **Terrain:** Desert
> **Climate:** Extremely hot and dry summers, short, cool winters
> **Annual Growth Rate:** 4.5%
> **Ethnic Groups:** Arab 84%
> **Religion:** 95% Sunni Islam, Christianity, Hinduism
> **Language:** Arabic (official), English widely spoken
> **Economy:**
>   **GDP:** (1986) $17.3 billion
>   **Per Capita Income:** $10,175
>   **Natural Resources:** Petroleum; fisheries
>   **Agriculture:** 1% land cultivated; Most food is imported
>   **Industry:** types- Petroleum extraction and refining, fertilizer, chemicals, some construction materials, water desalinization capacity 215 million gallons/ day
> **Official Name:** State of Kuwait
> **Date of Independence:** June 19, 1961

Kuwait University researchers divide the country into four sections: (i) the coastal dunes, (ii) the salty marsh and saline depressions around Kuwait Bay, (iii) the sparsely vegetated desert plateau in the west, and (iv) desert plain with patches of coarse grasses littering the sand which occupies the vast bulk of the country. All of it is mostly flat or gently undulating; *wadis* are on the northwest. On the north shore of the bay is the Zor Hills, a geological fault where an uplift has broken the plain and left an impressive scar.

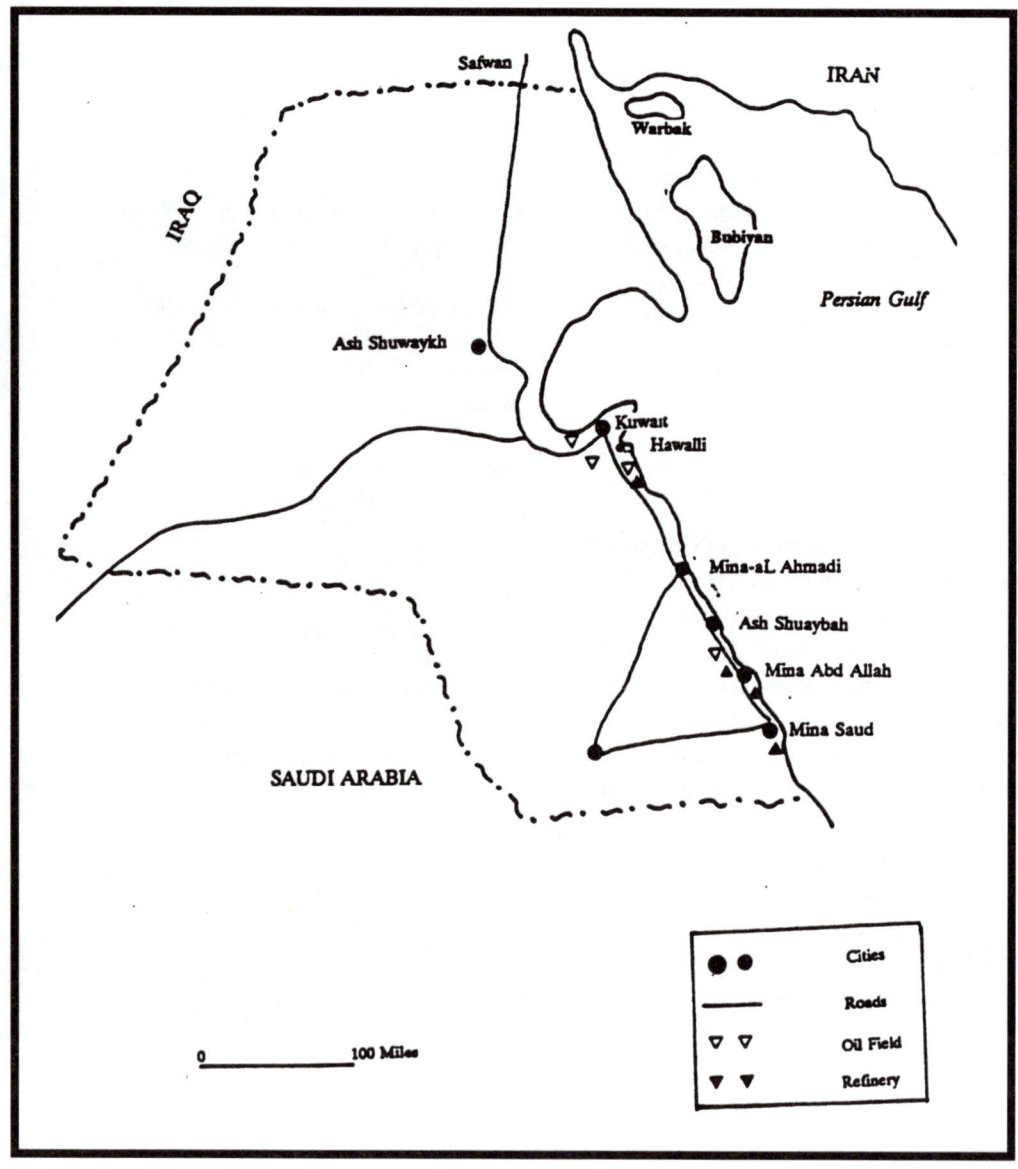

Map 26: Kuwait

Climatically, Kuwait falls in desert region which is characterized by long dry hot summers and short warm winters. According to some meteorologists, summer runs in Kuwait from May 21 to November 4, with scorching weather occurring in July and August. Sometimes, summer temperatures reach as high as 120°F (50°C) in the shade, with a summer average of 113°F (45°C). During the summer, hot, dry winds may create sandstorms. The humidity is low during this period, often as low as six percent, averaging in the 20s.

Fig. 35: A Mosque in Kuwait City

Between September and early November, the mercury falls to the mid-30s, although a marked increase in humidity makes it the most uncomfortable period of the year. A month of pleasantly warm days and cool nights follow before the onset of winter from December to February. During winter, the temperatures drop down to about 57°F (14°C). In January, the night temperatures drop to freezing point, sometimes producing frost. The minimum temperature so far recorded was 39°F (4°C) at Kuwait International Airport on January 20, 1964. Rainfall in the winter follows a crude seven-year cycle. In 1961, 7 inches (19 cm) of rain fell, which was a very wet year. At the bottom end of the cycle, only 1 inch (2.6 cm) of rain fell in 1964.

PEOPLE AND POPULATION

The people of Kuwait are primarily Arabs, but only 40% of them are indigenous. Many Arabs from nearby states of Lebanon, Jordan, Palestine, Syria, Iraq, Egypt have migrated to Kuwait, especially after oil production brought prosperity in the 1940s. Before the affluence, its population of less than 100,000 was either nomadic, or worked as seamen on the sailing vessels that plied the Gulf and went as far as India and East Africa. In 1994, Kuwait's population stood at 1.6 million, increasing at a rate of 3.0%. In addition to natural annual increase, the oil wealth attracts teachers, engineers, lawyers, doctors, and skilled and unskilled workers from nearby states. Now, more than half of the population lives in the modern capital city of Kuwait which has completely replaced the old town of mud houses that existed two generations ago. Kuwait is now almost totally air-conditioned, and virtually every building in the capital is less than 35-years old. It is a magnificent city with broad boulevards, circles, and trees. There is no better example of how a hostile environment has been transformed by man, including such fundamental elements as water and temperature (Fig. 37). In addition to houses, modern colleges and universities have been built (Fig. 38). The oil wealth has also attracted many Europeans and Americans, who work mostly in the oil industry.

Fig. 36: Saudi Arabia - Kuwait Border

EVOLUTION OF KUWAIT

Excavations on Failaka Island by a team of archaeologists from Denmark have unearthed fascinating links of Kuwait with ancient civilization, which goes back to more than four thousand years. The Failaka discoveries have added weight to the theories that the Gulf formed an early civilization contemporary with those of Mesopotamia and Pakistan.

Fig. 37: A view of Kuwait City

Kuwait has been an Arabic-speaking Muslim community since 639 AD, when the Arabs defeated the Sasanids and took the region. Early in the eighteenth century, the town of Kuwait was founded by the members of the Sabah family, which still rules Kuwait today. Like dozens of towns around the coast of Arabia, it sometimes drifted under the rule of stronger neighbors and sometimes was left to itself. When Basra was occupied by the Persians in 1776, many merchants moved headquarters to Kuwait. They were joined by the East India Company which began sending its mail from India to Kuwait, and from there to Aleppo by the renowned "Desert Express" camel caravans which could do the journey in two to three weeks.

Fig. 38: Shuwaikh University, Kuwait

In 1899, Sheikh Mubarak of Kuwait made a secret treaty with the United Kingdom to oppose the Ottoman Empire, which had exercised nominal control over Kuwait during much of the nineteenth century. The treaty also implied that Sheikh Mubarak and his successors would not secede any territory nor receive agents or representatives from any foreign power without the consent of the British Government. In return, the British agreed to give an annual subsidy to support the Sheikh and his heirs. At the outbreak of World War I, Britain made Kuwait its protectorate. The Sabah family retained internal authority over the town, which was still an uninviting lonely little trading center administered from Basra in Iraq.

Mubarak was followed by his son, Jabir (1915-17), and then by another son, Salim (1917-21). Subsequent *amirs* descended from these two brothers. Sheikh Ahmad al-Jabir Al-Sabah ruled Kuwait from 1921 until his death in 1950, and Sheikh Abdullah al-Salim Al-Sabah from 1950 to 1965. Kuwait had special treaty relations with the United Kingdom, which handled Kuwait's foreign affairs and was responsible for Kuwait's security. On June 19, 1961, Kuwait became independent following an exchange of notes with the United Kingdom. Before the British left in

1961, they defined Kuwait-Iraq boundary, which was not accepted by Iraq. In July, 1961, Kuwait became a member of the League of Arab States, a regional organization with headquarters in Cairo, Egypt.

The first elections were held in December 1961 to elect twenty representatives of the Constituent Assembly to draft a constitution with members of the ruling family. This Assembly was formed because a few months earlier Iraq had claimed that Kuwait was a province of Iraq. At that time, British troops landed in Kuwait, in case Iraq attempted to annex the territory by force.

In May 1963, Kuwait became a member of the United Nations. In October 1963, Iraq recognized the independence of Kuwait, and several agreements were signed between the two countries, including a plan for construction of a canal from Iraq to Kuwait. A border clash in March 1973 stopped the project and renewed Kuwaiti suspicions of Iraq's intentions. In 1990, Iraq invaded and annexed Kuwait after articulating an escalating series of grievances and demands. The royal family and a large population escaped to Saudi Arabia. Led by United States and supported by Britain, France, and twenty-two other countries, Iraqi forces were attacked in Kuwait and Iraq. Military conflict broke out on January 17, 1991, when coalition air forces began to systematically bomb military targets. After 45 days of one-sided war, Iraq was overwhelmingly defeated and ousted from Kuwait. The royal family returned from exile to take control of the country.

ECONOMY

In Kuwait, agriculture is limited by the lack of water. Virtually no food crop is produced, but horticulture is becoming increasingly important in areas near the Saudi and Iraqi borders. The government is trying to develop hydroponic agriculture (a technique of growing plants in solutions instead of soils). In addition, only goats and dates are raised. Fish and shrimp are plentiful in territorial waters, and large-scale commercial fishing has been undertaken locally and in the Indian Ocean.

Oil

In 1937, Kuwait granted an oil concession to the Kuwait Oil Company (KOC), which was jointly owned by the British Petroleum Company and Gulf Oil Corporation. In 1970, the Kuwaiti Government nationalized the KOC. The following year, Kuwait took over onshore production in the Divided Zone, between Kuwait and Saudi Arabia. There, KOC produced jointly with Texas Incorporated, which acquired the Saudi concession onshore in the Divided Zone, when it purchased Getty Oil Company in 1984.

The Kuwait Petroleum Corporation (KPC) is the parent company of all the government's operations, which includes Kuwait Oil Company, Kuwait National Petroleum Company, and others. It refines and manages the domestic sales and manages other companies like Petrochemical Industries Company which produces ammonia and urea. Kuwait Foreign Petroleum Exploration Company has several concessions in the developing countries. Shipping is handled by the Kuwaiti

Oil Tankers Company. This company purchased the Santa Fe International Corporation outright in 1982, which gives KPC a worldwide presence in the petroleum industry.

KPC has also purchased refineries and associated service stations in the Benelux and Scandinavian countries from Gulf Oil Company, including its storage facilities and a network of service stations in Italy. In 1987, KPC also bought a 19% share in British Petroleum. KPC markets its products in Europe and is interested in acquiring refineries and service stations in the United States and in Japan.

Kuwait has more than 66 billion barrels of recoverable oil, only exceeded by Saudi Arabia. Due to the soft world oil market, Kuwait reduced its production. However, even this reduced production and price yields a large profit margin. In addition, Kuwait is expanding its refineries so that most petroleum exports will be in the form of refined products.

Industry and Development

In May 1964, a royal decree established the Shuaibia Industrial Development Board (now the Shuaibia Area Authority) to develop industries in Kuwait. Its priorities were to build a commercial harbor, develop industries, and increase important services, which include two huge water and power plants. The water plants provide pumped water for industrial and domestic uses. Other facilities include the liquid products pier at Shuaibia built in 1968 and liquid ammonia from the Petrochemical Industries Company. In addition, Kuwait has three oil refineries and a range of small manufacturers. It also includes ammonia, desulfurization, fertilizer, brick, block, and cement plants. Plans for expansion and modernization include major projects in oil refining, petrochemicals, electricity, water supply, highway construction, housing, and telecommunications. Shipping is done by Kuwait Oil Tankers Company. The company has 22 crude oil and refined product carriers and is the largest tanker company in an OPEC country. Kuwait also is a member of the United Arab Shipping Company.

CHAPTER 24
KYRGYZSTAN

Once part of the Muslim Turkic empire, Kyrgyzstan fell to the Russians during the nineteenth century when it was a remote frontier land. Once under Soviet control, the impact of religion dissipated, and it gained identity as a socialist republic. Since the dissolution of the Soviet Union and independence of Kyrgyzstan, people are reverting back to their roots in religion.

GEOGRAPHY

Kyrgyzstan is bordered by China on the southeast, Kazakhstan and Uzbekistan on the north and west. Tajikistan borders it on the south and west. The country is mountainous with lofty peaks, mighty glaciers and beautiful valleys. In the northwest are the Tian Shan, known as "Heavenly Mountains," while the southwest has the Pamir Ranges, known as the "Roof of the World." At the extreme end of the southern border of Kazakhstan begins the Podeka peak. Podeka peak rises to 24,409 feet (7,439 m) on the Chinese border (Map 27).

The high mountains prevent southern warm air currents from bringing heat or moisture to the land. Being in the rain shadow area or leeward side, Kyrgyzstan becomes a topographical desert. Only the highland captures some moisture from the air currents originating in the Mediterranean Sea in the winter. These create a snow pack and add moisture to the glaciers in the high mountains. As the ice and snow melts in the summer, the waters feed the rivers. The *Kara Darya* from Tien Shan joins *Narya Darya* from the Altay Mountains in the Fergana Valley to form *Syr Darya*.

Its capital was formerly known as "Frunze," named after General Mikhail Frunze, who helped establish the control of the Red Army. When Kyrgyzstan became independent, one of its first acts was to change the name back to the original name of Bishkek, meaning "churning staff."

Geographical Profile

Area: 76,642 sq. mile (122,627 sq. km)
Population: 4.6 million (1994); 5.4 million (2000); 6.6 million (2010)
Capital: Bishkek
Other City: Przhavalsk
Neighboring Countries: China, Kazakhstan, Uzbekistan, Tajikistan
Ethnic Groups: Approximately Kirgiz (52%); Russians (22%); Uzbeks (13%)
Language: Kirghiz
Religion: Sunni Islam 80%, Orthodox Christianity 20%
Economy:
  GDP: not known
  Per Capita Income: $1,550
  Natural Resources: Coal, lead, mercury, tungsten, uranium, oil, natural gas
  Agriculture: Cotton, sugar beets, tobacco, grapes and other fruits
  Industry: Textile, machinery, sugar and tobacco
Official Name: Republic of Kyrgyzstan
Year of Independence: 1991

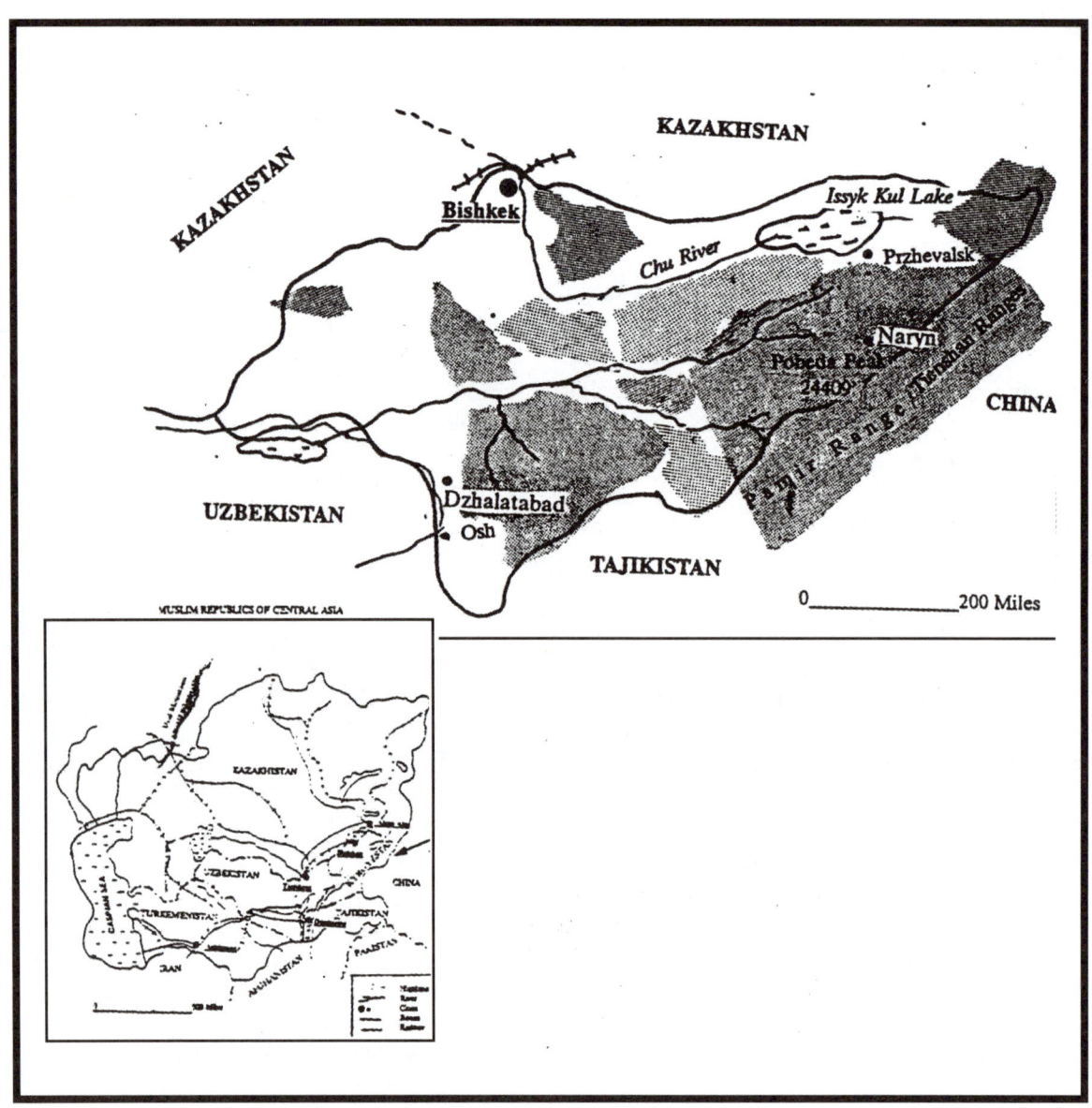

Map 27: Kyrgyzstan

PEOPLE AND POPULATION

Kyrgyzstan's boundaries were defined on the basis of nationality as interpreted by Soviet planners in the 1920s. The people are divided into Kirgiz, Russians and Uzbeks. In 1994, the population of Kyrgyzstan was reported as 4.6 million people. The Kirgiz represent 52 percent of the population; 22

percent are Russians and 13 percent Uzbeks. Ukranians, Tatars, Kazakh Dungans and Uygurs make less than 1 percent. The Kirgiz are Sunni Hanafi Muslim. More than 50% of the population live in the cities of Bishek, Osh and Przhevalsk. Biskek and Osh are connected by a highway that cut through mountains. Numerous urban centers have grown, although lowland areas cover only 15% of the total area. More than a third of the population is clustered in large and small urban communities.

EVOLUTION OF KYRGYZSTAN

The Kirgiz migrated to the region from Upper Yenisey, where they had lived from the 7th to the 17th century. Famine and a freezing cold climate brought them farther south. These people came under the rule of the Kokand *Khanate* in the 19th century. This was a system of government in which one strong ruler, the *Khan*, was placed in charge of a large territory. The Uzbek *Khans* built a fortress in Bishkek in 1845, which formed the nucleus around which the city developed. The Kokand *Khanate* was annexed by Russian in 1876. It was an area of political unrest until the Red Army brought stability in 1922. During the same year, a famine reduced the population by more than half a million.

ECONOMY

Pastoralism is the republics economic mainstay. In addition to sheep and cattle, the Kirgiz raise yaks for meat and milk. The yak can survive on high altitude pastures unsuitable for other livestock. There are about one and a half million cattle on the pasture lands and over ten million sheep.

Agriculture

Irrigation-agriculture accounts for one-third of the Gross National Product (GNP). Irrigation is facilitated by the Issuk Kul lake, located almost on the Kazakhstan border in the northeast. The name means "hot lake", because most of its water comes from the thermal springs deep underground. This hot water mixes with melted glacier water and keeps the lake temperature above normal. Water flowing from the lake forms the Chu River which is used for irrigation until it eventually disappears in the desert sand. Fodder crops, barley and corn, cotton and tobacco are grown. Potatoes, vegetables and fruits are cultivated on about 6% of the arable land. At present, more than 80% of the agricultural lands are owned by state and collective farms. The majority of the state and collective farms are insolvent and depend on state subsidies.

In December 1991, a program of privatization of land and resources was introduced. To manage privatization, the State Property Fund (SPF) was established in July 1992. The first phase of the program involved the privatization of small scale retail and service enterprises with 35% state owned assets sold by the end of 1993. In May 1993, the United States Agency for International Development sent advisers for the privatization program. They introduced coupons redeemable in cash to further popularize the privatization scheme.

Minerals and Industry

Natural resources include coal, lead, mercury, tungsten, gold, oil and natural gas. Industries produce agricultural machinery, textiles, sugar from beets, and tobacco. Meat-processing and leather are also important. Some metal refining is done, but generally the ores are exported. Uranium oxide and molybdenum are produced in the Kara-Balta Concentrating Combine (Chu valley), the largest in Kyrgyzstan. Aluminum and antimony are mined in Osh region.

The agriculture industry is the second important sector of Kyrgyzstan's economy. Presently the industries are under a centralized system of economic management, which is likely to change. The most significant industry is textiles, including wool. Other industries relate to leather and light manufacturing.

CHAPTER 25
LEBANON

Culturally, Lebanon is complex and different from other Arab States. It has a highly fragmented society, divided along religious and ethnic lines. Ethnically, it is divided into Christians, Muslims, Druze, and other groups.

GEOGRAPHY

Located on the eastern shore of the Mediterranean Sea, Lebanon is bordered in the north and east by Syria, and on the south by Israel. Its principal topographic features are a narrow coastal plain, behind which are the high Lebanon Mountains, the fertile Biqa valley, and the Anti-Lebanon Mountains extending to the Syrian border (Map 28). Latani is Lebanon's main river, which flows into the sea north of Tyre. It is the only river in the Arab Near East that does not cross a national boundary. The Helmand River, one of the sources of the Jordan River, rises within Lebanon.

PEOPLE AND POPULATION

People have been attracted as refugees or traders to Lebanon's rugged mountainous interior for a long time. The very mountains that promised protection also limited the economic growth based on agriculture. As a result, the Lebanese moved out of the poor agricultural lands to become merchants and entrepreneurs in other parts of the world. Until recently,

---

Geographical Profile

Area: 4,015 sq. mi. (10,452 sq. km)
Population: 3.6 million (1994); 4.1 million (2000); 4.9 million (2010)
Capital: Beirut; Other cities: Tripoli, Sidon, Tyre, Zahleh
Neighboring Countries: Jordan, Syria, Israel
Terrain: Narrow coastal plain, backed by Lebanon Mountains, Biqa Valley, and Anti-Lebanon Mountains
Climate: Typically Mediterranean
Annual Growth Rate: 1.1% (1989)
Ethnic Groups: Arab 93%, Armenian 6%, and others 1%
Religions: Islam (Shi'ah, Sunni, Druze), Christians (Maronite, Greek Orthodox, Greek Catholic, Roman Catholic, Protestant, Armenian Apostolic)
Language: Arabic (official), French
Economy:
  GDP: $1.8 billion (1988)
  Avg. Inflation Rate: 155%
  Natural Resources: Limestone
  Land: 61% Urban, desert, or waste; 21% agricultural, 8% forested
  Agriculture: (33% of GDP 1984)
  Products: Citrus fruit
  Industry: (13% of GDP): Types: Cement production, light industry, refining
Official Name: Republic of Lebanon
Year of Independence: 1943

most of the traders in many African countries were Lebanese, as were the bankers of the Arab world.

The population of Lebanon is comprised of Muslims and Christians. No official census has been taken since 1932, reflecting the political sensitivity in Lebanon over religious balance. Although there has been no census, it is well-known that Muslims outnumber Christians by nearly 2 to 1. Various Christian sects make up the non-Muslim portion of the population. In the early 1970's, Muslims claimed that they were in the majority and were entitled to a fair share in political and economic power. This contributed to the tensions preceding the 1975-76 Muslim-Christian civil strife. Even the present crisis is based on demands for a more powerful Muslim voice in the government.

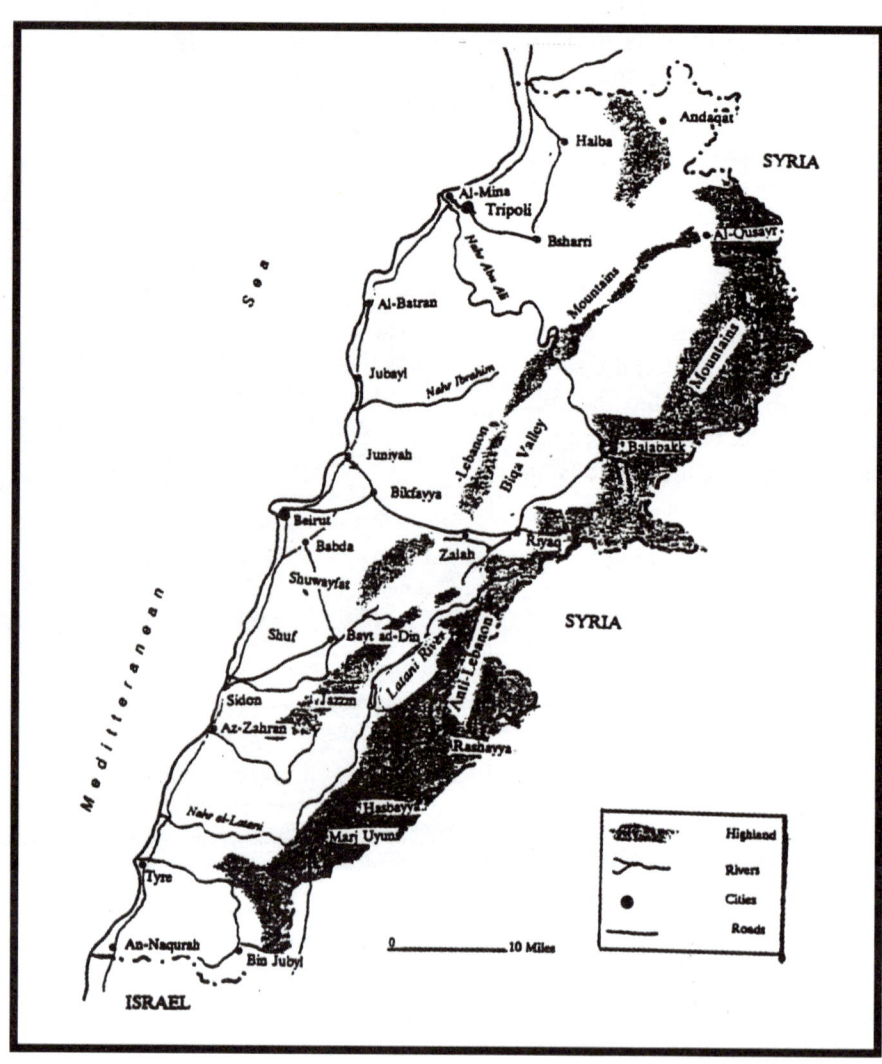

Map 28: Lebanon

The Christian sects in Lebanon include Maronite, Greek Orthodox, Greek Catholic, Armenian Apostolic, Roman Catholic, and Protestant. The Maronites, affiliated with the Roman Catholic Church, make up the largest Christian group. They are usually strongly opposed to any increase in power exercised by the Muslims. Islam is represented by members from the Sunni and Shi`ah sects. *The Twelver Shi'ah* constitutes the largest religious community in Lebanon. The Druze sect constitutes another significant minority. The Druze are an offshoot of the Shi'ah Isma'ili sect. The Druze faith is extremely esoteric and has little in common with the original tenents of Islam. Besides their stronghold in Southern Lebanon, they are also found in *Jabal al-Druze* in southern Syria, around the large town of Suwaida.

With no official figures available, it is estimated that 600,000-900,000 Lebanese fled their country during the 1975-76 civil strife. Although some returned, the instability in the late 1970s, Israeli invasion in 1982, and renewed internal conflict in 1983-84 and 1989-90 sparked further waves of emigration, adding to uncertainty over population figures.

EVOLUTION OF STATE

Lebanon is the historical home of the Phoenicians and Semitic traders who based a maritime culture there for more than 2,000 years. In later centuries, mountains of Lebanon were a refuge for Christians, when the Crusaders established several strongholds in Lebanon. After World War I, following the collapse of the Ottoman Empire, the five Ottoman provinces that comprised the present day Lebanon were mandated to France by the League of Nations. The country was ruled by France until it gained independence in 1943.

Although Muslims were in the majority, the French rule denied them a dominant role in the government. Even after independence, the charter guaranteed a dominant political and economic role for Christians, particularly the Maronites. The Maronite Church is unique in Lebanon. Originating as a distinct group in Syria in about the sixth century, the Maronites have preserved many ancient customs.

Although the national constitution of Lebanon recognizes seventeen religious communities, the four dominant communities are (i) Christians (Catholics and non-Catholics), (ii) *Sunni* Muslims, (iii) *Shi'ah* Muslims, and (iv) Druze. Muslims hold a demographic majority, as did the Christians when the first and last census of Lebanon was taken by the French in the 1930s. That census was used as the statistical basis of religious government called Lebanon's "confessional" style of government. According to this arrangement, the President of Lebanon was required to be a Maronite, whereas the prime minister had to be a *Sunni* Muslim. Other important and administrative positions were also distributed on the basis of religious and ethnic affiliations. Jobs were also distributed according to a community formula, which led to resentment and constant friction.

Generally, Christians are at the top of the ladder, the Druze are in the middle, and the *Sunni* and *Shi'ah* Muslims are at the bottom. For forty years since their independence, these communities lived uneasily with their confessional style government. In the 1970s, the system of confessional government began to disintegrate. Age-old social identities came to the surface as the unequal apportionment of political power became increasingly divisive. Adding to the unrest was a large Palestinian population that lived in Lebanon.

In 1975, a civil war broke out between Muslims and Christians, and the effective central government collapsed. Over thirty private armies were fighting for control. Sporadic fighting between Catholic and non-Catholic Christians, *Sunni* and *Shi'ah* Muslims, Druze, Palestinian refugees, and Israelis has devastated Lebanon. Prior to the civil war, Lebanon was a prosperous and wealthy country. Its capital, Beirut, was a fulcrum of the world economy and was often called the "Paris of the Middle East."

Fighting between the Israelis and Palestinians in July 1981 ended with a cease-fire arranged by President Reagan's special envoy, Philip C. Habib. The cease-fire was respected during the next 10 months, but a string of incidents led to an Israeli ground attack on June 6, 1982, to remove PLO (Palestine Liberation Organization) forces from Lebanon. In August, an agreement was reached that the Syrian troops and the PLO fighters would leave Beirut. Then, under Israeli protection, Christian Lebanese militiamen massacred hundreds of Palestinian civilians between September 16 and 18 in the Sabra and Shatila refugee camps in West Beirut.

The general security situation in Beirut remained calm through late 1982 and the first half of 1983, when Christian militiamen invaded the Druze-controlled Shuf area southeast of Beirut. The situation was exacerbated by the deterioration of internal security. The clashes between the Palestinians and Christian militia continued until 1988. In January 1989, the Arab League appointed a six-member committee led by the Kuwaiti foreign minister. Later, the Arab League empowered a Higher Committee on Lebanon, composed of King Fahd of Saudi Arabia, President Bendjedid of Algeria, and King Hassan of Morocco, to work toward a solution in Lebanon. The committee arranged for a seven-point cease-fire in September, followed by a meeting of Lebanese parliamentarians in Taif, Saudi Arabia. The deputies approved the Taif agreement on November 4, which gave some presidential powers to the Council of Ministers, expanded the National Assembly, and equally divided those seats between Christians and Muslims. The President of Lebanon continues to be a Maronite Christian.

ECONOMY

Lebanon was considered the financial and commercial capital of the Middle East before the outbreak of the civil war in 1975. Because of its location, mercantile heritage and the Christian-Muslim population, it was regarded as a bridge between the West and the Middle East. The preeminence of Lebanon in the region's commercial services seemed to confirm this perception. It's principal port is Lebanon, followed by Tripoli, then Jounrich, and Sidon. During the civil war, the Beirut port remained almost inactive for commercial operations, but since March 1991, when the Lebanese army regained control of the port, it reopened for shipping. In 1992, the traffic at Beirut port had greatly increased. The number of ships docking at Beirut port rose by more than 37% over 1991, the number of containers rose by more than 37%, and tonnage unloaded rose by more than 56%.

The civil war between the Christians and Muslims weakened this traditional leadership immensely. In the intervening years, the war has inflicted massive damage on Lebanon's economic infrastructure. Beirut, the Shuf, and Southern Lebanon have been particularly hard hit. Industry, housing, roads, electrical and water supply systems, telecommunications, and public health facilities were largely destroyed.

Since the outbreak of the war, no reliable statistics on growth rates are available, but the consensus is that the economy expanded only marginally. In recent years, economic growth rates have probably been negative, given the heavy fighting in 1988-90, which resulted in the destruction of much of the economic infrastructure of Beirut and its environs. Industrial production has also been severely reduced as a result of destruction of most industrial areas, especially that of Shuwayfat on the southeast edge of Beirut. It is only now that Lebanon's industry is beginning to recover with metal goods, processed foods, textiles, and pharmaceuticals. Particularly since the civil war, agriculture has suffered greatly, especially in Southern Lebanon. A disturbing phenomenon is the increased production and trafficking of drugs, particularly cannabis and opiates.

Lebanon is basically an agricultural country, although only 38% of its total area is cultivated, owing to its physical character. Agriculture, including forestry and fishing, contributes 8.5% of the Gross Domestic Product. The principal crops are wheat, sugar beets, potatoes, oranges, and olives.

Lebanon has no strong agricultural base, although bananas and citrus grown in the coastal plain and deciduous fruits from the upland area form the basis of an export trade with surrounding Arab areas. The urban population, concentrated mainly in Beirut and Tripoli, is noted for its commercial enterprise, but chronic instability in much of the country has had a strong negative impact on both agriculture and commerce. Lebanon has a higher proportion of skilled labor than any other Arab country.

The service sector, particularly banking, is the most important sector of the Lebanese economy. Prior to the late 1970s, Lebanon was a major center for Arab banking and other services, which accounted for 70 percent of the Lebanese national income and produced jobs for 55 percent of the active population. The oil *sheikhs*, who were reluctant to invest in non-Arab countries, invested their surplus capital in Lebanese real estate. Thus, Lebanon was a classical crossroad economy; its location resulted in a good standard of living and an expanding economy as the Arab hinterland grew in wealth. Although 15 years of strife have weakened this area, the banking industry has maintained its vitality throughout the difficult years. A large number of Lebanese professionals have emigrated. The remittances they send to the country assist in the balance of payments, but their services would benefit Lebanon directly if the security situation permitted them to return.

Today, Lebanon's long-term future remains uncertain. Torn by conflicting internal pressures, it suffers from a major identity crisis. Thoroughly Arab, it is neither fully Christian nor fully Muslim. Until these conflicts are resolved, Lebanon will continue to be destabilized by internal security problems.

NOTES

CHAPTER 26
LIBYA

In 1934, Italy adopted Libya as the official name of the country, which was used by the Greeks for all of North Africa, except Egypt. Libya was the first country to achieve independence through the United Nations as a constitutional and a hereditary monarchy in 1952. In 1969, the monarchy was replaced by a republic.

GEOGRAPHY

Socialist People's Libyan Arab Janahiriya is located midway along the Mediterranean Sea where the sea laps the Sahara desert (Map 29). Its narrow coastline is about 1,110 miles (1,770 km). The remaining 93% of the land is desert or semidesert. Between Cyrenaica and Tripolitana is a waste of bleached desert and scrub. Cyrenaica bulges northwards into the Mediterranean Sea. South of Tripoli and to the east of Benghazi are hilly areas which rise to 3,000 ft. (900 meters) above sea level. A further zone of hills and mountains lies in the south and southwest which rise to 10,335 ft. (3,150 m). Between these are largely barren, rock strewn plains and vast deserts. Libya has no permanent rivers. Except for scattered oases, only the narrow coastal strip and the slopes of the two northern hill areas are suitable for cultivation. An estimated 7% of the land is devoted to agriculture and nomadic herding.

Rainfall averages less than 20 inches (50 cm.) on the coast and less than 8 inches (20 centimeters) in the interior, with occasional dry spells. The temperature in coastal areas is influenced by the Mediterranean, but the interior

---

Geographical Profile

Area: 679,536 sq. mi. (1,758,610 sq. km)
Population: 4.8 million (1994); 5.7 million (2000); 4.9 million (2010)
Annual Growth Rate: 3.08%
Capital: Tripoli;
Other City: Benghazi
Terrain: Desert and semi-desert, hills south of Tripoli and east of Benghazi; rocky plains and sand in the center, mountains in the south
Climate: Mediterranean on the coast, dry, extreme desert in interior
Ethnic Groups: Arab, Arab/Berber 80%, Berber 15%, Touareg, Tebous Arab, some Greeks, Maltese, Italians, Egyptians, Pakistanis
Religion: Sunni Islam 97%
Economy:
  GDP: (1986) $20.5 billion
  Per Capita Income: $5,500
  Natural Resources: Petroleum, natural gas
  Agriculture: Products: Wheat, barley, olives, citrus fruits, vegetables, dates
  Industry: Types: Crude petroleum, refined products, food processing, textiles, cement, handicrafts
Official Name: Socialist Republic of Libyan Arab Jamahiriya
Date of Independence: December 24, 1951

experiences the hot, wider ranging extremes of the desert climate. A special feature of the Libyan climate is the *ghibli*, a hot, dry, dust-laden southern wind lasting from one to four days. The *ghibli* usually occurs in spring and fall and can raise the temperature within hours to more than 40ºC (110ºF).

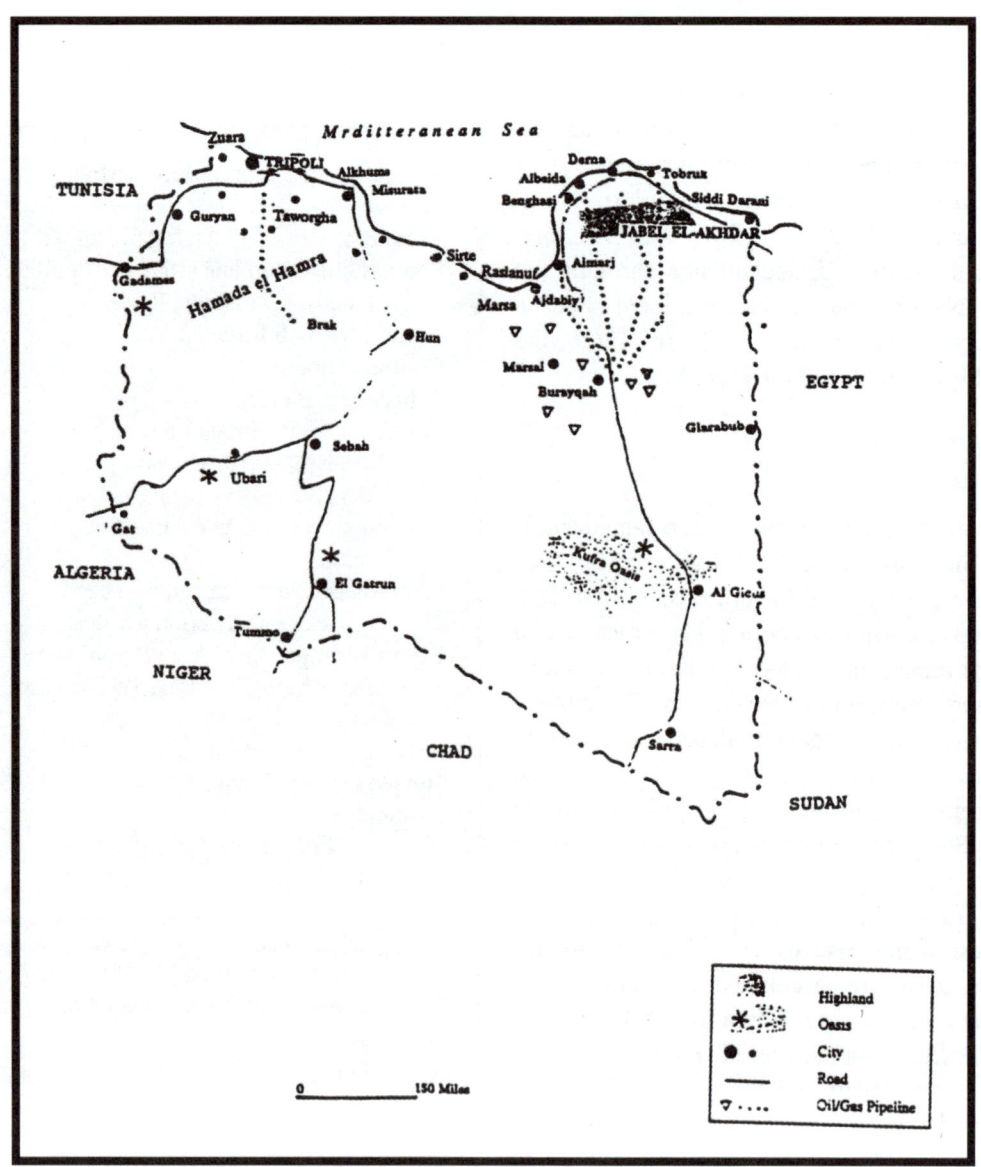

Map 29: Libya

PEOPLE AND POPULATION

Libyans are primarily a mixture of Arabs and Berbers. Small Tebou and Tuareg tribal groups in Southern Libya are nomadic or semi nomadic. Among foreign residents, the largest groups of people are from Egypt, Turkey, Pakistan, India, Sudan, Morocco, South Korea, and Thailand. A substantial number of Tunisians worked in Libya before relations were severed in 1985 and the Tunisians were expelled. However, since the border was reopened in December of that year, Tunisians have since returned to Libya. Other foreign residents include 110,000 persons from Europe and a significant number of Palestinians, Filipinos, Bangladeshis, and Jordanians. More than half of the population of Libya is urban, mostly concentrated in the three largest cities along the coast, Tripoli, Benghazi and Misurata (Fig. 39). The population is young; 50% is under the age of 15 years.

Fig. 39: Libya's Coastal Settlement

Libya has a small population of 3.2 million people and a large land area. Population density is about 5 persons per square mile (2.2 persons per sq. km). Ninety percent of the people live in less than 10% of the area, primarily within 19 miles (30 km) of the sea. Of these, 2.1 million live in the coastal areas of Tripolitania, 1 million along the coast in Cyrenaica, and only 100,000 in the desert interior of Fezzan. A part of the population of Fezzan (about 15%) is nomadic and semi- nomadic (Fig. 40).

Fig. 40 : A Nomad

EVOLUTION OF LIBYA

The people of Libya have been subjected to varying degrees of foreign control for most of their history. The Phoenicians, Carthaginians, Greeks, Romans, Vandals, and Byzantines ruled all or parts of Libya. Although the Greeks and Romans left impressive ruins at Cyrene, Leptis Magna, and Sabratha, little else remains today to testify to the presence of these ancient cultures.

The Arabs conquered Libya in the seventh century, following which, most of the people adopted Islam, Arabic language, and culture. The Ottoman Turks administered the country from the 16th century. Libya loyally remained part of the Ottoman Empire until Italy invaded it in 1911. After years of resistance by the people, Italy succeeded in incorporating Libya as its colony.

Between the two World Wars, the *Amir* of Cyrenaica, King Idris I, led Libyan resistance to Italian occupation. After the war, Tripolitania and Cyrenaica came under British administration, and France controlled Fezzan. In 1944, King Idris returned from exile in Cairo but declined to resume permanent residence in Cyrenaica until the removal of certain aspects of British and French control. Under the terms of the 1947 peace treaty with the allies, Italy relinquished all claims to Libya.

On November 21, 1949, the UN General Assembly passed a resolution stating that Libya would be independent before January 1, 1952. King Idris represented Libya in the subsequent U.N. negotiations. When Libya became independent on December 24, 1951, it was the first country to achieve independence through the United Nations. Libya was proclaimed a constitutional and a hereditary monarchy under King Idris.

The discovery of significant oil reserves in 1959 was one of the most important events in Libyan history. Income from oil enabled Libya to become an extremely wealthy country, whereas previously it had been one of the world's poorest measured in terms of resources. King Idris ruled the Kingdom of Libya, until the government was overthrown in a military-led coup on September 1, 1969. The new regime headed by a Revolutionary Command Council (RCC) abolished the monarchy, and subsequently, proclaimed the new Libyan Arab Republic. Colonel Mu'ammar al-Qadhafi emerged as leader of the RCC and eventually as dictator, a position he currently retains, though he holds no official position.

Seeking new directions, RCC's motto became "freedom, socialism, and unity." It pledged itself to remove backwardness, take an active role in the Palestinian Arab cause, promote Arab unity, and encourage domestic policies based on communism with social justice, non-exploitation, and an equitable distribution of wealth as its main points of propaganda. Qadhafi also instituted changes in the religion of Islam in order to make it more "modern".

An early objective of the new government was the withdrawal of all foreign military installations from Libya. Following negotiation, British military installations at Tabruk and nearby El Adem were closed in March 1970, and US facilities at Wheeler base near Tripoli were closed in June 1970. In July 1970, the Libyan Government ordered the expulsion of several thousand Italian residents. By 1971, libraries and cultural centers operated by foreign governments were ordered closed.

During the years since the revolution, Libya has asserted its credentials as the leader of the Arab and African revolutionary forces and sought an active role in various international organizations. In the late 1970s, Libyan embassies were redesignated as "Peoples Bureaus." The peoples bureaus, aided by Libyan religious, political, educational, and business institutions overseas, have exported Qadhafi's revolutionary philosophy abroad and taken direct action to control Libyans in other countries.

ECONOMY

Libya's economy remains dependent upon revenues from exported crude oil. After the first major oil discovery in 1959, the economy expanded rapidly. As a result of oil, Libyan per capita gross domestic product (GDP) rose from $40 in 1950 to more than $4,900 in 1975, and to nearly $11,000 in 1980, but declined to $5,500 in 1986. Total GDP in 1980 exceeded $34 billion but fell back to $25 billion by 1984 and $20 billion by 1986. Direct oil earnings were $22-35 billion in 1985 and approximately $6 billion in 1988. Agriculture is the second largest sector in the economy.

Agriculture

High summer temperatures, desiccating desert winds, lack of rainfall, and poor soils contribute to the scantiness and poverty of Libyan agriculture. Less than one percent of Libyan land is productive, and three-quarters of this is suitable only for grazing. Tripolitania is agriculturally the most productive area. The coastal zone from the western border to Homs receives about 10 inches (250 mm) of rain annually, and locally this is supplemented by irrigation. The Jeffara is the most favored area and is the major producer of barley wheat and vegetables. Tree crops, olives, almonds, citrus fruits, and vines increase in importance, the olive being the chief crop on the Jebel behind Tripoli. Cyrenaica has a third of the arable land but has the largest area of pastoralism. The *Bedouin* move south in the winter to graze steppe pastures and return to *Jebel* in late spring for grazing. They then harvest the cereal patches planted the previous autumn. Barley is the major cereal, while fruit and vegetables grow along the coast and benefit from springs emerging from the base of the limestone Jebel.

Agriculture in the Fezzan is confined to the oases, which contain many million date-palms. In addition to dates, millet and vegetables are the other staples of diet. In recent years, increasing demand from oil camps and northern towns has stimulated the production of fruit and vegetables.

The state now operates some farms previously owned by the Italian companies. Some have become cooperatives. Since the revolution, agriculture has received the largest share of the development investment for a high degree of self-sufficiency. Thus, the development plans put in motion a green revolution aimed at expanding and modernizing farming. Among its measures were the provision of grants and loans to small farmers for seeds, machinery and farm buildings, the organization of cooperatives, the purchase of local produce at favorable prices, and the promotion of agricultural research and establishment of major projects.

Over a hundred agricultural projects have been started. The most spectacular of these projects is the Wadi Kufra oasis in the desert southeast of Libya. Early in the 1960s, oil exploration here resulted in the discovery of fresh water aquifers in the Nubian sandstone at depths of 980 ft. (200 m). The oil company began an experimental agriculture project, since taken over and expanded by the government. From the Kufra production project, about 24,710 acres (10,000 ha) of irrigated fodder is being produced for sheep breeding and fattening, and nearby, 2230 acres (900 ha) of small irrigated farms grouped into sixteen hamlets are well established. Such a project in the heart of the desert presents innumerable difficulties and is accomplished only at huge cost. Libya is undertaking a multi-billion dollar "Man-made River" project to tap water resources deep under the Sahara to meet water needs of the coastal population in the 1990s. However, technical difficulties have delayed the completion of the first phase, while the postponement of building deadlines has hindered the beginning of the second phase of the project.

Libya is self-sufficient in a few foods. Domestic food production meets only about 35% of the demand. A long-term objective is to become self-sufficient in agriculture, although the scarcity of water is a serious obstacle in reaching this ambitious goal. Higher incomes and a growing population have also caused food consumption to rise. The livestock is also not sufficient to meet the food requirements. According to 1990 figures, there were 0.25 million cattle, 0.193 million camels, 5850 million sheep, 0.975 million goats, and 38 million poultry. The livestock products are beef (55,000 tons), mutton and lamb meat (59,00 tons), goat meat (1,000 tons), cow milk (79,000 tons), sheep and goat milk (68,000 tons), and hides and skins (19,900 tons).

Oil and Development

Oil in commercial quantities was first discovered in Zelten in 1959, about 186 miles (300 km) south of Benghazi. These discoveries were the first of a series in the Sitre Basin. Pipelines connect the many fields with newly created coastal terminals at Ras Sidra, Ras Lanouf, Marsa Brega, Zuetina, and Tubruk. Six refineries are in operation, and four more are being constructed. Oil operations have been restricted to the Sitre Basin, but oil exploration is now extending to western Libya, the offshore areas, and to the south. Crude oil exports account for 99 percent of Libyan total exports. Since 1969, liquid gas has been exported to Spain and Italy.

With oil money, Libya continues to pursue the RCC's goals, which include a more equitable distribution of income and services, greater government control of the economy, and independence from foreign influence. Boosted by oil revenues, the government invested in various development projects. Since 1965, several 5-year plans have been implemented which focus on specific economic problems and particular areas of development. The first plan gave priority to communications and public works. The second emphasized agriculture, transport, housing, and local government. This plan, however, was ended before its completion and replaced by a 3-year development plan from 1972-75. The third plan (1976-80) projected expenditures of about $29 billion and stressed the development of agriculture, schools, transportation, housing, electrification, and industrial projects outside of the oil sector. With little success, the final plan (1981-85) emphasized diversification of the country's economy away from dependence on the oil sector. Another plan was scheduled to begin in 1986, but falling oil prices forced cuts in programs and a reassessment of goals.

Beginning in 1961, crude oil production rose rapidly and peaked at 3.7 million barrels per day (b/d) in the spring of 1970. Following the RCC's extended renegotiation of concessions with oil companies and Libya's joining the Arab embargo during the October 1973 Arab-Israeli war, production dropped to less than 2 million b/d by early 1974. Sustained production limits from the Organization of Petroleum Exporting Countries (OPEC) and unrealistic Libyan pricing policies temporarily dropped output as low as 600,000 b/d by early 1982. Currently, production is close to Libya's OPEC-assigned quota of 990,000 b/d.

Since 1981, fiscal difficulties, associated with declining oil revenues combined with the effects of various socialistic schemes, have been a disadvantage to merchants and other business professionals, among others. Although Libyans have experienced a dramatic rise in the standard of living during the past 20 years, economic austerity measures as well as tighter internal security controls caused a general deterioration in the quality of life for many Libyans in the 1980s. Nonetheless, distribution of national wealth remains more equitable in Libya than in many other developing countries.

Manufacturing and Service Activities

Before oil, the non-agricultural activities of Libya were mainly limited to the processing of agriculture products, flour milling, oil processing, fish canning, and artisan work in leather and textiles. With immense wealth from oil, a construction and expansion of towns has taken place, so enlarging the construction industry. The manufacturing of consumer goods (clothing, footwear, paper making, and metal working) was also encouraged. However, with limited new materials and a tiny home market, no great enlargement of secondary activities was likely, and hence, emphasis on import substitution was abolished in the 1981-1985 development plan. Instead, increasing investment in industry is now directed to metallurgy (iron, steel and aluminum products), petrochemicals, and plastics. Seven coastal centers (Zuara, Misurata, Sirte, Marsa, Brega, Ras Lanouf, and Abu Kammash) have been designated as industrial centers.

──────────**NOTES**──────────

CHAPTER 27
MALAYSIA

Malaysia bridges mainland and peninsular Southeast Asia. Its two parts are separated by 404 miles (650 km) of the South China Sea. Most of Malaysia occupies the southern tip of the Malay peninsula south of Thailand. Islam was first introduced in Malacca by the Arab traders, and from there, it spread to other parts of Malaysia.

GEOGRAPHY

Most of Malaysia is mountainous, with the exception of some coastal areas and a few inland undulating plains. In peninsular Malaysia, the highest peak is Gunong Tahan, 7,175 ft. (2,187 meters). The mountains of peninsular Malaysia extend in a north-south direction; there are six ranges, which rise to more than 5,000 ft. (1,500 m). The southern-most hills gradually disappear beneath the sea and reappear in the Indonesian territories on Longga, Riau, and Bangka islands, which are 10 miles (16 km) south of Singapore. The central range is the longest watershed. The ranges lying to the east and west of the central range are broken by drainage lines. Before the advent of modern road building in the Malay peninsula, the main mountain range was a great physical barrier preventing contacts between the east and west coasts. Now, the mountains are crossed at four major points (Map 30).

Geographical Profile

Area: 127,310 sq. mi. (329,749 sq. km)
Population: 19.7 million (1004); 22.9 (2000); 27.1 (2010)
Neighboring Countries: Thailand, Singapore, Indonesia
Capital: Kuala Lumpur
Other Cities: Penang, Petaling Jaya, Ipoh, Malacca, Johore Baharu, Kuching, Kota Kinabalu
Terrain: Malaysia is separated from East Malaysia in Borneo by 400 miles (644 km) of the South China Sea; Coastal plains, jungle-covered mountains
Climate: Tropical
Ethnic Groups: Malay and other indigenous 61%; Chinese 30%, Indians 8%, Others 1%
Religion: Sunni Islam 65%, Hinduism, Buddhism, Taoism, Christianity
Languages: Malay, Chinese dialects, English, Tamil, other indigenous
Economy:
  GDP: $41 billion (1990)
  Natural Resources: Petroleum, liquefied natural gas, tin, minerals
  Agriculture: Products- Palm oil, rubber, timber, cocoa, rice, pepper, pineapples
  Industry: Types - Electronics, electrical products, rubber products, automobile assembly, textiles
Official Name: Malaysia
Date of Independence: September 16, 1963

Along the coasts of peninsular Malaysia and inland between mountain ranges are plains produced by erosion. The plains are generally low and flat, with swamps and marshes in places. The coastal plains are generally between 5 to 40 miles (8 to 64 km) wide in the west and 20 miles (32 km) in the east. The rivers are generally short, the longest being the 270 mile (435 km) Pahang River. The Perak River, with a length of 252 miles (406 km), is the second longest. These rivers flow in a north-south direction following the mountain ranges before turning towards the sea.

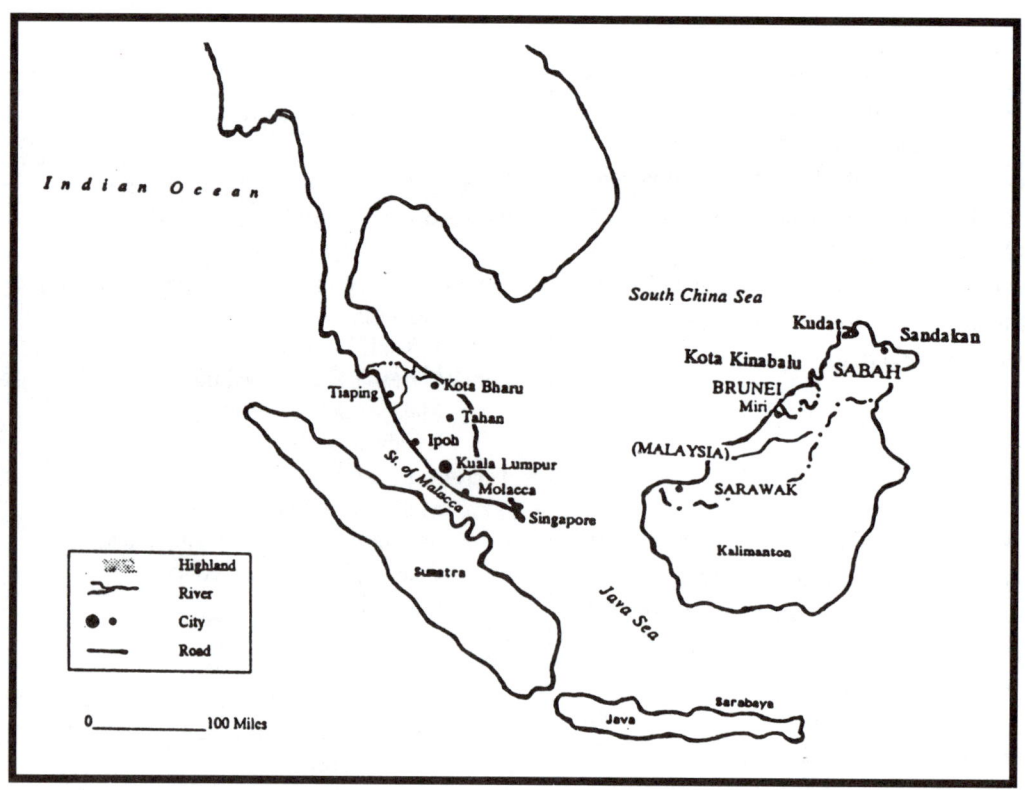

Map 30: Malaysia

In East Malaysia, Sabah has a very irregular coastline. Here, only one river, Kinabatangan, is navigable far inland. Sabah consists of mountains interspersed with upland plateaus, except in its coastal area. The mountains include Malaysia's highest peak, Gunong Kinabalu. Sarawak has three regions: (i) a swampy coastal plain, (ii) an area of rolling country, and (iii) a mountainous region in the interior. The largest of several rivers is the Rajang, which is navigable by small ships for 160 miles (260 km) upstream. Three-fourths of the land is covered by rain forest.

Malaysia has a rainy, tropical climate. In the lowlands, temperatures seldom exceed 90°F (32°C) during the day and generally fall to about 70°F (21°C) at night. In the mountainous area, temperatures are lower and, at 4,000 to 5,000 ft. (1200-1500 m.) above sea level, are quite pleasant. There is no dry period in Malaysia, and the humidity is always high.

The average annual rainfall is 100 inches (2,500 mm) in peninsular Malaysia, and 150 inches (3,750 mm) in Sabah and Sarawak. Because of the interplay of northeast and southwest monsoons, rainfall varies greatly from place to place. In general, the weather is stormier on the east coast of peninsular Malaysia and in Sarawak, than on the west coast of peninsular Malaysia and in Sabah. Some areas in western peninsular Malaysia and in Sabah receive only 60 inches (1,500 mm) of rainfall a year. The greatest annual rainfall of 236 inches (6,000 mm) occurs at Long Atar in Sarawak.

PEOPLE AND POPULATION

Malaysia's population is an amalgam of diverse, unassimilated ethnic groups. In 1994, Malaysia's population stood at 19.7 million people, and it has been growing at a rate of 2% per year. About 37% of the people are under 15 years of age. Population distribution is uneven, with some 15 million residents concentrated on peninsular Malaysia lowlands in an area slightly smaller than the state of Michigan.

Fig. 41: The Central Mosque, Kuala Lumpur

Malaysia's population is composed of many ethnic groups with Malays as the majority. The politically dominant Malays are indigenous and by constitutional definition, all Muslims. Malaysia is enthusiastically trying to Islamize its society (Fig. 41). Nearly one-third of the Malaysians are Chinese. They are mainly urban and, by virtue of their important role in trade, business, and finance, possess considerable economic power. The majority of them are Buddhists, Taoists, or Christians.

Malaysians of Indian descent comprise just over 8% of the population. About 85% of the Indian community are Tamils. They are divided among Hindus, Buddhists, and Muslims. They have created their own cultural landscapes in Malaysia, in which Muslims have constructed mosques (Fig. 42) and Hindus have constructed temples. Malaysian Indians are well represented in the professions as well as in agriculture and trade. Non-Malay indigenous groups make up more than 50% of Sarawak's population and about 66% of Sabah's population. They are divided into dozens of distinct ethnic groups, but they share some general patterns of living and culture. Until the 20th century, most practiced traditional beliefs; now many have become Christians or Muslims.

About 85% of Malaysia's population speak Malay, the "national language." English is used widely in government and business. Chinese dialects (Cantonese, Mandarin, Hokkisn) are also used. Tamil, Punjabi, and Urdu are spoken by about 8% of the people.

Fig 42: An Indian Mosque, Kuala Lumpur

EVOLUTION OF MALAYSIA

In the first century AD, two far-flung but related events in India and China helped stimulate Malaysia's emergence in international trade in the ancient world. At that time, India had two principal sources of gold and other precious metals: (i) the Roman Empire and (ii) China. The overland route to and from China was cut by marauding Huns. At about the same time, the Roman Emperor cut off shipments of gold to India. As a result, the Indians sent large and seaworthy ships to Southeast Asia, including the Malaysian Peninsula, to seek alternate sources. In the centuries that followed, tin deposits assumed great significance in Indian ocean trade, and the region prospered. As maritime trade among Middle Eastern, Indian, and Chinese ports flourished, the peninsula benefited from its location as well as from development of its diverse resources, including tropical woods and spices. Malay ports served as transshipment centers. Indian trade brought Indian culture, economy, religion, and politics, with historic results for what eventually became Malaysia. Some of these Indian Hindus still maintain their religious practices different from present-day India, which they say has changed greatly.

Until the 15th century, Malaysia was ruled by powerful outside powers. The Buddhist kingdom of Srivijaya based in Sumatra, dominated much of the Malay Peninsula from the 9th to the 13th centuries AD. In the 14th century, a Hindu kingdom based in Java gained control of the Malay Peninsula. Acceptance of Islam by the people of Malay, beginning in the early 14th century, accelerated with the rise of the state of Malacca under the rule of a Muslim prince in the 15th century. Trade made Malacca the greatest international center of the eastern world and the main center of diffusion of Islam in Southeast Asia. Through Malaccan influence, the smaller states of the peninsula and north Java accepted Islam.

Malacca was a major regional entry port where Chinese, Arab, Malay, and Indian merchants traded precious goods. Drawn by the rich trade, a Portuguese fleet conquered Malacca in 1511, marking the beginning of European expansion in Southeast Asia. Impressive churches were built as an expression of new power. The Dutch ousted the Portuguese from Malacca in 1641. In 1795, the Portuguese were replaced by the British, who had occupied Penang in 1786.

In 1886, the British settlements of Malacca, Penang, and Singapore were combined to form the Colony of the Straits Settlements. From these strong points, in the 19th and early 20th centuries, the British established protectorates over the Malay *sultanates* on the peninsula. Four of these states were consolidated in 1895 as the Federation of Malay States.

The Japanese occupied the Peninsula from 1942 to 1945 and encouraged nationalism against the British. Popular sentiment for independence swelled during and after the war, and in 1957, the Federation of Malaya negotiated independence from the United Kingdom. The British colonies of Singapore, Sarawak, and Sabah (called North Borneo) joined the Federation of Malaya to form Malaysia on September 16, 1963. The merger with Singapore did not work satisfactorily. Malays regarded Singapore as a threat to its political position, fearing that Singapore's two million Chinese would upset their majority. As a result, Singapore withdrew on August 9, 1965, becoming an independent republic.

Following World War II, local communists, nearly all Chinese, launched a long, bitter insurgency, prompting the imposition of a state of emergency in 1948, which was lifted in 1960. Small bands of guerrillas remained in bases along the rugged border with southern Thailand, occasionally entering northern Malaysia. These guerrillas finally signed a peace accord with the Malaysian Government in December 1989. A separate small insurgency began in the mid-1960s in Sarawak, which also ended with the signing of a peace accord in October 1990.

Malaysia is a constitutional monarchy, nominally headed by an *Agong* (paramount ruler), customarily referred to as king. Kings are elected for 5-year terms from among the nine *sultans* of the peninsular Malaysian states. The king is also the leader of the Islamic faith in Malaysia.

ECONOMY

At the time of independence, Malaysia inherited an economy dominated by two commodities - rubber and tin. In the 35 years since, Malaysia's economic record has been one of the most successful in Asia. From 1965 to 1990, the economy experienced a period of broad diversification and sustained rapid growth averaging between 7% and 8% annually. Per capita gross national product (GNP) reached nearly $2,000 in 1984. By 1990, the figure was $2,300. Palm oil, timber, cocoa, pepper, and clover were added to Malaysia's export crops. Malaysia is the world's leading producer of rubber and palm oil, the number four producer of tin and the largest exporter of tropical timber. The production sector expanded rapidly after 1980, making Malaysia a significant exporter of oil and liquefied natural gas (LNG). New foreign and domestic investment in manufacturing, much of it from the United States, Japan, Taiwan, and Singapore, led to increasing exports of electronic components, electrical consumer goods, textile products, and other manufactures. Manufacturing grew from 13% of gross domestic product (GDP) in 1970 to an estimated 27% in 1980.

Malaysia's recovery from its recession began in late 1986 and gained during 1987. Improved commodity prices and strong growth in exports of manufactured goods led the recovery. The economic expansion since 1987 has been led by foreign demand for Malaysia's exports, with net exports accounting for more than three-quarters of growth. In 1988, the strong export performance resulted in Malaysia's first current economic surplus since 1979.

Agriculture

Agriculture is the economy's second largest sector, accounting for an estimated 19% GDP in 1990 and 30% employment. Agriculture products (including forest products) account for an estimated 31% of exports. Malaysia is the world's largest producer of natural rubber, accounting for 25% of world production. In Malaysia, about 60% of the cultivated area is devoted to rubber production.

In the 1980s, palm oil began to overshadow rubber as the "golden" crop. Palm oil is a vegetable oil used for a variety of purposes, like cooking oil, soap, and as an ingredient in margarine. Malaysia produces 60% of the world's palm oil, and production will continue to increase as new acreage is developed and trees mature.

Timber and timber products account for 17% of all exports in 1990. Malaysia is the world's largest exporter of tropical hardwood. Most of the raw timber exported from Malaysia comes from Sabah and Sarawak. Peninsular Malaysia exports plywood, moldings, and other wood products.

Malaysia is now the world's fourth largest producer of cocoa. It also exports pepper (from Sarawak), coconut products, and fresh fruits. It is a net exporter of chicken but relies on imports of beef, dairy, vegetable, wheat, and some fruit products.

Rice is the main food crop. About 87% of the crop is grown in peninsular Malaysia. A government program, designed to promote self-sufficiency, expanded the rice-growing area from 1.3 million to 1.9 million acres (530,000 to 760,000 ha.) between 1964 and 1979.

Minerals

The petroleum sector became increasingly important during the 1980s, as periodically high prices and rising production volumes increased Malaysia's export revenues. In 1990, oil, LNG, and petroleum products accounted for 18% of total exports. Oil production in 1990 averaged 626,400 barrels per day. Major customers for Malaysia's crude oil are Singapore, Japan, and South Korea. Some of the oil exported to Singapore is imported back into Malaysia as refined products. All of Malaysia's LNG exports are shipped from Sarawak to Japan, although Malaysia expects to expand LNG exports to include Taiwan and South Korea. Oil production is roughly split between fields in the South China Sea off Borneo and those off peninsular Malaysia. Gas reserves, located off the peninsular Malaysia, are being developed to fuel power stations and to supply industries in Peninsular Malaysia and Singapore. All exploration is conducted under production-sharing contracts between the national oil company and foreign oil companies. The only foreign oil companies currently producing oil and gas are Exxon and Shell.

Malaysia is no longer the world's leading tin producer. The collapse of the International Tin Council in 1985 decreased prices and forced many of Malaysia's smaller mines to close.

Since 1971, efforts have been made through the National Economic Program (NEP) to eradicate poverty in Malaysia and to restructure the economy to end the identification of economic function with race. In particular, it was designed to enhance the economic standing of ethnic Malays and indigenous peoples (collectively known as "*bhumiputras*" in Malay). Rapid growth in the 1970s and early 1980s made it possible to expand the share of the economy for *bhumiputras* without reducing the economic attainments of the other groups.

Manufacturing

Manufacturing is now the Malaysian economy's largest sector, accounting for an estimated 27% of GDP in 1990. Major products include electronic components (Malaysia is the world's largest exporter of semiconductor devices), electrical goods, air conditioners, textiles, and apparel.

NOTES

CHAPTER 28
MALDIVES

The Republic of Maldives is the southernmost country of South Asia, southwest of Sri Lanka. It extends in the Indian Ocean on a chain of atoll islands. The entire population of Maldives is Muslim and Islam is its official religion.

GEOGRAPHY

The Republic of Maldives is a chain of atolls in the northern Indian ocean between 7°N latitude to 1°S latitude (Map 31). These atolls are 400 miles (650 km) from India, and are the southernmost political entity of the South Asian realm. They are a chain of 1,200 islands extending over 502 miles (764 km) from north to south, with a combined area of just 115 square miles (less than 300 sq. km). The Republic is 74 miles (120 km) wide at its widest point. The capital, Male, is located on an island which has an area of about one square mile (2.6 sq. km) about 415 miles (670 km) southwest of Sri Lanka. The highest elevation in the country is less than 6 feet (2 m) above sea level. In April 1987, high tides swept over Maldives, destroying much of Male and the nearby islands.

The climate is equatorial (hot and humid) with little daily variation. The average temperature is 80°F (27°C), with a relative humidity of 80%. Most of the area is subject to the "wet" southwest monsoon (May-October) and the "dry" northwest monsoon (December-March). Annual rainfall averages 100 inches (254 centimeters) in the north and 150 inches (281 centimeters) in the south. Tropical storms often hit the islands with disastrous effect. The lowest rainfall is between January and March.

Geographical Profile

Area: 115 sq. mile (398 sq. km)
Population: 200,000 (1994); 300,000 (2000); 400,000 (2010)
Capital: Male
Terrain: Flat Islands
Climate: Hot and humid
Ethnic Groups: South Indians, Sinhalese, Arabs
Religion: Sunni Islam 100%
Languages: Dhiveli, English
Economy:
    GDP: $95 million
    Per Capita Income: $494 (1987)
    Domestic Economy: (1967): Tourism, (17%); fishing (16%); agriculture (11%); industry (6%); trade, fish, garments
Official Name: Republic of Maldives
Date of Independence: July 26, 1965

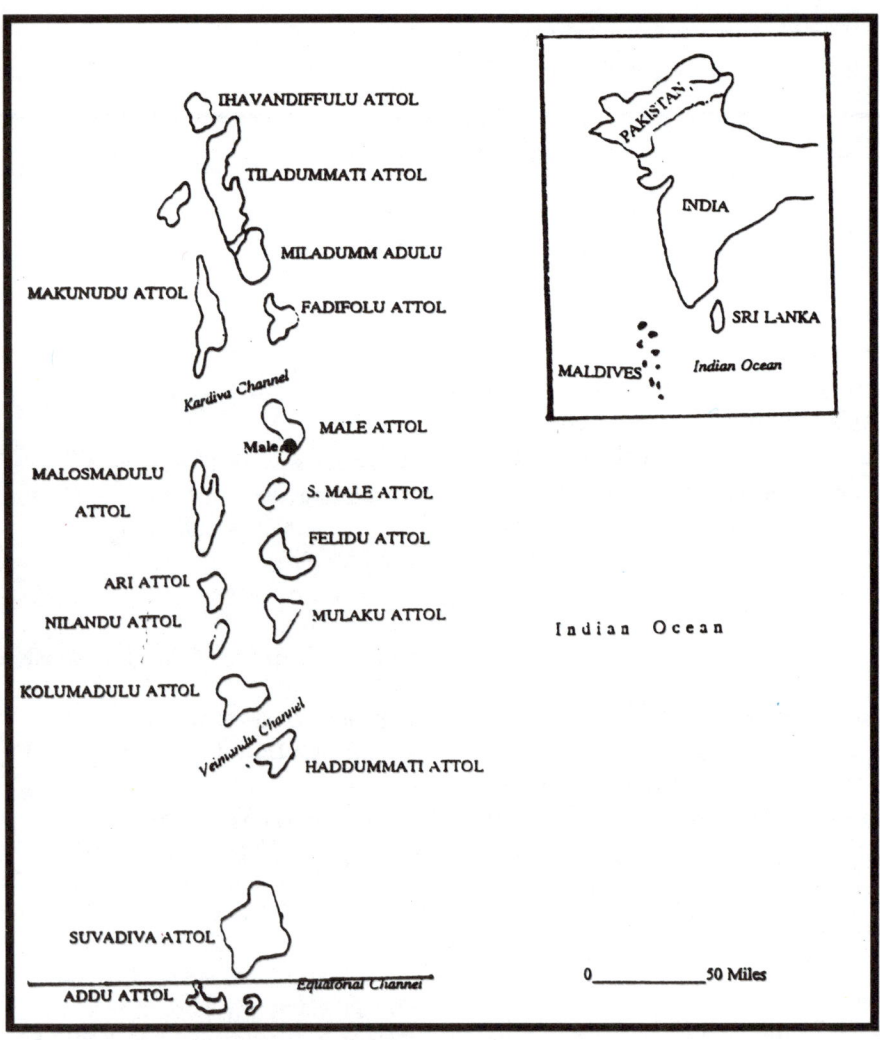

Map 31: Maldives

Small boats ply the waters, linking the inhabited islands (about 200 of them are inhabited) to each other and to the capital. The capital's townscape is dominated by a large mosque, and a few buildings rise above two stories. Here, buildings have replaced the palm trees that almost completely cover the other islands.

PEOPLE AND POPULATION

The earliest settlers were probably from Southern India, speaking languages of the Dravidian family. They were followed by Indo-European speakers from Sri Lanka in the fourth and fifth centuries BC. In the 12th century, sailors from Arab countries and East Africa came and introduced

Islam in the islands. Today, Maldivian ethnic consciousness is a strong blend of these cultures, reinforced by religion and language.

Of the 1,200 islands, only 202 are inhabited (Fig. 43). The population is scattered throughout the country, with the greatest concentration on the capital island, Male. Only four islands have a population of more than 3,000. Although most islands are uninhabited, absence of potable water and arable land limits population expansion. The official religion is Islam and official language of Maldives is Dhiveli. Dhiveli is an Indo-European language which is related to Sinhala, the language of Sri Lanka.

Fig. 43: A Settlement in Maldives

EVOLUTION OF MALDIVES

The early history of Maldives is obscure. According to Maldivian legend, a Sinhalese prince was stranded in a Maldivian lagoon with his wife, who was the daughter of the king of Sri Lanka. The prince stayed on the island and became a ruler. In the ninth century, Sulaiman the Merchant described the islands as ruled by a queen. The people were probably already Buddhists, as is shown by the stupas on various islands. In 1163, the Maldives king converted to Islam, either by Yusuf Shamsuddin of Tabriz or by Abul Barakat the "Berber." From this time onwards, there is a written history of the country compiled in Arabic.

A lengthy description of the islands is given by Ibn Batuta, who resided there for two separate periods in 1343-44 when he became *Qadi* or Chief Justice in 1346. The Portuguese became involved in Maldives and occupied the island from 1558 to 1573. They were eventually driven away by the warrior-patriot Muhammad Thakurufar Al-Azam. Al-Azam's birthplace in a small northern island is kept as a shrine today.

A full survey of the islands was made in 1835 by the British Indian Navy, and in 1887, a British protectorate over Maldives was declared. On November 11, 1968, the *Sultanate* was abolished, and the country assumed its present name. In 1956, a bilateral agreement gave the United Kingdom the use of Gan (in Addu Atoll) in the far south as an air facility in return for British aid for 20 years. The agreement ended in 1976, shortly after the British closed the Gan air station.

ECONOMY

A little agriculture is done for subsistence. Rice is grown on the sandy and shallow atoll soils. In addition to rice, coconut palm, and a variety of fruits, shrub and other useful plants are grown. Around the houses, bread fruit, jack fruit, mango, lime, papaya, banana, manioc, corn, eggplant, taro, sweet potato, pumpkins, and other vegetables are grown.

Maldivians have always depended on trade for supplies of grain and textiles from other countries in return for fish, coconut products, ambergris, and cowries. Cowries were once used in huge quantities as international currency. Now Maldivian economy is based on tourism and fishing. Poor soil and unavailable arable land limit agriculture to a few subsistence crops. Traditional industry consists of boat building and handicrafts, while modern industry is restricted to a cannery and a few garment factories and consumer products.

Fig. 44: Fishing Activity in Maldives

Fishing employs about one-third of the labor force (Fig. 44). Production was more than 60,000 metric tons in 1988, most of which was tuna. More than one-half of the annual harvest is frozen, canned, or dried and exported to Thailand, Sri Lanka and other countries. In recent years, Maldives has successfully marketed its natural assets for tourism -- its beautiful beaches on small coral islands, blue waters, abundant with tropical fish, and glorious sunsets. Since the first resort was established in 1972, 58 resort hotels have been developed - each on its own island. The number of tourists, mainly from Europe and Japan, increased from 1,100 in 1972 to 155,758 in 1988. To facilitate tourism, Male International Airport has been expanded to accommodate wide-bodied aircraft.

——————————— **NOTES** ———————————

NOTES

CHAPTER 29
MALI

As a dry, landlocked country, Mali was hardest hit by the drought in the early 1970s. Things were so grim that the people were forced to change their traditional way of life from nomadism to rudimentary farming.

GEOGRAPHY

Mali is focused on the Niger River, its main artery. The Niger divides the country into several distinct sections. Southwest of Bamako in the higher land is the Upper Valley, with numerous headwaters and fairly narrow valleys (Map 32). From Koulikoro to Sansanding the river is broader but has a narrow flood plain. East of Sansanding is the inland delta. The area of the former middle Niger is still marked by a braided river and much indeterminate drainage. A distinction is sometimes made between the 'dead' delta from Sansanding to Diafarabe, where the Niger divides. The 'live' part is eastward toward Timbuktu with a complex network of water courses and seasonally flooded depressions. Below Kabara, port for Timbuktu, the Niger again becomes a single river in a seven to ten mile (12 to 15 km) wide valley. The Niger's main tributary, the Bani, also provides a zone of better-watered land.

In the extreme south of Mali, the rainfall is more than four inches (100 mm) in five to seven months of the year. At Bamako, the

---

Geographical Profile

Area: 474,754 sq. mi. (1,240,278 s. km)
Population: 9.1 million (1994); 10.8 million (2000); 14.2 million (2010)
Capital: Bamako
Other Cities: Segou, Mopti, Kayes, Gao
Terrain: Savannah and desert
Climate: Semitropical in the south, arid north
Ethnic Groups: Mande (Bambara or Banama, Malinke, Sarakole) 50%, Peul 17%, Voltaic 12%, Songhal 6%, Tuareg and Moor 5%
Religion: Sunni Islam 90%, Indigenous Pagan 9%, Christian 1%
Languages: French (official) and Bambara
Economy:
  GDP: (1991) $2.8 billion
  Per Capita Income: (1991) $300
  Natural Resources: Gold, phosphate, kaolin, salt, and limestone currently mined, deposits of bauxite, iron ore, manganese, lithium, and uranium are known or suspected
  Agriculture: (40% of GDP)
  Products: Millet, sorghum, corn, rice, livestock, sugar, cotton, peanuts, and tobacco
  Industry: (19% of GDP)
  Types: Food processing, textiles, cigarettes, light manufacturing, plastics, and beverage bottling
Official Name: Republic of Mali
Date of Independence: September 22, 1960

total is 48 inches (1200 mm). North of Timbuktu, the climate is Saharan type with negligible rainfall. Therefore, most of the country is moisture deficient for a large part of the year, which determines the agricultural practice.

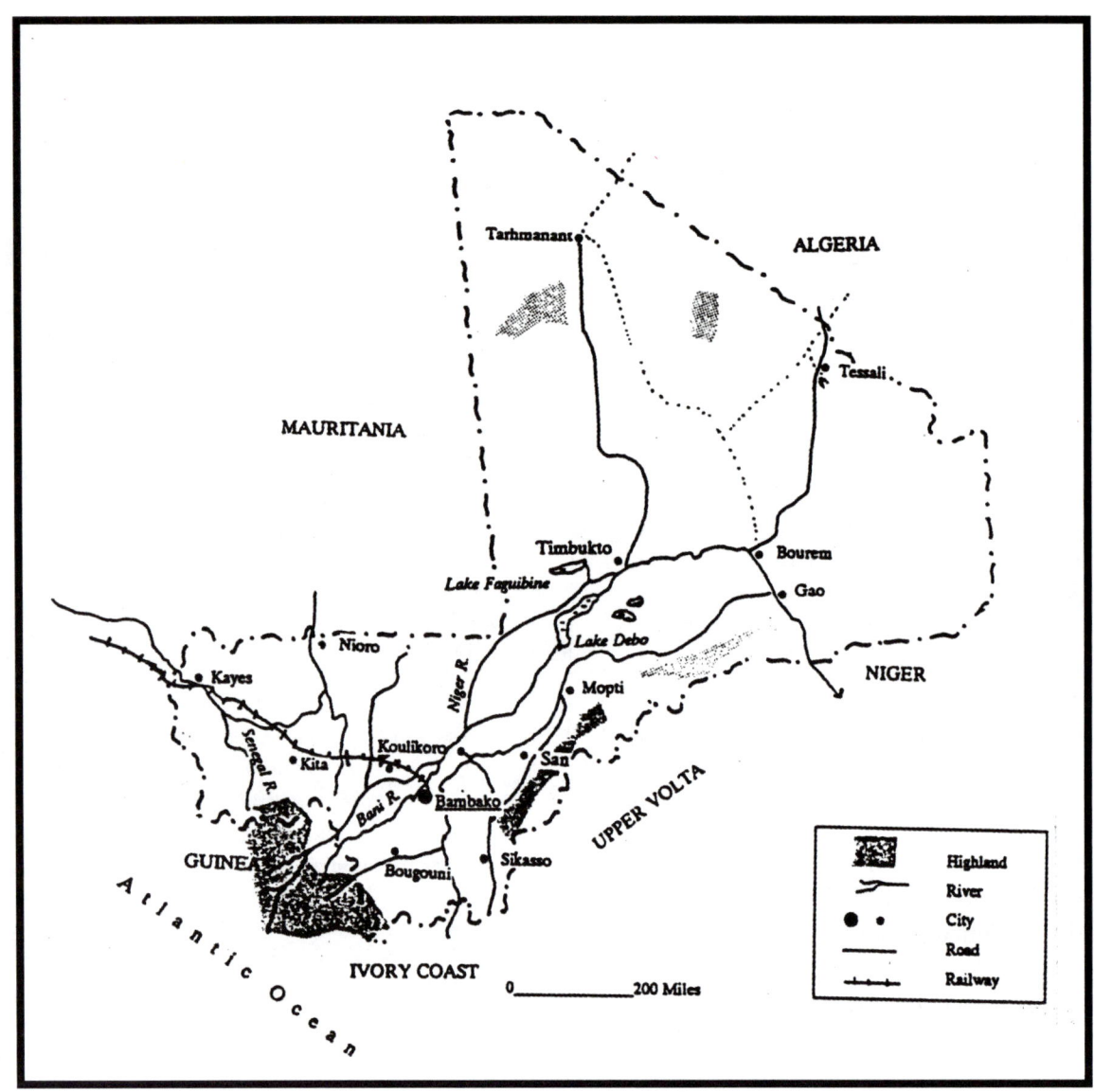

Map 32: Mali

EVOLUTION OF MALI

The Malinke Kingdom of Mali had its origins in the 11th century on the upper Niger River. Rapidly expanding in the 13th century under the leadership of Soundiata Keita, it reached its height about 1325 AD, when it conquered Timbuktu and Gao. Thereafter, the kingdom began to decline, and by the 15th century, it controlled only a fraction of its former domain.

During the period from 1465 to 1530, the Songhai Empire expanded from its center in Gao. Under Askia Mohammad I, it conquered the Hausa states as far as Kano (in present day Nigeria) and much of the territory of Mali Empire in the west. It was destroyed by a Moroccan invasion in 1591.

French military penetration began around 1880. Ten years later, the French made a concerted effort to occupy the interior. A French civilian governor of Soudan (French name of the area) was appointed in 1893, but resistance to French control did not end until 1898. The French attempted to rule indirectly, but in many ways, they downgraded the traditional authorities. As part of the colony of Soudan, Mali was administered with other French colonial territories as the Federation of French West Africa.

In January 1959, Soudan joined Senegal to form the Mali Federation, which became fully independent within the French Community on June 20, 1960. The Federation collapsed on August 20, 1960, when Senegal seceded. On September 22, Soudan proclaimed itself the Republic of Mali and withdrew from the French community.

On November 19, 1968, a group of young officers staged a bloodless coup. These military leaders renounced socialism. A constitution was approved in 1974, but Mali continued to suffer from political instability. On June 8, 1992 new elections were held to bring democracy and stability to the country.

PEOPLE AND POPULATION

Mali's population consists of diverse, sub-Saharan ethnic groups, sharing similar historic, cultural, and religious traditions. Exceptions are the Tuaregs and Maurs, desert nomads, related to the North African Berbers. The Tuaregs traditionally have opposed the central government. Starting in June 1990, armed attacks in the North by Tuaregs and bandit groups led to clashes against the military in an effort to gain greater autonomy. In April 1992, the government and most opposing factions signed a pact to end the fighting and restore stability in the north. Its major aims are to allow greater autonomy to the north and increase government resource allocation to what has been a traditionally impoverished region.

Historically, good inter-ethnic relations throughout the rest of the country were facilitated by easy mobility on the country's vast savannas. Each ethnic group was traditionally tied to a specific occupation, all working within close proximity. The Bambara, Malinke, Sarakole, and Voltaic were farmers; the Peuth, Moor, and Tuareg, herders; and the Bazo, fishers. In recent years, this linkage has shifted as ethnic groups seek diverse, non-traditional sources of income. Along the Niger River between Timbuktu and Gao, the Songhal farm and fish. Until droughts in the mid-1970s, the Tuaregs were the principal herders in this region.

Although each ethnic group speaks a separate language, nearly 80% of Malians communicate in Bambara, the common language of the market place. Malians enjoy a relative harmony rare in African states.

ECONOMY

Mali's potential wealth lies in mining and in the production of agricultural commodities, livestock, and fish. Agricultural activities occupy 75% of Mali's labor force and provide 40% of the GDP.

Agriculture

Mali is 1.5% arable, 3.7% woodland, 7% grazing land, 27% sub-desert, and 60.3% desert. Of the arable land, 80% is devoted to food production, 8.6% for peanuts, and 3.2% for cotton cultivation. The productivity of the traditional cultivation is low, as is the ratio of cultivated to cultivable land.

Nomadic herding is the main element of the economy, with about five million cattle, ten million sheep and goats and 165,000 camels at its peak. In the 1960s, live animals invariably provided the leading export in terms of value, with cattle moving by road or railroads to Ivory Coast, Senegal, and other neighboring countries. Kayes, Bamako, and Mopti are large cattle centers. In the drought of 1970-72, 40% of Mali's herds were lost, disrupting the herding economy. Animals that survived were taken by herdsmen to the south. In 1984, it was reported that 1.6 million heads of cattle converged on to the Mopti region where there was grazing for half the number. Herds that had been greatly depleted at the height of the drought were restocked by 1982, only to be reduced again in 1983-84. The largest concentrations of cattle are in areas north of Bamako and Segou, extending into the Niger delta. However, herding activity is shifting to the south, due to the effects of previous droughts. Sheep, goats, and camels are raised to the exclusion of cattle in the dry areas north of Timbuktu.

The most productive agricultural area lies along the banks of the Niger River between Bamako and Mopti and extends south to the borders of Cote d'Ivoire and Burkina Faso. This area is most important for the production of cotton, millet, corn, vegetables, tobacco, and tree crops. Peanuts are grown throughout the country but are concentrated in the area around Kita, west of Bamako. Before independence, peanut cultivation was an important activity, especially from Bamako to Kayes, but it lost its primacy after the 1960s.

The Niger River is also an important source of fish, providing food for riverine communities; the surplus is smoked, salted, dried, and then exported. Due to drought and diversion of river water for agriculture, fish production has steadily declined since the early 1980s. Sorghum is planted extensively in the drier parts of the country and along the banks of the Niger in eastern Mali, as well as the lake beds in the Niger delta region.

Minerals and Industry

Mining is a rapidly growing industry in Mali, with gold accounting for 80% of mining activity. There are considerable proven reserves of other minerals also, which are not presently exploited. Gold has become Mali's third largest export, after cotton and livestock. In Mali, the largest private investment in gold mining is BHP Minerals, a multinational American-Australian company. An agreement was signed in 1992 for an expansion of the company's mine at Syama in southern Mali.

During the colonial period, private capital investment was virtually nonexistent, and public investment was devoted largely to the Office du Niger irrigation scheme and to administrative expenses. Following independence, Mali built some light industries with the help of various donors. Manufacturing, consisted principally of processed agricultural products like peanut oil mills, sugar refinery, cotton and textile mills, meat processing, fruit conservancy, tobacco, and others. The industries accounted for about 8% of the GDP. As a landlocked country, industrial development is hampered by the distance and cost of transportation to external markets.

──────────────── **NOTES** ────────────────

NOTES

CHAPTER 30
MAURITANIA

Islam was introduced in Mauritania by the Berber tribes in the 11th century AD. The Berbers traveled widely across the desert, which led them to develop trading towns and religious centers. Today, almost the entire population in Mauritania is Muslim.

GEOGRAPHY

The vast, Islamic Republic of Mauritania is situated in Northwest Africa. It is larger than France and Spain combined and occupies the Atlantic facade of the Sahara Desert from the Senegal River northwards to Cape Blanc. It is bounded by Senegal in the south, Mali in the south and east, Algeria in the northeast and Western Sahara in the northwest (Map 33). There are three distinct geographic regions in Mauritania: (i) in the south is a narrow belt along Senegal River Valley, where soils and climatic conditions permit settled agriculture; (ii) in the center is a broad, central east-west band characterized by vast sand plains and fixed dunes held in place by sparse grass and trees; and (iii) in the north is an arid region which fades into the Sahara Desert and is characterized by shifting dunes, rock outcrops, and rugged mountainous plateaus with elevations of more than 1,500 feet (456 m) (Map 33).

The climate is hot throughout Mauritania. In most of the country, daytime temperatures exceed 100°F (38°C) for more than half of the year, but the cool nights bring relief. In the south it is cooler, with a little difference between day and night temperatures. Rainfall is limited and concentrated in the south from July through October. There is no permanent surface water, but

> **Geographical Profile**
>
> **Area:** 419,212 sq. mi. (1,085,760 sq. km)
> **Population:** 2.2 million (1994); 2.6 million (2000); 3.5 million (2010)
> **Capital:** Nouadhibou
> **Other Cities:** Kaedi Zouerate; Kiffa; Rosso
> **Terrain:** Northern four-fifths barren desert; southern 20% mainly Sahelian landscape
> **Climate:** Predominantly hot and dry
> **Ethnic Groups:** Arab-Berber, Arab-Berber-Negroid, Negroid
> **Religion:** Sunni Islam
> **Languages:** Arabic (official), Hassaniya Arabic, French, Pular, Wolof, and Soninke
> **Economy:**
>   **GDP:** $1 billion (1990)
>   **Per Capita Income:** $520
>   **Natural Resources:** Iron ore, gypsum, fish
>   **Agriculture:** Products: Livestock, millet, corn, wheat, dates, rice
>   **Industry:** Types: Iron mining, fish processing
> **Official Name:** Islamic Republic of Mauritania
> **Date of Independence:** September 1958

depressions may hold some moisture, and capillary action produces salt pans at the surface. Annual rainfall of less than 4 inches (100 mm) prevails over some two-thirds of the country, mainly in the north and east.

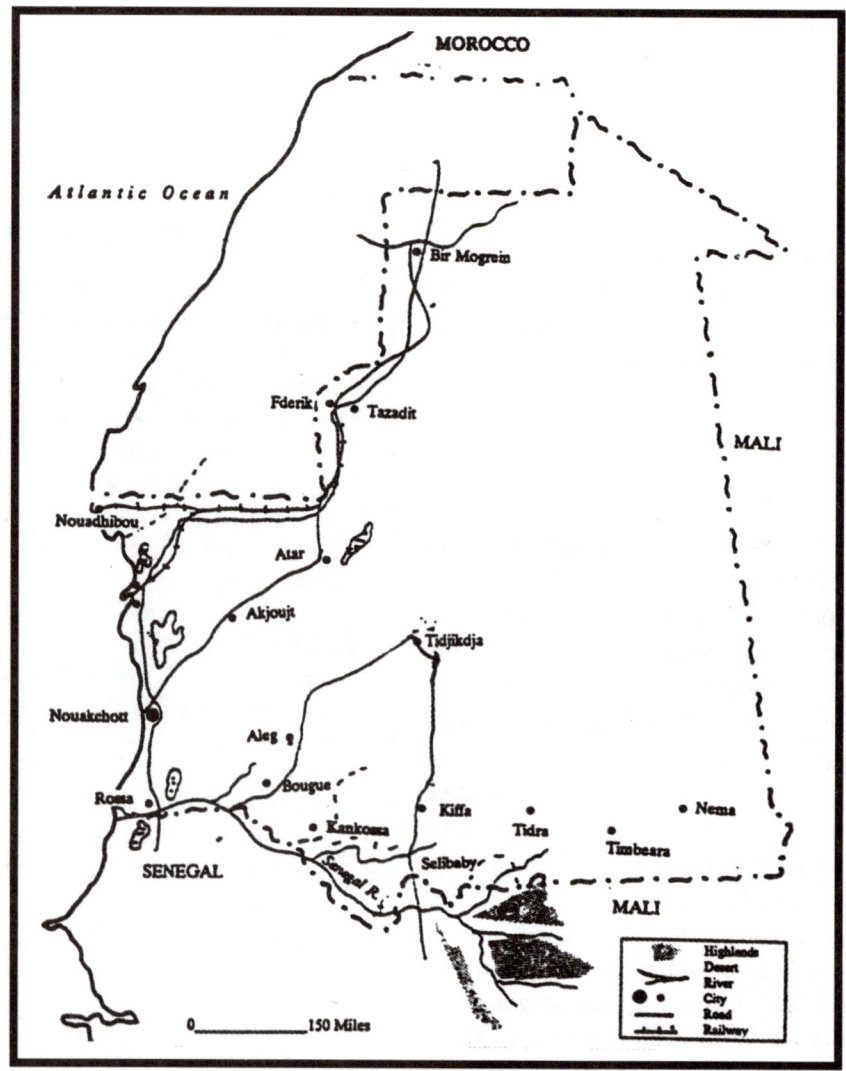

Map 33: Mauritania

PEOPLE AND POPULATION

Eight percent of the people of Mauritania are Moors of Arab-Berber descent who speak dialects of Hassaniya Arabic. Social status is determined by either Arab-Berber or caucasoid-negroid origins. In general terms, the society is divided as Moorish "white" and Berber "black." Non-Moors, non-Arabs, or Berber-speaking black Africans, including the Toucouleur, Fulbe, Wolof, and Banbara people, comprise about 20% of the population and live in the south. About three-quarters of the population are of Arab-Berber stock, divided into a superior Bidan group and an inferior group along the Senegal River.

As a result of recent endemic drought, large numbers of former nomads and oasis dwellers have migrated to urban areas (Nouakchott, Nouadhibou, Kaedi, and Rosso), swelling the population of the cities and the surrounding shanty towns. In a country where two-thirds of the population is nomadic, taking census is not easy. But in 1994, the population of Mauritania was estimated at 2.2 million. Large parts of the north and east are virtually uninhabited. In the south are negro peoples who are mainly sedentary cultivators.

EVOLUTION OF MAURITANIA

In Mauritania, the migration of people increased in the third and fourth centuries AD, when Berber groups arrived from the north, seeking pasture for their herds and safety from war. The use of the camel allowed them to travel widely across the expanding desert, leading to the development of a caravan trade system. Gold, slaves, and ivory went north; whereas salt, copper, cloth, and other items came to Timbuktu (presently in Mali) and beyond in the south. Important trading towns were established wherein people readily accepted Islam. In the 11th century AD, the conquest of western Sahara regions by the Al-Murabitun, a Berber tribe, firmly established Islam throughout Mauritania. Al-Murabitun tribes were then defeated by the Arab Moors, led by Beni Hassanm in the 16th century.

Descendants of the Arab warriors became the upper stratum of Moorish society, and Arabic generally displaced Berber dialects as the language of the country. Beneath the Hassan tribes were the Marabout tribes, whose leading figures served as the teachers of Islamic tradition. Some of the more important Marabouts (Sufi holy men) founded *tariqats* (brotherhoods), whose influence extended well beyond their tribe.

The French proclaimed a protectorate over the "Moorish country" in 1903 and declared it a colony in 1920 but the area was not brought under French control until about 1934. Until independence, the French governed the country largely by relying on the authority of the tribal chiefs. The colony area was increased substantially in 1945, when the Hodh region of French Soudan (now Mali) was administratively transferred to Mauritania. Certain parts of this territory were ceded back to Mali in territorial adjustments in 1964.

The colonial period had enormous consequences for relations between and among Mauritania's various ethnic groups. Under French occupation, slavery was legally abolished, and the payment of tribute was either reduced or eliminated, but Mauritanians continued to accept the notion of a servile class even after independence. Slavery was again abolished in 1980, but the social status and economic situation of freed slaves have not improved much.

The French occupation also led to a return of sedentary negroid people across the Senegal River into southern Mauritania, an area from which they had been expelled gradually in earlier years by the warlike Maure nomads. To this day, conflict between Moor and non-Moor ethnic groups, centering on language, land tenure, and other issues, continues to be the dominant challenge to national unity.

Mauritania became independent in 1960. It withdrew from the French Community in 1966. The Islamic Republic of Mauritania was proclaimed in November 1968. Shortly thereafter, the process of transferring Mauritania's administrative services from Senegal to the new capital of Nouakchott began.

ECONOMY

Mauritania has a dual economy, with little interaction between the traditional and modern production sectors. Most Mauritanians are either nomadic herders or settled farmers who live within a subsistence economy. They occasionally supplement their incomes as wage earners or by selling produce in local markets. Livestock raising has traditionally generated about 24% of the GDP and involved nearly two-thirds of the total working population. However, since 1983, when about 80% of the pasture lands were lost to the desert, livestock were decimated. Estimates for total herds for 1990 are 1.4 million cattle, 8.5 million sheep and goats, and 950,000 camels. Camels are dominant in the central part of the country, cattle in the south, and sheep and goats in the north.

Agriculture

Mauritania's agricultural sector has also been devastated by a series of droughts that have left the country heavily dependent on food aid. Even after relatively abundant rainfall in 1989-90, Mauritania grew only 37% of its cereal needs. Some wheat, tobacco and vegetables are grown in the shade of the date palms. Date production is confined to the oasis areas (principally those of Atar, Tidjika and Kiffra), but it has always been a minor export.

Gum arabica was collected from acacia trees mainly in the southern part of the country, and exports reached 5000 tons in 1968. The drought has reduced acacias by about two-thirds in a zone within 65 miles (100 km) of the Senegal River.

The cool offshore waters provide valuable fishing grounds, traditionally fished by Canary Islanders, many of whom based their operations and landed their catch at Nouadhibou (formerly Port Etienne). Because of the over-fishing by trawlers in Northwest Africa, the government of Mauritania has entered into a fishery conservation agreement with neighboring countries. The government is also encouraging marine research and has signed an agreement with Algeria. Mauritania's Higher Institute of Fish Farming in Nouadhibou will undertake joint projects with the Algerian National Institute of Mauritania Sciences and Territorial Development. The total fish catch was 99,000 metric tons, which dropped to 98,000 metric tons in 1988, and to 93,000 metric tons in 1989. The very low relative humidity and almost complete lack of rain made simple sun-drying an effective form of processing. Dried fish was exported as far as Gabon and the Congo. Many other countries have started fishing in Mauritania's waters, but arrangements have been that they also land and process their fish at Nouadhibou. About a half-dozen fishing companies have been set up for this purpose and exports reach to respectable figures in good years. In addition, there is fishing in the Senegal River and its tributaries.

Minerals and Industries

One of Mauritania's most important natural resources is the high-grade iron ore. To exploit this resource at F'Derick, the Miferma Iron Company went into production in 1963. The mining concessions were controlled by French, British, Italians, Germans, and local interests that were nationalized in 1974. There are other mines near the north-central town of Zouerate. The semi-autonomous mining company *Societe Nationale Industrielle et Miniere* (SNIM) exploits these deposits. This high-grade iron ore is the country's leading export.

Industry (including mining, manufacturing, construction, and power) provided 24% of Gross Domestic Product in 1989. An estimated 8.9% of the labor force was employed in industrial sectors in 1980. During 1980-89, industrial Gross Domestic Product increased by an annual average rate of 5.2%. The manufacturing sector contributed 5.4 percent of the Gross Domestic Product in 1987. Fish processing is the most important activity.

In 1991, work began on another large high-grade iron deposit at M'Haoudhat and a small deposit in the original Kedia group of mines. Exports of copper concentrates from a mine located at Akjouji began in April 1971, but declining world copper prices and technical difficulties led to the mine's takeover by the government in 1975. Three years later, the government discontinued exploitation of the mine. In the early 1980s, efforts by an Arab consortium of Kuwait, Saudi Arabia, Qatar, and Abu Dhabi tried to revive the mine but failed. However, in April 1992, a joint venture with an Australian company was inaugurated in Akjoujt for reprocessing the old copper mine debris for gold. This is leading to the resumption of copper mining. The mine at Akjoujt is linked by road with the state's capital, Nouakchott, where the Peoples Republic of China built a new harbor and gave technical assistance in the construction of cement works and sugar refinery.

Years of drought in the 1970s and 1980s have brought Mauritania to the edge of financial collapse. Drought reduced livestock population and domestic food production, forcing hundreds of thousands of Mauritanians to forsake traditional activities and migrate to urban areas. Participation in the Western Sahara War, from 1975 to 1978, proved a costly debacle. Declining commodity prices undermined the country's mineral industry. The external factors were compounded by inappropriate macro economic policies that discouraged exports and agricultural production. The future of the country looks bleak unless the world situation improves for the better.

NOTES

CHAPTER 31
MOROCCO

Three major Berber groups inhabited Morocco when the Arabs came in the 7th and 11th centuries. With the fusion of Berbers and Arabs, the Islamic faith created a new order in Morocco. It was from Morocco that Islam was also introduced in Europe.

GEOGRAPHY

Morocco, or *El-Maghreb El-Aqsa*, is the only country that borders the Mediterranean Sea and Atlantic coasts. *Jabal al-Tariq* (Strait of Gibraltar) separates it from Europe by about 12 miles (18 km). On the east it is bordered by Algeria, and on the south, by Western Sahara. Its frontier with Algeria is desert and has never been defined exactly, although Morocco and Algeria signed a border agreement in 1977 (Map 34). Morocco claims the Western Sahara as an integral part of the country. The United States and many other nations do not recognize Morocco's claim, considering that the issue of sovereignty remains to be determined.

On the basis of topography, climate, and way of life, Morocco can be divided into four distinctive parts: Atlantic Morocco, Western Sahara, the Atlas Mountains, and the plateau land to the east. Atlantic Moroccan plains fronting the 350 miles (560 km) in the northwest are agriculturally productive. They are the most densely populated, most advanced

---

Geographical Profile

Area: 172,413 sq. mi. (446,550 sq. km)
Population: 27.7 million (1994); 32.0 million (2000); 32.0 million (2010)
Capital: Rabat
Other Cities: Casablanca, Marrakech, Fez, Tangier
Neighboring Countries: Western Sahara, Mauritania, Algeria
Terrain: Coastal plain, mountains, desert
Climate: Mediterranean and desert
Ethnic Groups: Arab-Berber
Languages: Arabic (official), French, three Berber languages
Religion: Sunni Islam (99.97%), Jewish and Christian .03%
Economy:
   GDP: $18.7 billion (1988)
   Per Capita Income: $770 (1988)
   Natural Resources: Phosphate, fish, iron, manganese, lead, cobalt, silver, copper
   Agriculture: Product: Wheat, barley, citrus fruits, wine, vegetables, olives, livestock, fishing
   Industry: Types: Phosphate mining, manufacturing and handicrafts, construction and public works, energy
Official Name: Kingdom of Morocco
Date of Independence: March 2, 1956

economically, and most "Arab" in their landscape. Most of Morocco's major cities are in this area, cut off from the interior by the encircling mountains in the east and south. Peaks of the High and Middle Atlas ranges reach 15,100 ft. (4,650 m) above sea level, and peaks of the Rif Massif rise sharply from the coast to 7,840 ft. (2,150 m) above sea level.

Beyond the mountains are a series of arid, rolling plateaus in the eastern part of Morocco, forming a continuation of the Algerian high plateaus, gradually dipping into the Sahara Desert in the south and southeast. This area has scattered oases along the Draa and Souss Rivers. The Moroccan rivers are large and run for a longer period in the year; some are perennial and many reach the sea. The oases have spawned numerous migrations across the mountains into inner Morocco, and several of the ruling dynasties rose from these mountains.

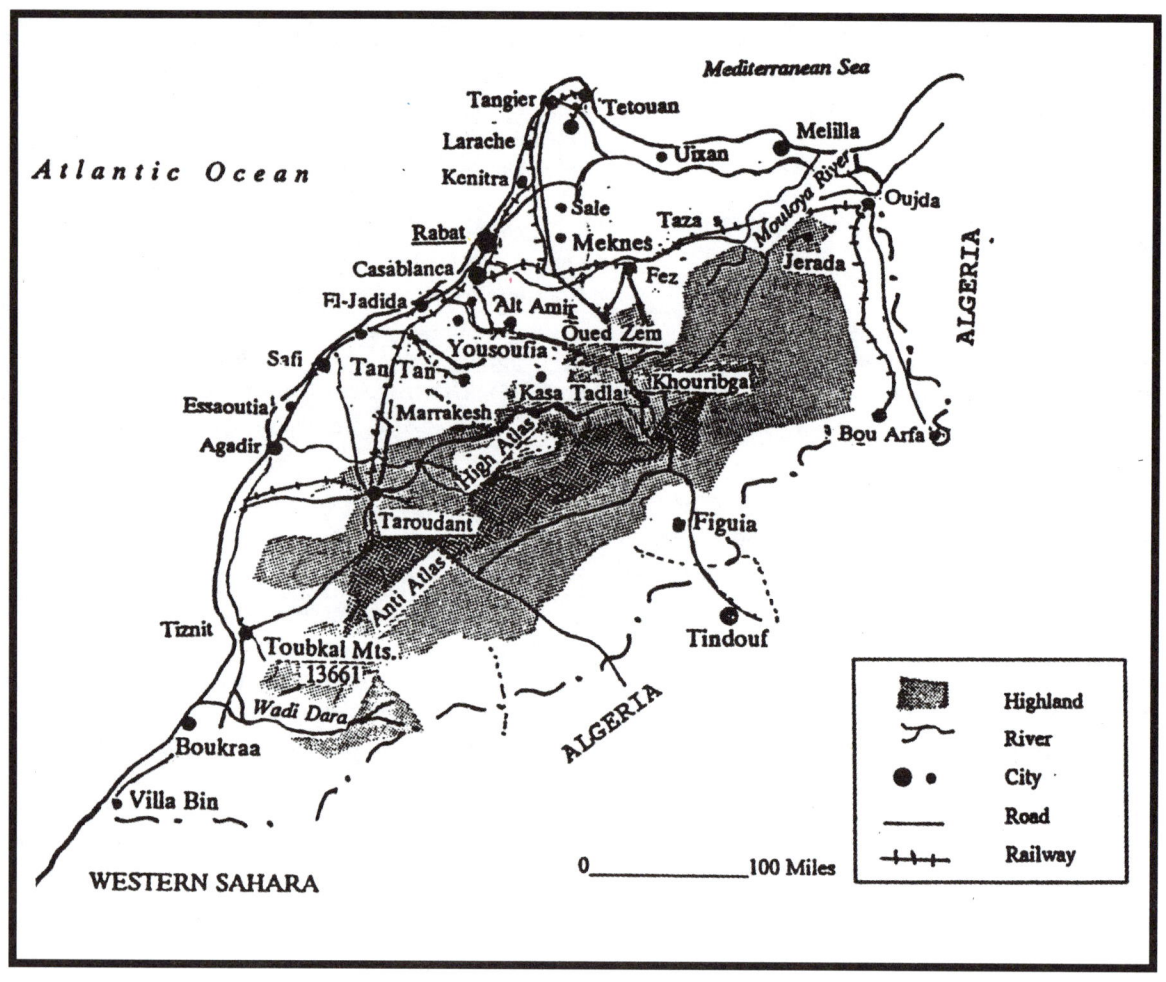

Map 34: Morocco

Morocco has been called "a cold country with a hot sun." The interior climate becomes increasingly extreme in temperature with sudden variations. The mild, semitropical climate on the coast becomes a desert climate beyond the mountains. The desert blooms in March. From April to October is usually a dry season.

PEOPLE AND POPULATION

Most people in Morocco are Muslims of Arab, Berber, or mixed Arab-Berber stock. Morocco's Jewish minority numbers about 12,000 people, and they have lived peacefully among their Arab neighbors. About 100,000 foreign residents are French or Spanish, most of who work as teachers or technicians. Most people live west of the Atlas Mountains, a range that insulates the country from the Sahara Desert. Casablanca is the center of commerce and industry and the leading port. Rabat is the seat of government; Tangiers is the gateway to Morocco from Spain and also a major "port." "Arab" Fez is the cultural and religious center, and "Berber" Marrakech is a major tourist center (Fig. 45).

Fig. 45: Hotel Mamoura, Marrakech, Morocco

The principal language is Arabic, although Berber dialects are spoken widely in rural areas. The division between Berbers and Arabs is very subtle. Physically, the two people are scarcely distinguishable, although European features are somewhat more evident among the non-Arabs. The greatest number of Berbers is in the interior of Morocco, with other concentrations on the coastal highlands of Algeria. Recent archaeological and geographical research has shown that Berber people were quite thickly settled on the Saharan Atlas.

In 1994, the population of Morocco stood at 27.7 million, with a highly uneven distribution. Most of the people live west of the Atlas Mountains, which covers almost one-third of the country and supports nearly two-fifths of the population.

EVOLUTION OF MOROCCO

Morocco's strategic location has shaped much of its history. Many people came to this area to trade or settle, while others came as invaders to dominate it. Romans, Vandals, Visigoths, and Byzantine Greeks successively ruled the area. Arabs came in the seventh century AD and brought with them the Arabic civilization and Islam. The Alawid dynasty, which has ruled Morocco since 1649, claims direct descent from the fourth *khalifah*, 'Ali.

Morocco's location and resources led to early competition among European powers in Africa, beginning with successful Portuguese efforts to control the Atlantic coast in the 15th century. France showed a strong interest in Morocco as early as 1830. Following recognition by the United Kingdom in 1904 of France's "sphere of influence" in Morocco, Algeria's Conference (1906) formalized France's "special position" and entrusted policing of Morocco to France and Spain jointly. The Treaty of Fez (1912) made Morocco a protectorate of France. By the same time, Spain assumed the role of protecting power over the northern and southern (Saharan) zones.

The first nationalist movements for independence based their arguments on the Atlantic Charter, a joint statement issued by U.S. President Franklin Roosevelt and British Prime Minister Winston Churchill that set forth the right of all people to choose the form of government under which they will live. Following this joint statement, one of the first demands for independence was made in 1944. Morocco was granted independence on March 2, 1956, as a kingdom. By agreements with Spain in 1956 and 1958, control over certain Spanish-ruled areas was restored to Morocco. On October 29, 1956, the signing of the Tangier Protocol politically reintegrated the former international zone. Spain, however, retained control over the small enclaves of Cueta and Melilla in the north, and the enclave of Ifni in the south. Ifni became a part of Morocco in 1969, following efforts by King Muhammad V (Fig. 46).

ECONOMY

Morocco is rich in human and natural resources and is beginning to develop a socioeconomic structure. Like most developing nations, its economy has two distinct and unequal parts. Traditional economy is based on agriculture. The modern economy dates back to French occupation, investment, and settlements. The modern economy accounts for over two-thirds of the country's total production.

Fig. 46: Mausoleum of King Mohammad V, Rabat

Agriculture

Agriculture is crucial to the economy of Morocco. It employs about 50 percent of the work force, produces about four-fifths of the nation's food requirements, and contributes nearly one-third of the total exports. There are two types of farming: the large traditional agriculture and the smaller modern sector, derived from the European settlement and concerned with cash and export crops. The climate, particularly rainfall, influences the pattern of agriculture and leads to considerable fluctuations in yields from year to year. The Atlantic seaboard and mountain valleys are the scenes of cultivation and settled ways of life. As the rainfall diminishes from north to south and from east to west, the emphasis on stock-rearing increases under semi-nomadic or nomadic regimes.

The traditional agriculture is concerned with producing basic foods, and some 80 percent of the cultivated land is under wheat and barley. In recent years, increasing quantities of food have been imported. Arable agriculture, with permanent settlements, lies mainly in the better-watered northern half of the Atlantic plain, with irrigation at the foot of the mountains. In the semi-arid steppe areas, the ground is scratched, rather than ploughed, and cereals planted. The bulk of the population seeks summer pastures for the sheep and goats. There are also similar movements within the mountains. There are rich reserves of fish in the cold water of the Canary current, off Morocco's coast, but these are mainly exploited by foreign fleets. The principal varieties caught are the sardine, bonito, and yunny. The nearly 1,200 mile long (1950 km) coastline along the Mediterranean Sea and Atlantic Ocean is one of the world's richest fishing grounds.

Minerals and Industry

Mining is an important industry in Morocco. It is efficiently organized for an export market, and minerals account for 16 percent of total exports by value. The principal mineral is phosphate of lime, and Morocco is the world's leading exporter and third producer after United States and former Soviet Union. Other minerals are coal, iron ore, lead, zinc, and manganese. Iron ore is mined at Uixan and Ait Amir, and coal comes from Djerada in eastern Morocco.

Since independence in 1956, there has been a substantial increase in industries. The modern industrial region is the Chaouma, which centers at Casablanca. About 70 percent of the industries are in and around this city. Many industries are associated with the country's primary production, and for the most part serve a home market. They include milling, brewing, tobacco manufacturing, soap and candle manufacturing, in addition to automobile assembly, plastics, cement, chemicals, and paper.

———————————— **NOTES** ————————————

CHAPTER 32
NIGER

The landlocked Republic of Niger is predominantly Muslim and, perhaps, the richest of the interior Sahelian countries, even though it was hit hard by the draught in the early 1970s. About 60% of its cattle and 28% of its sheep perished, and approximately one-quarter of its population either died or emigrated to neighboring states. During the extreme difficulties and severe drought stress, cultural pride gave courage and endurance to these people.

GEOGRAPHY

Niger lies on the southern edge of the Sahara Desert, 1,200 miles (1,900 km) from the Mediterranean and 1,000 miles (1,600 km) inland from the South Atlantic. It is a large country of 490,000 square miles (1,267,000 sq. km), with an extreme north-south extent of 750 miles (1200 km) and extreme east-west extent of 875 miles (1,400 km). In comparative terms, the country is three times the size of California. Niger is bordered on the north by Algeria and Libya, on the east by Chad, on the west by Mali and Burkina Faso, on the south principally by Nigeria, and for a short distance, by Benin (Map 35).

Two-thirds of the country is

Geographical Profile

Area: 490,000 sq. mi. (1,267,000 sq. km)
Population: 8.9 million (1994), 10.7 million (2000), 15.1 million (2010)
Neighboring Countries: Algeria, Libya, Chad, Nigeria, Benin, Burkina Faso, Mali
Capital: Niamey
Other Cities: Tahoua, Maradi, Zinder, Arlit, and Agadez
Terrain: About two-thirds desert and mountain; one-third savanna
Climate: Hot, dry, and dusty
Ethnic Groups: Hausa 50%; Djerma 22%; Fulani 8.5%; Tuareg 8%; Beri 3%, Arab, Toubou, and Gourmantche 1.2%
Religions: Predominantly Sunni Islam and some Christianity
Languages: French (official), Hausa, Djerma
Economy:
   GDP: $1.622 billion (1985)
   Per Capita Income: $265
   Natural Resources: Uranium, coal, iron, tin, phosphate
   Agriculture: Products: Millet, sorghum, peanuts, beans, cotton, rice, cowpeas
   Industry: Types: Textiles, cement, agricultural products
Official Name: Republic of Niger
Date of Independence: August 3, 1960

uninhabited desert, except for scattered oases and mining camps. The remainder is savanna land, suitable mainly for livestock and limited agriculture. The Niger River flows for 300 miles (480 km) along the southwest border, permitting the cultivation of rice and vegetables.

The climate is entirely Saharan and Sahelian: hot, dry, and dusty, especially in the months of April and May. Annual precipitation ranges between 4 to 32 inches (10 to 82 centimeters). Niamey, the capital, receives about 21.6 inches (550 mm) of rainfall. Further north, the rainfall drops to 13.7 inches (350 mm) in Tahouna, 5.9 inches (150 mm) in Agades, and gives a negligible amount north of Bilma. Water is scarce everywhere, except in the southwest. Artesian water has been developed in the Tahoua area and northwest of Lake Chad. Generally, men and animals depend on wells for over half the year.

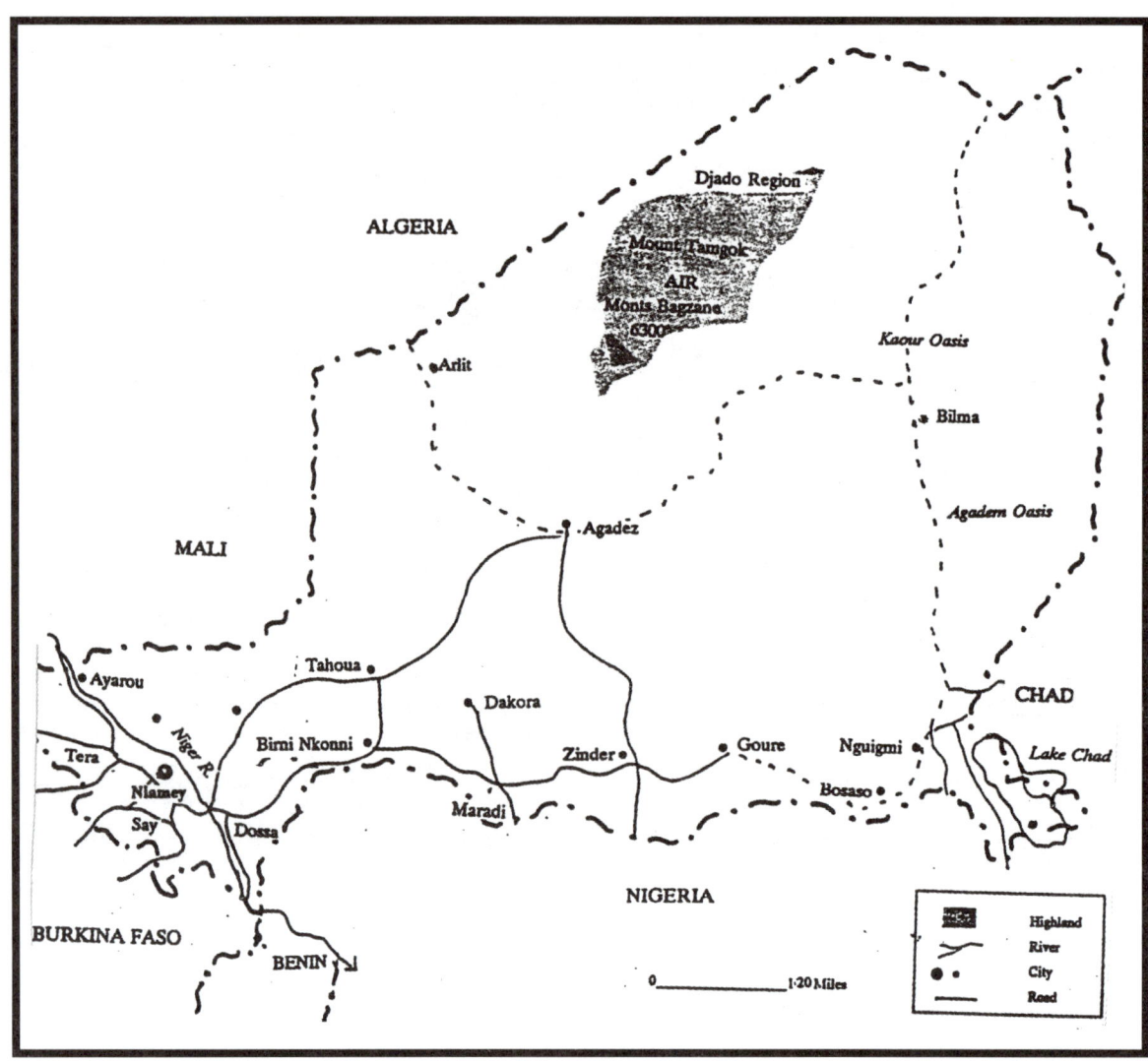

Map 35: Niger

PEOPLE AND POPULATION

About 96 percent of the population of Niger is rural, but only 3 percent of the land is cultivated. Two of the largest ethnic groups are the Hausa and the Djerma-Songhai. Both are sedentary farmers who live in the arable land in the south. Only in the extreme south, along the Niger River and in the Maradi District, is there permanent settlement. Agadez is the largest settlement in the Air Massif, where Tuaregs and other nomads keep considerable livestock in the vicinity. About 10% of the people are nomadic Fulani in the south and in the Sahara are Tuareg, Kanouri, and Toubou.

In 1994, Niger's population stood at 8.9 million with a 3.2% annual rate of natural increase. Life expectancy at birth was 45 years, and the doubling time of the population was 22 years. About 55% of the national area had only 2 percent of the population. Over 32 percent of the population was located in the extreme southwest, close to the Niger River, and a further 56 percent was dispersed along a fairly narrow zone including the towns of Taboua, Maradi, and Zinder, which are close to the Nigerian border.

EVOLUTION OF NIGER

During recent centuries, the nomadic Tuaregs formed the large confederations, pushed southward, and clashed with the Fulani Empire of Sokoto, which had gained control of much of the Hausa territory in the late 18th century. In the 19th century, contact with the West began when the British and Germans explored the area searching for the mouth of the Niger River. French efforts to control the North began before 1900, but dissident ethnic groups, especially the desert Tuaregs, could not be subdued until 1922, when Niger became a French colony.

Niger's colonial history and development parallel that of other French West African territories. French West Africa was administered from Paris through a governor general at Dakar, Senegal, and governors in the individual territories, including Niger. The 1946 French constitution, in addition to conferring French citizenship on the inhabitants of the territories, provided for decentralization of power and limited participation in political life for local advisory assemblies.

On December 4, 1958, Niger became an autonomous state within the French Community. On August 3, 1960, it became fully independent.

ECONOMY

Niger's economy grew rapidly from 1977 through 1980, but receded due to the falling prices of its minerals. Agriculture is the main occupation, but it is faced with the recurrent droughts.

Agriculture

Agriculture supports 90 percent of the population. In spite of successive droughts, Niger alone was self-sufficient in food among the Sahelian states in 1984. Domestic harvests in 1985 and 1986 were significantly better than 1984. In 1970, traditional agriculture and pastoralism accounted for two-thirds of the GDP. The principal food crops are millet and sorghum. However, it was badly affected in the drought of the early 1970s. In addition a widespread crop loss occurred due to disease and predators. Peanut production increased steadily in the 1960s and by 1969, accounted for 60 percent of the value of exports. Cotton cultivation was introduced in 1956, but production has increased only slowly. In recent years, peanut production and cotton have not been sufficient to keep local processing plants fully employed. Cowpea production has grown significantly, spurred by strong demand from Nigeria Government policy gives top priority to increased grain production to meet domestic needs. The rest of the economic support comes from livestock.

Minerals and Industries

Niger is rich in uranium. Its uranium production increased significantly between 1978 and 1981. This increase is attributable almost entirely to a second uranium mine at Akouta which opened in 1978. The mine is operated by a consortium that includes Nigeria, France, Japan, and Spain as partners. Niger's first mine, Arlit, is operated by another consortium with Nigerian, French, German, and Italian partners. Both mines are located in the remote, northern Air region near the town of Arlit. All uranium companies in Niger have been asked to help finance the Tahoua-Arlit "Uranium Road," an important part of the trans-Saharan route and a link to Niger's mineral-rich, isolated north.

Niger has tin, phosphate, copper, and iron ore reserves. The phosphate deposits in the Park W Game Reserves are being explored for possible commercial value, but copper and iron ore reserves are not commercially exploitable at this time. The demand for petroleum products, created by an expanding economy, makes Niger's oil exploration in the eastern Lake Chad area and northern Djado regions vital. To date, no oil has been found, but strikes in neighboring Chad offer some promise.

Niger receives substantial amounts of concessionary grant assistance. Major donors are France, the United States, the Federal Republic of Germany, Canada, Saudi Arabia, the European Community, the World Bank, and the United Nations Development Fund.

CHAPTER 33
NIGERIA

When Nigeria achieved its independence in 1960, it consisted of more than 200 ethnic groups. These ethnic groups had their own religion and language. The Hausa and Fulani Muslims dominate the north, while Yorubas predominate the southwest. Ethnic and religious affiliations impede the economic and political progress.

GEOGRAPHY

Located on the west coast of the African continent, Nigeria is Africa's most populous state. It is bounded on the south by the Gulf of Guinea, and on the landward side by Cameroon, Chad, and Benin (Map 36). The environmental diversity of Nigeria is usually distinguished into four regions: (i) the hot, humid coastal belt of mangrove swamps; (ii) tropical rain forest and oil palm belt, 50 to 100 miles (80-160 km) wide; (iii) the high, relatively dry central plateau of open woodland and savanna 6,000-7,000 feet (1830 to 2150 m) above sea level; and (iv) semi-desert in the extreme north.

Nigeria has several navigable rivers, notably the Niger and Benue and the Cosba. The Niger and Benue Rivers form a Y-shaped system. The elevation pattern of most of Nigeria consists of a gradual rise from the coastal plain to the northern savanna regions, generally reaching an elevation of 1800 to 2100 ft. (600 to 700 m). Higher altitudes, reaching more than 4500 ft. (1200 m), are found in the isolated area of Jos plateau. The coastal plain

---

Geographical Profile

Area: 356,700 sq. mi. (923,768 sq. km)
Population: 95.6 million (1994); 113.9 million (2000); 152.2 million (2010)
Neighboring Countries: Cameroon, Chad, Niger, Benin
Capital: Lagos
Other Cities: Ibadan, Kano, Enugu
Ethnic Groups: 250 tribal groups; Hausa, Fulani, Ibo, Yoruba are the largest
Religions: Sunni Islam 51%, Christianity, Indigenous Paganism
Languages: English (official), Hausa, Yoruba, and Ibo
Economy:
  GDP: $28 billion (1989)
  Per Capita Income: $390
  Natural Resources: Petroleum, tin, columbite, iron ore, coal, limestone, zinc
  Agriculture: Products: Cocoa, palm oil, yams, cassava, sorghum, millet, corn, rice, livestock, peanuts, cotton
  Industry: types: Textiles, cement, food products, footwear, metal products, lumber, beer, car assembly
Official Name: Nigeria
Date of Independence: October, 1960

region penetrates inland for about 50 miles (75 km) in the west, but extends further in the east. The eastern and western sections of the coastal plain are separated by the Niger Delta, which extends over an area of 3860 square miles (10,000 sq. km). Much of this area is a swampland, separated by numerous islands. Separating the two segments of the coastal plain and extending to the northeast and northwest are the broad river basins of the Niger and Benue Rivers. To the north of the Niger and Benue basins are the broad, stepped plateau and mountains that characterize much of northern Nigeria.

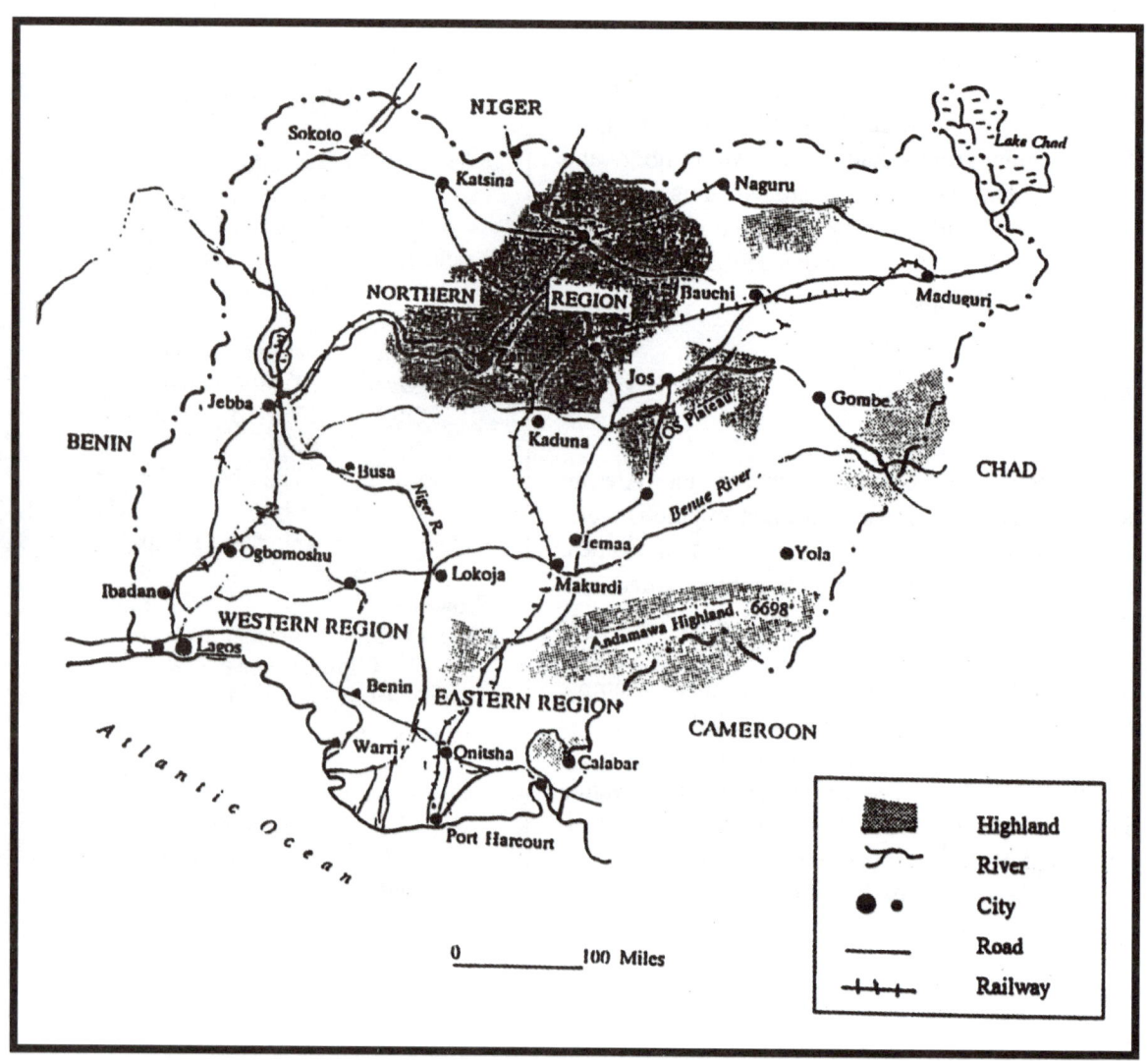

Map 36: Nigeria

Nigeria's climate is characterized by strong latitudinal zones, becoming progressively drier as one moves north from the coast. Rainfall is the key climatic variable. Two air masses control rainfall - one from Atlantic ocean and the other from African land mass. In the coastal and southeastern portions of Nigeria, the rainy season usually begins in February or March. The peak of the rainy season occurs in August, when air from the Atlantic covers the entire country. From September through November, the country has clear skies, moderate temperatures, and lower humidity under the influence of northeast trade winds. From December through February, however, the northeast trades blow strongly and often bring with them a load of fine dust from the Sahara.

PEOPLE AND POPULATION

The ethnic variety of Nigeria's people is dazzling and confusing. The number of ethnic groups vary from 250 to 400. The most widely used marker is that of language. People who speak a distinct language are viewed as ethnically different. Markers other than language are also used to define ethnicity.

The people of the northern two-thirds Hausa region of Nigeria are Muslims. Smaller ethnic groups of the north include the Fulani, Nupe, Tiv, and Kanuri. Yoruba Muslims and Christians dominate the southeastern part of the country. Some of these people engage in traditional dancing even in the market places (Fig. 47). In the southeast are the Ibos. Most Ibos are Christians, who exercised great influence in trade, bureaucracy, and professions. Efika, Ibos, and Eastern Ijaws also are sizable groups in the area. Several smaller linguistic groups are found in the midwest such as the Benin and Western Ijawa. Communication between persons of varying ethnic backgrounds frequently takes place in English, although knowledge of two or more Nigerian languages is widespread.

Fig. 47: Traditional Dancing, Nigeria

EVOLUTION OF NIGERIA

The known history of Nigeria dates back to more than 2,000 years. At this time, the Nok culture in the present plateau state worked iron and produced sophisticated terra-cota. In the north, recorded history dates back to 1000 AD, where Islam came in the 11th century AD and penetrated toward the south.

In the southwest, the Yoruba kingdom of Oyo was founded in about 1400 AD, and at its height, from the 17th to 19th centuries, attained a high level of political organization. It encompassed a domain extending as far as modern Togo. During the 17th and 18th centuries, the impact of the slave trade and other factors produced stagnation and political disintegration. In the early 19th century, the Qadiri Sufi shaykh Usman dan Fodio launched a *jihad* in which he defeated the neo-pagan Hausa kingdoms. From the city of Sokoto, he controlled an empire that included 100,000 square miles (258,998 sq. km) in Northern Nigeria.

Following the Napoleon wars, the British expanded their trade with the Nigerian interior. In 1885, British claims to a sphere of influence in that area received international recognition. In 1886, the Royal Niger Company was chartered. In the 1890s the company's territory came under the control of the British government, which consolidated its hold over the area of modern Nigeria. In 1914, the area was formally united as the "Colony and Protectorate of Nigeria."

Administratively, Nigeria remained divided into the northern and southern provinces and Lagos colony. Following World War II, Nigerian nationalism grew and demands for independence intensified. Nigeria was granted full independence in October 1960 as a federation of three regions (Northern, Western and Eastern) under a constitution that provided a parliamentary form of government. In 1963, the country altered its relationship with the United Kingdom by proclaiming itself a federal republic and promulgating a new constitution. A fourth region (the Midwest) was established that year.

In 1966, the military, having control, gave greater autonomy to minority groups by replacing four regions with 12 states. The Ibo rejected attempts at constitutional revisions and insisted for full autonomy for the east. Finally, in May 1967, the military governor of the Eastern Region declared the independence as the "Republic of Biafra." The civil war that ensued was bitter and bloody, ending in the defeat of Biafra in 1970. Following the civil war, reconciliation was rapid and effective.

In July 1975, Gen. Murtala Muhammad staged a bloodless coup. The General replaced thousands of civil servants and announced a timetable for the resumption of civilian rule by October 1, 1979. He also announced the government's intention to create new states and to construct a new federal capital in the center of the country. General Muhammad was assassinated on February 13, 1976, and his chief of staff, Lt. Gen. Olusegun Obasanjo, became the head of the state. Seven new states were created by him in 1976, bringing the total to 19. Two more states were added in 1987. After 1987, the government changed a number of times, promulgating new constitutions.

ECONOMY

Prior to 1860, Nigeria was exporting slaves in large numbers, but in the middle of the nineteenth century, the palm-oil trade developed rapidly. In the beginning, palm nuts were gathered from wild trees and shipped to the port through inland waterways. The trade was so widespread that the east-central area became known as the "oil rivers."

Agriculture

After the 1880s, cocoa cultivation spread rapidly in the southwest, and the kola nut, a valued stimulant for West Africans, became important. Cultivation of this tree crop was encouraged by the extension of the railway inland from Lagos after 1898, and Lagos developed as the primary port, city, and economic center. In 1951, the railway reached Kano in the north, and the export of peanuts, which were grown for local consumption, increased. Cultivation has since declined because of drought and virus infection. Distinct export regions were developed in Nigeria: the palm-oil from the southeast, rubber and timber from the central-southern area, cocoa from the southwest and peanuts from the north. In addition to Lagos, Ibadan is an important city (Fig. 48).

Fig. 48: A General View of Lagos, Nigeria

Minerals and Industry

Oil exploration was first started in 1927, but the first significant reserves were found in 1956 at Olobiri near Port Harcourt. Onshore wells now account for 73 percent of the total and offshore wells for 27 percent. The oil boom shifted Nigeria from an agriculturally based economy to one that now relies on oil for more than 95% of export earnings. The greater opportunities made possible by the oil discovery induced massive rural-urban migration, which has had a devastating impact on agriculture. However, the country has experienced severe economic difficulties since 1982 because of the dramatic fall in export revenues and heavy debt service payments.

In 1980, industry accounted for only 5 percent of the GDP and consisted mainly of small-scale traditional crafts (wood, textiles, leather, and metal), food processing, vegetable oil, timber, and tobacco. Clearly, the economy has undergone considerable change since 1960, with agriculture declining giving way to oil exports.

──────────── **NOTES** ────────────

CHAPTER 34
OMAN

Islam was introduced in Oman during the lifetime of Prophet Muhammad. By the eight century, Ibadism, a form of Islam tracing its roots to the Khawarij movement, became a dominant religious sect in Oman.

GEOGRAPHY

Oman is located in the eastern part of the Arabian Peninsula (Map 37). The borders with Saudi Arabia and the United Arab Emirates are still undemarcated, while the border with Yemen is under dispute. Despite the fact that Oman's border is under dispute, the Sultan of Oman exercises jurisdiction over villages in the northwest Buraimi area. Oman faces the Gulf of Oman on the northeast and the Arabian Sea on the south, with a coastline of nearly 1,000 miles (1,600 km). Oman's territory also includes the tip of the strategically important Musandam Peninsula that juts into the Strait of Hormuz and is separated by the United Arab Emirates from the rest of Oman. Oman's geography also encompasses the island of Masirah off the eastern coast. While the country is not divided into precise districts, the following regions may be noted: the tip of the Musandam Peninsula, the Batinal coastal plain stretching south to Muscat, the Muscat-Matrah coastal area, the mountainous interior

Geographical Profile

Area: 82,000 sq. mi. (212,457 sq. km)
Population: 1.7 million (1994); 2.1 million (2000); 3.0 million (2010)
Neighboring Countries: United Arab Emirates, Saudi Arabia, Yemen.
Capital: Muscat
Other Cities: Matrah, Ruwi, Nizwa, Salalah, Sohar
Terrain: Mountains, Plains, and Plateau
Climate: Hot, humid along the coast; hot and dry in interior; summer monsoons in far north
Ethnic Groups: Arab, Balochi, Zanzibari, Indians, Pakistanis
Religion: Ibadi Islam, some Hinduism
Language: Arabic (official), English, Balochi, Urdu, Indian dialects
Economy:
  GDP: $7.3 billion (187)
  Per Capita Income: $5,600 (1986)
  Natural Resources: Oil, natural gas, copper, marble, limestone, gypsum, chromium
  Agriculture: Products: Dates, limes, bananas, mangoes, alfalfa, other fruits and vegetables, fisheries
  Industry: Types: Crude petroleum, fisheries, construction, petroleum refinery, copper mine and smelter, cement factory and various light industry
Official Name: Sultanate of Oman
Date of Independence: Independent since 1650

capped by the high Green Mountain region, the foothills and desert stretching south and west of these mountains, the Province of Dhofar in the far south, and the off-shore island of al-Masirah.

The summer season in Oman is hot and humid. Average low and high temperatures for January range between 65ºF to 77ºF (18ºC to 25ºC). Interior temperatures are higher, but the air is much drier. Annual rainfall averages 1.5 to 4 inches (4-9 cm) with wide fluctuations throughout the country. Dhofar experiences a strong monsoon from May to September, with frequent mists. Precipitation in several parts of the country is sufficient for cultivation without irrigation.

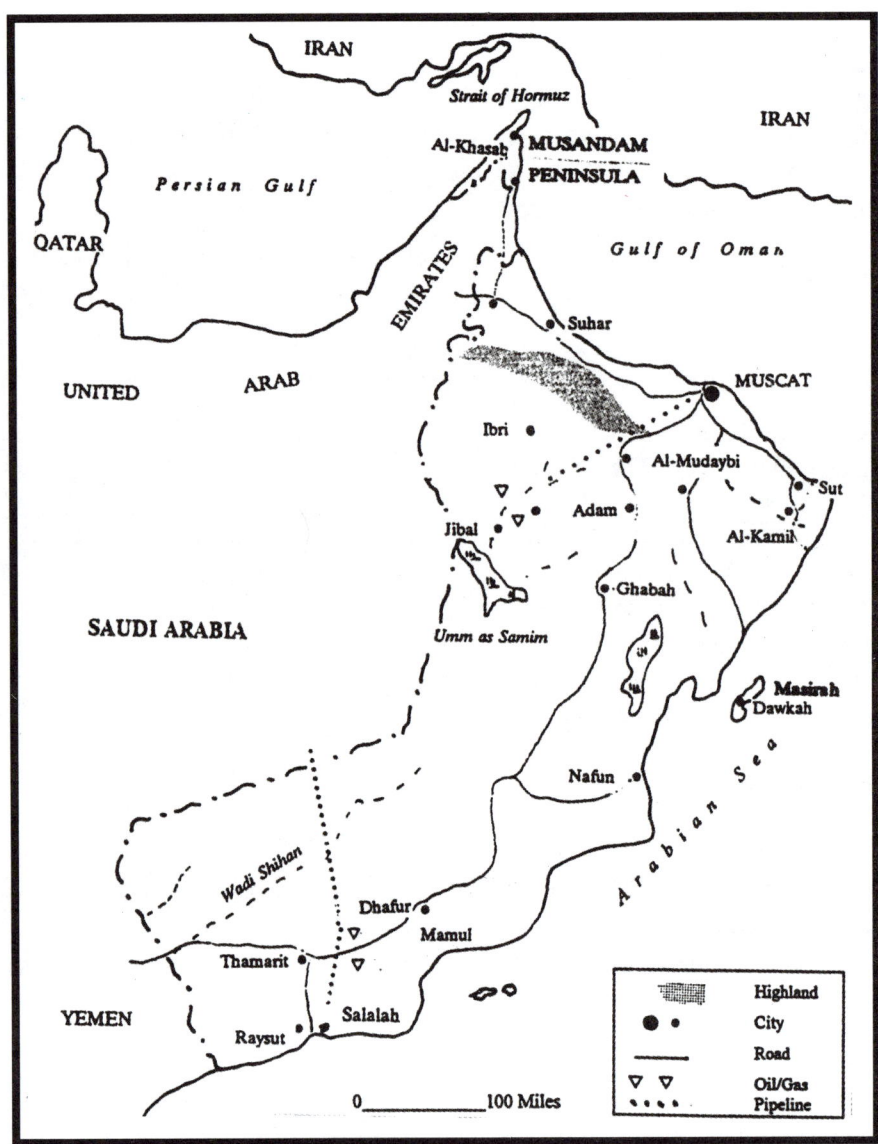

Map 37: Oman

PEOPLE AND POPULATION

Native Omanis are Arabs who dominate the population. About one-third of the population lives in Muscat and the Batinah Coastal Plain northwest of the capital; more than half the people live in small towns, primarily in the interior; some 60,000 live in the southern province of Dhofar, and about 15,000 live in the remote Musandam Peninsula on the Strait of Hormuz. Significant minorities of Iranians, Balochis, Indo-Pakistanis, and East Africans live along the northeast coast and are primarily merchants, soldiers, civil servants, and laborers. Foreigners comprise about 25% of the population and 50% of the nonagricultural work force. About 300,000 expatriates live in Oman, most of whom are guest workers from India, Pakistan, Bangladesh, Sri Lanka, Egypt, Jordan, and the Philippines.

In 1994, the population of Oman stood at 1.7 million, with a 3.5 percent annual rate of natural increase. With such a high rate of natural increase, the population is expected to double in 20 years.

EVOLUTION OF OMAN

In 1508, the Portuguese conquered parts of the coastal region of Oman. Their influence predominated for more than a century, with only a short interruption when the Turks ruled Oman. The fort built during the Portuguese occupation can still be seen in Muscat. After the Portuguese were expelled in 1650, Muscat and Oman extended their conquests to Zanzibar and other parts of the Eastern Peninsula. During this period, political leadership gravitated from the Ibadhi *imams*, who were elected religious leaders, to hereditary *sultans*, who established their capital in Muscat. By the early 19th century, Muscat and Oman was the most powerful state in Arabia and on the east coast of Africa. The Muscat rulers established trading posts on the Iranian coast and also exercised a measure of control over the Makran coast (now in Pakistan). Gawadar was the last remnant of the holding that was ceded to Pakistan in 1958.

Except for a brief period of Iranian rule, the country has remained independent since 1650. Muscat and Oman was the object of Franco-British rivalry throughout the 18th century. The British developed a paramount position in 1798 through an arrangement of friendship. Two years later, the *Sultanate* agreed to receive a resident British representative. During the 19th century, the British and Muscat and Oman concluded several treaties of friendship and commerce. A new treaty of friendship was signed in 1951 by which Britain recognized the *Sultanate* as a fully independent state.

When *Sultan* Sa'id Sayyid died in 1856, his sons quarreled over the successions. As a result of this struggle, the empire was divided in 1861 into two separate principalities - Zanzibar, with the East African dependencies, and Muscat and Oman. Zanzibar paid an annual subsidy to Muscat and Oman until it became independent in early 1954.

During the late 19th and early 20th centuries, the *Sultan* in Muscat faced rebellion by members of the Ibadhi sect residing in the interior who wanted to be ruled exclusively by their religious leader, the *Imam* of Oman. The conflict was resolved when the Imam was granted autonomy in the interior, while recognizing sovereignty of the *Sultan*.

In 1964, a separatist revolt began in Dhofar province. Aided by communist and separatist governments such as former South Yemen, the rebels formed Dhofar Liberation Front, which later merged with the Marxist-dominated Popular Front for the liberation of Oman and the Arab Gulf states. However, the movement was not successful. In 1970, the name of the country was changed to Oman.

ECONOMY

When Oman declined to be an entry port for arms and slaves in the mid-19th century, much of its former prosperity was lost. The economy relied almost exclusively on agriculture, camel and goat herding, and traditional handicrafts. Agriculture and fishing is the traditional way of life in Oman. Dates and limes, grown extensively in the Batinah Coastal Plain and the highlands, make up most of the country's agricultural exports. Coconut palms, wheat, and bananas also are grown and cattle are raised in Dhofar. Other areas grow cereals and forage crops. Poultry production is steadily rising. Fish and shellfish exports reached $25 million in 1988.

Oil and Modern Development

Oil was first discovered in the interior near Fahud in the western desert in 1964. Petroleum Development Oman Ltd. (PDO) began production in August 1967. Now 60% of its production is owned by the government and 40% by the Netherlands and France. With the collapse of oil prices in 1986, revenues dropped dramatically.

Oman does not have the immense oil resources, but they are the key to Oman's economy. In recent years, Oman has found more oil to last for about 20 more years. The outlook for further discoveries is promising. Natural gas reserves, which will increasingly provide fuel for power generation and desalination is also promising.

The government is undertaking many development projects to modernize the economy and improve the standard of living. Increase in agriculture, and especially fish production is believed possible with the application of modern technology. In the Muscat capital area, a modern international airport at Seeb and a deep-water port at Matrah have been constructed. An airport at Salalah at nearby Raysut has been completed. A national road network is being built, including a recently constructed highway linking the northern and southern regions. In an effort to diversify, the government built a copper mining and refining plant at Sohar. Marble, limestone, and gypsum may prove commercially valuable in the future.

CHAPTER 35
PAKISTAN

Pakistan is an acronym of five names, in which P is for Punjab, A for Afghana Province (Northwest Frontier Province), K for Kashmir, S for Sindh, and "Tan" for Balochistan. The letter I was added later for easier pronunciation to make it Pakistan. It was an idea in the 1930s, a goal in the 1940s, and became a reality on August 14, 1947. Pakistan, the only Muslim state created on the basis of ideology, represents a manifestation of Islam and its power to mobilize the Muslims to achieve a political goal.

GEOGRAPHY

In comparable terms, Pakistan is as large as France and Britain combined. The eastern limit of the Middle East is reached in Pakistan. In the southwest it is bordered by Iran and in the west and north, by Afghanistan. The boundary with India runs for about 800 miles (1,280 km). The southern province of Sindh is separated from the salt flats of the Rann (wilderness, or desolation) of Kutch. The Rann of Kutch boundary was demarcated by the Indo-Pakistan Western Boundary Tribunal in 1968. A narrow strip of Afghanistan, known as Wakhan peninsula, separates Pakistan from Tajikistan by 10 to 12 miles (16 to 19 km) at its narrowest point. In the northeast, Pakistan shares a common border with the Peoples Republic of China. The Arabian Sea and the Rann of Kutch form the southern boundary of Pakistan (Map 38).

Geographical Profile

Area: 310,527 sq. mi. (803,943 sq. km)
Population: 129.2 million (1994); 154.7 million (2000); 154.7 million (2010)
Neighboring Countries: India, Iran, China, Afghanistan
Capital: Islamabad
Other Cities: Karachi, Lahore, Faisalabad, Multan, Sukkur, Hyderabad, Peshawar, and Quetta
Ethnic Groups: Punjabi, Sindhi, Pathan, Baloch, Muhajirs
Religion: Islam 97% (Sunni 85%, Shi'ah 15%); small minorities of Christians, Hindus, and others
Economy:
  GDP: $43 billion
  Per Capita Income: $380 (1990)
  Natural Resources: Arable land, natural gas, limited petroleum, substantial hydropower potential, coal, iron ore
  Agriculture: (26% of GNP): Types: Wheat, cotton, rice, sugarcane
  Industry: (18% of GNP): Types: Textiles, fertilizer, steel products, food processing, oil, and gas products
Official Name: Islamic Republic of Pakistan
Date of Independence: August 14, 1947

Pakistan is composed of four federated provinces: Balochistan, Punjab, Sindh, and the Northwest Frontier Province. In addition, there is a federally administered tribal area adjacent to the Northwest Frontier Province, Northern Areas (former states of Gilgit, Chitral, Dir, and Swat), and Azad Kashmir.

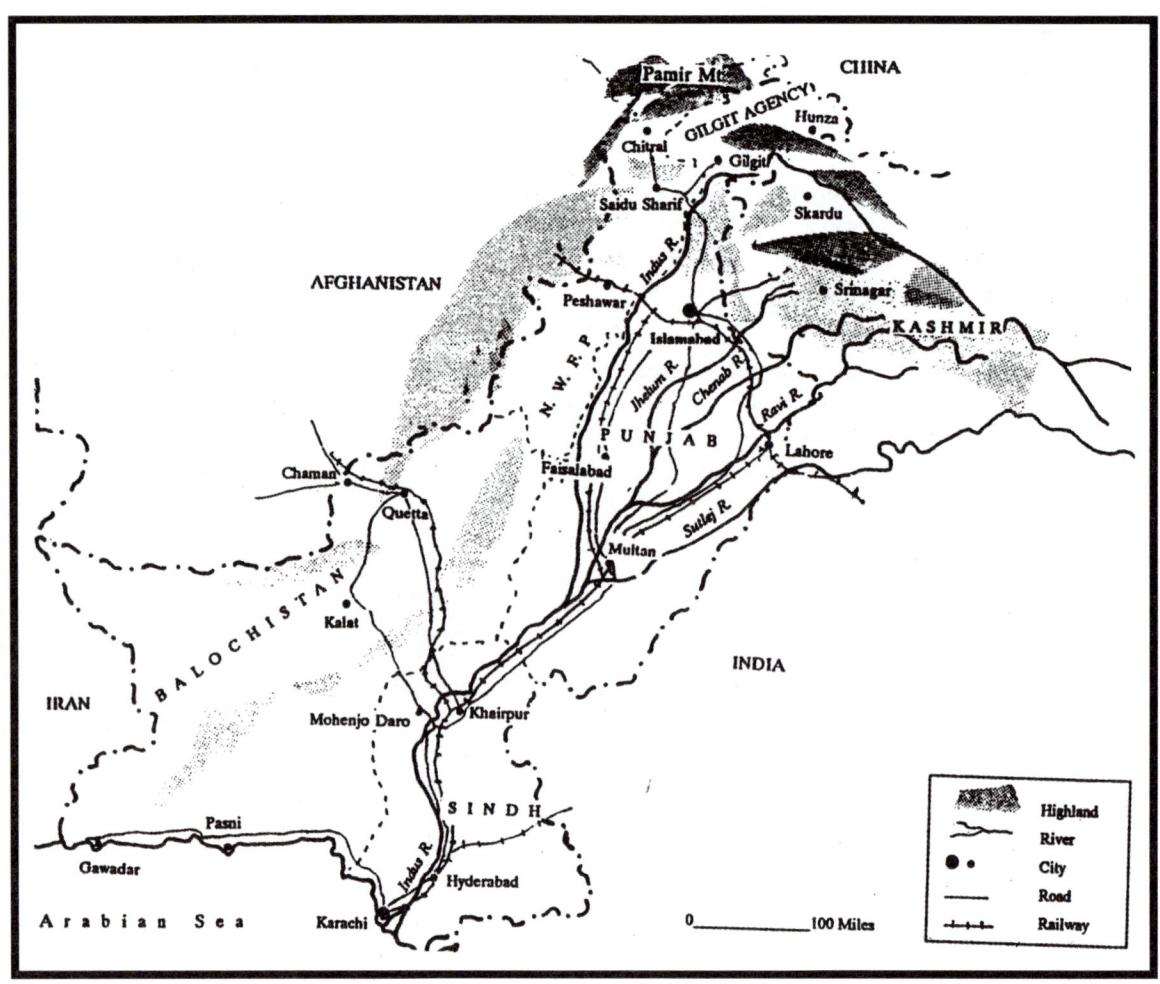

Map 38: Pakistan

On the basis of surface configuration and irrigation-agriculture, Pakistan is divided into four ecological resource regions: (i) mountains and plateaus, (ii) desert, (iii) Indus plains, and (iv) Indus delta. Rugged mountains, foothills, and narrow valleys cover about half of Pakistan. A lifeless sandy desert extends from the Rann of Kutch in the south to Cholistan in the north. The Indus valley plain is a part of a broad downwarp, which extends from the Bay of Bengal westward to the Arabian Sea. The western half of the downwarp has been filled by material brought by the Indus and its tributaries: Jhelum, Chenab, Ravi, Sutlej, and Beas. Of these, the Indus has been, by far, the largest contributor. The Indus delta begins south of the historic Tatta city. It is a complicated geomorphic area due to frequent lateral shifting of the river, earthquakes, and the Arabian Sea tides.

About 20 percent of Pakistan receives less than 5 inches (120 mm) of rainfall, 75 percent receives 10 inches (250 mm), and only about 7 percent of the area located in the Himalayan foothills and in the northern parts receive over 29 inches (500 mm) of rainfall. Rain falls mostly from June through October. In the winter months, Pakistan receives less than 3 inches (76 mm) of rainfall from the western depressions.

Fig. 49: The city of Lahore, WAPDA House: Punjab Assembly to its left

PEOPLE AND POPULATION

Most people in Pakistan live in the Indus River valley especially along an arc formed by the cities of Faisalabad, Lahore, Rawalpindi/Islamabad, and Peshawar or the port city of Karachi (Fig 49). The people are divided into five ethnic groups. Punjabis are in majority, and their province is Pakistan's largest and most populous province. Sindh is the second largest, which experienced considerable upheaval in the years following partition. Millions of Hindus and Sikhs left for India to be replaced by roughly seven million Muslims. These people speak Urdu, which is the national language of Pakistan, and identify themselves as the third group, known as the *Muhajirs*. The fourth group of people are the Pathans or Pakhtuns. They live in the Northwest Frontier of Pakistan. Their history and ethos glorify the martial virtues. The fifth group is those of Balochis, who live in an exceedingly inhospitable habitat. Their province is Pakistan's largest in area, but smallest in population. There are several smaller ethnic groups that inhabit the high mountains in the Hunza and Baltistan.

Since independence in 1947, Pakistan has had four national censuses: in 1951, 1961, 1972 and 1981. In 1951, the total population was 33.70 million; in 1961, it was 42.98 million; in 1972, 64.9 million, and in 1981, 84 million. In 1994, the population of Pakistan was estimated at 129 million. With its current rate of 3.1 percent annual growth, it is likely to increase to 154 million in 2000 and to 195 million in 2010.

EVOLUTION OF PAKISTAN

Pakistan's Islamic history began with the arrival of Muslim traders in the 8th century AD. During the 16th and 17th centuries, the Mughals (Persian for Mongols) united most of South Asia in an empire marked both by its administrative effectiveness and cultural refinement. British traders arrived in 1601, but the English Empire did not consolidate its control there until the later half of the 18th century. After 1850, the British governed virtually the entire subcontinent, including most of what is now Pakistan.

In the early 20th century, the Hindu and Muslim leaders began to press for independence. Growing concern about Hindu domination led Muslims to form the All-India Muslim League in 1906. The idea of a separate Muslim state emerged in the 1930s. In 1940, *Quaid-i-Azam*, Mohammed Ali Jinnah, publicly endorsed the "Pakistan Resolution," which called for the creation of an independent state in regions where Muslims were a majority. To commemorate the occasion, Pakistan has constructed a tower in Lahore exactly at the place where *Quaid-i-Azam* Jinnah and other leaders stood to speak in support of the resolution (Fig. 50).

Fig. 50: Minar-i-Pakistan, Lahore

Weakened by World War II, the British government announced in June 1947 that the subcontinent would be partitioned and full independence will be granted to two successor states - India and Pakistan. Pakistan would consist of the contiguous Muslim-majority districts of western British India, plus parts of Bengal. This arrangement resulted in a bifurcated Muslim nation, separated by more than 1,000 miles (1600 km) of Indian territory. The partition of India, particularly the Punjab, was accompanied by communal rioting, resulting in the loss of tens of thousands of lives. About 7 million Muslims came to Pakistan, and a like number of Hindus and Sikhs left for India.

The death of *Quaid-i-Azam,* Mohammed Ali Jinnah, in 1948 (Fig. 51) and the assassination of his political successor in 1951, Prime Minister Liaquat Ali Khan, deprived Pakistan of its two most able leaders, dealing a serious blow to the nation's political development. In 1958, a group of senior military officers took control of the nation. After a number of changes, a new constitution, and national elections, a second martial law was imposed on April 1, 1969. Due to continued unrest and political problems, the eastern wing of Pakistan seceded with the help of the Indian Army in 1971 to become Bangladesh. The western wing, which was formerly West Pakistan, remained as Pakistan. The guiding principles of Pakistan were unity, faith, and discipline. People have constructed a monument in Karachi, Pakistan's largest city, where three swords represent the three guiding principles of Pakistan (Fig. 52, Fig. 53).

The president is the head of the state and acts on the advice of the prime minister, both of whom are elected for a period of five years. The National Assembly consists of 207 directly elected Muslim members. An additional ten seats are reserved for the minorities, who also serve for five years. The Senate has 87 members who are elected for a term of six years, with 1/3 retiring every two years.

Fig. 51: Mausoleum o f *Quaid-i-Azam* Jinnah, Karachi, Pakistan

Fig. 52: Three Pillars Representing Three Principles (Unity, Faith and Discipline)

Fig. 53: Port City of Karachi, Pakistan

ECONOMY

Pakistan is a relatively poor country but has the resources and entrepreneurial skill to support rapid economic growth. The growth of the gross domestic product (GDP) has averaged between 6 to 8 percent between 1981-1994, with generally moderate inflation.

Agriculture

Agriculture accounts for about 26 percent of the GDP and employs more than 50 percent of the labor force. About 25 percent of the total land area is under cultivation. Wheat, rice, cotton and sugar cane are the major crops cultivated in *kharif* and *rabi* seasons by irrigation. In addition, mangos, citrus fruits, and a large variety of other fruits, known for their quality, are grown in certain regions of the country. Pakistan has the largest contiguous irrigation system in the world. Irrigation, intensive farming, and a liberal use of mechanized farming and green revolution technology have enabled Pakistan to become a net food exporter. Pakistan exports rice, fish, fruits, and vegetables and imports wheat, vegetable oil, and sugar.

Minerals and Industry

Pakistan has extensive energy resources, including fairly sizable natural gas reserves, some proven oil reserves, and large hydropower potential. Exploitation of energy resources has been slow, and domestic demand for power continues to outstrip supply. Coal contributes about 5.9% of the overall energy requirement of the country. The total coal reserves are estimated at 580 million tons. Ninety percent of the coal produced in Pakistan is used in the brick kilns. The government is developing new thermal and hydropower generation capability and is encouraging private investment in power development. Oil is also mined in Pakistan, but their quantity is not sufficient to meet local demands. The main products are cotton yarn and cloth, art silk and synthetic cloth, garments, carpets and rugs, leather and leather products, fish processing and canning, hosiery and gloves, vegetable oil, sugar, molasses, cement, urea and phosphate fertilizers, iron and steel products, sport goods, surgical instruments, marble and onyx products, and wool and jute textiles.

Cotton, textile, and apparel manufacturing is Pakistan's largest industry, accounting for nearly 20 percent of total manufacturing output and 40 percent of total exports. Other major industries include cement, fertilizer, edible oil, sugar, steel, machinery, and food processing. Large scale manufacturing units account for about 70 percent of total output value. The public sector, which includes many enterprises, nationalized in the 1970s, producing about 30 percent of manufactured output in 1991. The public sector, however, is expected to decline sharply as state industrial units are sold to private investors.

To encourage further industrialization, the government has recently adopted a program of privatization. One of the objectives of privatization is to reduce the drain on government resources caused by the operational losses of the state owned enterprises and to create greater opportunities for the private sectors. Another objective of privatization is to expand and modernize their enterprises, to improve productivity, efficiency, and profitability. Privatization covers a wide range of fields like industries, banks, trade, shipping, airlines, and others. So far three banks have been privatized in Pakistan. The telephone and telegraph department has been converted into a corporation.

CHAPTER 36
PALESTINE

Palestine includes the area between the Jordan River and the Mediterranean Sea. The name originated from the ancient people known as the Philistines. Its present boundaries are uncertain, but it is expected that soon a sovereign independent state of Palestine will emerge in Gaza strip and the occupied West Bank with East Jerusalem as its capital. The future of this state hangs in the balance, but the Palestinians' right to establish its own state in the Arab territory occupied by Israel in the 1967 war is now universally recognized. One hundred and twenty-six states recognize Palestine as a state, and most Arab-Islamic and African nations have Palestinian embassies in their capital.

Palestine's significance has always been greater than its size. Because of its crossroads location, bridging Southwest Asia, Africa, and Europe, Palestine has been fought over for control by the great powers all through its history. Its historical significance is linked to three major religions - Judaism, Christianity, and Islam. The city of Jerusalem is especially important to these religions. To Jews, Palestine is the site of the ancient kingdom of Israel and the land supposedly promised to them by God. Jerusalem contains the site of the Temple of Solomon, the central site of Jewish worship. To Christians, Jerusalem is sacred as the site of the life and ministry of Jesus and the early Christian Church. For the Muslims, Jerusalem is the third sacred city, after Makkah and Madinah for various reasons. Muslims claim rightful succession to the heritage of Israelite prophets: Moses, David, and Solomon and of Jesus, the central figure in Christian faith. It is the site of Prophet Muhammad's night journey

---

Geographical Profile

Area: 27,000 sq. km; Gaza Strip is 30 miles long and 10 miles wide; West Bank is 80 miles long and 40 miles wide.
Population: Total number of Palestinians: 5,250,336 (1985) of which 2,965,873 were living in Arab States, 117,730 in United States of America, and 476,000 in Gaza Strip and 945,000 in West Bank
Capital: Jericho
Other Important Cities: Beitshean, Haifa, Jaffa, Rsmlah, Naplouse, Hazareth, Akka and Gaza
Neighboring Countries: Lebanon, Syria, Jordan, Egypt
Climate: Cool summers in the mountains, and hot along the coast. The temperature ranges from 24°C TO 27°C in summer and from 13°C to 18°C in winter
Rivers: Jordan River (252 km), Yarmuk River (40 km), Al-Auja (26 km), and Al-Maqta (13 km)
Official Language: Arabic
Ethnic Background: Arabs
Religion: Sunni Islam, Christianity, Judaism
Economy:
　GNP: $2,134 million (West Bank) $864 million (Gaza)
　Per Capita Income: $2,175 (West Bank) $1,310 (Gaza)
　Official Name: Palestine
Declaration of Principles: Sept. 13, 1993

('*Isra*') from Makkah to the Aqsa Mosque (the site of Solomon's temple) and then his ascension to heaven (Map 39).

After a long and bitter conflict between the Palestinians (both Muslims and Christians) and the Jews of Israel, a new promise of peace was initiated on September 13, 1993. The Palestine Liberation Organization (PLO) and the Israeli Government signed a Declaration of Principles on Palestinian self-rule in the Gaza Strip and Jericho. This initial arrangement is likely to lead to a comprehensive settlement of Arab-Israeli conflict, making parts of historic Palestine an independent state in future. At present, the future as well as immediate past for Palestine is linked with that of the Jewish state of Israel. This chapter discusses Palestine and Israel as a geographic entity. The Evolution of Palestine section surveys the history of the land from ancient to present times.

GEOGRAPHY

The historic land of Palestine lies at the heart of the Arab world, between Jordan River and the Mediterranean Sea where Africa, Europe, and Southwest Asia meet. It is composed of the districts of Gaza, Lod, Al-Quds, Samara, Haifa, and Galilee. Palestine was an Ottoman province until General Allenby conquered it for the allies in 1918.

Palestine is neighbored by Lebanon and Syria to the north and northeast, Jordan to the East, Egypt to the southwest, and Israel to the

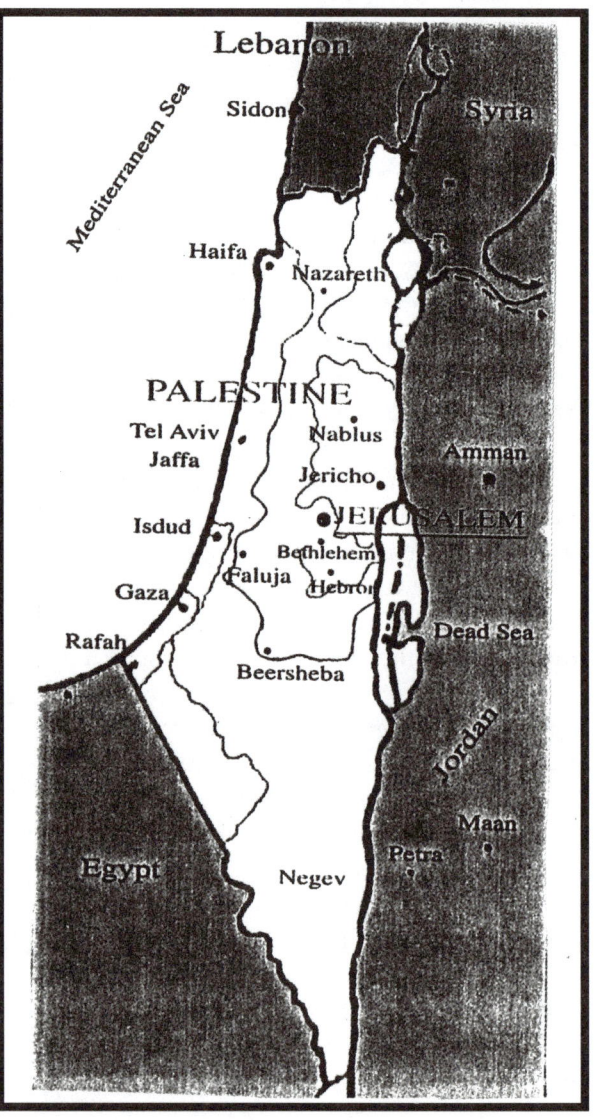

Map 39: Palestine

West. Climatically, Palestine is cooler in the winter season, with a temperature ranging between 13°C and 18°C. On the mountains, the temperatures average between 5°C and 15°C. In the summers the temperatures range between 24°C and 27°C along the coast.

Palestine's rich variety of landscape makes it geographically unique. Within the compass of an area measuring 280 miles (420 km) by 66.6 miles (100 km), seas, lakes, mountains, valleys, lowlands, and deserts are all found. The climates range from subalpine through temperate to Mediterranean and tropical types with corresponding contrasts in vegetation and agricultural potential. The nature of relief, soils, and climate offer an environment of high productivity, but are vulnerable to serious ecological deterioration, if neglected or mismanaged. In fact, Palestine is a part of a physiographic region, which was folded to form a long anticline running roughly parallel with the Mediterranean coast. Through most of Palestine the axis lies almost north to south, curving southwest towards the Sinai frontier in southern Palestine. Strong vertical movements have occurred in the area, resulting in the formation of the deepest inland depression on the earth, containing the Jordan valley, the Dead Sea depression (over 2500 feet (790 m) below the level of the Mediterranean Sea in some places), the Aqaba, and the Gulf of Aqaba. Surface drainage is largely by a few east-west flowing streams, some of which have cut deeply into the highlands with their numerous headstreams. Notable rivers are Jordan River (405 miles, 252 km), Yarmuk (64 miles, 40 km), Al-Auja (41 miles, 93 km), and Al-Muqta. The mountains include the historic areas of Upper and Lower Galilee, Samaria, and Judea.

POPULATION

The population of Palestine was 70% Muslims, 20% Jewish, and 10% Christian in 1948 when the Jewish-Arab war erupted. This proportion was virtually reversed when the state of Israel was carved out, and the Arab population was expelled from Jewish-occupied territory. In the state of Israel, Muslims now represent only 18% of the population with Jews nearly 80%. However, the 1985 census reported the total numbers of Palestinians (Muslims and Christians) as 250,330, living in different countries of the world. More than half of these Palestinians were living in the Arab States and the rest in United States. The area of the Gaza Strip is about 1,000 square miles, and its population is close to 1 million (1997). The West Bank is 2,300 square miles with a population of 1.6 million (1997). The Gaza Strip is an extremely crowded land with a density close to 10,000 persons per square mile, whereas the density of population in the West Bank is 690 persons per square mile. Most of the population here is Muslim.

EVOLUTION OF PALESTINE

Palestine was settled by Semitic tribes at a very early date. It was then called Canaan. Canaanite tribes controlled the area for more than 1,000 years. About 1500 BC, Hebrew tribes began to enter the area. They later came into conflict with a people known as Philistines. It is from them that the term Palestine is derived. The Hebrew tribes ultimately defeated the Philistines and established a monarchy under the leadership of the family of Prophet David in about 1000 BC known as the kingdom of Israel. This monarchy flourished for some 75 years. It then split into two weaker kingdoms: Israel and Judah, which survived for approximately 200 and 400 years respectively. Both kingdoms fell under the rule of more powerful neighbors - Assyria, Babylonia, and Persia. At the time of Jesus, the Jews still aspired for political independence, but by then, the region had become a part of the powerful Roman Empire.

After 70 AD, the Romans destroyed much of Jerusalem in retaliation for Jewish rebellions. In a particularly brutal response to a Jewish revolt in 132 AD, the Romans killed more than a half million people in more than 1,000 villages. With the conversion of the Byzantine, or Eastern Romans, Palestine and Jerusalem particularly became centers of Christian pilgrimage in the 4th century. Christians formed the majority of the population, and Jews were not allowed to settle in the city.

Inspired by their new faith, Islam, Muslim armies conquered the area in the 7th century. The city of Jerusalem surrendered peacefully to Caliph 'Umar himself who, in return, guaranteed religious freedom to all its residents. Except for a century of Christian dominance during the Crusades, Palestine remained under Muslim control, either Arab or Turkish, from 7th to 20th century. It was part of the Ottoman Empire, centered in Istanbul from 1517 to 1918, when British forces took command of the region during World War I. Following the war, Britain was awarded the right to administer Palestine under a League of Nations mandate that committed Britain to preparing the population of Palestine for future self-rule.

In the 20th century, Palestine was a unique case under the mandate system. All of the areas governed by European powers were assured that they would be granted independence after a period of tutelage. With respect to Palestine, Britain assumed the mandate promising a Jewish homeland without violating the rights of the Palestinians. The British assisted the growth of Jewish population in Palestine through immigration making them viable for future self-rule.

During the latter half of the nineteenth century more than half the Jews in the world lived in Eastern Europe and Tsarist Russia. Their presence in these lands was resented, and they were subjected to humiliating pogroms. In 1887, Theodore Herzl proposed to the Zionist council the idea of Judenstat, a Jewish state in Palestine. The idea was welcomed by the world Jewry and accepted by many Western nations as promising a solution to the Jewish problem. In the 1880s there were a series of anti-Jewish riots in southern Russia which resulted in large-scale emigration establishment of rural settlements in Palestine. Neither Ottoman rulers nor local Palestinians resented the fact, and they did not see any political motive in it.

In 1904, a second wave of immigrants began to arrive in Palestine from Russia. The Jews even sought to purchase the province of Palestine from the *Khalifah* Sultan 'Abdul-Hamid II, who refused this offer. The scattered distribution of Zionist villages in these early years was largely a reflection of both Jewish attachment to the land and Arab acceptance of their long lost cousin in their midst. The Jews have always been part of the Arab-Muslim society, and their culture and religion flourished along with the Arabs.

The situation changed, however, after the First World War, when the British occupied Palestine as a mandated territory. On November 2, 1917, during the First World War, Lord Arthur Balfour, British Foreign Secretary, issued the famous Balfour Declaration, promising the Jews homeland in Palestine without violating the rights of its inhabitants, the Palestinians. The promise of Jewish homeland came in direct conflict with various promises of independence that Britain had made to the Arabs in general and Palestinians in particular, naturally raising both resentment and fear. The Palestinians immediately recognized that the homeland was just another name for the establishment of the state of Israelis laid down in the Zionist declaration of 1887, and hence, they clearly saw their impending displacement from their homeland.

Soon after the Balfour Declaration, two further groups of immigrants reached Palestine. The first group consisted of people from Eastern Europe, already prepared by Zionist Organization to establish a Jewish community. A second group began to arrive in 1924, chiefly from Poland. By 1931, the Jews numbered about 175,000 in a total population of 1,036,000 (17 percent). The activities of the Jewish National Fund led to the purchase, reclamation and colonization of large areas by almost continuous claims of Jewish villages. Then, a pre-1948 wave of immigration began to reach Palestine in 1931 as a result of the Nazis persecution of Jews in Germany. By the end of 1939, 230,000 immigrants had entered Palestine, chiefly from Germany and Austria. The estimated population of Palestine in 1940 was 1,530,000 of which 457,000 (22 percent) were Jews.

From the beginning of the British mandate in Palestine, the Arab population had understandably become anxious about the political future of their country. They rightfully feared that their interests and aspirations would be held secondary to those of the Jews, since they had been cheated by the European powers; but most of all, they deplored the growing number of Jewish immigrants after 1939. After 1936, when the Jewish numbers increased markedly, Arab exasperation led to rioting and rebellion against the British. A Royal Commission was sent to Palestine to investigate the causes of Arab unrest. The Commission recommended the partitioning of Palestine into Jewish and Arab states under British sovereignty, with certain regions retained under direct British control. The Arabs rejected the partition and favored a secular democratic state in which all citizens, regardless of religious affiliations, could live together in peace. The conflict led to further violence. The British government also rejected partition, announcing new policies for Palestine and appointing a new commission (Woodhead Commission) to resolve the dispute. While they regarded partition as unworkable, the Commission drew up several alternative plans, all of which assigned a part of northern Palestine to the Jewish state. The whole of the south would be either part of the Arab state, or remain under British administration. Also rejecting the propositions of the Woodhead Commission, the British announced new policies for Palestine in a White Paper published in 1939. Palestine was to become an independent Arab-Jewish state within ten years. Jewish immigration would be limited to 75,000 over the next five years, enough to bring the Jewish population to one-third of the total. Any subsequent immigration would require the consent of the Arabs. Finally, the purchase of land was restricted to a small part of western Palestine.

Between 1940 and 1948, when Israel was established, Jewish immigration into Palestine was officially restricted, but more than 110,000 people managed to enter the country, the vast majority of whom were from Eastern Europe. The Jewish settlements multiplied overnight.

The British unilaterally decided to terminate their mandate in Palestine on May 14, 1948, and the State of Israel was proclaimed by the David Ben Gurion at a meeting held at the Municipal Hall in Tel Aviv. The United States Government recognized the new state, followed by former Soviet Union and Eastern European countries. Several months of desperate fighting between the new entity of Israel and surrounding Arab states followed. In 1949, armistice lines were agreed with Egypt, Jordan, Syria, and Lebanon, roughly reflecting the front lines, when military operations ceased. By May 1948, on the eve of civil war, the population of Palestine, including 650,000 Jews (about 31 percent), was about 2,065,000. However, only 15 percent of the cultivable land was owned by the Jews. In November 1948, following the flight and expulsion of approximately 650,000 to 700,000 Arabs from within the borders of Israel and the immigration of over 100,000 Jews, the population of Israel reached 873,000, 82 percent of whom were Jews. By 1988, the population reached an estimated 4.4 million, excluding 1.6 million in territory conquered and occupied by Israeli forces in the Six-Day Arab-Israeli War of June 1967 and the subsequent October War in 1973.

Since 1948, the status of Jerusalem (*Yerushalayim* in Hebrew meaning "City of Peace" and *al-Quds* in Arabic meaning "The Holy") has been intensely disputed between Israel and the Palestinian Muslims. The dispute originates in the fact that Jerusalem is a holy place for three Abrahamic faiths: Jews, Christians and Muslims. The three most sacred objects in Jerusalem are the Church of Holy Sepulcher, *Al-Aqsa* Mosque (with Dome of the Rock at the center), and the Wailing Wall.

As a result of the first Arab-Israeli war, Jerusalem was partitioned between Israel and Jordan. In the 1967 war, the Israelis also took the Jordanian part of the city. The Jews maintain their position that all of Jerusalem is the eternal capital of Israel, and they shall neither return it nor share it with the Palestinians.

The Arab-Israeli War of 1967, in which the Arabs suffered a crushing defeat, allowed Israel to enlarge its territory, adding the West Bank and Gaza strip. The defeat of 1967 made the Palestinians even more determined to launch a freedom struggle using their own human resources. Out of this movement grew the Palestine Liberation Organization (PLO) in 1964, under the leadership of Yassir Arafat, which carried the struggle both internally and externally. Another more dramatic development was the rise of the Palestinian youth and women under *Hamas* and *Intifada,* the uprising of 1987.

The continuous Palestinian struggle and bloody Arab-Israel conflict has led to a new realism. Led by the United States, Israel and Palestine Liberation Organization signed the Oslo Accord in 1993, agreeing to resolve their differences peacefully and negotiating Israeli withdrawal from the occupied territory. As of January 1997, Oslo Accord has called for Israeli withdrawal from most of the urban areas of Palestine, and in spite of various setbacks, both the Palestinian Authority and Israel are moving toward a final settlement, which would hopefully usher in an independent, sovereign Palestinian state.

ECONOMY

At present, the economy of the newly emerging Palestinian state is closely tied with the economy of Israel and Jordan, and independent figures are not available. Some pledges of outside aid provide subsistence to Palestinian refugees as well as help developmental efforts within Palestinian self-rule territories. In 1990, 38 countries, including Pakistan, pledged nearly $188 million to programs of the UN Agencies to support the Palestinian refugees in the Middle East. In addition, the European Community provided $33 million in emergency food aid to the Palestinians in Israeli occupied territories. However, total support dropped to $40 million after 1991, because funding was stopped by Saudi Arabia and Gulf States as a sequel to Gulf war.

At present, most Palestinians work in Israeli farms and factories. In 1990, 32,000 Palestinians were registered with Israeli Employment Agency to work, a number which increased to 70,000 in 1991, despite the fact that 2,000 Palestinians were replaced by the immigration of Russian Jews.

The formation of a Palestinian state is in a flux even at the time this section was written. The Declaration of Principles on Palestinian self-rule signed on September 13, 1991 is now disputed, as its interpretations questioned by the new right-wing government in Israel. Many of the Israeli government's actions have intensified the conflict.

CHAPTER 37
QATAR

Qatar is an Arabic word which literally means "long island." It lies parallel to the Iranian coast, from which it is separated by the Clarence Strait. Nearly all the people of Qatar are Muslims. Islam is the official religion, and Islamic jurisprudence is the basis of Qatar's legal system.

GEOGRAPHY

Qatar consists of a peninsula of 4,400 square miles (11,400 sq. km.), jutting out into the Persian (Arabian) Gulf as a featureless sandy wasteland (Map 40). Its land boundaries meet Saudi Arabia and the United Arab Emirates. It has 350 miles (560 km) of coastline. Bahrain is 18 miles (29 km) west of the peninsula. Qatar's basically flat terrain is marked by a gradual rise from the east to a central limestone plateau. There are hills in the south which reach a high point of only 345 ft., (105 m) at Aba Al-Bawl Hill. Windblown sand covers much of the south, and sand dunes predominate in the southeast. Most of the rest of the country is stony, sandy, and barren, consisting of salt flats, dune desert, and plains. Of the numerous islands and coral reefs which belong to Qatar, Halul, in the Persian Gulf 60 miles (90 km) east of Doha, is of special importance. It is the collecting and storage point for the country's three offshore oil fields.

The climate is unpleasantly hot and humid during the summer and mild in the winter; midday temperatures in July and August can reach 104°F (40°C), with a humidity of 85 percent or more. In the winter, there is less humidity, and the

---

Geographical Profile

Area: 4,427 sq. mi. (11,437 sq. km)
Population: 0.5 million (1994); 0.6 million (2000); 0.7 million (2010)
Neighboring Countries: Saudi Arabia, United Arab Emirates
Capital: Doha
Other Cities: Umm Said, Al-Khor, Dukhan, Ruwais
Terrain: Mostly desert, flat, and barren
Climate: Hot and dry
Ethnic Groups: Arabs 55%, South Asians 33%, Iranians 6%
Religion: Mainly Sunni Islam, some Shi'ah
Economy:
    GDP: $5.2 billion (1992)
    Per Capita Income: $13,000
    Natural Resources: Oil, natural gas, fish
    Agriculture: Products: Fruits, vegetables (most food is imported)
    Industry: Types: Oil production and refining, natural gas, fishing, cement, petrochemicals, power/desalinization plants, steel, fertilizer
Official Name: State of Qatar
Date of Independence: September 3, 1971

temperature ranges between 50º and 68ºF (10º and 20ºC). The winter season is characterized by chilly nights and rainfall averages between 2 to 3 inches (50 to 75 mm) a year.

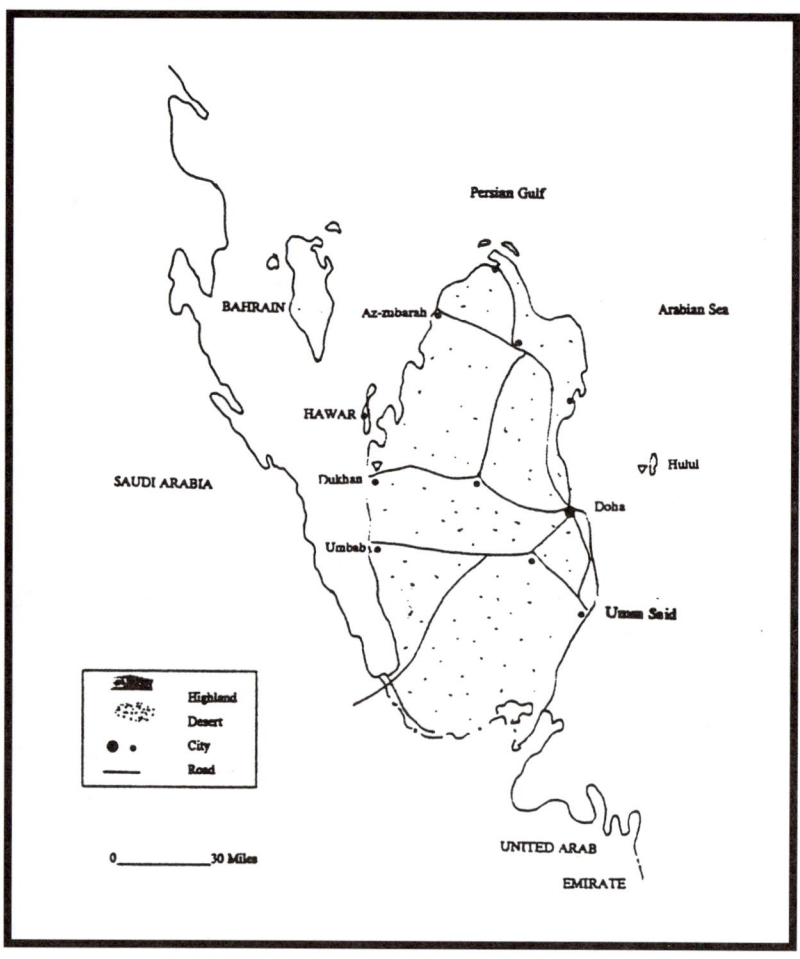

Map 40: Qatar

PEOPLE AND POPULATION

The majority of the Qatari people are descendants of nomadic tribes who came to Qatar in the 18th century to escape the harsh conditions of the neighboring areas of Najd and Al-Hasa. Some Qataris are descendants of Omani tribes. Qataris are mainly Sunni Muslims. The ethnic divisions include 20 percent native Qataris, 25 percent other Arabs, 34 percent South Asians, 16 percent Iranians, and 5 percent others. The ratio of men to women stands at approximately 2 to 1. Nearly 60 percent of all Qataris live in Doha.

In 1994, the population of Qatar stood at 0.5 million with an annual rate of natural increase of 2.5 percent. With such a rate of increase, the population will double in 28 years. There are many urban centers in Qatar. However, many people still live a nomadic life style (Fig. 54).

Fig. 54: A bedouin

EVOLUTION OF QATAR

Qatar is first mentioned in literature by several 10th century Arab writers. In the 18th century, Al-Khalifah (the Khalifah family) migrated from their homes farther west and north on the Arabian Peninsula, to az-Zubarah, in Northwestern Qatar. The Persians thought that the Al-Khalifah family was a threat and invaded Qatar in 1783. The Al-Khalifah defeated them and moved their headquarters to Bahrain Island, ultimately becoming rulers of the independent State of Bahrain. They also claimed the territory surrounding az-Zubarah. The rift between the *sheikhs* of Bahrain and their nominal subjects on Qatar grew, and in 1867, full-scale war broke out. Bahrain, aided by the *Sheikh* of Abu Dhabi routed the Qataris. In the following year, the British negotiated the termination of the Bahraini claim. This resulted in an arrangement that would require Qatar to pay tribute to Bahrain. The tribute ended when Qatar was occupied by Ottoman Turks in 1872. Later, the British installed Muhammad ibn Thani Al Thani, who lived in Qatar as a ruling *sheikh*. He signed an agreement that he would refer all matters of dispute between Qatar and his neighbors to the British resident for settlement.

In 1871, the Ottoman Empire endeavored to station troops in Qatar, being nominal suzerain of most of the Arabian Peninsula. Their unsuccessful efforts led to an armed conflict in 1893, resulting in a Turkish defeat by the forces of the *Sheikh*. This was done with the help of the British. After the outbreak of World War I in 1914, Turkish influence in the Persian Gulf came to an end, and in November 1918, Britain and Qatar concluded a treaty, whereby Qatar became a British protectorate state, like that of the Trucial States (now the United Arab Emirates).

Qatar, together with nearby Bahrain, was scheduled to join with the seven *emirates* of Trucial coast to form the United Arab Emirates when Britain left the Persian Gulf area in 1971. However, Bahrain and Qatar chose to become independent states.

ECONOMY

Qatar has a policy of "Qatarisation," under which all joint venture industries and government departments strive to move Qatari nationals into positions of greater authority as soon as they are educated and available. As a result, a greater number of foreign-educated Qataris, including many educated in the United States, are returning to Qatar to assume key positions.

Agriculture

Less than one percent of Qatar's land is arable, and less than five percent is suitable as pasture land. Vegetation is found only in the north, where irrigated farming is located and where desert plants briefly blossom during the spring when rain falls. Animal life in Qatar includes the gazelle, jerboa, sand rat, gerbil, hare, and other animals.

High mineral content makes the underground water unsuitable for drinking. The distillation of seawater now provides more than half the country's water supply. Agriculture was introduced into the barren desert of Qatar only 20 years ago. Despite the scant rainfall, irrigation from deep underground wells produces good crops of fruits and vegetables.

Oil and Minerals

Oil revenues are the basis of Qatar's economy and provide more than 80% of government revenue. The production of oil began in 1949, when a British firm began shipping oil from the oil field at Dukhan, southwest of the peninsula, to the oil harbor at Doha. In 1966, Shell Company began offshore oil production. In 1973, oil production and revenues increased sizably, moving Qatar out of the ranks of the world's poorest countries and providing it with one of the highest per capita incomes. In 1976-77, oil production was taken over by the Qatar National Production Company.

Qatar's economy was in downturn from 1982 to 1989. OPEC (Organization of Petroleum Exporting Countries) quotas for crude oil and the generally unpromising outlook on international oil markets reduced the earnings. The resulting recessionary local business climate caused many firms to lay off expatriate staff to cut costs. With the economy finally beginning to recover, the expatriate population, particularly from Egypt and South Asia, is growing again. The economy boosted again in 1991 with the completion of a $1.5 billion Phase I of North Field gas development. North Field reserves are among the world's largest.

Industry

Qatar's heavy industrial projects, based in Umm Said, include a refinery, a fertilizer plant for urea and ammonia, a steel plant, and a petrochemical plant. All these industries use gas or fuel. Most of them are joint ventures between the European and Japanese firms and the Qatar government. Although the United States is a major equipment supplier for Qatar's oil and gas industry, to date, there has been little American investment in Qatar.

--- **NOTES** ---

NOTES

CHAPTER 38
SAUDI ARABIA

Saudi Arabia contains the heart of the Muslim World and is a place where the first Islamic state was formed in the seventh century. From here began the religion of Islam, which changed the course of human history and affected the destinies of people in many parts of the world. The modern state of Saudi Arabia was, however, established in the 1920s through the organizational abilities of King Abdul Aziz.

GEOGRAPHY

Saudi Arabia occupies about four-fifths of the Arabian Peninsula. Boundaries are not fully defined in the south and southeast. From mountain ranges near the Red Sea, the land slopes gently eastward toward the Arabian (Persian) Gulf. The topography is mainly desert, including the Rub al Khali (Empty Quarter), a vast, uninhabited expanse of sand. Saudi Arabia has no permanent rivers or bodies of water. Major regions include (i) The Hijaz, (ii) The Asir, (iii) Nejd, (iv) Eastern Province, and (v) the Northern region.

The Hijaz parallels the Red Sea where the holy cities of Islam (Makkah and Madinah) are located. Asir is a mountainous region along the southern Red Sea coast. Nejd is the heartland of the country. The Eastern Province (also known as Al-Hasa) borders the Arabian (Persian) Gulf and contains the largest concentration of proven oil reserves in the world. The northern region has the greatest concentration of nomads (Map 41).

Geographical Profile

Area: 830,000 sq. mi. (2,331,000 sq. km)
Population: 17.2 million (1994); 21.1 million (2000); 31.1 million (2010)
Neighboring Countries: Yemen, Oman, United Arab Emirates, Qatar, Kuwait, Iraq, and Jordan
Capital: Riyadh
Other Cities: Jeddah, Makkah, Taif, Dammam, Madinah
Terrain: Mainly desert, with rugged mountains in southwest
Climate: Arid with great extremes of temperatures
Ethnic Groups: Arabs (90%), Afro-Asians, immigrant workers
Religion: Islam
Economy:
  GDP: $70 billion (1988)
  Per Capita Income: $7,700
  Natural Resources: Oil, iron ore, gold, copper
  Agriculture: Dates, grains, livestock, vegetables; cultivated land 0.3%
  Industry: Types: Petroleum production, petrochemicals, cement, fertilizer, light industry
Official Name: Kingdom of Saudi Arabia

Rainfall in Saudi Arabia is erratic, averaging 2-4 inches (5-10 cm) a year, except in the Asir, which averages 12-30 inches (30-75 cm.) in the summer. During the summer, the heat is intense over much of the country, frequently exceeding 120°F (48°C) in the shade, with high humidity along the coasts. In the winter, temperatures sometimes drop below freezing in the central and northern areas, but snow and ice are rare.

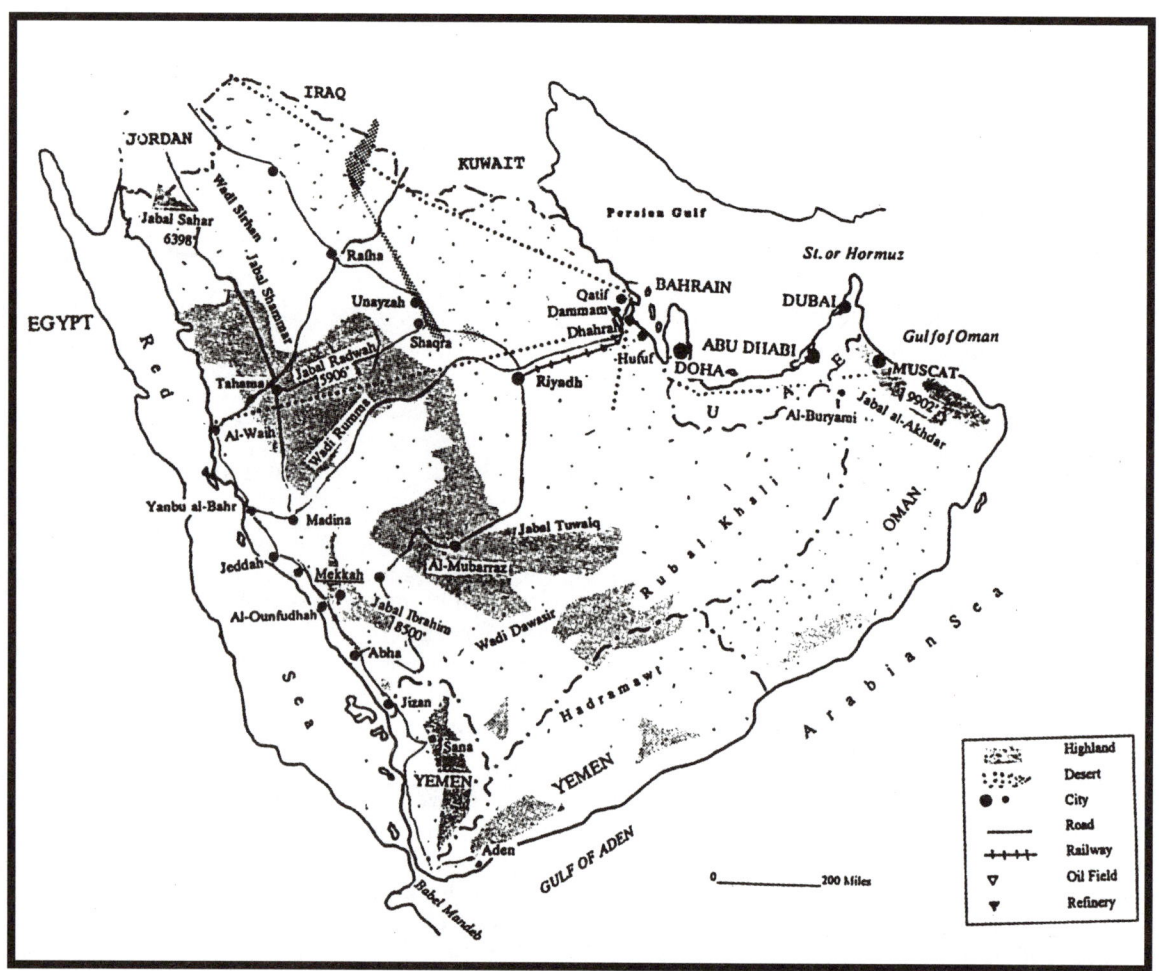

Map 41: Saudi Arabia

PEOPLE AND POPULATION

Saudis are a race of Arabs, while some are a mixture of Turks, Iranians, Indonesians, Indians, and Africans, most of whom immigrated as pilgrims and reside in the Hijaz along the Red Sea coast. Many Arabs from nearby countries are employed in the kingdom. In addition, there are expatriate workers from North America, South Asia, Europe, Africa, and the Far East. With the exception of some people who come from the western countries or Far East, the overwhelming majority of the people are Muslims. The Muslims regard the Ka'bah in Mecca (Makkah) (Fig. 55) as the most sacred place and the center of their religious lives. The Prophet's mosque in Madinah is the second most important sacred place.

Fig 55: The Ka'bah in the city of Makkah, Hijaz

Recent estimates show that Saudi Arabia's population stood at 17.2 million (1994). Until the 1960s, most of the population was nomadic or seminomadic; however, under the impact of rapid economic growth, urbanization has advanced swiftly, and about 95% of the people are now settled. Some cities and oases have densities of 2000 persons per sq. mile (770 per sq. km).

The society in Saudi Arabia was based on tribes and extended families. After centuries of tribal living, two factors galvanized the disparate tribes, nomads, and townspeople of Saudi Arabia into unaccustomed unity and brought the new nation onto the center stage of world affairs. These two factors were the charismatic leadership of Abd al-Aziz from 1902 until his death in 1953 and the discovery of the world's largest proven reserves of oil.

EVOLUTION OF SAUDI ARABIA

The Saudi state first arose in Central Arabia about 1750, when a local bedouin chief, Muhammad bin Saud, joined forces with the religious rabble rouser and founder of the '*Wahhabi*' movement, Muhammad ibn Abdul Wahhab, to create a new political entity. Over the next 150 years, the fortunes of the Saudi family rose and fell several times as Saudi rulers contended with Egypt, the Ottoman *Khalifah*, and other Arab tribes for control within the peninsula. From the very outset, the Saudi family received the support of the British and later the United States in maintaining their hegemony. The Saudi-Wahhabi state did much to cause rebellion against the Ottoman *khilafah* and on several occasions sacked the Holy Cities of Makkah and Madinah. It took the armed might of the Ottoman general, Muhammed Ali Pasha, to crush this ongoing sedition, which was manipulated by the power centers of Europe.

The modern Saudi state was founded by the late King Abd al-Aziz Al-Saud (known internationally as Ibn Saud). At the age of 21, Abd al-Aziz recaptured Riyadh with a force of 50 men in a dramatic dawn raid on the rival Al-Rashid family. Continuing his conquests, Abd al-Aziz vanquished Al-Hasa, the rest of the Najd and Hijaz, between 1913 and 1926. In 1932, these regions were united as the Kingdom of Saudi Arabia. The country's southern border with Yemen was partially defined by the Treaty of Taif in 1934, which ended a brief border war between the two states, but the border remains undemarcated in many areas. Boundaries with Jordan, Iraq, and Kuwait were established by a series of treaties negotiated in the 1920s. The "neutral zones" - the one with Iraq and the other with Kuwait - were created at that time. The Saudi-Kuwaiti neutral zone was administratively partitioned in 1971, with each state continuing to share equally the petroleum resources of the former zone. A tentative agreement on the partition of the Saudi-Iraqi neutral zone was reached in 1981, and partition was finalized in 1983. The border between Saudi Arabia and the United Arab Emirates was agreed upon in 1974.

ECONOMY

Saudi Arabia's economy is heavily dependent on oil. It accounts for about 88% of the country's exports by value. Proven reserves are estimated at one-fifth of all proven reserves in the world. Agriculture contributes to only 5% of the Gross Domestic Product.

Agriculture

Over a period of thousands of years, the people of the Saudi Peninsula developed the skills and social structure needed to extract a rewarding, if not bountiful, living from an extremely hostile environment. In the absence of any lakes or rivers, water was a precious commodity. Production was nearly subsistence in nature - much different than that required at the present time.

Of the country's total area of 568 million acres (230 m. ha), an estimated 1,643,000 acres (665,000 ha) were cultivated in 1980, which amounts to much less than one percent of the land area. Total grazing land was estimated at 210 million hectares (most of the country), but only five percent was considered excellent and 31 percent as good. Forested areas were estimated at 395,360 acres (160,000 ha), essentially in the mountains of the southwest.

Only in the mountains of Asir in the southwest was rainfall sufficient to support cropping. Cropping in the rest of the country was scattered and dependent on irrigation. Where water was available, nearly autonomous economic units emerged long ago, consisting of mutually supported farming, livestock raising, and arts and crafts. Long distances of rough arid terrain separated these scattered centers. The camel was best suited to serve man in such conditions. In the 1980s, commercial farming was an objective. Saudi officials wanted farmers to produce a substantial part of the country's basic food needs and maintain a prudent level of self-sufficiency in food production. Since the 1950s the agricultural sector expanded at a slower rate than the rest of the economy. By 1982, agriculture, including a little fishing, contributed only one percent to the GDP.

Oil

Oil was discovered in the 1930s. Large-scale production, however, did not begin until after World War II. More than 95% of all Saudi oil is produced by the Arabian American Oil Company (ARAMCO) on behalf of the Saudi Government, which is now being transformed into a Saudi company under the name of Saudi Arabian Oil Company. ARAMCO previously held a concession in Saudi Arabia, but since its purchase by the Saudi Government in 1980, it has functioned solely as a service company responsible for the exploration, development, production, and export from the government-owned reserves at levels of output established by the government.

The Japanese-owned Arabian Oil Company (AOC) and the U.S. based Gettys Oil Company (now owned by Texaco) operate in the former Saudi Arabia-Kuwait neutral zone and provide the rest of Saudi crude oil production.

With 5-year development plans, the government has sought to allocate its petroleum income to transform its relatively undeveloped oil-based economy into that of a modern industrial state while maintaining the kingdom's traditional Islamic values and customs. Dependence on oil revenues continue, but industry and agriculture now account for a larger share of total economic activity.

Industry

As an economic diversification instrument, industries were encouraged, The Saudi Industrial Development Fund established in 1974 supplied interest-free, medium to long-term financing for up to 50 percent of project cost for firms with at least 25 percent Saudi ownership. In 1981, nearly 1,200 industrial plants were operating. Most were small, often little more than shops. Some were larger, such as bakeries, printing establishments, and small factories turning out wood and metal products. The large establishments included automobile assembly plants, petrochemicals, iron and steel, copper wire, cables, and others.

NOTES

CHAPTER 39
SENEGAL

In colonial times, Senegal was the anchor of the French West African Empire. It is still a leading state in the region with a predominant Muslim population.

GEOGRAPHY

Senegal is located in the bulge of West Africa, bounded by the Atlantic Sea, Mauritania, Mali and Guinea-Bissau. The Gambia penetrates more than 200 miles (321 km) into Senegal (Map 42).

Senegal lies in the path of Sahel's environmental onslaught. As a result, the country's north suffers severely from drought and dislocation. Most of the country has low, rolling plains with savanna type vegetation. In the southeast however, plateaus rise to the elevations of 1,640 feet (500 m) above sea level to form the foothills of Fouta-Djillon Mountains. Marshy swamps interspersed with tropical rain forest are common in the southwest. Senegal is drained by the Senegal, Saloum, and Casamance Rivers, each of which is navigable by ocean-going vessels for a substantial distance.

The well-defined dry and humid seasons are the result of alternating winds, southeast in the winter and southwest in the summer. Dakar's annual rainfall is about 2 inches (61 cm), which occurs between June and October when maximum temperatures average 82°F (27°C).

Geographical Profile

Area: 76,000 sq. mi. (196,840 sq. km)
Population: 8.4 million (1994); 9.9 million (2000); 13.1 million (2010)
Neighboring Countries: Guinea, Mali, Mauritania, Guinea-Bissau
Capital: Dakar
Other Cities: Thies, Kaolack, Saint-Luis, Ziguinehor
Terrain: Flat or rising to foothills
Climate: Tropical/Sahelain-desert or grassland in the north, heavier vegetation in the south and southeast
Ethnic Groups: Wolof 43%, Fulani and Toucouleur 23%, Serer 15%, Diola, Mindingo, and others 22%
Religion: Sunni Islam 94%. Christianity (5%), Paganism (1%)
Languages: French (official), Wolof, Pulaar, Diola, Mandingo
Economy:
  GDP: $5 billion (1989)
  Per Capita Income: $630
  Natural Resources: Fish, phosphate
  Agriculture: (22% of GNP): Products: Peanuts, millet, sorghum, manioc, rice, cotton
  Industry: (24% of GNP): Types: Fishing, agricultural product processing, light manufacturing, mining
Official Name: Republic of Senegal
Date of Independence: August 20, 1960

The maximum temperature from December to February is about 63°F (17°C). The minimum temperature from December to February is about 63°F (17°C). Temperatures in the interior are higher than along the coast, while rainfall increases further south, exceeding 60 inches (102 cm) a year in some areas.

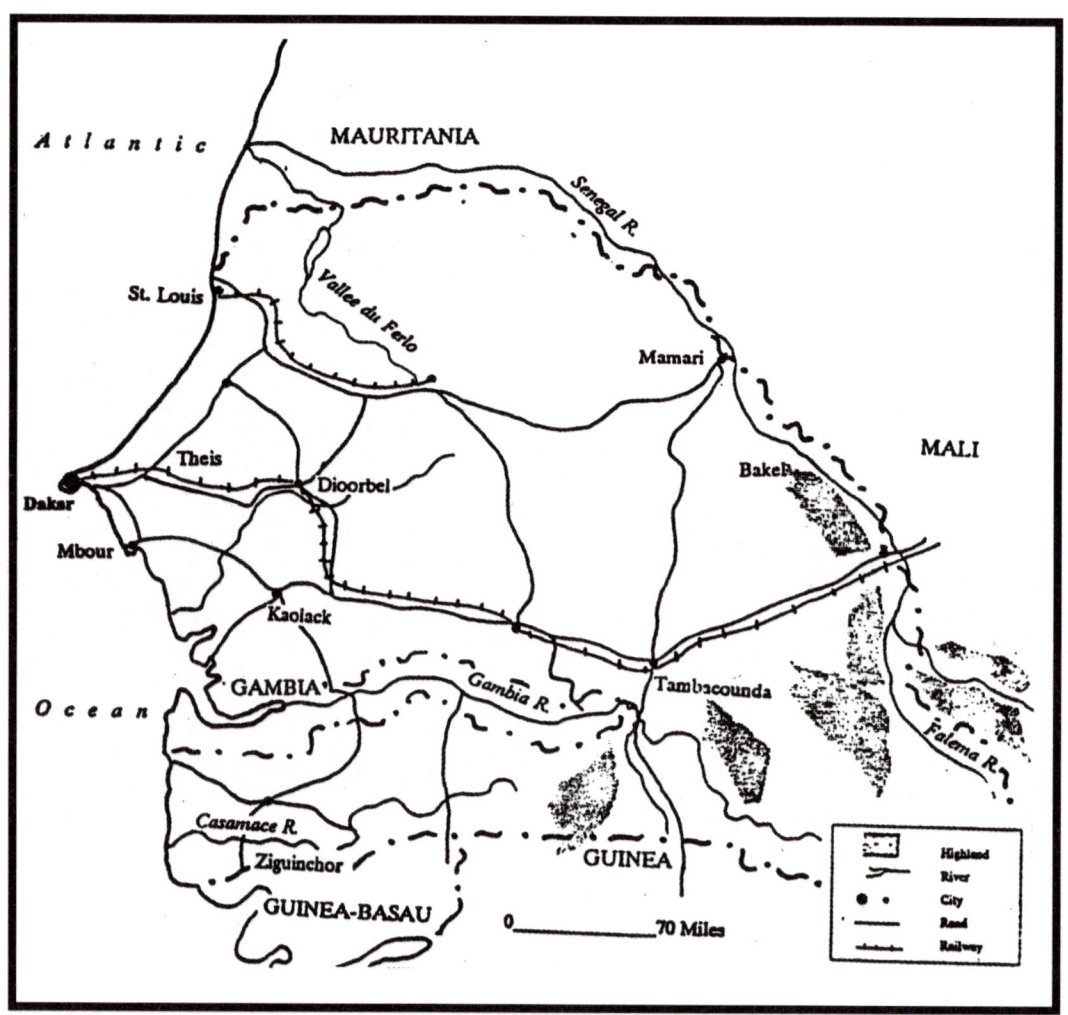

Map 42: Senegal

PEOPLE AND POPULATION

Most Senegalese belong to Wolof, Rulani, Toucouleur, Serer, and Diola tribes and speak their ethnic languages. French is the official language spoken by literate persons. Nearly 40,000 Europeans (mostly French) and Lebanese reside in Senegal. Despite the rapid migration of literate to the cities, Senegal is predominantly rural. About 70% of its people live in villages. In these areas, density varies from about 200 per sq. miles (77 per sq. km) in the west-central region to five persons per sq. mile (two persons per sq. km) in the arid eastern section.

In 1944, Senegal's population stood at 8.4 million, with a 2.8 percent annual rate of natural growth. With this rate of growth, the population was likely to double in 25 years.

EVOLUTION OF SENEGAL

Archaeological findings indicate that Senegal was inhabited in prehistoric times. Islam first came to the Senegal River Valley in the 11th century. It spread to other parts of the country from there. Today, 94% of the Senegalese are Muslims. In the 13th and 14th centuries, the area came under the influence of the Mandingo Empire to the east. The Doloff Empire to the east was also founded at this time. The empire comprised the states of Cayor, Baol, Oualo, Sine, and Solum until the 16th century, when they revolted for independence.

Arriving in the 15th century, the Portuguese were the first Europeans to trade in Senegal. They were followed by the Dutch and the French. During the 18th century, the French gradually established control over the interior regions and administered them as a protectorate until 1920 and as a colony thereafter. There were many Islamic movements (mostly led by Sufi *shaykhs*) tried in vain to resist the armed might of the French. After 1902, Dakar became the capital of the French West Africa. In 1946, a territorial assembly was elected by a restricted franchise and given advisory powers. These were gradually expanded, and the franchise broadened in succeeding years. Senegal became a member of the French Community with virtually complete internal autonomy.

In January 1959, Senegal and French Soudan merged to form the Mali Federation, which became fully independent on June 20, 1960. Due to the internal political difficulties, the federation broke on August 20, 1960. Senegal and Soudan (renamed the Republic of Mali) each proclaimed independence.

ECONOMY

Senegal's economy remains fragile; the country depends on the export of peanuts, and phosphate and on its fishing industry. Its resource-poor economy is vulnerable to droughts, environmental degradation, and international price fluctuations.

Agriculture

Senegal is overwhelmingly agricultural, with more than 70% of the labor force engaged in farming. The most widespread food crops are millet, guinea corn, cassava, and corn, with rice in the moister areas of Casamance or along river valleys. Most of the cultivation is rain-fed, and it has often been said that "when the rains fail or are late, no one can work or be productive in rural

Senegal." Along the Senegal River, there is flood-plain cultivation, but this too is dependent on the vagaries of river level and subsequent rainfall.

Senegal has an estimated 2.7 million head of cattle, with concentrations in the Diourbel-Kaolack region where the Serere people practice to a form of mixed farming. In the drier parts of the interior plains, pastoralism is mainly practiced by semi-nomadic Fulani people.

Peanuts (Groundnuts) provide the main cash income for many of the peasant farmers and is the country's main export crop. The widespread sandy, low-clay content soils are particularly suitable for peanut cultivation, but tend to become impoverished fairly rapidly. Rainfall variability results in wide fluctuations in annual production. About half of the peanut crop is delivered to oil mills at Dakar, Longa, Dioubrel, Kaolack, and Ziguinchor. In normal years, peanut, peanut cakes, and peanut oil make up 50 percent of the export value.

The only attempt to move away from rain-fed farming was made during the colonial era. The Richard Toll irrigation scheme of the late 1940s involved a barrage across a water-course connecting Lake Guiers with the Senegal River. The stored water is distributed by pumping to 14,826 acres (600 ha) of rice cultivated by mechanical methods. Since the 1960s, sugar cultivation has been added. Another dam was completed for the purpose of controlling saline water from the delta and lower Senegal River so that irrigation can ultimately be extended to as much as 494,200 acres (200,000 ha).

Industries and Minerals

Because it served as the industrial base for the whole of French West Africa, and also because it has an urban market in Dakar with 40,000 Europeans and Lebanese, Senegal has long had a wider range of industries than most other West African states. At independence in 1960, manufacturing grew at 7 percent a year. Initially, industry was based on the processing of local commodities (vegetable oils, cereals, fish, and sugar), but it has now diversified into textiles, clothing, paints, engineering, vehicle assembly, ship construction and repairs, and oil refining. A high proposition of the industry is concentrated in the Dakar area.

Until 1964, there was extraction of zircon and titanium from beach sand in the Saloum River area, but the principal mining activity is now for phosphate at Taiba and Thies. At present, the phosphate is exported in an unprocessed form, but there are plans for a fertilizer and phosphoric acid plant at Taiba. In 1963, a company was established to develop iron-ore mining at Koudakourou in the extreme southeast of the country.

The fishing sector has become a bright spot on the Senegalese economic horizon. The sophistication of Dakar, the winter dry season, numerous good beaches, possibilities for sport fishing and game hunting, and an existing level of infrastructure including well-developed port facilities are facilitating economic growth. A major international airport serving 24 international airlines, direct and expanding telecommunication links with major world centers, and a good road and railway system strengthens tourism and economy and offers the possibility of future development.

The industrial Free Trade Zone, a government-owned and operated free-trade zone, offers liberal tax advantages and exemptions from customs duties for investors manufacturing for export.

CHAPTER 40
SOMALIA

The Somalis are a Hamitic speaking people, predominantly pastoral, homogenous in language and culture. They are bound together by a strong sense of nationalism and the Islamic religion. Islam dates back to the seventh century AD when it was a part of an Arab sultanate founded by Quraish immigrants from Yemen.

GEOGRAPHY

Somalia is located on the east coast of Africa, north of the Equator, and along with Ethiopia and Djibouti, it is often referred to as the Horn of Africa. It extends along the south shore of the Gulf of Aden to Cape Gardafui, and then south to Ras Chiamboni beyond the Gibu (Juba) River (Map 43). It comprises Italy's former Trust Territory of Somalia and the former British Protectorate of Somaliland. The coastline extends for 1,700 miles (2,720 km).

The northern part of the country is hilly, dominated by the rugged Ogo and Mijuretein (Medjourtine) mountains. In many places, the altitude ranges between 3000-7000 ft. (900 and 2,100 meters) above sea level. The central and southern areas (which comprise the bulk of the territory) are low-lying, almost featureless, with an average altitude of less than 500 ft. (180 m). The Juba and the Shebelle Rivers rise in high Ethiopian Massif and flow south across the broad, low-lying coastal plain country toward the Indian Ocean. The Juba enters the Indian Ocean at Kismaiyu, but the Shebelle does not reach the sea, except during periods of exceptionally heavy rains.

Geographical Profile

Area: 246,000 sq. miles (680,800 sq. km)
Population: 8.8 million (1994); 10.5 million (2000); 13.9 million (2010)
Neighboring Countries: Kenya, Ethiopia, Djibouti
Capital: Mogadishu
Other City: Hargeisa
Terrain: Central and Southern Somalia are flat; Northern Somalia is hilly
Climate: Hot and dry with seasonal monsoon
Ethnic Groups: 98.8% Somali; 1.2% Arab and Asian
Religion: Sunni Islam 99%
Economy:
  GDP: (1985) $1.8 billion
  Per Capita Income: $300
  Natural Resources: Undetermined quantities of various minerals including petroleum
  Agriculture: Products: Livestock bananas, corn, sorghum, sugar
  Industry: Types: Sugar, textiles, packaging, oil refining
Official Name: Somali Democratic Republic
Date of Independence: June 26, 1960

Major climatic factors are a year-round hot climate, seasonal monsoon winds, and irregular rainfall with recurring droughts. The mean daily maximum temperatures range from 85°F-105°F (30° to 40°C) except at higher elevations and along the east coast. The mean daily minimums usually vary from about 60°F-85°F (15°C to 30°C). The southwest monsoon, a cool sea breeze, makes the period from about May to October the most pleasant season at Mogadishu. The December-February period of the northeast monsoon is also comfortable. The "Tangambill" periods that intervene between the two monsoons (October-November and March-May) are hot and humid.

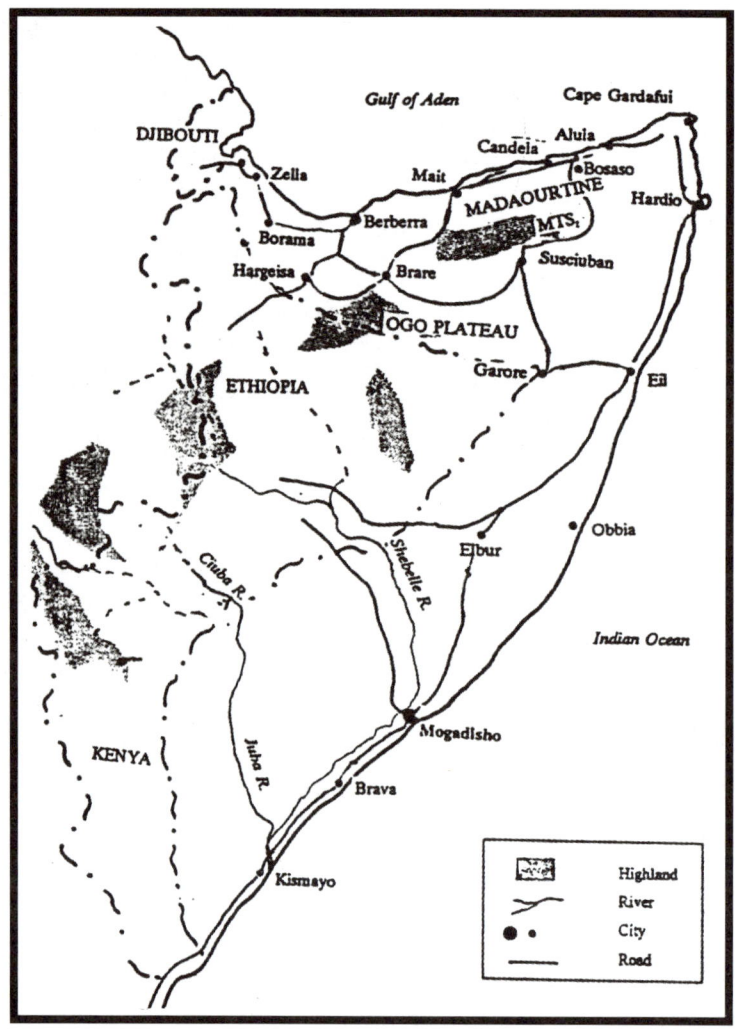

Map: 43: Somalia

PEOPLE AND POPULATION

Somalis have a remarkably homogenous culture and identity. As early as the seventh century AD, indigenous Cushitic peoples began to mingle with Arab and Persian traders who had settled along the coast. Interaction over the centuries led to the emergence of a Somali culture bound by common traditions, a single language, and the Islamic faith. Somali nationalism extends far beyond the legal state, and for years, the Somalis have sought to include all their people in Ethiopia, Djibouti, and other areas in a single nation-state.

Sizable ethnic groups in the country include some 35,000 Arabs, about 2,000 Italians, and 1,000 Indians and Pakistanis. Nearly all inhabitants speak the Somali language, which remained unwritten until October 1973, when the government proclaimed it the nation's official language and decreed an orthography using Italian letters. Somali is now the language of instruction in all schools. Arabic, English, and Italian are also used extensively.

In 1994, the total population stood at 8.8 million people, with an annual rate of natural increase at 2.9 percent. With this rate of increase, the population is expected to double in 24 years.

EVOLUTION OF SOMALIA

Early history traces the development of the Somali people to an Arab sultanate, which was founded in the seventh century AD by Quraish immigrants from Yemen. Somalis displaced their ethnically related Galla peoples and small bands of Bantu, known to the early Arab geographers as the Zanj. As the Somalis swept south, Yemenite Arabs set up coastal city states such as Zeila, Berbera, Mogadishu, and Brava. By the tenth century, a ring of coastal emporia had been established through which Muslim expansion followed. The towns were captured by the Portuguese in the sixteenth century when they sacked the port of Berbera. In turn, they were replaced by the Turks, Egyptians, and the Sultan of Zanzibar and by the end of the nineteenth century by France, Britain, and Italy.

The British East India Company's desire for unrestricted harbor facilities led to the conclusion of treaties with the Sultan of Tajura as early as 1840. With the opening of the Suez Canal in 1869, the Red Sea became a major avenue of European trade with Asia and the object of colonial aspirations. At the time, the Red Sea coast was subject to the nominal suzerainty of the Ottoman Empire, but governed by local potentates. In 1870, an Egyptian governor was appointed over the whole coast from Suez to Cape Gardafui, and Egyptian garrisons were established at Zeila, Berbera, and later at Harrar. But in 1885, the troubles stemming from the Mahdist revolt in the Sudan, led Egypt to withdraw, and the "scramble" of the Horn of East Africa began.

The British gained control over northern Somali chiefs in 1886, who were guaranteed British protection. British objectives centered on safeguarding trade links to the east and securing local sources of food and provisions. The boundary between Ethiopia and British Somaliland were established in 1897 through treaty negotiations between Britain and King Menelik of Ethiopia.

In 1885, Italy obtained commercial advantages in the area from the Sultan of Zanzibar and in 1889 concluded agreements with the Sultans of Obbia and Caluula, who placed their territories under Italy's protection. Between 1897 and 1905, Italy made agreements with the Ethiopians and the British that marked out the boundaries of Italian Somaliland. The Italian Government assumed direct administration, giving the territory colonial status.

During the first two decades of this century, British rule was challenged through persistent attacks led by the Islamic leader and Sufi, *shaykh* Mohammad Abdullah. A long series of intermittent engagements and truces ended in 1920, when British warplanes bombed Abdullah's stronghold at Taleex. Since then, Abdullah has been lauded as a popular hero and stands as a major figure of Somali national identity.

Italian occupation gradually extended inland. In 1924, the Jubaland Province of Kenya, including the town and port of Kismayu, was ceded to Italy by the United Kingdom. The subjugation and occupation of the independent sultanates of Obbia and Mijertein began in 1925 and were completed in 1927. In the late 1920s, Italians and Somali influence expanded into the Ogaden region of eastern Ethiopia. Continuing incursions climaxed in 1935, when the Italian forces launched an offensive that led to the capture of Addis Ababa and the Italian annexation of Ethiopia in 1936. Following Italy's declaration of war on United Kingdom in June 1940, Italian troops overran British garrison. In 1941, British forces began operations against the Italian East African Empire and quickly brought the greater part of the Italian Somaliland under British control. In 1948, Britain turned the Ogaden and neighboring Somali territories over to Ethiopia.

In Article 23 of the 1947 peace treaty, Italy renounced all rights and titles to Italian Somaliland. In accordance with treaty stipulations, the Four Powers referred the question of disposal of former Italian colonies to the UN General Assembly on September 15, 1948. On November 21, 1949, the General Assembly adopted a resolution recommending that Italian Somaliland be placed under international trusteeship system for 10 years, with Italy as the administering authority, followed by independence for Italian Somaliland. In 1959, at the request of the Somali Government, the UN General Assembly advanced the date of independence from December 2 to July 1, 1960. The British Somaliland also got independence on June 26, 1960 and joined Italian Somaliland to become one country as Somalia.

Since that time, Somalia has suffered by misrule and dictatorship. In recent times, the Somali people have paid a heavy price for this mismanagement. In the late 1980's, several warlords divided the country between themselves and plunged the nation into anarchy. As a result, tens of thousands died from the fighting and the famine that ensued. In 1993, the United Nations sent peace keepers into Somalia to put an end to the famine and to make peace between the factions.

ECONOMY

About 60% of all Somalis are nomadic or seminomadic pastoralists who raise cattle, camels, sheep, and goats. About 25% of the population are settled farmers who live mainly in the fertile agricultural zone between the Juba and Shebelle Rivers in southern Somalia.

Agriculture

Agriculture is severely restricted by the harsh environment. Less than one percent of the area is cultivated, and nearly 13 percent is cultivable, most of which is in the Giuba and Shebelle valleys. There, the emphasis is on staple crops (sorghum, corn, and cassava), although irrigated cash crops such as sugar and bananas are also important. Bananas were once Somalia's leading export, the plantations being established by the Italians.

Somalia's predominant economic sector is pastoral, but it is handicapped by low and erratic rainfall, periodic droughts, overgrazing, inferior stocks, frequent invasion of locusts, and conservative attitudes towards the marketing and ownership of livestock. Despite these limitations, livestock products contribute 55% of the export earnings. Live goats, sheep, and camels form the bulk of these exports, most being shipped to Saudi Arabia and Kuwait (Fig. 56).

Fig. 56: Livestock in Somalia

Minerals and Industry

Minerals, including petroleum, natural gas, and uranium, are found throughout the country, but none have been exploited commercially. Several oil companies are exploring for petroleum. With the help of foreign aid, small industries such as textiles, handicrafts, meat processing, and printing are being established.

The European Community and the World Bank jointly financed construction of a deep-water port at Mogadishu. The former Soviet Union improved Somalia's deep-water port at Berbera in 1969. Facilities at Berbera were further improved by a U.S. military construction program completed in 1985. The United States is currently renovating a deep-water port at Kismayo that serves the fertile Juba River basin and is vital to Somalia's banana export industry. Smaller ports are located at Merca, Brava, and Bosaso.

A small fishing industry has begun in the north where tuna, shark, and other warm-water fish are caught (Fig. 57). Aromatic woods - frankincense and myrrh - from a small forest area also contribute to the country's exports.

The government has assumed a direct role in developing the national economy. In 1970, foreign banks and several other foreign-controlled firms were nationalized. Since 1981, the government has undertaken a series of major economic reforms in compliance with three successive International Monetary Fund standby agreements.

In spite of its strategic location, the lack of infrastructure transportation (roads, railways, airports, and seaports) impedes Somalia's development.

Fig. 57: Somalia: Fishing

There is no railway in Somalia. Roads are few and far between. A 76-mile (122 km) road between Berbera and Buras was provided by the United Arab Emirates in 1981. Another 161-mile (257 km) road between Mogadisho and Kismayu, completing a link between Guba and Gelib and providing a link between Mogadishu and Kismayu was completed in 1985 with financial assistance from the Arab Fund. In 1988, the United States also funded construction of a 75-mile (120 km) road between Mogadishu and Cadali. Then, in 1989, the European Development Fund granted a sum of $54 million for construction of a 144-mile (230 km) road between Gelib and Barbera to provide access to the Juba valley. All together, Somalia had 13,926 miles (22,281 km) of roads in 1988.

CHAPTER 41
SUDAN

Sudan is a geographical bridge between the Arab north and African south. The transition between the north and south lies along 12º N parallel. In the north are Muslims who dominate the government, politics and economy. The south consists mostly of Christians and tribal people.

GEOGRAPHY

Located in the northeastern part of Africa, Sudan is the largest country of the continent. Its northern and northwestern boundaries with Egypt, Libya, and northern Chad are geometrical, which for a greater part lie in a desolate dry terrain. In the west are the Central African Republic and Uganda. In the east, the boundary corresponds to the western limit of Ethiopian massif. In the south are Kenya and Uganda (Map 44).

Sudan is located in the tropics and features Saharan conditions in the north and equatorial conditions in the south. With minor exceptions, Sudan is dry and characterized by high temperatures and little rainfall. Southern Sudan is humid with milder temperatures and heavy rains. Sudan can be divided into six geographical regions: (i) northern Sudan, (ii) semi-desert steppe, (iii) western Dafur, (iv) the Quz, (v) the clay plain, and (vi) southern Sudan. Northern Sudan is part of the Sahara, an extension of Libyan desert,

---

Geographical Profile

Area: 967,500 sq. mi. (2.5 million sq. km)
Population: 28.2 million (1994); 33.9 million (2000); 42.2 million (2010)
Neighboring Countries: Egypt, Libya, Chad, Central African Republic, Zaire, Uganda, Kenya, Ethiopia
Capital: Khartoum
Other Cities: Juba, Port Sudan, Kassala, Kosti
Terrain: Generally flat with mountains in the east and west
Climate: Desert in north to tropical in south
Ethnic Groups: Arab-African, black African
Religions: Sunni Islam, Paganism (southern Sudan), Christianity
Languages: Arabic (official), English, tribal languages
Economy:
  GDP: 9 billion (1988)
  Per Capita Income: $300 (1990)
  Natural Resources: Modest reserves of oil, iron ore, chrome, and other industrial metals
  Agriculture: Products: Cotton, peanuts, sorghum, sesame seeds, arabic gum, sugar cane, livestock
  Industry: Types: Textiles, cement, cotton ginning, edible oil, and sugar refining
Official Name: Republic of Sudan
Date of Independence: January 1, 1956

which stretches in a straight line with Egypt. West of Khartoum and Butana is the semi-desert steppe. This area offers sparse grazing to a number of nomadic camel and sheep-owning Arab tribes. Western Dafur is volcanic, with an elevation ranging from 2,100 ft. (700 m) and 3,000 ft. (1,000 m). East of Darfur is a great stretch of undulating sand, which stretches to the White Nile and is known as Qoz. Clay plains extend from the junction of the White and Blue Nile, and east from Nuba Mountains to the Ethiopian border. Southern Sudan is largely a "Sudd" (barrier) because of floating vegetation that occasionally block the navigable channels.

The orientation of Sudan's physiographic belts is latitudinal. A series of climatic zones is recognized from desert north to the moist savanna of the extreme south. North of El-Fasher latitude, vegetation becomes nonexistent, and the rainfall drops down to 10 inches (254 mm). Across the Kordofan Plateau the rainfall ranges between 25 to 30 inches (635-762 mm), and in the southwestern margins, it exceeds 50 inches (1,270 mm).

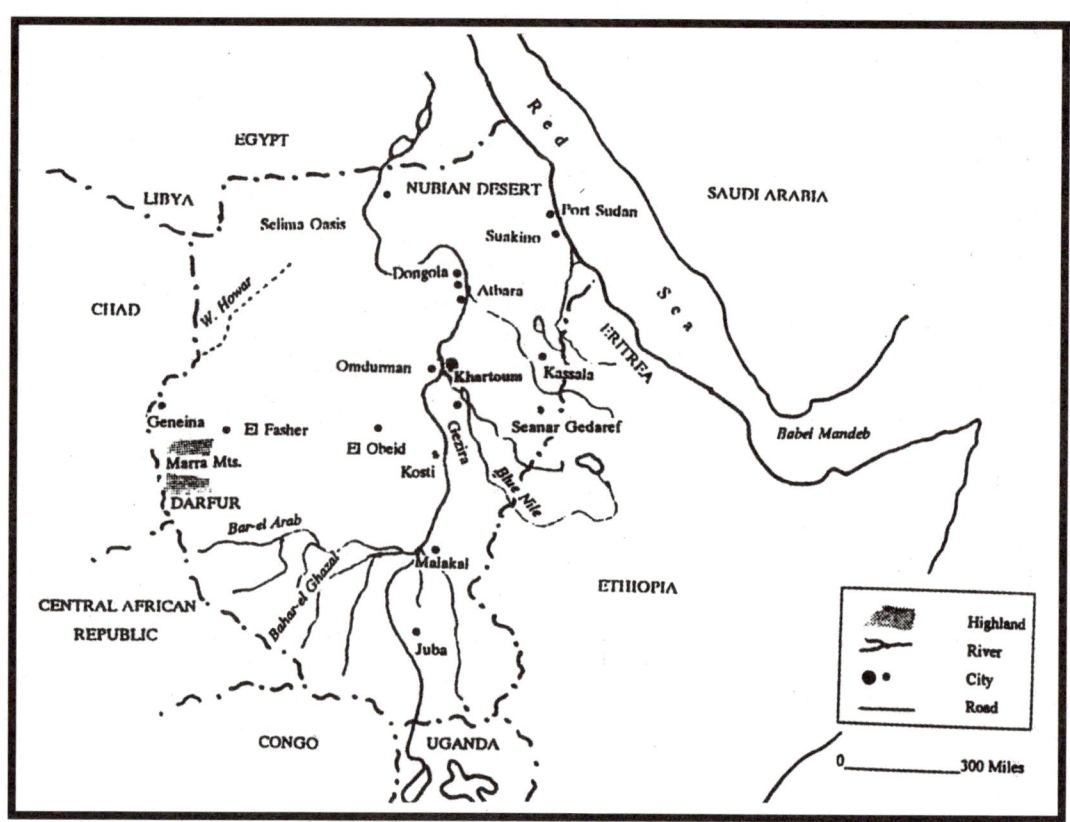

Map 44: Sudan

The great longitudinal unifier is the White Nile. In the extreme south, it enters Sudan via a series of rapids, all of which are upstream from Juba. Below Juba, the Nile is navigable to Khartoum. The gradient is very low, as the river braids its way through the Sudd, re-entering a well-defined valley in the area of Malakal. It is along the Nile that the "bridge" character of Sudan between black and Arab Africa becomes clear.

PEOPLE AND POPULATION

Sudan has two distinct cultural groups: Arab Muslims in the north and black Africans in the south, making an effective collaboration between the two a major problem. The five northern regions cover most of Sudan and include most urban centers. The population is concentrated in the Gezira, immediately to the south of Khartoum, and along the river further to the north. Other population clusters are remote from the capital in distance and in every other way. Most Sudanese who live in this area speak Arabic and are predominantly Muslim. Included in the minorities are several distinct tribal groups; the Kababish of northern Kordofan, a camel-raising people; the Jaalin and Shaigiyya groups of settled tribes along rivers; the semi-nomadic Baggara of Kordofan and Darfur; the Hamitic Beja in the Red Sea areas and Nubians of the northern Nile area. These people were heavily influenced by the Sufi teachings of Islam (Fig. 58).

Fig: 58: The *dhikr* of the dervishes of Khartoum

The southern region has a population of about 4-6 million and is a predominantly rural area with a subsistence economy. Here, the people mainly live with their indigenous, traditional beliefs, although Christian missionaries have made significant inroads. These people slaughter pigs and goats in their religious performance.

South Sudan also contains many tribal groups and uses many more languages than the north. The Dinka (population one million or more) is the largest of many black African tribes. Along with the Shilluk and the Nuer, they are among the Nilotic tribes. The Azande, Bor, and Jo Luo are Sudanic tribes in the west, and the Acholli and Lotuhu live in the extreme south extending into Uganda. Most of these people are rural and live in villages and small towns.

The first census was taken at the time of their independence in 1956 and reported a population of 10.3 million. In 1973, the population reached 14.1 million and in 1983, 20.6 million. In 1994, the population was estimated at 28.2 million people with 3.1 percent annual rate of natural increase. With such a rate of annual increase, the population would double in 22 years.

EVOLUTION OF SUDAN

Sudan was a collection of small, independent states from the beginning of the Christian era until 1820-21, when Egypt conquered and unified the northern portion of the country. Although Egypt claimed all of the present Sudan during most of the 19th century, it was unable to establish an effective control on southern Sudan, which remained an area of fragmented tribes, subject to frequent attacks by slave raiders.

In 1881, a Muslim *shaykh* named Muhammad Ahmad proclaimed himself to be the *Mahdi*, the messianic figure promised to appear at the end of time to bring peace and justice to the Earth. He began to unify the Muslim peoples of Western and Central Sudan. His followers were given the name *Ansar*, which they continue to use today. His movement culminated with the fall of Khartoum in 1885. Muhammad Ahmad died shortly thereafter, but his Islamic state survived until overwhelmed by an Anglo-Egyptian force in 1898. Sudan was proclaimed a condominium in 1899 under British-Egyptian administration.

In February 1963, the United Kingdom and Egypt concluded an agreement providing for Sudanese self-government and self-administration. With the consent of the British and Egyptian governments, Sudan achieved independence on January 1, 1956. In 1958, Chief of Staff, Lt. Gen. Ibrahim Abboud overthrew the parliamentary regime in a bloodless coup. Following the popular resentment against the Army rule, a civilian government took office in late October 1964. Elections were held in April 1965, and a new government was formed. Dissatisfaction with this government culminated in another coup on May 25, 1969. In September 1983, as a part of Islamization, the government incorporated the penal code Islamic punishment drawn from the *Shari'ah*. The code was not acceptable even to many Muslims, who reacted against the government. The government declared a state of emergency, in part, to ensure that *Shari'ah* was applied more broadly.

Early 1985 saw serious shortages of fuel and food in Khartoum, a growing insurgency in the south and an increasingly difficult refugee burden. In April, massive demonstrations broke out in Khartoum. On April 6, 1985, senior military officers mounted a coup and took over the government. Elections were held in April 1986, but the civilian governments were short-lived. In February 1989, the army again seized power.

Southern resentment of northern domination culminated in a civil war. The southerners took control of large areas of Equatoria, Bahr-al Ghazal and Upper Nile provinces and also of the southern portions of Dhafur, Kordofan, and Blue Nile provinces. The government of Sudan also controls a number of major southern towns and cities, including Juba, Wau, and Malakal. An informal cease-fire in May broke down in October 1989, and fighting between the government and southern rebels has continued since then.

ECONOMY

Sudan's primary resources are agricultural. Minerals are negligible, and industrial development is only just beginning.

Agriculture

About one-third of the total area is suitable for cultivation or grazing. Grain (sorghum) is the principal food crop, and wheat is grown for domestic consumption. People usually sell grain in front of their huts, which also serve as schools for religious education for the children (Fig. 59). Other crops like sesame seeds and peanuts are cultivated for domestic consumption and increasingly for export. Subsistence production occupies more than half the population and uses 80 percent of the cultivated area. Cotton accounts for nearly 50% of export earning. Another large export crop is arabic gum, which is used in pharmaceutical, food preparation, and printing. Sudan produces four-fifth of the world's supply of arabic gum. The areas of commercial production are in the Khartoum-Gezira area and along the river and rail lines, mainly in the northeastern quadrant of the country.

Minerals and Industry

Sudan lacks minerals. Industrial development has made some progress since the Second World War. It is concerned mainly with the processing of agricultural products to reduce imports. Khartoum North has emerged as the major industrial center, but the manufacturing industry is also important in Khartoum, Omdurman, Wad Medani, Atbara, and Port Sudan. Manufactured goods include clothing, shoes, soap, beer, furniture, cigarettes, rubber tires, and plastics. A cement factory was established at Atbara in 1949, and another was established at Rabak in the Blue Nile Province in 1964. A meat-canning plant was established at Kosti in 1952, textile mills at Nazara in 1950, and two aluminum plants and a glass factory in Khartoum-Omdurman.

In the middle 1970s, large-scale agricultural schemes were established with assistance from oil-rich Arab states. Sudan hoped to attain self-sufficiency in sugar, wheat, and coffee and also become the breadbasket of the Arab world. Unfortunately, the high hopes of the planners were not achieved due to infrastructure and technical problems.

Fig. 59: A Maderssa (School) for education of children

CHAPTER 42
SYRIA

The Arab world ends at Syria's northern border which joins Turkey. Muslims had come to the southern cost of Syria during the lifetime of Prophet Muhammad, but Islam was introduced to Syria in 635 AD.

GEOGRAPHY

The strategic crossroads location gives Syria an important position in the Middle East. The country is bordered by Turkey, Iraq, Jordan, Israel, Lebanon, and the Mediterranean Sea (Map 45). In historic times, the name Syria had been applied to the larger eastern Mediterranean coastal region, but its contemporary boundaries were created by France after the First World War.

The Anti-Lebanon Mountains (*Jabal ash-Sharqi*) are the most prominent topographic feature in Syria. The main ridge rises to a height of 8,625 feet (2,629 m) near an-Nabk, while the main height is between 6,000 and 7,000 feet (1,829 and 2,134 m). The Euphrates River Valley, traverses the country from north to the southeast. The *Jabal al-Druze* rises to 5,905 feet (1,800 m) in the extreme south, and the Jabal Abu Rajmayb (the Palmyra Range) stretches southeastward across the central part of the country. A semi-desert plateau characterizes the southeast. The eastern side of the Anti-Lebanon mountains is dotted with valley oases, the largest of which is Damascus. Damascus is considered to be largest continuously inhabited city. It is located on the banks of the Barada River and is the main center of education, culture, and industry.

Geographical Profile

Area: 71,500 sq. miles (185,170 sq. km)
Population: 14.8 million (1994); 18.9 million (2000); 25.6 million (2010)
Neighboring Countries: Turkey, Lebanon, Israel, Jordan, Iraq
Capital: Damascus
Other Cities: Homs, Aleppo
Ethnic Groups: Arabs (90%), Kurds, Armenians, Circassians, Turks
Religion: Islam 95% (Sunni 70%, Alawi 12%, Druze 3%, Isma'ili 1%, other Shi'ah); Christianity 5%
Languages: Arabic (official), French, Kurdish
Economy:
    GDP: (1984) $13.9 billion
    Per Capita Income: $1,388
    Natural Resources: Oil, phosphate, chrome and manganese ores, asphalt, iron ore, rock salt, marble, gypsum
    Agriculture: (17% of GNP): Products: cotton, wheat, barley, sugar beets
    Industry: Types: Mining, manufacturing construction
Official Name: Syrian Arab Republic
Date of Independence: April 17, 1946

The undulating plain, occupying most of the country, is known as the Syrian desert. In general, their elevation lies between 980 feet and 1,640 feet (300 and 500m). The area is not a sand desert but comprises rock and gravel steppe. A mountainous region in the south central area is known as al-Hamad.

The Mediterranean Sea moderates temperatures along the coastal plain, which experiences warm humid summers and mild damp winters. The climate can be compared to that of Phoenix, Arizona. Summer days are dry and hot, with mean maximum temperatures above 80°F (27°C). From December to March, the weather is quite cold, but seldom reaches freezing. Precipitation is about 30 inches (25.4 cm) in the western desert area. The rainy season generally lasts from November to April. Few large rivers originate within Syria; the Euphrates, al-Khabur, and Balikh have their headwaters in Turkey, and the Oronstoes River rises in Lebanon. Tapping these rivers for irrigation, particularly the Euphrates, has been a priority of Syrian development plans.

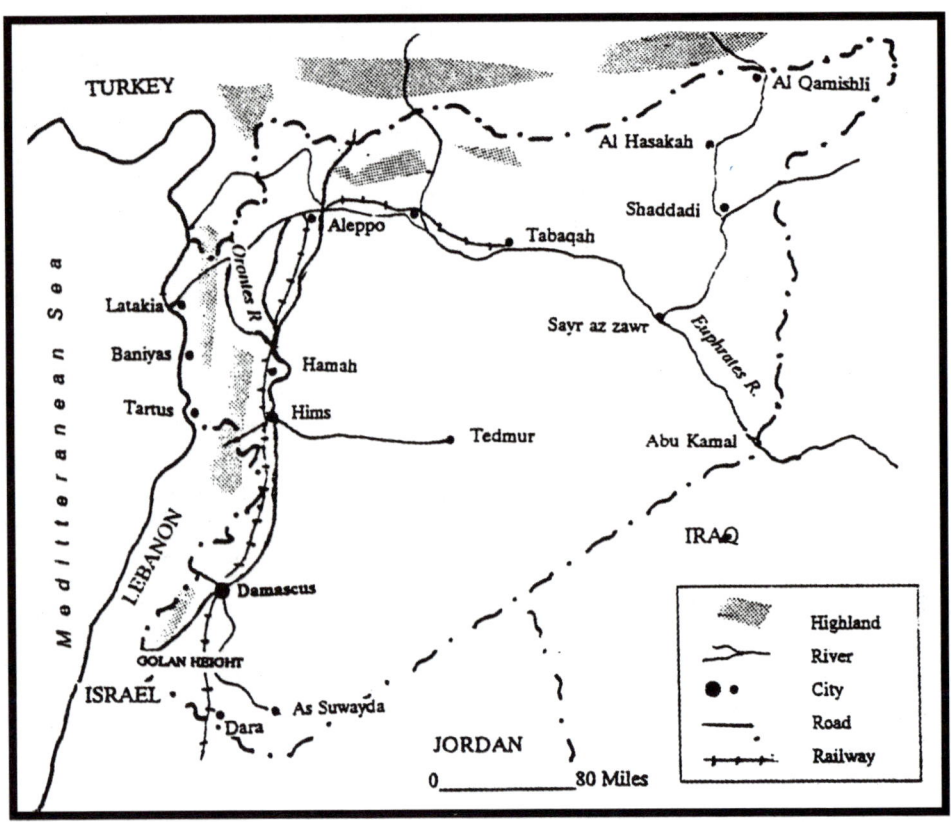

Map 45: Syria

PEOPLE AND POPULATION

Syrians evolved from several origins over a long period of time. The Greek and Roman ethnic influence was negligible in comparison with that of Semitic peoples of Arabia and Mesopotamia. Later, the Turks came like the Greeks and Romans before them. These people influenced political and economic structures but failed to produce any noticeable change in the dominant Arab character of Syrian people.

Some ethnic groups have been partially assimilated by the Arab majority that also include the Bedouins. Second in number to the Arabs are Kurds, who partially lost their mother tongue. The third are the Armenians who can be divided into two groups: the early settlers, who have now been largely Arabized, and the later immigrants, who arrived after World War I and retained their identity and language. Most people live (i) in the Euphrates River Valley, (ii) along the coastal plain, and (iii) in a fertile strip between the coastal mountains and the desert. Overall, the population density is about 109 persons per square mile (42 persons per sq. km).

The population of Syria is 95% Muslim, with a *Sunni* majority. Other Muslim groups include *Alawi*, *Shi'ah*, and *Druze*. Some 120,000 Christians live in Syria, and the Jewish community numbers about 4,000. Arabic is the official language. Many educated Syrians speak English or French, but English is more widely understood. The ancient language of Aramaic (spoken by Jesus Christ) is still spoken in a few villages.

EVOLUTION OF SYRIA

Archeologists have discovered that Syria was the center of one of the most ancient civilizations on earth. Around the newly excavated city of Elba in northern Syria, a great Semitic Empire existed from the Red Sea, north to Turkey, and east to Mesopotamia, from 2500 to 240 BC. The city itself had a population estimated at 250,000 people during that time, and the many tablets found there yield considerable information about this civilization.

Syria was occupied successively by Canaanites, Phoenicians, Hebrews, Armenians, Assyrians, Babylonians, Persians, Greeks, Nabatacans, and Byzantines. In the first half of the 11th century, Syria was absorbed into the Muslim *Khilafah*. In the second half of the 11th century, Syria fell into the hands of Seljuk Turks, who had established a *sultanate* in Anatolia. They occupied Aleppo and then Damascus. After the death of Sultan Malik Shah in 1092, the Seljuk Empire fell to pieces. Between 1090 and 1124 the crusaders occupied Antioch, Jerusalem, al-Karak in Transjordan, and the coast. Syria was significant in the history of Christianity as the self-proclaimed apostle, Paul, established the first organized Christian Church at Antioch.

Damascus, settled about 2500 BC, is one of the oldest inhabited cities in the world (Fig. 60). It came under Muslim rule in 636 AD. Immediately thereafter, the city's power and prestige reached its peak. From 661 AD to 750 AD, Damascus became the capital of Umayyad Empire, which extended from Spain to India.

In 1920, an independent Arab Kingdom of Syria was established under King Faysal of the Hashemite family, carving out the Ottoman *vilayet* of Aleppo, Beirut, Damascus, and Zor-al-Jezira in the aftermath of the First World War. Later, King Faysal became King of Iraq. However, his rule ended after a few months, following the clashes between his Syrian Arab forces and regular French forces. French troops then occupied the country in accordance with a League of Nations mandate. With the fall of France in 1940, Syria came under the control of the British and the Free French in July 1941 after a fierce battle with the pro-German Vichy French forces occupying the country.

Fig. 60: Damascus

Continuing pressure from Syrian nationalists groups, however, forced the French to evacuate their troops in April 1946, leaving the country in the hands of a republican government that had been formed during the mandate. Following the declaration of independence on April 17, 1946, Syrian policies were marked by upheaval and instability until 1970, when a bloodless coup installed the present government which is under the Alawi general, Hafiz al-Asad.

ECONOMY

From the very beginning, Syria's economy has been founded on the twin pillars of agriculture and commerce. The Euphrates and other small rivers, together with rainfall, have allowed northern

Syria to produce grains and cotton. The Syrian cities of Damascus and Aleppo have always owed much of their stature in commerce passing through them (Fig. 61).

Fig. 61: Aleppo

Agriculture

Agriculture dominated the Syrian economy until recently. Cotton, the major cash crop was the leading export until the mid-1970s. Other crops include vegetables, citrus fruits, olives, tobacco, and sugar beets. Wheat is the most important food crop, although its production is constantly subjected to great fluctuations because of irregular rainfall. Wheat and barley together account for two-thirds of the cultivated area. A number of irrigation projects help in cultivation. Peasants often also herd sheep, goats, and camels to supplement their incomes.

Minerals

Minerals include oil, natural gas, phosphate, iron ore, asphalt, limestone, basalt, chrome, and manganese. Oil in commercial quantities was first discovered in the northeast in 1956. The most important oil field is that of Suwadiyah, followed by those of Qaratshuk and Rumaylan. The fields are a natural extension of Iraqi oil fields of Mosul and Kirkuk. Oil became Syria's leading natural resource and chief export after 1974. It accounts for some 40 percent of total exports. Because much of Syria's oil is heavy and high in sulfur, it imports light crude oil from Iran for blending in the refineries at Home and Baniyas. Natural gas was discovered at the field of Jhessa in 1940.

Raw phosphate was discovered in 1962; the four richest beds are located at Khumayfia, Ghandir, al-Jamal, Swwanah, and *Wadi* ar-Rakhim. Iron ore is found in the Zabadani region, and asphalt has been found northeast of Latakia and west of Dayr az-Zawr. Syria is rich in limestone, basalt, and marl and has scattered reserves of chrome and manganese.

Industry

Most of Syria's earliest industries processed agricultural products or turned out light consumer goods. Damask steel, swords and blades, brass and copper work, wood engravings, gold and silver ornaments, mother-of-pearl inlays, and silk brocades were the most common. In the 1970s, the government initiated a policy of rapid industrialization, particularly in such areas as iron and steel, fertilizers, textiles, chemicals, and the assembly of such items as refrigerators and television sets. Wool, cotton, and nylon textiles are the most important. The mills are mainly in Aleppo, Damascus, Hims, and Hamah. Natural silk is produced in Latakia. Industrial output increased by about 1.4 percent between 1980 and 1988, but many state farms are inefficient.

CHAPTER 43
TAJIKISTAN

When the Soviet Union was disintegrating, Tajikistan was the first Central Asian country to pull down Lenin's statue and replace it with a statue of Qasim Firdausi. Abul Qasim Firdausi was a tenth century Muslim poet. Muslim identity was also expressed by the people of Tajikistan in many other ways after the independence. In Tajikistan, more than 85 percent of the people are Muslim.

GEOGRAPHY

The Republic of Tajikistan, (formerly known as the Tajik Soviet Socialist Republic), is situated in the southeast part of Central Asia. To the north and west, it borders Uzbekistan, and to the northeast Kyrgyzstan. To its east is the Peoples Republic of China and to the south is Afghanistan. Its eastern region is dominated by the gigantic Pamir Mountains, commonly known as the "Roof of the World." Mt. Communism (24,590 feet; 7,495 m), and Lenin Peak (23,405 ft; 7,139 m) are among the highest mountains on earth. These peaks will probably have different names soon, as the country is shifting from communism to Islam. From these high glacier-sustaining mountains begin Amu and Syr *Daryas* (literally rivers) with their swift streams, which are used to produce hydro-electricity. These rivers and their tributaries are the main

---

Geographical Profile

Area: 54,019 sq. mi. (139,855 sq. km)
Population: 5.9 million (1994); 7.1 million (2000); 9.1 million (2010)
Neighboring Countries: Kyrgyzstan, Uzbekistan, Afghanistan, China
Capital: Dushanbe
Other City: Khodzhent
Terrain: Mountains, plateaus, small section of the Fergana valley
Climate: Varies considerably according to altitude
Ethnic Groups: Tajiks (62%), Uzbeks (24%), Russians
Religions: Islam 90% (Sunni 90%, Isma'ili 10%); Orthodox Christianity 10%
Languages: Tajik, Russian
Economy:
  GNP: $2,723 million (1992)
  Per Capita Income: $480 (lowest among all former Soviet republics)
  Natural Resources: Gold, aluminum, iron, lead, mercury, and tin
  Agriculture: Products: Cotton, grain, vegetables, and fruits
  Industry: Types: Mineral extraction, aluminum production and power generation
Official Name: Republic of Tajikistan
Date of Independence: 1991

sources of irrigation water for the neighboring desert republics of Uzbekistan and Turkmenistan (Map 46).

In the south and east, mountains are located in a high and dry plateau. In the north is a small section of the Fergana valley. In the southwest are the hot, dry Gissar and Vakhsh valleys. The highest dam is at Rogun on the Vaksh River, more than 1000 ft. (310 m.) high. Another large dam is located downstream at Nurek. Together, they provide more electric power than Dushanbe and other surrounding towns can use, so the excess power is transmitted to Turkmenistan and Uzbekistan.

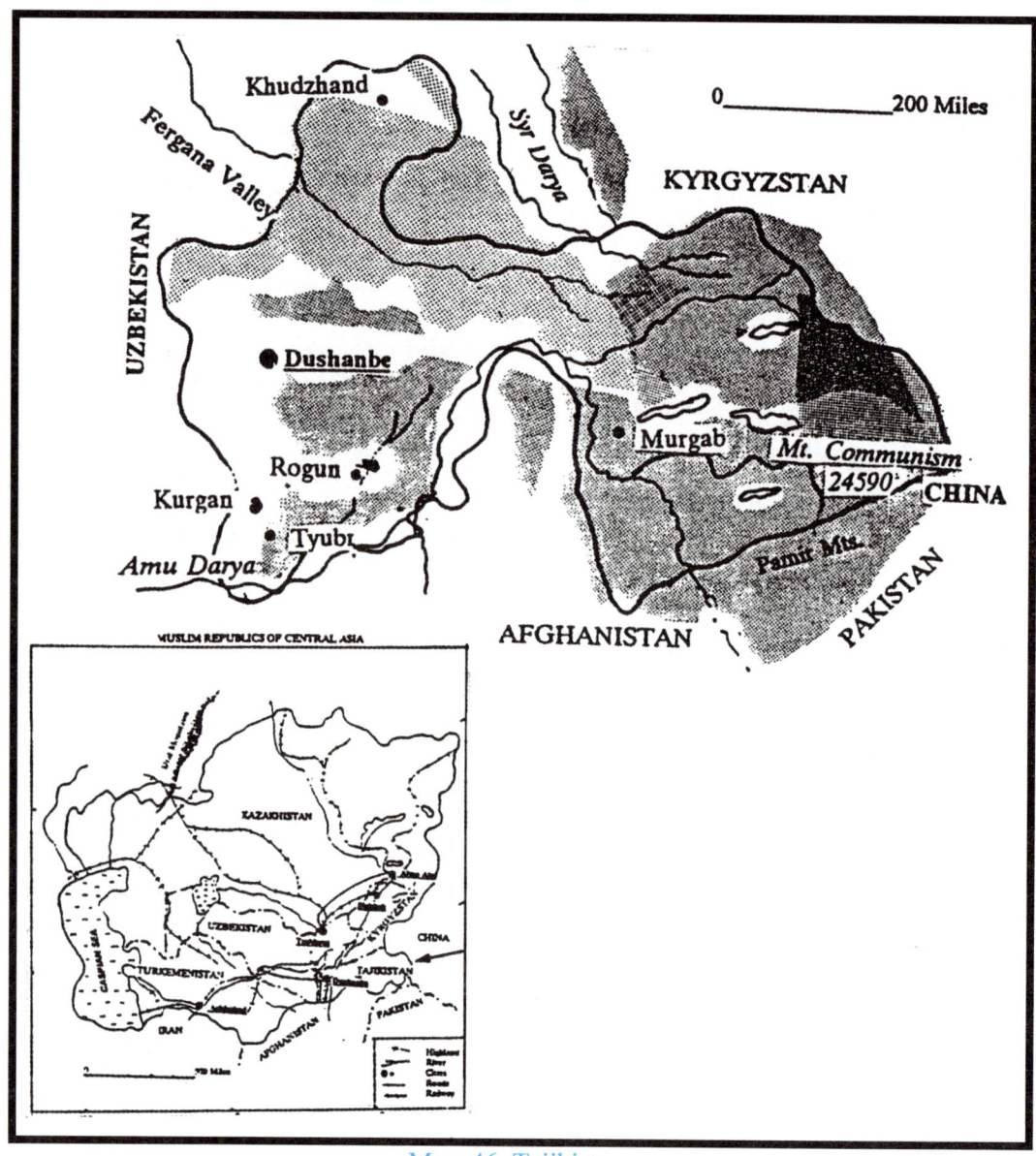

Map. 46: Tajikistan

The climate varies considerably according to altitude. The average temperature in January in Khojand (lowland) is 30.4°F (-0.9°C). In July, the temperature average is 81.3°F (27.4°C). In the southern lowlands, the temperature variation is somewhat more extreme. In the mountain areas, the winter temperature can fall below -51°F (-45°C). The average January temperature in Murgab in the mountains of southeast Gorno-Badakshan is -3.3°F (-19.6°C). Precipitation in the valleys is in the range of 6 to 10 inches (150-250 mm) per year. Levels of rainfall are very low in mountain regions and seldom exceed 2.36 to 3.14 inches (60-80 mm) per year.

PEOPLE AND POPULATION

The Tajiks are different from the other nations of Central Asia in that they are of Iranian origin, not Turkic. They are descendants of the inhabitants of ancient Sogdiana, which was centered south of Bukhara. They speak the Tajik language, which is closely related to Persian. Since 1940, the Cyrllic script has been used. In 1989, Tajik replaced Russian as the official language of the republic. The major religion is Islam. Most Tajiks and ethnic Uzbek residents follow the *Sunni* tradition, but in the Pamirs, people belong to the *Ismaili* sect. There are also representatives of the Russian Orthodox church and a small community of Jews.

Tajiks make up 62 percent of the population, but a larger part of the Tajik nation inhabits neighboring Afghanistan (there also is a Tajik minority across the border to the east in China). In their republic, Tajiks share their land with Uzbeks, (which are 24 percent of the population) and Russians (a shrinking 7 percent of the population). Armenians and others, including the small *Ismaili* Muslims, for whom the Gorno-Badakhshan Autonomous Region was created by the Soviets reside in several Pamir valleys.

EVOLUTION OF TAJIKISTAN

By about the eighth century AD, the Tajiks were a distinct ethnic group. They were distinguished from their Turkic neighbors by their sedentary way of life and the Iranian language. In the 16th century, Tajikistan became a province in a group of Turkish republics. Later, under Uzbek rule, they formed several semi-independent territories. After the 1917 Revolution, regions of Tajik principalities came under Russian rule. Tajikistan resisted the Russians until 1921, but in 1929, it became a Soviet republic.

As the Soviet Union began to disintegrate, Tajikistan declared its independence in 1991, along with four other central Asian states. But the transition to independence almost immediately deteriorated into rioting, bloodshed, and civil war. As Moscow's grip relaxed, Muslims rebelled against the entrenched communist leadership and seized the upper hand through much of 1992. Tajikistan's newly independent non-Muslim neighbors and Moscow, alarmed by the prospect of the forging of a Tajik Islamic republic, with strengthening ties to nearby Iran and adjacent Afghanistan, gave support to the old rulers to counterattack the Muslims. This effort soon succeeded, and by early 1993, the former communists had regained control of the country. The United States had also sent a five-person embassy staff to Dushanbe, but it had to leave the country, due to unsettled conditions.

In October 1991, Tajikistan signed a treaty with seven other former Soviet republics to establish an economic community. On December 21, it also signed the Alma Ata Declaration, by which the Commonwealth of Independent States was established.

ECONOMY

According to the World Bank, Tajikistan's national product (GNP) in 1992 was US $2,723 million, which is equivalent to $480 per person. This per capita income is the lowest among all former republics of the Soviet Union.

Agriculture

Despite the fact that only 7% of land in Tajikistan is arable, the economy of Tajikistan is primarily agricultural. In 1991, agriculture contributed 48.9% of net material product (NMP) and provided 44.6% of the employment. The principal crop is cotton, followed in importance by barley, corn, wheat, vegetables, apples, peaches and grapes. About 75% of the country's arable land is irrigated. In 1991, agricultural NMP decreased by about 10% compared with the previous year. Silk culture (sericulture) is an ancient enterprise, which is still flourishing. The grazing slopes support about a million and a half dairy cattle and three and a half million Karakul sheep. Camels and yaks are also raised in small numbers.

Minerals and Industry

Lignite is mined at several locations but main deposits are in Kyzylkiya. It is used in local industries. Uranium is found in the northern section of the country, in association with vanadium deposits in volcanic areas.

Industries include silk spinning, cotton ginning, fruit canning, leather tanning, wine-making, carpet weaving, metal working, and machine building. Cotton, wool, and silk textiles are also important. Dushanbe, the capital, is the major industrial and cultural center. Coal is mined nearby, as well as lead and arsenic. The city produces cotton, silk, phosphate fertilizers and wool textiles. In order to further improve the industries and forge a unity with Pakistan, Afghanistan, Iran and other Muslim countries, two rail and road links are under construction. One will join Samarkand-Termez-Mazar-i-Sharif-Kabul-Torkham and Karachi, while the other will pass through Termez-Mazar-i-Sharif-Shebargan-Herat-Kandhar-Chaman and Karachi.

On the headwaters of Syr *Darya* is Khodzhent City, a major center for silk production. Other industries include clothing, footwear, and food products. Khodzhent was located on the old caravan route between China and the Mediterranean Sea. It was completely destroyed by the army of Genghis Khan. In 1936, it was renamed Leninabad. With independence, it returned to its old name.

CHAPTER 44
TUNISIA

Islam was introduced in Tunisia by the Arabs early in the seventh century AD. Since then, it has been one of the leading Muslim countries, although the French tried to change it during their colonial rule. It led other Arab countries in the promotion of equal status for women and is the only Arab country which prohibited polygamy in 1957.

GEOGRAPHY

Tunisia is the smallest country in North Africa. As part of the Arab *"Maghreb,"* it is located between Algeria on the west and Libya in the southeast. It has a coastline running 1,000 miles (1,600 km) long on the Mediterranean Sea. At its closest point from Europe, Tunisia lies 90 miles (144 km) across the Strait of Sicily (Map 47).

Western Tunisia is higher, with the highest land in the northwest. The Eastern or Maritime part of Tunisia is low. Topographically, the country can be divided into three subregions: (i) Northern Tunisia, (ii) Central Tunisia, and (iii) Southern Tunisia. Northern Tunisia is comprised of a sequence of ridges and valleys generally trending in the north-southeast direction. The valley of the River Medjerda has a series of closed basins, which are well-watered and fertile. These basins support dense forests of cork and Portuguese oak, in addition to being the

> **Geographical Profile**
>
> **Area:** 63,378 sq. mi. (164,149 sq. km)
> **Population:** 8.8 million (1994); 9.9 million (2000); 13.1 million (2010)
> **Neighboring Countries:** Algeria, Libya
> **Capital:** Tunis
> **Other City:** Sfax
> **Terrain:** Arable land in the north and along the central coast; south is mostly semiarid or desert
> **Climate:** Hot, dry summers and mild, rainy winters
> **Ethnic Groups:** Arab (98%), Berber (1%), Europeans (1%)
> **Religion:** Sunni Islam 99%; Christian and Jewish less than 1%
> **Languages:** Arabic (official), French
> **Economy:**
>   **GDP:** $8,7 billion (1989)
>   **Per Capita Income:** $1,253 (1989)
>   **Natural Resources:** Oil, phosphate, iron ore, lead, zinc
>   **Agriculture:** (16% of GDP): Products: Olives, wheat, citrus fruits, grapes, truck crops, fish
>   **Industry:** (33% of GDP): Types: Crude oil, food processing, construction
> **Official Name:** Republic of Tunisia
> **Date of Independence:** March 20, 1956

source of most of Tunisia's agricultural production. South of the High Tell and Dorsale region begins the Tunisian steppe land, which gradually blends into the Sahara desert. Camel and sheep owning nomads traditionally occupy this steppe land. Southern Tunisia accounts for over one-third of Tunisia. This area lacks sufficient rainfall, and only has sparse grazing and semi-nomadic people.

Several ranges of the Atlas Mountains extend into Tunisia from neighboring Algeria. The average elevation of these mountains is about 4,000 feet (1,200 m) above sea level. Northern and central Tunisia have a Mediterranean climate, with mild, rainy winters and hot, dry summers. The period of greatest rain is from December until March. In the south, the climate is hot and dry year round.

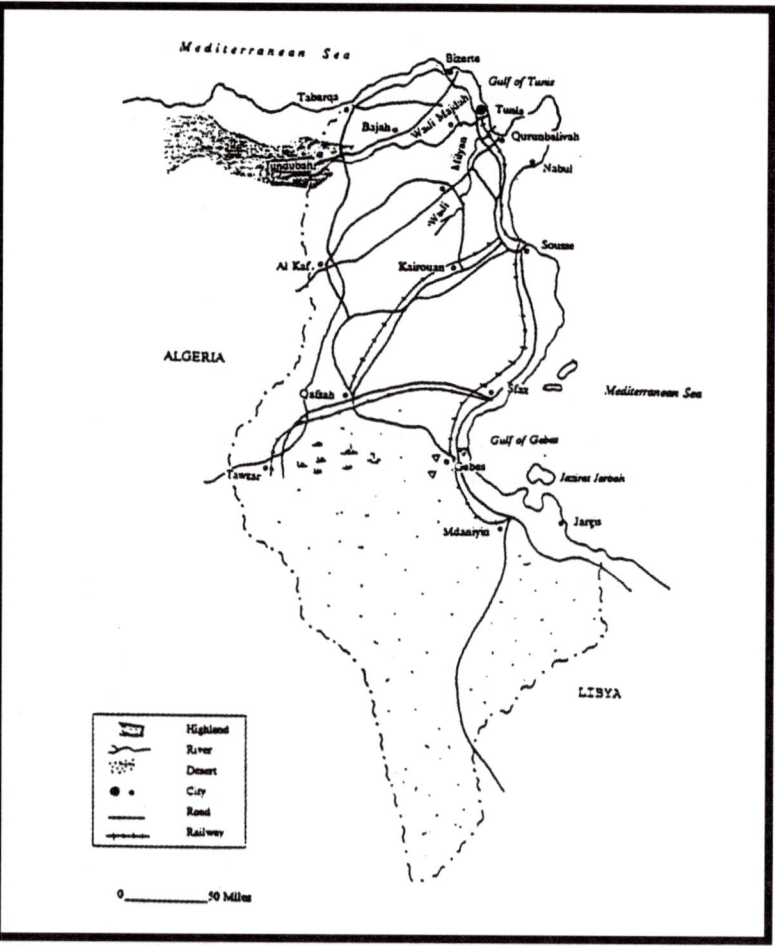

Map 47: Tunisia

PEOPLE AND POPULATION

Tunisians are descendants of the indigenous Berbers and Arabs who brought Islam to North Africa in the seventh century AD. The predominant language of Tunisia is Arabic, although French is also spoken widely in business and governmental circles. About 98 percent of the population is Muslim.

Four-fifth of Tunisia's population lives in the northern half of the country. A general relationship between density of settlement and annual rainfall can be discerned, with a rural density of more than 139 persons per square mile (250 per sq km) in regions of sufficient rainfall. South of the chotts, the population density is very low. Most densely populated areas are in the plains around Tunis and Bizerta, in the coastal bulge; Sousse-Monastir-Moknine, around Sia; and the Isle of Djerba.

Tunis (pop. one million) is the capital, industrial center, principal port, and the largest city in the country. In 1994, the population of Tunisia stood at 8.8 million people, with 2.1 percent as the annual rate of natural increase. With such a rate of annual increase, the population of Tunisia would be likely to double in 33 years (Fig. 62).

Fig. 62: Tunis

EVOLUTION OF TUNISIA

Tunisia's location on the threshold of the western basin of the Mediterranean Sea and its close proximity to Europe (less than 90 miles or 145 km from Sicily) led to its early colonization by the Europeans. Phoenicians were the first, who founded Carthage and other North African settlements. Ancient Carthage lies close to Tunis. There are many other important Roman ruins in and around Tunis. Carthage was defeated by the Romans in 148 AD. The Romans ruled North Africa until they were defeated by the tribesmen in fifth century AD. In the seventh century, Arabs introduced Islam in Tunisia and transformed Tunisia and other parts of North Africa. Tunisia became a center of Arab culture until its assimilation into the Turkish Ottoman Empire in the 16th century.

Like Algeria, Tunisia came under the French control in 1881. The French established a protectorate there, which led to a rise of nationalism among the Tunisians. Eventually, Tunisia became independent in 1956. At the time of independence, Tunisia was extremely poor and devastated. About 70 percent of the people were making a precarious living with agriculture and fishing, consuming most of what they produced. Any surplus was bartered instead of going into any kind of monetary transactions. In 1956, per capita income was as low as $100, which in 1956 increased to $1,253 as a result of immense changes and reorientation in ways of life,

As a result of major structural changes and reorientation of Tunisia's economy, disputes and tensions developed between France and Tunisia. These disputes were finally resolved after France withdrew its naval base at Bizerte in 1962. In 1964, Tunisia nationalized foreign interests, and relations with France again deteriorated. After a couple of years, cooperation was reestablished in 1968. Since then, France and Tunisia share good relations, so much so that France has extended important economic credits and established many technical assistance programs in Tunisia.

ECONOMY

Tunisia is primarily an agricultural nation, producing typical Mediterranean steppe and desert crops. Since independence in 1956, Tunisia is also expanding its industrial sector, including steel and automobile assembly.

Agriculture

Before independence, almost all large modern farms situated on the most fertile parts of Tunisia were owned by the Europeans. In 1964, these farms were nationalized. Some farms were split and given to farmers; others were consolidated into 1,200 acre (500 ha) cooperatives. Despite fierce opposition by large Tunisian farmers, the program of land reform by collectivization was imposed mainly on the rich farms in Northern Tunisia. The policy of collectivization was combined with crop diversification, irrigation, and mechanization. Initially, there was success, but the succession of droughts, excessive collectivization, and general lack of effort among farmers forced a change in the policy.

Currently, three types of land holdings co-exist in Tunisia: public farms, cooperatives, and private farms. Among private holdings, there are a large number of small holdings. Farms around Tunis and Cap Bon in the north produce vines, vegetables, and citrus fruits in surplus quantities. In the central steppe area, olive cultivation predominates. Further south, dates are dominant. Wheat and barley are cultivated widely throughout the country, but yields are poor and imports are necessary.

Minerals and Industry

Tunisia's natural resources are limited to phosphate, iron ore, lead, and a small quantity of oil and natural gas. Recent oil discoveries, including the one by an American oil company that can provide 20 percent of Tunisia's daily needs, have been put off until Tunisia becomes a net importer of oil. Discovery and exploitation of further hydrocarbon reserves remains imperative, especially given the uncertain timing of any joint exploitation of the Libyan-owned reserves on the continental shelf. Much investment has gone into the exploitation in the Gulf of Gebes and other shore areas. Phosphate production has doubled in the last 15 years, although production of other minerals has declined (Table 8).

Table 8
Mineral Production (000 Tons)

	1975	1978	1980	1982	1984
Phosphate	3,512	3,712	4,502	4,729	5,600
Iron Ore	326	185	212	270	-
Lead	11	8	8	5	-
Zinc	6	7	9	8	-
Crude Oil	4,300	5,400	5,500	5,800	5,800

The French policy during the colonial days and the lack of fuel resources limited the range of the manufacturing industry mainly to the processing of agricultural products. Since independence, planned development of the economy has seen a considerable expansion of mining-energy manufacturing, which accounts for two-fifths of the GNP. The first three 4-year plans gave priority to infrastructure development (roads, railways, and port development) and basic industry (oil exploration, production, refining, and metallurgy). The principal industries are food processing, textiles, chemicals, building materials, paper and electrical equipment. The growing chemical industry is based upon the petrochemicals from the Bizerte oil refinery and local phosphate deposits.

NOTES

CHAPTER 45
TURKEY

Turkey is at the heart of what was once the vast Ottoman Empire that brought Islam to the very doorstep of Christian Europe. About 98% of the people of Turkey are Muslim, but since the early 1920s, the country has been officially secular. However, Islam has been reemerging in recent years on the center stage of political and social life in Turkey.

GEOGRAPHY

Bridging Europe and Asia Minor, Turkey is a land of geographic, economic, and social contrasts. It lies partially in Europe (3%) and partially in Asia, sharing common borders with Greece and Bulgaria on the northwest, Russia and Iran on the east, and Iraq and Syria on the south. The Bosphorus, the Sea of Marmara, and the Dardanelles, known collectively as the Turkish Straits, connect the Black and the Mediterranean Sea. Turkey contains two islands near the Dardanelles and tiny ones around the western coast, but the major islands of the Aegean Sea belong to Greece (Map 48).

From a physical standpoint, Turkey is composed of (1) coastal regions of hills, mountains, valleys and small plains bordering the Black, Aegean, and the Mediterranean Seas and (2) the Anatolian Plateau and associated mountains, occupying the interior of the country. The plateau lies at 2,000 to 6,000 feet (600-1,800 m); it is highest in the east where it adjoins the high

---

Geographical Profile

Area: 296,000 sq. mi. (766,640 sq. km)
Population: 61.9 million (1994); 70.5 million (2000); 81.2 million (2010)
Neighboring Countries: Bulgaria, Russia, Iran, Iraq, Syria, Bulgaria, Greece
Capital: Ankara
Other Cities: Izmir, Adana
Terrain: Inland plateau, narrow coastal plain
Climate: Moderate in coastal areas, harsher temperature inland
Ethnic Groups: Turks, Kurds, Laz, Balkan *muhajirs*
Religions: Islam 99% (Sunni 90%, Alevi Shi'ah 10%), Christians, Jews
Languages: Turkish (official), Kurdish
Economy:
  GDP: $80.5 billion (1989)
  Per Capita Income: $1,433 (1989)
  Natural Resources: Coal, chromite, copper, boron, oil
  Agriculture: Products: Cotton sugar beets, hazelnuts, wheat, barley and tobacco
  Industry: Types: Food processing, textiles, basic metals, chemicals, and petrochemicals
Official Name: Republic of Turkey
Date of the Establishment of the Republic: October 29, 1923

mountains of the Armenian knot. Its surface is rolling, treeless, and windswept. Along its northern side, the Anatolian Plateau is bordered by the Pontic Mountains. These ranges lie generally at 3,000 to 6,000 feet (915 to 1,830 m) high in the west but rise to a maximum of over 12,000 feet (3,658 m) in the east. The Taurus Mountains bordering the plateau on the south are somewhat higher than the Pontic Mountains. The highest mountains in Turkey are Agri Dagi (Mt. Arafat) at 17,275 feet (5,265 m) and Uludag (Mt. Olympus) at 8,343 feet (2,543 m). The coastal plains and valleys along or near the Aegean Sea, Sea of Marmara, and the Black Sea are, in general, Turkey's most densely populated and productive areas.

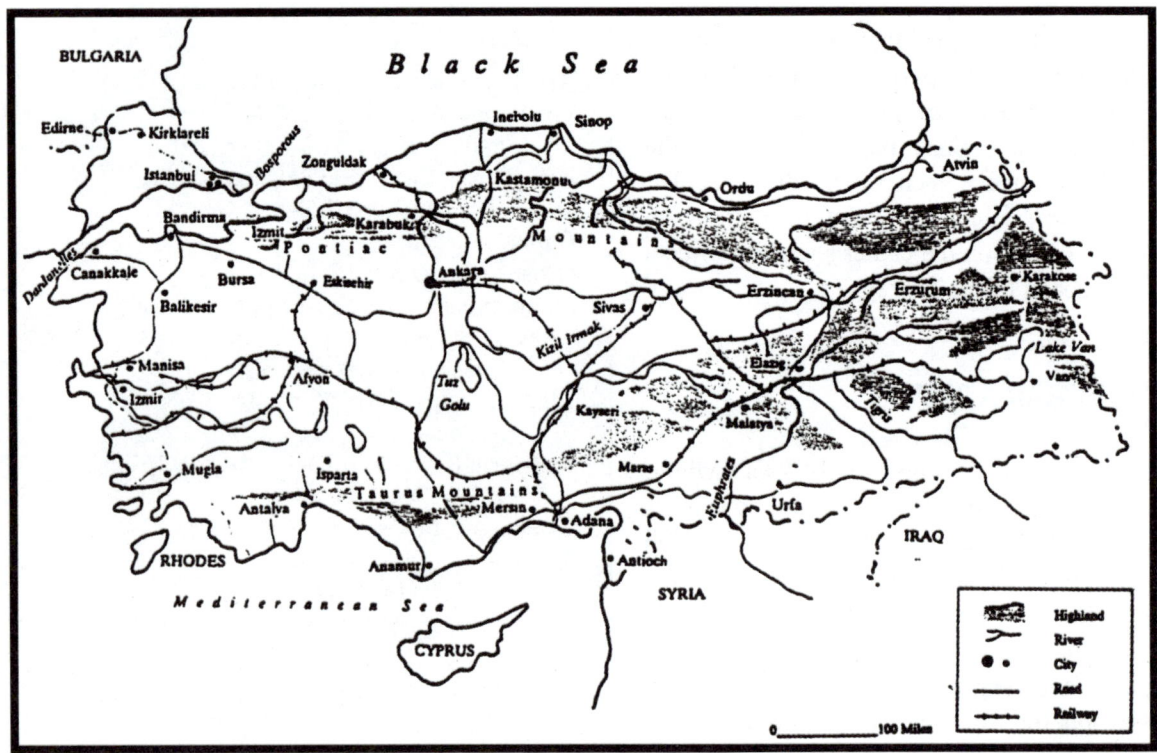

Map 48: Turkey

The two most useful rivers are the Kizil Irmak and the Sakarya, both of which drain into the Black Sea. The Seyhan, which empties into the Mediterranean, runs through the fertile plain around Adana, on which much of Turkey's cotton is grown. Both the Tigris and Euphrates rise in Turkey, but they pass through steep mountain gorges and cannot be utilized for irrigation until they enter the plains of Syria and Iraq.

The western part of the country generally has good winter rains, as does the southern range, known as Taurus Mountains. The Pontus Mountains along the north coast have moderate rains throughout the year, especially in the spring. Ankara and the central plateau lack adequate rainfall. The eastern highlands have an abundance of precipitation, but the rugged terrain is not suitable for agriculture. At higher elevations, snow covers the ground for at least four months of the year.

PEOPLE AND POPULATION

The majority of the people in Turkey are Muslim, but officially, they have been secular since the early 1920s. The state exercises no legal discrimination against its non-Muslim minorities, primarily Armenian and Assyrian Christians and Jews. The Kurds (who are mostly Sunni of the Shafi' school) constitute an ethnic and linguistic group. In Turkey, Kurds are estimated to number close to 10 million. They have lived in the isolated, mountainous regions of the Middle east for more than 3,000 years. Although an increasing number of Kurds have migrated to the cities, the traditional homes of the Kurds are in poor, remote areas of the east and southeast, where incomes are less than half the national average and economic development lags. Most Kurds are loyal citizens to their country. However, the communist, atheist Kurdish People's Party (PKK) is quite active in terrorism.

Istanbul is Turkey's main metropolis, industrial center, and port. One of the world's most historic and cosmopolitan cities, Istanbul was, for many centuries, the capital of the Eastern Roman (Byzantine) Empire. It became the capital of the Ottoman Empire when it fell to the Turks in 1453, after withstanding many sieges. Istanbul is located at the southern entrance of Bosporus, the northernmost of the three water passages (Dardanelles, Sea of Marmara, and Bosporus) that connect the Mediterranean and the Black Seas and are known as the Turkish Straits (Fig. 63). However, the capital of the Turkish Republic was established in 1923 at the more centrally located city of Ankara on the Anatolian Plateau. Turkey's third largest city, Izmir is a seaport on the Aegean Sea.

Fig. 63: One of the beautiful mosques of Istanbul

EVOLUTION OF TURKEY

Largely, because Turkey is the link between Europe and Asia and has served as a bridge for the migration of countless peoples, it has been the home of successive civilizations that reach back to the dawn of history. Many cultural traits that came to Europe from Asia passed through Turkey, including perhaps farming and animal domestication. Radiocarbon dates at Hacilar (a few miles southwest of Kayseri in the center of the country) indicate that the site was settled in 7040 BC. Farming dates back in Turkey from at least this period. Among the many ancient civilizations, the better known include the Hittites (1450-1200 BC), who shared the mastery of the Near East with the Egyptians; the civilizations of Phrygia, Lydia, Lycia, and Caria (750-300 BC), upon which eastern Greek culture Iona was built; the Persians, who overran the region in the sixth century BC; the Greeks, who defeated the Persians in 334 BC and remained dominant until the reign of the Roman Emperor Augustus (30 BC); the Romans (30 BC-395 AD); and the Christian Byzantines (395-1453 AD).

In the 14th and subsequent centuries, Turkish tribes established the Ottoman (`Uthmani) Empire. From the 16th to 19th centuries, this empire was an important power. At its height in the 16th century, its territories extended over some 7,772,200 square miles (20,000,000 sq. km.) over three continents which included North Africa as far west as Algeria; the south as far as Sudan; and most of southeastern Europe, the Fertile Crescent, and parts of the Arabian Peninsula. In the center of the Empire was the large Anatolian Peninsula between the Mediterranean, Aegean, and Black Seas. Presently, the Anatolian plateau forms most of the national territory of the modern Republic of Turkey.

The 18th century marked the beginning of the decline of Ottoman power. Weakening power continued until World War I (1914-1918) when Ottoman armies fought and lost on several fronts throughout the empire. Eventually, Anatolia was divided and occupied by allied forces. The modern Republic of Turkey rose from the ruins of the Ottoman Empire, which was defeated and dismembered at the close of World War 1. The Arab parts of the empire fell to Britain and France, but the Turks defended Anatolia with great ferocity. Secret agreements, made during the war, divided many areas among the victors, leaving only a very small Turkey in northern Asia Minor.

In 1920, with Christian Greek troops landing in Izmir, the French army in southern Turkey, and British forces in occupation of Istanbul, the Grand National Assembly met in Ankara and elected an energetic and determined army officer, Mustafa Kamal, as its leader. With a poor but determined new army, Ghazi Mustafa Kemal, pushed the French back to Aleppo, captured Armenia (which had proclaimed itself a Muslim free republic), persuaded the Italians to withdraw from southwest Asia Minor, and began a struggle with Greece, which had invaded Anatolia in a bid to establish the old empire of Alexander the Great. A bitter war was fought with the Greeks. The invading army proved no match for the tenacious Turks, and they were forced to withdraw back to Greece. The Greeks destroyed everything they found along the way and committed atrocity after atrocity upon Muslim towns and villages. Later, France was the first nation to recognize the new Turkish government.

After eliminating Greece from Asia Minor, the Turks turned northward to Istanbul, where a small British force was left to defend the city. The British decided to withdraw, and in 1923, the Treaty of Lausanne gave Turkey full sovereignty over most of the territory it now possesses. On

October 29, 1923, the Grand National Assembly proclaimed Turkey a republic and elected Ghazi Mustafa Kemal Ataturk as its first President. The name *Ataturk,* meaning "Father of Turkey," was given to the newly elected President by the Turkish National Assembly.

Almost single-handedly, Kemal Ataturk began the process of modernizing Turkey. The capital was shifted from Istanbul (formerly Constantinople) to Ankara. The Caliphate was abolished in 1924, and a republican constitution was enacted. In 1925, the traditional male headgear of fez and turban were banned (the *hijab,* however discouraged, was not outlawed), and Sufi Orders were outlawed (as they have always been a source of resistance to secularism). The Muslim *Hijri* calendar was replaced by the western Gregorian calendar. In 1928, the Latin alphabets were adopted in place of Arabic script, which was one of the most radical changes ever made by a Muslim government. The constitutional provision that declared Islam as the official state religion was deleted the same year. In 1934, Turkish women were given the franchise with a right to seek elective offices.

These drastic measures did little to destroy the Islamic sympathies of the vast majority of Turks. In the 1950's, the new president Adnan Menderes lifted many of these stringent codes against Islam. In recent times, Islamic-oriented movements have been gaining a greater voice in society and public politics, most notably the movement led by Necmettin Erbakan. There has also been a resurgence in the popularity of the Sufi *tariqats,* namely the Naqshibandi.

ECONOMY

The Turkish economy is unusual among the Middle Eastern countries in two ways. First, it has a greater percentage of usable land than any other country in the region, and second, it possesses sufficient iron and coal to develop its own heavy industry. These advantages, combined with virtual self-sufficiency in oil, have helped to create the most powerful and integrated economy in Turkey.

Agriculture

Since 1970, agricultural activity has increased considerably, employing almost half of the total labor force in the production of cotton, tobacco, grains, fruits, and vegetables. Because of the productivity of Turkey's soil and the efforts of Turkish farmers, the country was one of the few in the world that was self-sufficient in food during the 1980s. Ambitious government projects, including the irrigation programs to create a new "fertile crescent" in the semiarid southeast, stress the important role of agriculture. Because most of Turkey's farmland is privately owned, continued growth depends on farmers' recognition of positive economic benefits accompanying a change from subsistence to commercial agriculture.

Though much of interior Turkey is suitable for cereal cultivation and animal husbandry, there are serious constraints. High elevations and steep slopes, cool temperatures, short growing seasons, and semiarid conditions limit the productivity of much of the more traditional agricultural zones. In addition, gains in permanent cropland are made at the expense of permanent pastureland and the dry farmland included in the arable land (Table 9). The only category of agricultural land that declined between 1972 and 1987 was the pastureland. The shift results in both overgrazing on the remaining pastureland and encroaching on degrading remaining forest land.

Table 9
Land Use (in thousand hectares) in Turkey

	1972	1977	1982	1987
Total land area	76,963	76,963	76,963	76,963
Arable land	75,573	25,063	24,199	24,964
Permanent Cropland	2,655	2,866	2,892	2,965
Permanent Pasture	10,600	10,100	9,400	8,700
Forest	20,170	20,155	20,199	20,199
Others	17,967	18,779	20,273	20,137

Minerals and Industry

Mineral resources of Turkey include oil, coal, iron, chromite, copper and boron. After the Turkish Republic was formed in 1923, its leaders eagerly sought to stimulate industrial development. As private capital was lacking or nonexistent, the state moved in to finance the industries. As such, many of the present industries are state-owned. In recent years, many state-owned industries were sold to private owners to lessen state control and state protection of the economy as a means of achieving expanded production, greater exports, and lower inflation.

Turkey's predominant industries are those customarily found in developing nations: textiles, agricultural processing, cement manufacture, simple metal industries, assembly of vehicles from imported components, and so on. The country is very dependent on imports for much of its machinery as well as many other types of manufactured goods, although enough oil is refined in Turkey to supply domestic needs for refined products. An iron and steel mill in the northern interior is the largest heavy-industrial establishment. Coke is manufactured here from coal supplied by a nearby coal basin. High-grade iron ore comes by rail from deposits 500 miles (800 km) away. In addition to coal and iron ore, Turkey has valuable deposits of chromium and a variety of other metallic and nonmetallic minerals.

CHAPTER 46
TURKMENISTAN

In the southwest of Central Asia lies the desert Republic of Turkmenistan. This area was a part of Muslim Turkestan before it became a Soviet republic in the 1920s. It won independence from the Soviets in 1991.

GEOGRAPHY

Turkmenistan (formerly the Turkmen Soviet Socialist Republic) is the most southern republic of Muslim Central Asia. It is bordered to the north by Uzbekistan, to the northwest by Kazakhstan, to the west by the Caspian Sea, to the south by Iran, and to the southeast by Afghanistan (Map 49). This area was part of the Muslim Turkestan before it became a Soviet Republic in 1925. Turkmenistan's southern border is located over a fault zone creating a geothermal power close to the surface. This is an untapped energy source.

Turkmenistan is mostly a lowland desert (Kra-Kum) with some highlands to the southwest and southeast. Streams that originate in these highlands disappear into the desert except for the Amu *Darya* which flows along the border of Uzbekistan. A large arm of the Caspian Sea, the Kra-Boguz-Gol Bay extends into Turkmenistan. Kara-Boguz-Gol means "Black Throat Lake." In the last twenty years, the level of the Caspian Sea is falling, and the size of the bay has been halved. Drying sediments from the bay are rich in Flaubers Salts and petroleum resources.

Geographical Profile

Area: 188,417 sq. miles (488,100 km)
Population: 4.1 million (1994); 4.8 million (2000), 5.5 million (2010)
Neighboring Countries: Uzbekistan, Kazakhstan, Afghanistan, Iran
Capital: Ashkabad
Other Cities: Khiva, Marg, Nebit Dag
Terrain: Kara Kum desert occupies 90% of country
Climate: Continental, with extremely hot summers and cold winters
Ethnic Groups: Turkmen (72%), Uzbek (9%) Russians (9%)
Languages: Turkmen, Russian
Religions: Sunni Islam 95%, Orthodox Christian
Economy:
    GNP: $4,895 million (1992)
    Per Capita Income: $1,270
    Natural Resources: Oil, Natural gas, coal, sulfur, salt
    Industries: Types: Mining, textiles
    Agriculture: Products: Cotton, grain, vegetables and fruits
Official Name: Republic of Turkmenistan
Date of Independence: October 27, 1991

The climate of Turkmenistan is severely continental, with extremely hot summers and cold winters. The average temperature in January is 25°F (-4°C), but winter temperatures can fall as low as -27°F (-33°C). In the summer, temperatures often reach 122°F (50°C) in the southeast Kara-Kum desert; the average temperature in July is 82°F (28°C). Precipitation is slight throughout much of the country; average annual rainfall ranges from only 3 inches (80 mm) in the northwest to about 11.8 inches (300 mm) in mountainous regions.

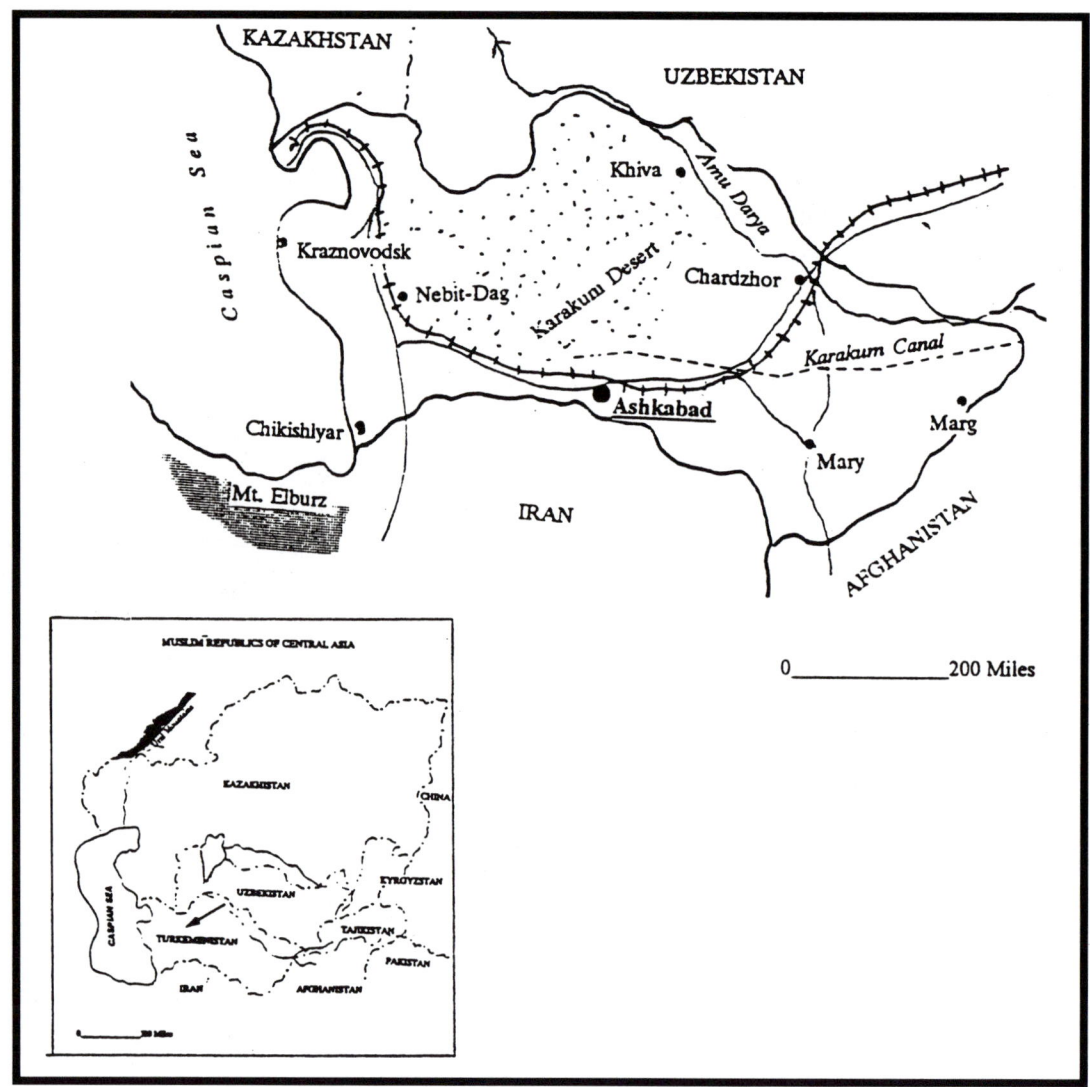

Map 49: Turkmenistan

PEOPLE AND POPULATION

Turkmenistan was the frontier domain of many nomadic peoples when Soviet efforts to modernize the area began. Turkmen make up 72 percent of the population. They are descendants of medieval Oghuz tribes to which the Seljuk and Osmani Turks also belong. They still retain their tribal and clan divisions. In addition, they are completely Muslim and strongly attached to the Sufi order of the Naqshibandiyyah. Russians are about nine percent of the population who mostly live in towns. Uzbeks are another 9 percent. Other minorities are Kazakhs, Tatars, and Ukranians.

During the disintegration of the USSR, the Soviet regime accused Iran of irredentism towards Turkmenistan's Muslims, but there was no validity to the claim. In 1989, these Muslims gave asylum to thousands of Azeri Muslims who fled across the Caspian Sea to escape from Armenian persecution in Nagorno-Karabakh.

When the USSR invaded Afghanistan in the 1980s, they sent in the Muslim units of the Soviet army, many of them from Turkmenistan. The Soviets hoped the Muslims, who understood the culture, would quickly win the war. However, this did not prove to be the case as most of the Muslims refused to shoot at the Afghan fighters.

In 1929, the traditional Arabic script was replaced by Latin script, which was in turn replaced by the Cyrillic script in 1940. In 1990, Turkmen was declared official language of the republic. Turkmen is a member of the Southern Turkic group. In 1993, it was announced that the republic would change to a Latin-based Turkish script by early 1996.

In 1994, the population of Turkmenistan stood at 4.1 million people, with a 2.7 percent annual rate of natural increase. With this rate of annual increase, the population of Turkmenistan is expected to double in 26 years. About half of the population lives in towns and cities, of which the biggest is Ashkabad, the capital of the republic.

EVOLUTION OF THE PEOPLE

The Turkmen are descendants of the Oghuz tribes who migrated to Central Asia in about the 10th century AD. By the 15th century, they had emerged as a distinct ethnic group, but were divided by tribal loyalties and territorial division between neighboring powers. From the 15th to 17th centuries, the southern tribes of barren desert of Turkmenistan were under Persian rule, while the north was under the suzerainty of the Uzbek Khanates of Khiva and Bukhara. In the early 18th century, the Persians annexed Khivan and Bukharan territories. Bukhara regained its power in the latter half of the century, capturing Marv (now Mary) and deporting its entire population to Bukhara. Meanwhile, the Russians had begun their expansion into Central Asia, and during the 19th century they gradually reduced the Khanates to the status of protectorates. In 1895 Russian control was confirmed by agreement with the British; the international boundary, thus established, divided some Turkmen under Russian rule from others in the British sphere of influence.

After the Bolshevik Revolution, Turkmen Soviet Socialist Republic was established on October 27, 1924. In May 1925, it became a constituent republic of the Union of Soviet Socialist Republics. A large number of Turkmen fled to Iran and Afghanistan during the Stalin years. It became independent in 1991, with other Central Asian republics. Nationalists claim that the entire Central

Asia, including the other four republics, is really Turkmenistan territory. They base their claim on the ancient region known as Turkestan.

On August 22, 1990, the Turkmen Supreme Soviet decided to secede and become independent. In late 1990 and early 1991, Turkmenistan participated in negotiations towards a new Union Treaty, which would redefine the status of the republics within the structure of the USSR. A referendum was held in which 94.1% of the electorate voted for independence. On the following day, the Turkmen Supreme Soviet adopted a law for independence, declaring October 27, 1991, to be the day of independence.

ECONOMY

In 1992, Turkmenistan's gross national product (GNP) was US $5,895 million, equivalent to $1,270 per person. Its economy is predominantly agricultural, with irrigation on more than 90 percent of the agricultural land. Although heavily dependent on irrigated-agriculture and livestock, the country virtually has no cattle or pigs.

Agriculture

Soviet efforts to stabilize the population and to make it more sedentary centered on the massive Kara Kum canal project. This project began in the 1950s. It brings water from the mountains to the east into the heart of the desert, In 1993, a major part of the canal which eventually will reach the Caspian Sea, was more than 700 miles (1,100 km) complete, and about 3 million acres had been brought under cultivation. Two important rivers, the Zeravshan and Kashka *Darya*, start high in the mountain glaciers and disappear in the desert sands. The Zeravshan irrigates a belt about twenty miles wide on its 200 mile journey from the Altay Mountains. It passes through the Uzbek cities of Samarkand and Bukhara before disappearing into the sands. The Kashka *Darya* is smaller than the Zerasvshan, but it creates several oases and irrigates fields of wheat, cotton, rice, as well as orchards of peaches and apricots. Cotton is the dominant crop. However, in recent years, over-intensive cultivation of cotton together with massive irrigation projects, have led to serious ecological damage. Two oases produce wheat, barley, corn, millet, sesame, melons, grapes, jute and alfalfa. Wheat and corn are also produced by dry farming methods on non-irrigated lands.

The country maintains a herd of about five million sheep. One of the products from the sheep is the Karakul hides for which the area is famous. The hides are taken from three day old sheep. Mature sheep provide wool for the carpet industry. Camels are raised, but the numbers do not match those of one hundred years ago. There are some dairy cattle which are fed irrigated alfalfa and corn.

Minerals and Industry

Important resources of the country are oil, natural gas, phosphate, salt, sulfur, iodine, bromine, bentonite, lignite coal, barites, various salts, clay and gypsum. There are twenty small hydroelectric stations scattered along the mountain foothills and the Kara-Kum canal.

Turkmenistan's major industries include fish canning, cotton ginning, railroad car repairing and silk spinning. Ashkabad, a city founded in 1881 as a Russian fortress, was developed as a halfway point for stopping on the Trans-Caspian railway from the Caspian Sea to Tashkent. It has textile, small machine, glass, carpets, leather, printing, and a small motion picture industry. Ashkabad is located on a major fault zone and was destroyed in 1948 and was later rebuilt.

Located on the Amu *Darya*, Chardzhou is an inland port with shipyard facilities handling small vessels. It is the center of the cotton and silk industry. It also produces fertilizer from phosphate rock, which is used in most of the Central Asian countries. Like Ashkabad, the capital, Chardzhov was founded by the Russians in the late 19th century as a fortress.

Another city, Krasnovodsk located on the Caspian Sea, was once an important fishing center. It still has a fish canning industry, but today, it is more important as a terminus for oil and natural gas pipelines and the Trans-Caspian railroad.

NOTES

CHAPTER 47
UNITED ARAB EMIRATES

The United Arab Emirates is a federation of seven emirates formed in 1971 out of the seven Trucial *Sheikhdoms* with whom Britain had treaties of defense and friendship. They are strongly Muslim and culturally similar to their neighbors.

GEOGRAPHY

Seven states with the capital on the Arab Gulf and one with a capital on the Gulf of Oman, comprise a federation known as the United Arab Emirates (UAE). The word *emirate* is an English formation from the Arabic *emir* or *amir*, which means "chieftain," or "prince." However, the title is not generally used with the names of the rulers of these states. Rather, the title of honor, *Sheikh*, is used with their names, as is traditional with the names of prominent men in Arabian society (Map 50).

The UAE lies in the east of the Arabian peninsula. It is bordered by Saudi Arabia to the west and south, and by Oman to the east. In the north, UAE has a short frontier with Qatar and a coastline of about 400 miles (650 km) on the southern shore of the Arabian (Persian) Gulf, separated by a detached portion of the Omani territory from the small section of the coast on the western

Geographical Profile

Area: 30,000 sq. miles (82, 880 sq. km)
Population: 2.7 million (1994) 3.1 million (2000) 4.9 million (2010)
Neighboring Countries: Saudi Arabia (south and west) Oman (northeast and southeast), Iran (north)
Capital: Abu Dhabi
Other Cities: Dubai, Sharjah, Al-Ain
Terrain: largely desert with some agricultural areas
Climate: Hot, humid, low annual rainfall
Ethnic Groups: Arabs, Pakistanis, Indians, Iranians, Filipinos. Only 15-20% of the residents are UAE citizens
Religion: Sunni Islam 90%, Christianity, Hinduism
Languages: Arabic (official), English, Hindi, Urdu, Persian
Economy:
    GNP: $34 billion (1990)
    Per Capita Income: $21,335 (1990)
    Natural Resources: Oil
    Agriculture: (1.5% of GNP)- Products: Vegetables, dates, dairy products, poultry
    Industry: Petroleum (46% of GNP)
    Other Industry: (7.5% of GNP)
Official Name: United Arab Emirates
Date of Independence: December 2, 1971

shore of the Gulf of Oman. Each of the seven states bears the same name as its capital city. The territory of Abu Dhabi, largely a desert is three times as large as the other six states combined. Each of these states exercises internal autonomy under its hereditary ruler (Fig. 64).

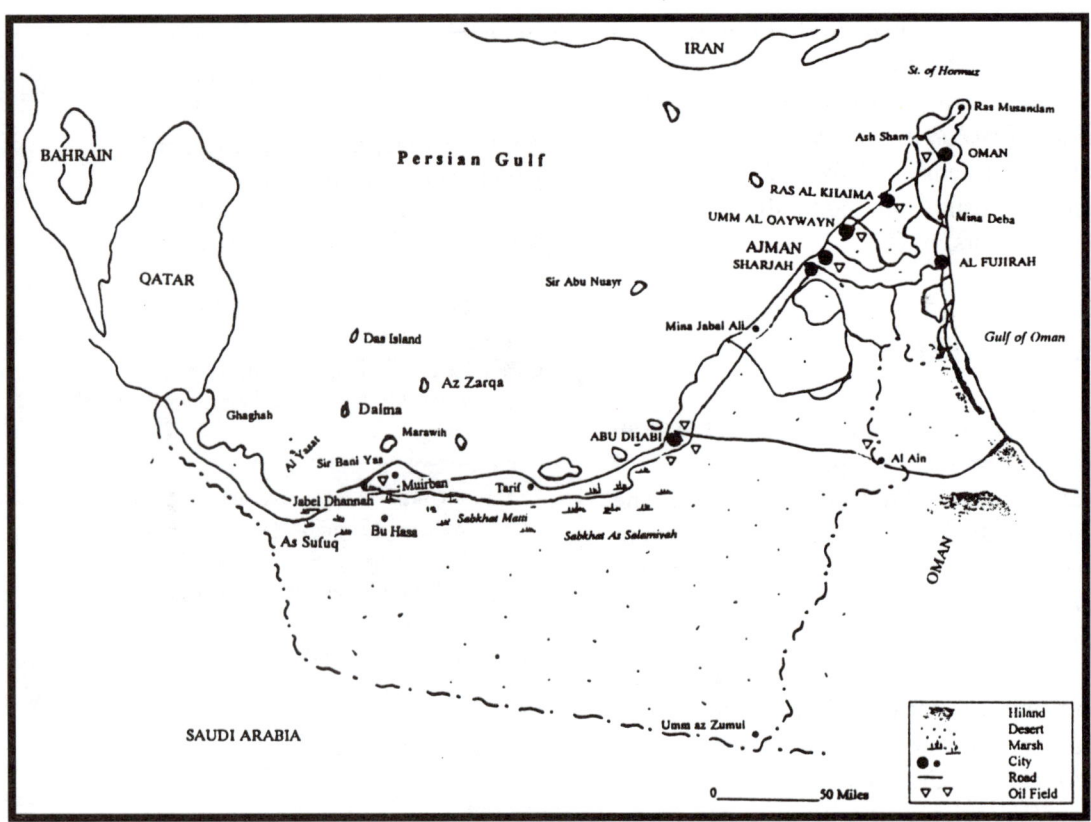

Map 50: UAE

The climate is exceptionally hot in the summer, with average maximum temperatures exceeding 104°F (40°C), and humidity is very high. Winter is mild, with temperatures ranging from 62.6°F (17°C) to 68°F (20°C). Average annual rainfall is very low: between 4 inches (100 mm) to 8 inches (200 mm).

Fig. 64: General view of Abu Dhabi

PEOPLE AND POPULATION

Of the total population of 2.7 million (1994), only 15 to 20 percent are the citizens of UAE. The rest include significant numbers of immigrants or guest workers who include Palestinians, Egyptians, Jordanians, Yemenis, Omanis, Iranians, Pakistanis, Indians, Filipinos, and West Europeans. Arabic is the official language, spoken by almost all of the native population. English is used as the second language.

The majority of UAE citizens are Sunni Muslims with a small Shi'ah minority. Most foreigners are also Muslim, although Hindus and Christians make up a portion of UAE's foreign population. In 1994, the annual rate of natural population increase was 2.8 percent. With this rate of increase, the population should double in 25 years. Table 10 gives the 1991 population by Emirates.

EVOLUTION OF UAE

The UAE was formed from the group of tribally-organized *sheikhdoms* located along the southern coast of the Persian Gulf and the northwestern coast of the Gulf of Oman. The *Sheikhdoms* and this area were converted to Islam in the seventh century. For centuries it was embroiled in dynastic disputes. It became known as the Pirate Coast because of the raiders who lived there and raided foreign shipping, despite the fact that both European and Arabic navies patrolled the area from 17th to 19th centuries.

Table 10
Population by Emirates (1991)

	Area (sq. km.)	Population	Density (per sq. km.)
Abu Dhabi	67,350	798,000	11.8
Dubai	3,900	501,000	128.5
Sharjah	2,600	314,000	120.8
Ras al-Khaimah	1,700	130,000	70.5
Ajman	250	70,000	304.0
Fujairah	1,150	63,000	54.8
Umm al-Qaiwan	750	27,000	36.0
Total	77,700	1,909,000	24.0

From 1982, Britain assumed responsibility for the *sheikhdoms'* defense and external relations. Otherwise, the *sheikhdoms* remained autonomous and followed the traditional form of Arab monarchy, with each ruler having virtually absolute power over his subjects. Because of the treaty with Britain, the UAE was known as the Trucial States or Trucial Oman.

In 1952, a local body known as the Trucial Council was established and consisted of rulers of seven *sheikhdoms*. The object of the Council was to encourage the adoption of common policies in administrative matters, possibly leading to a federation of states. In January 1968, the United Kingdom announced its intention of withdrawing British military forces from the area by 1971. In March 1968, the Trucial States joined nearby Bahrain and Qatar, which were also under British protection, in what was named the Federation of Arab Emirates. It was intended that the Federation should become fully independent, but the interests of Bahrain and Qatar proved to be incompatible with those of the smaller sheikhdoms, and both seceded from the Federation to become independent states. In July 1971, six of the Trucial States (Abu Dhabi, Dubai, Sharjah, Umm al-Qaiwain, Ajman, and Fujairah) agreed on a federal constitution for achieving independence as the United Arab Emirate (UAE). The United Kingdom accordingly terminated its special treaty relationship with the *sheikhdoms*, and the UAE became independent on December 2, 1971. The remaining *sheikhdom*, Ras al-Khaimah joined the UAE in February 1972.

As such, administratively, the UAE is a loose federation of seven *emirates,* each with its own ruler. The pace at which local government in each emirate evolves from traditional to modern is set primarily by the ruler. Under the constitution of 1971, each *emirate* reserves considerable powers, including control over mineral rights (notably oil) and revenues (Fig. 65).

Fig. 65: General View of Umm al-Qaiwan

ECONOMY

Prior to the first exports of oil in 1962, the economy of UAE was dominated by pearl production, fishing, agriculture and herding. Agriculture (including livestock and fishing) contributed an estimated 2.1 percent of the GDP in 1993. In 1992, an estimated 2.3 percent of the economically active population was employed in agriculture. The principal crops were dates, tomatoes, and aubergines.

Oil and Industry

Oil was first discovered in 1958, when deposits were located beneath the coastal waters of Abu Dhabi, the largest of the *sheikhdoms*. Onshore oil was found in Abu Dhabi in 1960. Commercial exploitation began in 1962. In neighboring Dubai (the second largest of the Trucial States), production began in 1969. In Sharjah, the production of oil began in 1974, although the output remains at a much lower level than that of Abu Dhabi or Dubai.

The UAE has huge proven oil reserves, estimated at over 100 billion barrels in 1990, 9.7 percent of the world reserves. The gas reserves are estimated at over 200 trillion cubic feet. At the present production rates, these supplies would last for well over 100 years.

Industry, including mining, manufacturing, construction, and power contributed an estimated 57.4 percent of GDP in 1993. Mining and quarrying contributed an estimated 38.4 percent of the GDP and employed an estimated 1.5 percent of the working population in 1990. Petroleum production is the most important industry in the UAE, providing 60.1 percent of the total exports in 1992.

The major heavy industries in the UAE are related to hydrocarbons. The most important products are residual fuels, liquefied petroleum gas and distillate fuel oils. There are two petroleum refineries in Abu Dhabi. In addition, over 200 factories operate at the Jebel Ali complex in Dubai, which includes a deep water port and a free-trade zone for manufacturing and distribution in which all goods for re-export or trans-shipment enjoy 100 percent duty exemption. A major power plant with associated water desalination units, an aluminum smelter, and a steel fabrication unit are prominent facilities in the complex. Except in the free trade zone, UAE requires at least 51% local citizen ownership of all businesses operating in the country as part of its attempt to place Emiris into leadership positions.

CHAPTER 48
UZBEKISTAN

Uzbekistan is a disjointed country, with the Uzbeks as the largest national group in Uzbekistan. They embraced Islam in the 8th century AD and ruled Central Asia until the *khanates* of Khiva and Bukhara were absorbed into Soviet Union in 1924. After the dissolution of the Soviet Union in 1991, the people of Uzbekistan began reviving Islam in their country.

GEOGRAPHY

The Republic of Uzbekistan (formerly the Uzbek Soviet Socialist Republic) lies at the heart of Turkestan in Central Asia. On the west, it is bordered by Kazakhstan, and on the south and west by Turkmenistan. Afghanistan is on the east and Kirgizistan is on the southeast (Map 51). The Karakalpak Republic is located within Uzbekistan. Most of Uzbekistan is a lowland country composed of the Kizil Kum desert. In the northeast are the foothills of the Tien Shan or "Heavenly Mountains." Uzbekistan encompasses about half of the Aral Sea and contains most of the Amu *Darya* system, which flows down from the mountains. The Aral Sea is rapidly drying up as a result of water diversion from the two rivers that flow into it. A small section of Syr *Darya* headwaters is found in eastern Uzbekistan. Much of the southeast is composed of wind-blown soil (loess), which is productive when irrigated.

The Karakalpak region is an enclave of Uzbekistan, with Nukus as its capital. It makes up 35 percent of Uzbekistan, occupying the entire western portion of the country. This region comprises

---

Geographical Profile

Area: 172,740 sq. miles (447,400 sq. km)
Population: 22.5 million (1994); 26.4 million (2000); 32.8 million (2020)
Neighboring Countries: Kazakhstan, Turkmenistan, Kirgizistan, Tajikistan, Afghanistan
Capital City: Tashkent
Other Cities: Samarkand, Namangan, Andizhan, Bukhara, Fergana, Kokand, Nukus
Ethnic Groups: Uzbek (71.4%), Russians (8.3%), Tajik (7%), Kazakh (4.1%) Tatar (2.4%), Others (9.1%)
Religion: Sunni Islam 90%, some Orthodox Christians, Jews
Economy:
  GNP: (1992) $18,377 million
  Per Capita Income: $860
  Natural Resources: Oil, natural gas, coal, zinc, copper, tungsten, molybdenum, lead, limestone, clay
  Agriculture: Products: Cotton, rice, wheat, corn, alfalfa, tobacco, sugar cane, sesame, fruits
Official Name: Republic of Uzbekistan
Date of Independence: November 1991

parts of the Kizil Kum desert and the Amu *Darya* delta on the Aral Sea. Karakalpaks are a Turkic-speaking people closely related to the Khazaks. There also live minorities of Uzbeks, Khazakhs, Turkmans, Russians, and Tatars.

The climate is marked by extreme temperatures and low levels of precipitation. Summers are long and hot with average temperatures of 90°F (32°C) in July. Daytime temperatures often exceed 104°F (40°C). Winters are extremely cold and dry. The average temperature in January is -4°C (25°F).

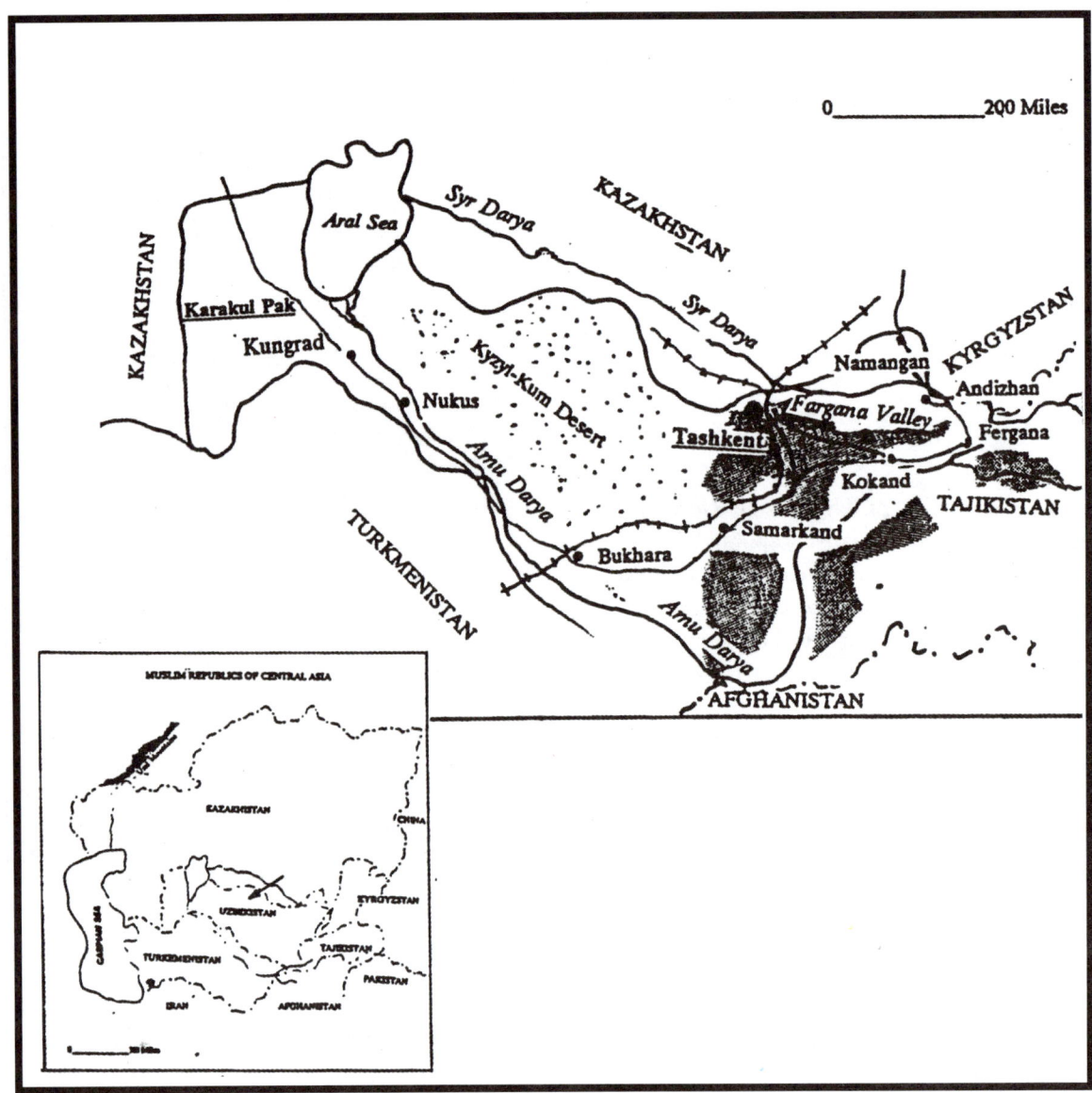

Map 51: Uzbekistan

PEOPLE AND POPULATION

The Uzbeks are descendants of nomadic Mongol tribes who mixed with the sedentary Persian inhabitants of Central Asia in the 13th century AD. Most of the Uzbeks are Sunni Muslims (Hanafi school). The Naqshibandi *tariqat* of Sufism is relatively well-established in Uzbekistan. There are also Orthodox Christians among the Slavic communities. In addition, there are 65,000 European Jews and 28,000 Central Asian Jews. Russians did not come here in great numbers and constitute about seven percent of the population today, a proportion that is declining.

During the Second World War, Stalin exiled several Muslim groups from the Caucasus region and elsewhere to Central Asia on charges that they collaborated with the Nazi invaders. These people were the Chechens, Ingush, Crimean Tatars, and Meshketians. Despite the hardships these people had to face, they were warmly taken in by the local Muslim population. Most have, since the end of communism in Russia, returned to their former homelands.

In 1994, Uzbekistan's population stood at 22.5 million people, with a 2.7 percent annual rate of natural increase. With such a rate of annual increase, the population of Uzbekistan is likely to be 26.4 million in 2000 and 26.4 million in 2010.

Tashkent, Samarkand, and Bukhara are important cities. Located in the foothills of Tien Shan, Tashkent is the largest and one of the important cities in Central Asia. It is the economic and cultural center of the region. Its old historical center features narrow, twisting streets and numerous mosques and *bazars*.

Samarkand is one of the oldest cities in the world and the oldest in Central Asia. Ruins just north of the city date back to the 4th century BC. The ancient Greeks called it Marakanda. Alexander conquered it in 329 BC, when it was a meeting place between Chinese and Western cultures. It became a part of the Arab world in the 8th century AD, after which it flourished as a trade center between Baghdad and China. The tomb of the Arab scholar Imam Bukhari, is on the outskirts of the city. The old section of Samarkand contains the Registan, a great square which has some of the most splendid monuments in Central Asia, including Tamerlane's Mausoleum and the Bibi Khan mosque.

Bukhara (also called Bokhara) is located on the Shkhrud irrigation canal of the Zeravshan River. Like other ancient Uzbek cities, Bukhara was on the trade routes between east and west. It became a major center of Islamic learning in the 9th century. Many great Islamic scholars and mystics were originally from this region.

EVOLUTION OF UZBEKISTAN

Uzbekistan is the site of one of the world's oldest civilizations. It was first identified as the province of Sogdiana in the ancient Persian Empire and was conquered in the 4th century BC by Alexander. Turkish nomads came during the 6th century AD. Uzbekistan was ruled by the Arabs, who introduced Islam in the 8th century. In the 12th century, it was captured by the Seljuk Turks of

Khorzem. During the 13th century, the forces of Genghis Khan overran the country. Tamerlane conquered most of Central Asia and the Caucasus in the 14th century. He made his headquarters at Samarkand in southeastern Uzbekistan, in the foothills of the mountains.

During this time, Uzbekistan was the major trade route between Europe and Asia. Marco Polo traveled through the area on his journey from Italy to India and China. The cities of Samarkand, Bukhara and Tashkent were prosperous. Later, the Uzbek leader, Abdullah, extended his empire to Persia, Afghanistan, and eastern Turkistan. This empire eventually broke into *Khanates* of Bukhara, Kokand, and Khiva. The *Khanates,* weakened by internal fighting, were conquered by Russia in the late 19th century.

In April 1918, the Turkestan Autonomous Soviet Socialist Republic (ASSR) was proclaimed, which included a vast region in Central Asia, including Uzbekistan. Bukhara and Siva were incorporated into the Turkestan ASSR by 1924. In May 1925, the Uzbek SSR became a constituent republic of the USSR, and in 1936, Karakalpak was transferred from the Russian Federation to the Uzbek SSR, maintaining its autonomous status.

For the first time, Uzbekistan was established as an independent nation-state in 1924-25. The state continued without significant changes until the policies of *glasnost* (openness) and *perestroika* were introduced in the 1980s. *Glasnost* and *perestroika* generated such politics that the continuation of the USSR as a federated entity was no longer possible. After its independence in November 1991, Uzbekistan sought to develop relations with other former Muslim neighboring states of Central Asia.

Like several other Soviet republics in the years prior to and immediately after the dissolution of the USSR, Uzbekistan experienced outbreaks of inter-ethnic strife, beginning in June 1989, when conflicts were reported between ethnic Uzbeks and the Meskhetian Turk minority. In February and March 1990, there was a resurgence of inter-ethnic conflict.

ECONOMY

About 60 percent of the land in Uzbekistan is covered by desert and steppe, while the remainder comprises fertile valleys watered by two river systems. Private farming was legalized in 1992.

Agriculture

Uzbekistan is the third largest producer of cotton in the world. It dominates the irrigated lands of Uzbekistan. Cotton is cultivated at the expense of food crops, most of which was exported to Moscow, where it was the backbone of the textile industry. Rice is grown in the irrigated valleys. Other crops include wheat, corn, alfalfa, tobacco, sugar cane, and sesame. Grapes, apples, peaches, and apricots are grown on the highland slopes.

In 1992, agriculture (including forestry) contributed to 35.9 percent of the Gross National Product. More than half of the country is covered by desert and steppe, while the remainder is comprised of fertile valleys watered by two major river systems. The massive irrigation of arid areas greatly increased the production of cotton but caused devastating environmental problems. The level of the Aral Sea has dropped by more than 40 feet (12 m). Other major crops include grain, vegetables, and fruit. In the north, wheat dominates the agricultural regimen. In addition, flax, hemp, millet, and sunflowers are cultivated. Silkworm breeding is also important, as is the production of *astrakhan* wool. Private farming was legalized in 1992; by December 1993, the process of transforming Uzbekistan's 715 state farms into cooperative and private farms, joint-stock companies and other forms of ownership was nearing completion.

The country raises about four million cattle, nine million sheep, and thirty six million chickens, in addition to horses, pigs, and goats. Products include wool and *karakul* sheep pelts.

Minerals and Industry

Uzbekistan is well endowed with mineral deposits, particularly oil, natural gas, and coal. Natural gas is an important export commodity and is also used domestically for industrial purposes and power generation in Bukhara, Samarkand, and Tashkent. The gas fields are in the southeast corner of the country. The gas runs most of the local industry and is carried by pipelines to all other Central Asian republics and even to European Russia. The country has large reserves of petroleum. More new fields are being exploited in the Ferghana Valley and Bukhara region.

Lignite coal is mined in the southeast. There are also large reserves of gold in the center of the Kyzyl Kum desert. Uzbekistan is the eighth largest producer of gold in the world, and the Murantau mine is the world's largest single, open-cast gold mine in the Kyzylkum desert. The Murantau mines produce about 70% of Uzbekistan's average annual output of 70 metric tons of gold. In addition to gold, silver, uranium, copper, lead, zinc, and tungsten is also found in Uzbekistan. Twenty-two hydroelectric plants add to the electric supply provided by thermal plants. A large thermal power plant is on line at Syr *Darya*, south of Tashkent, and a smaller unit operates at Navol, west of Tashkent. In 1991, 80.2 percent of electricity was generated by thermal power stations, while the remaining 10.8 percent came from hydroelectric sources.

Large cities in Uzbekistan have begun to manufacture textiles from cotton, silk, and wool. The intensive cotton industry has made Uzbekistan one of the most polluted places on earth. Pesticides and fertilizers, blown by strong winds, have made Uzbekistan a leader in cancer and birth defects. The Aral Sea, which once supported an important fishing industry, is now almost a lifeless lake. At the present time, boats remain stranded two hundred feet from the shoreline. Uzbekistan also has food processing factories, and more recently the country started manufacturing steel, tractors, and fertilizer.

NOTES

CHAPTER 49
YEMEN

Soon after Islam was introduced in Yemen, the Muslim *Caliphs* began to exert control over the area. After the *caliphate* broke up, the former North Yemen came under the control of the Zaydi *Imams*, who established a Shi'ah theocratic political structure that survived until the modern times.

GEOGRAPHY

The Republic of Yemen is situated in the south of the Arabian peninsula, bounded on the north by Saudi Arabia, to the east by Oman, to the south by the Gulf of Aden, and to the west by the Red Sea. The islands of Perim and Kamaran at the southern end of the Red Sea, the island of Socotora, at the entrance of the Gulf of Aden, and the Kuria Muria islands, near the coast of Oman are also part of the Republic (Map 52).

The geography of Yemen may be described in several zones from north to south. Along the coast is the Tihama plain, which is always hot with no rainfall and a lot of humidity because of its proximity to the Red Sea. About 30 miles (48 km) from the coast, the steep slopes of the scenic mountains begin to rise, running through the center of the country. Some mountain peaks reach more than 10,000 feet (3040 m) higher than the level of the Red Sea, which is only about 50 miles (80 km) distance one peak called Hadhur Shuayb is more than 13,000 feet (3950 m) high.

Geographical Profile

Area: 203796 sq. miles (527,970 sq. km)
Population: 11.1 million (1994); 13.6 million (2000); 19.0 million (2010)
Neighboring Countries: Saudi Arabia, Oman
Capital: Sanaa
Other Cities: Aden, Taizz, Hodeida, Al-Mukalla
Terrain: Mountainous interior; flat, sandy coastal plain
Climate: Extremely hot; humid on the coast
Ethnic Groups: Arab
Religion: Islam (mostly Zaydi Shi'ah, some Sunni)
Language: Arabic
Economy:
  GDP: $7.4 billion (1990)
  Per Capita Income: $617 (1990)
  Natural Resources: Oil, natural gas, fish, rock salt, small deposits of coal and copper
  Agriculture: (26% of GDP; Arable land 5%): Products: Qat (a mildly narcotic plant), cotton, coffee, millet, barley, fruits, poultry hides, skins, honey, livestock
  Industry: (18% of GDP): Types: Petroleum refining, mining, food processing, building materials
Official Name: Republic of Yemen
Date of Independence: May, 1990

East of the mountains is a high plateau which gradually slopes down toward the undefined eastern borders of the country. The capital, Sanaa, is at the western edge of this plateau at an elevation of 6,500 feet (1975 m); it is one of the highest capitals in the world. The people of high plateau and mountains wear long sheepskins in the winter to keep warm.

The climate in the semi-desert coastal strip is hot, with high humidity and temperatures rising to more than 100°F (38°C). Inland, the climate is somewhat less hot, with cool winters and relatively heavy rainfall in the highlands. The eastern plateau slopes into desert.

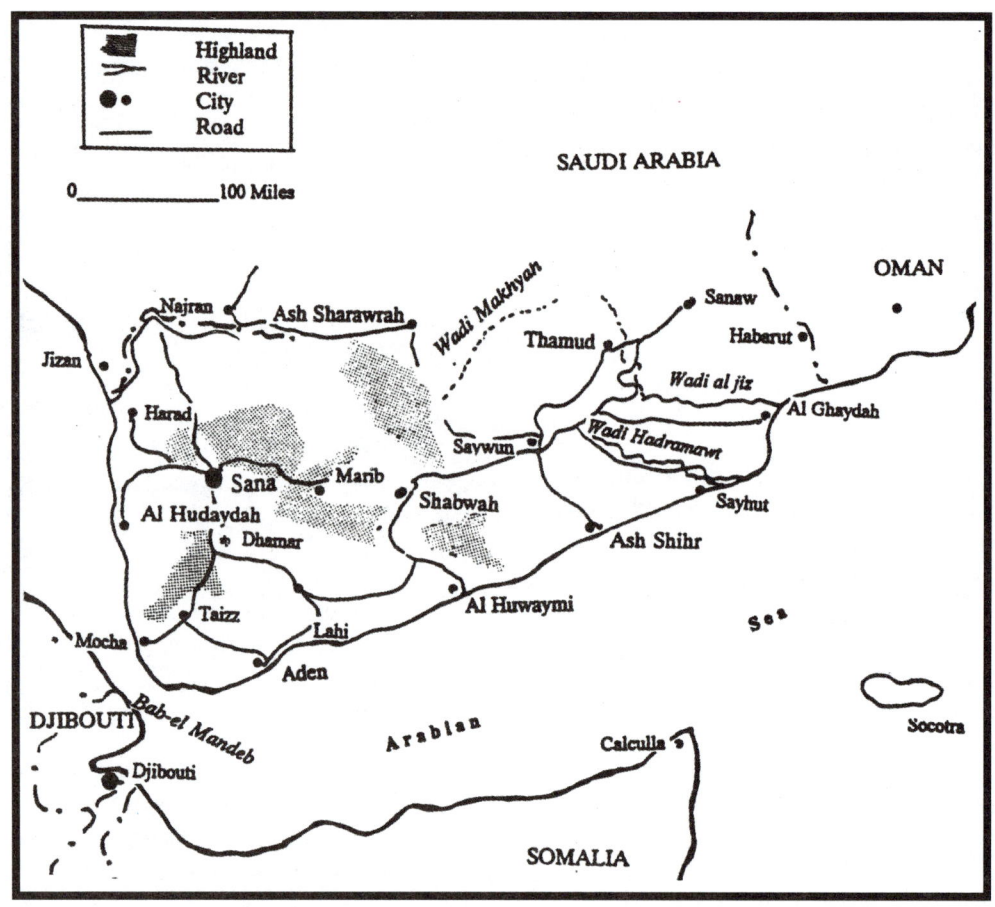

Map 52: Yemen

PEOPLE AND POPULATION

Virtually, all Yemenis are Arabs. The inhabitants of the mountains tend to be short and olive-skinned. Heavy African admixture is found on the coast. The population is almost entirely Muslim, and mainly of *Zaydi* sect. Traditionally, the people had lived in small towns, villages, and isolated clusters of houses, and until recently, most loyalties were local, mainly to family and clan. National patriotism is a rather new feeling, which is spreading slowly. A few people are nomads, mainly in the eastern part of the country, while considerably more live in the growing cities, where modern buildings clash with the greater dignity and appeal of traditional designs (Fig. 66).

Fig. 66: A Clay Fort in Al-Mukalla (Now used as a Museum)

While all Yemenis are Muslim (Fig. 67), there are two main divisions of approximately equal numbers. The coastal plain and much of the southern region is inhabited by *Sunnis*; the northern part is the homeland of the Zaydi sect of *Shi'ah* Islam. The total population of the country in 1994 stood at 11.1 million people with a 3.5 percent annual rate of population increase. With such an annual rate of increase, the population of Yemen would double in 20 years. In the year 2000, it would increase to 13.6 million and in 2010 to 19 million people.

EVOLUTION OF YEMEN

Between the 12th century BC and the 6th century AD, Yemen was a part of the Minaean, Sabaean, and Himyarite kingdoms. Later, it came under Ethiopian and Persian rule. In the 7th century, Muslims began to exert control over the area. Egyptian sultans occupied much of North

Yemen in the 11th century. By the 16th century, northern Yemen was a part of the Ottoman Empire.

Fig. 67: A Mosque in Jibla

Former North Yemen. Yemen had nominal sovereignty under the Ottoman Empire until World War I. Turkish forces withdrew in 1918, leaving Imam Yahya, leader of the *Zaydi* community in power. After brief military clashes with Saudi Arabia and the United Kingdom, which controlled Aden, its boundaries with Saudi Arabia and Southern Yemen were established. It became a member of the Arab League in 1945 and the United Nations in 1947.

In 1958, Yemen and the United Arab Republic (Egypt and Syria) formed a federation called the United Arab States, which was dissolved in 1961. In 1962, army officers staged a coup and declared a Yemen Arab Republic. Civil war ensued between royalist forces, supported by Saudi Arabia and Jordan, and republicans, aided by Egyptian troops. The republicans gained the upper hand, and Egyptian forces withdrew after the Arab-Israeli war in 1967. By 1968, most of the opposing leaders reached reconciliation; Saudi Arabia recognized the republic in 1970.

Former South Yemen. British influence increased in the south and eastern portion of Yemen after it captured the port of Aden in 1839. The area was ruled as a part of British India until 1937, when it was made a crown colony with designated East Aden and West Aden protectorates. By 1965, many of the tribal states within the protectorates of Aden colony proper had joined the Federation of South Arabia.

In 1967, British troops began withdrawing, and the Federation rule collapsed. The communist-dominated National Liberation Front seized control. After a series of negotiations with the British, and South Arabia, Aden was declared independent on November 30, 1967. On December 1, 1970, the country was named the People's Republic of South Yemen.

Movement Toward Union. In 1972, North and South Yemen declared that they approved a future union. However, little progress was made toward unification, and relations were often strained. During a summit meeting in Kuwait in March 1979, the presidents of both countries reiterated their support for unity. Deep-rooted animosity, however, led to fighting between the rival groups. In November 1989, both governments again agreed on a draft unity constitution originally drawn up in 1981.

In spite of such efforts, the differences and unrest continued for one reason or another. In March 1994, representatives from Oman and Jordan together with the US and French military attaches, succeeded in averting outright armed conflict between the two groups. Diplomatic initiatives continued throughout April 1994, while skirmishes between rival army units persisted. On April 27, a tank battle took place at Amran, near Sanaa. A series of pitched battles followed between battalions stationed in the territory of their neighbor. On May 4, hostilities erupted around Sanaa and Aden. The forces of the former Peoples Democratic Republic of Yemen had suffered serious defeat. On May 21, 1994, independence of the new Democratic Republic of Yemen was declared with Aden as its capital.

ECONOMY

Agriculture is at the center of Yemen's economy. In 1988, agriculture (including forestry and fishing) contributed 23 percent of the Gross Domestic Product.

Agriculture

On the coast, one finds date palms and grains suitable to hot climate. The upper slopes of the mountains that receive good rainfall are among the most intensively cultivated areas in the world. Through the centuries, the farmers have built elaborate terraces with stone walls - at some places right up to the crests of the mountains (Fig. 68). Some fruit trees are grown on the terraces, but coffee has been a more important crop. Since it used to be shipped by the British from the old port of Mukha, it became known as "Mocha coffee." Coffee is still an important export, but competition from the other countries has diminished its value. Many coffee plants have been replaced by *qat*. At present, *Qat* has a bigger return than coffee, and Ethiopian addicts are now the chief consumers of *qat*, although it is also used in Aden.

Animal husbandry is also an important part of the economy. Millions of sheep, goats, and humped cattle are raised for milk, meat, and hides. Donkeys and mules are still the most common beasts of burden, as camels are not suitable in the rugged mountains.

Minerals and Industry

Mining employed only 0.05 percent of the labor force of the Yemen Arab Republic in 1975. In 1984, oil was discovered in commercial quantities. Subsequently, more reserves were discovered along the border with the Peoples Democratic Republic of Yemen. Exports of crude oil began in 1987. In 1990, exports of oil and petroleum products provided 91 percent of total export earnings. There are significant reserves of natural gas. Salt is also exploited on a large scale.

Fig. 68: Terraced Agriculture, Yemen

In the Peoples Democratic Republic of Yemen, mining and quarrying contributed about 0.2 percent of the Gross Domestic Product in 1986. Oil was discovered in potentially commercial quantities in 1983. In addition, the region of the former Peoples Democratic Republic of Yemen has deposits of copper, gold, lead, zinc, and molybdenum.

Manufacturing contributed to 9 percent of the unified Yemen's Gross Domestic Product in 1991. The most important branches of manufacturing in Yemen are petroleum refining, building materials, food products, beverages, tobacco, and chemical products.

A port at Hudaida was completed in 1971 by the former Soviet Union. The Soviet Union also built a hard-surfaced highway southward from the port through the central plain. China built a road from Hudaida up through the rugged mountains to the country's capital Sanaa and another surfaced highway from Sanaa northward to Saudi Arabia. The rough road from Sanaa to Taizz and the old port of Mukha (Mocha) was built by the United States and later improved by West Germany.

NOTES

SELECTED BIBLIOGRAPHY

Afifi, H. "The Egyptian Experience of Algerian Reforms." *East African Journal of Rural Development* 5 (1972). 193-200.

"Africa: Scramble for Existence." *Time.* Cover Story. September 7 (1992). 40-46.

Ahmad, Akbar S. *Discovering Islam: Making Sense of Muslim History and Society.* Boston: Routledge and Kegan Paul International, 1987.

Ainer, Shinn. *Cultural Change and Community in Central Asia.* London and New York: Kegan Paul International, 1992

Baker, K.M. "Structural Change and Managerial Inefficiency in the Development of Rice Cultivation in the Senegal River Basin." *African Affairs* 81 (1982). 499-510.

Beaumont, Peter, et. al. *The Middle East: A Geographical Study.* 2nd rev. ed. New York: Wiley/Halsted, 1988.

Bell, Morag. *Contemporary Africa: Development, Culture and the State.* White Plains, New York: Longman, 1985.

Best, A.C.G. and H.J. deBlij. *African Survey.* New York: John Wiley & Sons, 1977.

Chapman, Grahman Paul and Kathleen, M. Baker. *The Changing Geography of Africa and Middle East.* London: Routledge, 1972.

Clarke, J.I., M. Khogali, and L. Konsinski. *Population and Development Projects in Africa.* Cambridge: Cambridge University Press, 1985.

Drysdale, Alasdair and Blanke, Gerald H., *The Middle East and North Africa: A Political Geography.* New York: Oxford University Press, 1985

Dunn, J. *West African States: Future and Promise.* Cambridge: Cambridge University Press, 1978.

Dunsmore, J.P. et. al. *The Agricultural Development of Gambia.* Surbiton: Ministry of Overseas Development - Land Resource Division, 1975.

Dutt, Ashok K. (ed.) *Southeast Asia: Realm of Contrasts*. Third rev. ed. Boulder, CO: Westview Press, 1985.

Fisher, William B., *The Middle East: A Physical, Social and Regional Geography*. Seventh rev. ed. London: Nathan, 1978

Grampton, P.D. "The Population Geography of Gambia." *Geography* 57 (1972), 183-88.

Grove, A.T. *Africa*. Third Edition. London: Oxford University Press, 1978.

Grove, A.T. "The State of Africa in 1980s." *Geographical Journal* 152 (1986), 193-203.

Grove, A.T. *The Changing Geography of Africa*. New York: Oxford University Press, 1989.

Haddad, Yvonne. *The Muslim World Today*. Washington, D.C.: The Islamic Affairs Program. The Middle East Institute, 1993.

Hamdan, G. "The Political Map of New Africa." *Geographical Review* 53 (1963). 418-39.

Hardojoni, Joan (ed.). *Indonesia: Resources, Ecology and Environment*. Singapore: Oxford University Press, 1991.

"Islam's Path East." *Aramco World Magazine*. Nov.-Dec. 1991. 1-67

Jeffe, Geogre (ed.). *North Africa: State and Region*. London: Routledge, 1993.

Johnson, B.L.C. *Bangladesh*. Second rev. ed. Totowa, N.J.: Barnes and Noble, 1982

Kirby, M.A. "Senegambia: A New and Future Nation." *National Geographic Magazine* 168:2 (1985). 224-51.

Knight, C. Gregory and James L. Newsman (ed.). *Contemporary Africa: Geography and Change*. Englewood Cliffs, N.J: Princeton Hall, 1976.

Manshard, W. *Tropical Agriculture*. London: Longmans, 1974

Mountjoy, Alan B. and David Hilling. *Africa: Geography and Development*. London: Hutchinson, 1988.

Noin, D. "Aspects dusous-development an Maroc," *Annals de Geographte* 75 (1966). 410-31.

O'Connor, M. "Guinea and Ivory Coast: Contrasts in Economic Development." *International Modern African Studies* 10:3 (1972). 409-26.

Organization of Islamic Conference. *Islamic Chamber Guide to OIC Member Countries.* Karachi: Chamber of Commerce and Industry on Commodity Exchange, 1993.

Radhwan, S. and E. Lee. *Agrarian Change in Egypt: An Anatomy of Poverty.* Croom: Helm, 1985.

Rahman, Mushtaqur. *Muslim World: Geography and Development.* Lanham, Maryland: University Press of America, 1987.

Rahman, Mushtaqur. *Muslim World: Geojournal.* September 1995.

Rahman, Mushtaqur. *Land and Life in Sindh, Pakistan.* Lahore: Ferozsons Ltd., 1993.

Rashid, Harun. *Geography of Bangladesh.* Boulder, CO: Westview Press, 1977.

Sayigh, Yusuf A. *Elusive Development: From Dependence to Self-Reliance in the Arab Region.* London: Routledge, 1971.

Sutton, K. "The Progress of Algeria's Agrrarian Reforms and its Settlement Implications." *The Maghrib Review* 2 (1978). 10-18

Swindell, K. "Industrialization in Guinea." *Geography* 54:4 (1969). 456-58.

United Nations. *Development Yearbook.* New York. (Annually)

United States Government. *Background Notes* (Published and revised periodically). Washington, DC.: Bureau of Public Affairs - Department of State, 1987-89

IQRA' International Educational Foundation, Chicago, is a non–profit Islamic educational trust, established by concerned Muslims in 1983, in response to the need for systematic Islamic education of our children.

We invite you to help IQRA' develop into a major Islamic educational research and production center by:

i. *Becoming an Anṣār (helper) of IQRA's Educational Program and making a regular contribution to its pioneering efforts.*

ii. *Joining the IQRA' Book Club and making a commitment to buy one newly-published IQRA' book each month.*

IQRA' Mail Order Service

7450 Skokie Blvd. Phone: (847) 673-7892
Skokie, IL 60077 Toll-Free: (800) 521-4272
U.S.A. Fax: (847) 673-4095

IQRA' Book Center

2701 W. Devon Ave.
Chicago, IL 60659
Phone: (773) 274-2665
Fax: (773) 274-8733
http://www.iqra.org

Lake Country School
3755 Pleasant Ave. S.
Minneapolis, MN 55409